KT-394-470

Acknowledgements

The research for this book began in 2000 when, as a postgraduate student at UCD, I began to investigate the issue of corruption in Irish politics. Having realised how difficult it would be to draw conclusions about this topic while its parameters were far from decided, I decided to look behind the issue, examining instead those institutions of state designed to prevent corruption.

The daily revelations of corruption in Irish politics nevertheless presented ongoing challenges to the research, and the PhD thesis on parliamentary accountability that emerged would not have been possible without the fantastic encouragement and confidence of my supervisor Niamh Hardiman, as well as Iseult Honahan, Jean Brennan and the hard-working staff at the then Department of Politics in UCD. Sincere thanks also to Philip Norton and Eunan O'Halpin who offered erudite comments on earlier drafts of this work.

I am grateful to the Irish Research Council for the Humanities and Social Sciences for the funding I received to undertake this work, as well as to the Geary Institute in UCD for the top-class facilities and environment in which to engage in my research. Thanks also to my colleagues at the IPA, particularly those in the Business Sector Development and Publications Divisions, and especially those involved in the final preparation of the book.

Along the way, a number of other people have offered support and friendship in spite of my obsession with this project. I am eternally grateful to my parents Sheila and Maurice, sisters Caroline and Deirdre and brother Conor, as well as the extended Duggan family, particularly Martin. Deepest thanks also to Barry and Rachel, Kevin and Niamh, Jane and Martin, as well as Brian, Katy, Kevin, Peter, Claire, Mark and Barry.

My final thanks go to my fiancée, Anna Bryson, who encouraged me to undertake this research in the first place and then stuck with me through the best and the worst of it. It really would not have been possible otherwise.

Introduction

> Laws are like cobwebs, which may catch small flies, but let wasps and hornets break through.
>
> Jonathan Swift, *A Critical Essay upon the Faculties of the Mind* (1707)

The quest for 'accountability' has become a pervasive feature of Irish political and administrative life. There is a consensus that whatever the institution or context, as much accountability as possible should be sought. However, as use of the term has broadened, so too has its meaning: as well as scrutiny and oversight, it now has connotations of control, responsibility and sanction, and is often preceded by terms such as 'public', 'regulatory', 'professional' or 'financial' according to the problem being addressed. This book focuses on a particular form of accountability that is central to Irish democracy yet remains one of the least studied – parliamentary accountability. Given the substantial changes in Irish society over the past two decades, it is timely to consider the role of parliament and parliamentary accountability in modern Irish life.

A healthy democracy requires an active legislature (parliament) and an efficient executive[1] that is subject to public examination. After all, the accountability of the government to the people, via parliament, is the most fundamental element of a democratic polity. However, for most of the Irish state's existence, its parliament has been seen as effectively powerless to challenge the dominant government that it elects. This volume argues that a closer examination of the development and dynamics of parliamentary accountability will illuminate some important features of contemporary Irish politics, including the need for extra-parliamentary investigative mechanisms such as tribunals of inquiry.

Rockman[2] distinguishes between executive scholars, who are concerned with effectiveness, direction and competence; and analysts of legislatures, who deal with issues of accountability, representation and responsiveness. This book falls into the category

---

[1] The executive, as the term is used here, consists of the Taoiseach, the cabinet of ministers and the associated administrative structures (such as departments) – see Chapter 1.

[2] Rockman, B. A. (1984) 'Legislative–Executive Relations and Legislative Oversight', *Legislative Studies Quarterly* Vol. IX(3), 388.

of analysis of legislatures, as it examines the challenges faced by the Irish parliament, Oireachtas Éireann[3] (hereafter 'the Oireachtas'), and in particular its Lower House, Dáil Éireann (or 'the Dáil'), in fulfilling its constitutional function of holding the executive to account. We have seen allegations and evidence of corruption and malpractice in Irish public life in recent decades, yet it remains unclear how corrupt Ireland really is. This is reflected in two reports referred to in the first annual report of the Standards in Public Office Commission in June 2003. Transparency International found that between 2001 and 2002, Ireland had dropped from the eighteenth to the twenty-third least corrupt state of 102 countries surveyed. However, the Council of Europe-funded GRECO (Group of States against Corruption) found that 'Ireland appears to belong to the group of … members that are least affected by corruption.'[4] The commission's annual report for 2003 noted that Ireland had moved back to eighteenth place in Transparency International's list, but was still seen as more corrupt than other member states of the European Union.[5]

This study considers the effectiveness of the most important national institution in preventing, identifying or punishing corrupt activities. It is argued that lacunae in the oversight capabilities of Dáil Éireann provided opportunities for the advancement of personal ambitions at the expense of the public good. Indeed, one of the most significant findings is that many of the most challenging and disturbing issues in contemporary Irish politics have their roots in parliamentary accountability and its shortcomings.

The blueprint for the modern Irish legislature is the British parliament at Westminster; in fact, Dáil Éireann's development in many ways has mirrored progress in the House of Commons. Following several recent public scandals and subsequent investigations in Britain, a number of monographs, books and syntheses have

---

[3]   Under Article 15.2 of the 1937 Constitution, the Oireachtas is the sole law-making body in the state and consists of the two chambers of parliament, as well as the office of the President. The term 'Oireachtas' is also used to refer solely to the Irish parliament (Article 15.1).

[4]   Standards in Public Office Commission (2003) *Annual Report 2002*. Dublin, pp. 4–5. A follow-up report by GRECO in 2003 welcomed the fact that a specialised anti-corruption unit had been established in the Office of the Director of Public Prosecutions earlier that year (GRECO (2003) *First Evaluation Round: Compliance Report on Ireland*. Strasbourg: Council of Europe, p. 4).

[5]   The index released in 2004 placed Ireland in joint seventeenth place, along with Belgium and the USA.

been produced on parliamentary accountability and its defects.[6] In Ireland, on the other hand, the recent analysis of corruption, political favouritism and abuses of public office has largely been conducted by journalists, on a case-by-case basis.[7] This volume provides a more comprehensive context and framework for the institutional and political nexus that failed to prevent the corrupt activities uncovered in recent years, and for the reform that has been introduced to increase accountability in Irish politics. It is informed by comparative legislative studies, and applies insights from contemporary international research: in particular, in order to demonstrate the links between structures and the activities of actors such as political parties, it draws on institutional theory. Legislative scholars have long appreciated the importance of institutions, but little substantive research using this theory has been applied to the Oireachtas.

Eight chapters are presented, in four parts. The chapter in Part I sets out the theoretical context of accountability issues and presents Dáil Éireann's difficulties in overseeing the executive. Part II establishes the distinguishing features of Dáil Éireann and maps its development since 1922. Chapter 2 considers the Irish parliament in comparative perspective, with a focus on legislative–executive relationships in Western Europe. Institutional theory is introduced and, in Chapter 3, is applied to the Oireachtas in order to explain some 'critical junctures' in Irish parliamentary accountability. Chapter 3 is also concerned with the development of the Irish party system and how the changing government formation preferences of the main parties have influenced, and in turn been influenced by, developments in the legislature.

---

[6] These include Oliver, D. (1991) *Government in the United Kingdom: the Search for Accountability, Effectiveness and Citizenship.* Milton Keynes: Open University Press; Woodhouse, D. (1994) *Ministers and Parliament.* Oxford: Clarendon Press; Pyper, R. (1996) 'Parliamentary Accountability' in R. Pyper (ed.) *Aspects of Accountability in the British System of Government.* Liverpool: Tudor Business Publishing, pp. 45–81; Flinders, M. (2001) *The Politics of Accountability in the Modern State.* Aldershot: Ashgate; The Hansard Society Commission (2001) *The Challenge for Parliament: Making Government Accountable.* London: Vacher Dod.

[7] See for example O'Toole, F. (1995) *Meanwhile, Back at the Ranch.* London: Vintage; Smyth, S. (1997) *Thanks a Million Big Fella.* Dublin: Blackwater Press; Keena, C. (2001) *Haughey's Millions: the Full Story of Charlie's Money Trail.* Dublin: Gill & Macmillan; Cullen, P. (2002) *With a Little Help from My Friends.* Dublin: Gill & Macmillan; Keena, C. (2003) *The Ansbacher Conspiracy.* Dublin: Gill & Macmillan.

Part III focuses on how political and administrative accountability is pursued in contemporary Dáil Éireann. As no systematic study of the internal workings of the Irish parliament has ever been undertaken, Chapter 4 is unique in its identification of the procedures and practices that permit executive domination of the legislature. Chapter 5 considers parliamentary committees, and in particular their use to inquire into matters of public concern.

Part IV analyses the alternative mechanisms of executive oversight created as a result of the failure of parliamentary methods detailed in Part III. Chapter 6 considers tribunals of inquiry and explains the necessity for judicial mechanisms of oversight. The relationship between parliamentary and judicial accountability is explored in this context. Chapter 7 is concerned with established and new 'public' oversight structures; Chapter 8 looks at the reforms that have occurred in Dáil Éireann and Seanad Éireann as a result of these. A concluding chapter considers the future of parliament and parliamentary accountability in Ireland.

PART I

What is accountability?

CHAPTER 1

Understanding accountability in Irish parliamentary politics

The contemporary Irish parliament

Dáil Éireann has traditionally been criticised for its weakness in holding government to account. As Gallagher points out, commentators on the Lower House of the Oireachtas have consistently found it to be one of the weakest chambers in Europe in terms of executive scrutiny.[1] Nonetheless, the Dáil continues to be a prominent public institution, legitimated by the fact that, apart from the relatively powerless presidency, it is the only directly elected national institution in Ireland. For this reason alone, an increasingly powerful executive must constantly ensure that the chamber in which it sits does not inhibit its work.

During the economically prosperous 1990s, many core institutions of traditional Irish society, such as the Catholic Church and the Gárda Síochána (police), changed from being closed, hierarchical and insular institutions to having their internal failings publicly exposed and scrutinised. The Oireachtas has also experienced this shift in public expectation: deficiencies in the process of parliamentary accountability became a matter of great public concern, and necessitated the introduction of new extra-parliamentary and parliamentary oversight institutions. Among other issues, these institutions have investigated payments to politicians by business interests, tax evasion, blood contamination, and corruption in the land planning process.

Since the early 1990s there have been almost daily revelations of political and administrative corruption and queries as to why there were no institutional safeguards against the abuse of public offices for personal gain. The public perception of parliament as the people's watchdog on government has been significantly eroded as investigative journalism and the law courts adopt the role of scrutinisers of the executive. Survey data reflect this huge decrease in public confidence

---

[1] Gallagher, M. (2005) 'Parliament' in J. Coakley and M. Gallagher (eds) *Politics in the Republic of Ireland.* London: Routledge/PSAI, p. 211.

in parliament and the Dáil: in 1990, public confidence in the Irish parliament was at 51 per cent,[2] eight points higher than the European average of 43 per cent.[3] By 1994 it had decreased to 24 per cent.[4]

·In fact, 1994 saw the Oireachtas reach a low point in terms of public perception of it and its work. Eurobarometer data for November–December of that year reveals that 40 per cent of people surveyed felt they could not rely on parliament, compared to 44 per cent who felt they could. At the beginning of 1996, 30 per cent of respondents said they could not rely on it while 53 per cent felt they could.[5] As Table 1.1 shows, between 1996 and late 2001 'lack of trust' in the national parliament went from being comfortably below the European average to slightly above it. This decline in trust coincides with the establishment of several tribunals of inquiry and the revelations of corrupt practices among parliamentarians that emerged during their hearings. The Eurobarometer survey released in Spring 2004 demonstrated that while trust levels in national political institutions were higher in Ireland than in the EU as a whole, trust in the Dáil remained low, with only four in every ten people claiming to trust it.

Using European Values Studies, Fahey *et al.*[6] find that between 1981 and 1999 there was a 'very marked' decline in confidence in the Irish parliament, from 52 per cent to 31 per cent. In a similar vein, the European Social Survey for 2002/3 revealed that among thirteen nations, trust in parliament was least evident in Ireland (Figure 1.1).[7]

Accountability and parliament

The starting point for this investigation must be the provisions for parliamentary oversight of the executive. 'The executive' has become an all-encompassing term in recent years, because of the many

---

[2]   The corresponding figure for 1981 was 53 per cent.
[3]   Hardiman, N. and Whelan, C. (1994) 'Politics and Democratic Values' in C. Whelan (ed.) *Values and Social Change in Ireland*. Dublin: Gill & Macmillan, p. 103.
[4]   Hardiman, N. and Whelan, C. (1998) 'Changing Values' in W. Crotty and D. E. Schmitt (eds) *Ireland and the Politics of Change*. London: Longman, p. 82.
[5]   Eurobarometer Survey, Vols 42, 44.2.
[6]   Fahey, T., Hayes, B. C. and Sinnott, R. (2005) *Conflict and Consensus: a Study of Values and Attitudes in the Republic of Ireland and Northern Ireland*. Dublin: Institute of Public Administration (IPA), pp. 193–4.
[7]   The European Social Survey looks at the issue of *trust* in parliament, while the European Values Survey considers *confidence*.

Table 1.1: Trust/mistrust in national parliament (%)

Survey	Ireland		EU average	
	Trust	Mistrust	Trust	Mistrust
Spring 1996	54	28	48	38
Autumn 1997	38	52	40	48
Spring 1999	36	48	41	46
Spring 2001	41	43	40	46
Autumn 2001	38	50	42	48
Spring 2004	40	48	35	54

Source: Eurobarometer Surveys

Figure 1.1: Trust in parliament, 2002/3 (0, no trust at all; 10, complete trust)

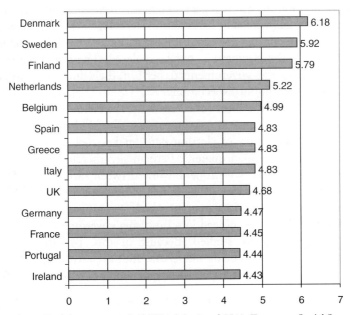

Source: Based on survey of 40,802 adults (aged 15+), European Social Survey 2002/2003

bureaucratic layers and meanings implied by it. For our purposes, and building on Dunleavy and Rhodes's definition of the 'core executive',[8] the executive consists of the Taoiseach (Prime Minister), the cabinet of ministers and the associated administrative structures (such as departments) that are charged with carrying out the processes of governing in the state. Where the Irish 'government' is referred to here, it denotes simply the Taoiseach and his ministers, who are elected to office by the Dáil and remain members of that chamber.

The accountability of the executive to the people is the most fundamental element of a democratic polity. Indeed, as Linz and Valenzuela argue, 'the most important difference among democratic regimes concerns the generation and accountability of executive authority.'[9] At one extreme in the understanding of accountability, government is held accountable to the public via national elections based on a secret, direct and equal ballot. In all Western parliamentary democracies, however, parliament acts on behalf of the electorate between elections when it elects a government and is constitutionally obliged to hold it to account. Indeed, in addition to producing legislation, controlling public expenditure and deliberating over policy, holding an elected government to account is one of the primary tasks performed by a legislature. Democratic theory envisages that a government that does not fulfil the wishes of parliament – and, by extension, the electorate – can be replaced. The threat of such sanction encourages governments to perform their duties broadly in accordance with public expectations.

Strøm refers to the ability of voters to use the ballot box to reward or punish governments as 'retrospective voting',[10] but later notes that the indeterminacy of election dates makes such *ex post* electoral accountability inadequate.[11] Parliament, therefore, must be equipped to oversee government work between elections and to ensure that the executive is held to account for its actions (or inactions). However, the extent to which parliaments in Western Europe and elsewhere succeed in scrutinising government has never been comprehensively studied. Because of this, parliaments are frequently criticised as being ineffectual and, as party whips ensure consistent government control, they are sometimes reduced to mere

---

[8] Dunleavy, P. and Rhodes, R. A. W. (1990) 'Prime Minister, Cabinet and Core Executive – Introduction', *Public Administration* Vol. 68(1), 3–28.

[9] Linz, J. J. and Valenzuela, A. (eds) (1994) *The Failure of Presidential Democracy*. Baltimore, MD: Johns Hopkins Press, p. x.

[10] Strøm, K. (1997) 'Democracy, Accountability and Coalition Bargaining', *European Journal of Political Research* Vol. 31(1–2), 47–62.

[11] Strøm, K. (2000) 'Delegation and Accountability in Parliamentary Democracies', *European Journal of Political Research* Vol. 37(3), 274.

'rubber-stamp' institutions, existing to give a democratic veneer to what is essentially the prerogative of the executive.

The 'decline of parliaments' and, with it, a decline in parliamentary oversight, has been prophesied since the start of the twentieth century[12] and has occurred in tandem with the development of disciplined parliamentary parties. To some extent, the increase in partisanship and the professionalisation of party politics have indeed turned parliaments into fora where adversarial politics takes precedence over parliamentary politics. Yet, in the early twenty-first century, legislatures remain core public institutions for legitimating political power, and it is the political parties that find themselves under threat from interest and pressure politics.

As the principal directly elected public institution in most democracies, legislatures act on behalf of citizens in ensuring that government is held to account for its actions. However, the growth of the executive state has made this role increasingly difficult in all Western democracies, with the result that extra-parliamentary mechanisms have been employed, often *post facto*, to act as oversight mechanisms. Simultaneously, in response to challenges posed by international political events such as EU integration, institutional innovation and adaptation have occurred within legislatures. These factors mean that our understanding of accountability, and particularly parliamentary accountability, needs to be re-examined.

Accountability in Westminster-type parliamentary systems

The Irish parliament has its structural and functional origins in its British equivalent at Westminster. In legislatures based on this model, collectively referred to as 'Westminster-style' parliaments,[13] the system of accountability is frequently understood as operating in a unidimensional manner with a clear chain of delegation. At the simplest level, principal–agent modelling is often used to explain the pattern of accountability that runs in the opposite direction to this delegation chain[14] (Figure 1.2). What this model does best is to show

---

12 Lord Bryce (1990 [1921]) 'The Decline of Legislatures' in P. Norton (ed.) *Legislatures*. Oxford: Oxford University Press, pp. 47–56.

13 Lijphart, A. (1984) *Democracies*. New Haven, CT: Yale University Press; Lijphart, A. (1999) *Patterns of Democracy: Government Forms and Performance in Thirty-Six Countries*. New Haven, CT: Yale University Press.

14 Strøm, K. (2000) 'Delegation and Accountability in Parliamentary Democracies', *European Journal of Political Research* Vol. 37(3), 267.

Figure 1.2: Ideal/typical chain of accountability in Westminster parliamentary system (where → means 'accountable to')

Public administration → Ministers → Government → Parliament → Electorate

---

that in such a system, the chain of accountability is only ever as strong as its weakest link.

The principal–agent model was developed to describe the theory of modern bureaucracy. The rationale is that the agent is better able to perform a function as it has special expertise not available to the principal. However, as Kiewiet and McCubbins point out, 'agency loss', where the agent is less than optimal in performing the function delegated to it, is a difficulty that all principals face.[15] These authors identify such hazards as 'hidden information' (the agent does not reveal all the information he or she should) and 'Madison's dilemma' (the more power given to the agent, the more danger there is) in principal–agent delegation processes. In fact, much of constitutional design is about minimising such liabilities in the democratic process, and the use of adequate checks and balances.

Of course, modern Irish government is infinitely more complicated than Figure 1.2 depicts: Figure 1.3 provides a more detailed description of its broad structures. In particular, the broadening range of activity with which the executive is involved provides great challenges for parliament in its role as watchdog. In theory at least, and despite its increasingly diffuse and complex nature, the Westminster system of government still attempts to provide clearer lines of accountability than many other forms of government. It is a far cry from the grid-like system of checks and balances that make up presidential forms of government, where the executive and legislative branches are institutionally separated.

The most complex and fundamental relationship in the Westminster system of governing is that between government and parliament. While the ascendancy of parliaments over monarchies predates the latter half of the nineteenth century, it is during this period that scholarly writing on the ascendancy of government, and its relationship to parliament, begins. Bagehot's *The English Constitution*

---

[15] Kiewiet, D. R. and McCubbins, M. D. (1991) *The Logic of Delegation. Congressional Parties and the Appropriations Process.* Chicago: University of Chicago Press, pp. 22–38.

Figure 1.3: Broad outline of the structures of the governing process in Ireland (arrow signifies 'accountable to')

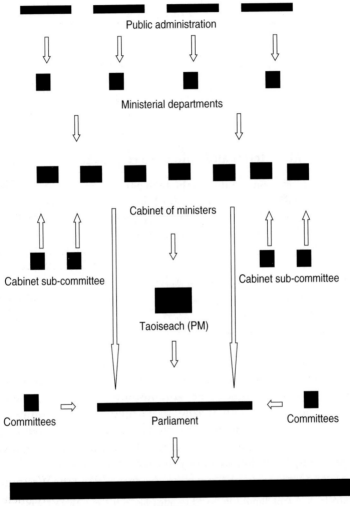

Public administration

Ministerial departments

Cabinet of ministers

Cabinet sub-committee   Cabinet sub-committee

Taoiseach (PM)

Committees   Parliament   Committees

Electorate

remains a classic work on the subject in which he famously refers to the close union of the legislative and executive powers in cabinet as 'the efficient secret'.[16] The relationship of these constitutional pillars

---

[16] Bagehot, W. (2001 [1867]) *The English Constitution*. Cambridge: Cambridge University Press.

of state is still subjected to much scholarly analysis internationally, but less so in Ireland.

The principle that the executive be accountable to parliament is vigorously asserted in most European constitutions, including the Irish Constitution, which envisages that the government shall be 'responsible' to Dáil Éireann,[17] a body elected by the people. This constitutional aspiration does not reflect the reality of modern party-dominated government, and the relationship between government and Dáil Éireann is increasingly complex. In order to analyse this relationship we must first consider the key concepts on which parliamentary accountability is founded.

Ministerial and collective responsibility

Parliamentary accountability in the Irish parliament, and particularly in Dáil Éireann, (the more powerful Lower House) is institutional-ised in two conventions: (a) ministerial responsibility for government departments, and (b) the collective responsibility of government for decisions made at cabinet.[18] In other words, individual ministers are responsible (or accountable) for the actions of their departments; and the college of ministers forms a government cabinet, each member of which is constitutionally bound to be collectively responsible for decisions taken by the government.[19]

Ministerial responsibility

In democratic systems, bureaucratic accountability extends upwards to the interface between the administration and the people's elected representatives. In Ireland, as in most other Westminster-style administrative systems, this interface occurs at the point of ministerial responsibility. The origins of the doctrine of ministerial responsibility lie in the attempt by nineteenth-century British liberal

---

[17] Article 28.4.1 of Bunreacht na hÉireann (the Irish Constitution) states that 'The Government shall be responsible to Dáil Éireann.' The Irish-language version, technically the official version of the Constitution, uses the term *freagrach*, whose literal translation is 'answerable'.

[18] Cabinet in this sense is the weekly meeting of ministers chaired by the Taoiseach (Premier), and not the consultative *cabinet* system common in other parliamentary systems, most notably France.

[19] Article 28.4.2: 'The Government shall meet and act as a collective authority, and shall be collectively responsible for the Departments of State administered by the members of the Government.'

democrats to reconcile the use of a salaried bureaucracy, which was not answerable to the people, with the requirements of democratic theory. As the state increasingly took on the role of regulator during this period, parliament in Westminster was content to delegate responsibility for various agencies to ministers who would be the final authority and fully answerable to the Commons. Therefore the mid-nineteenth century is often seen as the 'golden age' of the Westminster parliament, and writers such as Bagehot record it as a time when parliament held significant power over government and its ministers. Of course, as Flinders points out, even in Westminster there has never been agreement about the terms of that accountability and how it can be consistently enforced.[20]

Woodhouse, for example, claims that such a view of the origins of the doctrine is 'prescriptive' rather than 'descriptive'.[21] She argues convincingly that the development of ministerial responsibility occurred at the same time as the growth of disciplined political parties and the changing position of ministers from representatives of the Sovereign to representatives of such parties. In short, by the time ministerial accountability became an accepted part of Westminster politics, parliament was already in decline *vis-à-vis* the executive. Party discipline and bloc voting became parliamentary norms and eroded the ability of parliament to act as an effective check on government or to call for 'persons, papers and records'[22] that would allow it to scrutinise government work. In fact, in the era of party government, it may be argued that ministers became less accountable to parliament and more so to their own party backbenchers. The Westminster parliament at this phase of its development was used as a template for the development of the Oireachtas, as will be discussed in Chapter 3.

The statutory basis of ministerial responsibility

Since the enactment of eleven government departments under the Ministers and Secretaries Act, 1924, the Oireachtas has had no direct constitutional linkage with the civil service. Instead, civil servants are

---

20 Flinders, M. (2001) *The Politics of Accountability in the Modern State.* Aldershot: Ashgate, p. 42.
21 Woodhouse, D. (1994) *Ministers and Parliament.* Oxford: Clarendon Press, p. 5.
22 This power has its origins in the Westminster parliament's role as a High Court, which permitted it to punish for failure to provide information.

accountable to the various ministerial departments, which have been granted executive power by the Oireachtas. Since these departments needed to have a legal personality, this Act made the minister the 'corporation sole', thus separating the individual minister from the corporate entity of ministerial office. This was entirely consistent with the democratic doctrine that the administrative sphere be subordinate to the political one. However, the emphasis on the legal interpretation of the Act has come at the expense of political (and indeed managerial) conceptions of the doctrine, and defining what exactly ministers are accountable (as opposed to personally responsible) for continues to prove problematic.

In essence, the 1924 Act provided for the adoption of the convention of ministerial responsibility. In practice, Secretaries-General (as the most senior civil servants in each department) are also responsible for the financial accountability of the civil service to parliament. Each is an 'accounting officer',[23] responsible to the Committee on Public Accounts for the use of their departmental budget.

The growing range of activity by the public administration has necessitated several amendments to the Act since 1924. Most recently, the 1997 Public Service Management Act was a milestone in the development of the relationship between ministers and their departments. For the first time, the accountability of a Secretary-General to his or her minister was put on a statutory basis.[24] This accountability extended to matters such as implementing and monitoring government policies, the cost-effective use of resources and preparing strategy statements. Secretaries-General could now also appear before Oireachtas committees to answer questions on such statements.[25] These developments did not undermine or change the 'corporation sole' principle, however, which remains the basis for the accountability of ministers to parliament, and which underpins the Irish system of government. The 1997 Act concentrated on managerial and legal aspects of the relationship between the Secretary-General and the minister, as opposed to the political element. This complex relationship was further explored in a 2002

---

[23] While the term 'accounting officer' is long-standing, it was defined and put on a statutory basis only with the 1993 Comptroller and Auditor General (Amendment) Act.

[24] The Act also deals with the role of special advisers to ministers.

[25] Secretaries-General are also the accounting officers of their respective departments, and are therefore accountable to the Houses of the Oireachtas Committee on Public Accounts for the financial activities of their departments.

report produced by Secretaries-General concerning their dual role as Secretaries-General and accounting officers;[26] it is worthy of future examination in the context of a reforming public service.

Ministerial responsibility therefore forms a central element of the institutional structure of Irish parliamentary politics and government, yet it continues to provoke competing interpretations due to the changing nature of politics and the increased complexity of public administration. Whether or not ministers should resign for action for which they are not personally responsible is often the subject of intense debate. It may be argued that it is not always appropriate for the leader of an organisation to accept personal responsibility for matters that are clearly the fault of others, as doing so may protect those actually responsible. As Mulgan points out:

> In practice ... ministerial responsibility does not oblige ministers to resign for matters where they are not personally at fault. In such cases, they are merely required to undertake appropriate remedial actions, including the identification of those personally responsible, in other words to exercise the accountability obligations of their leadership role.[27]

While the doctrine's strength lies in its theoretical contribution to democratic accountability, its weakness lies in the reality of a dominant executive able to dictate what it is prepared to be accountable for. How far ministerial responsibility extends is periodically challenged: for example, a Supreme Court decision in 2002 on the powers of parliamentary committees found that the only route available to Dáil Éireann to investigate civil servants was through the appropriate minister (see Chapter 5). The consequences of Dáil Éireann's inability to develop its potential for effective executive scrutiny form the subject of this study.

Collective responsibility

Ministerial responsibility primarily entails the individual responsibility of ministers for the work of their departments, but, in theory at least, it also enables parliament to focus on the work of a particular minister rather than censuring the whole government. In addition,

---

[26] This was the *Report of the Working Group on the Accountability of Secretaries-General and Accounting Officers*, otherwise known as the Mullarkey Report, after its chairman.

[27] Mulgan, R. (2003) *Holding Power to Account: Accountability in Modern Democracies*. London: Macmillan, p. 206.

ministerial responsibility facilitates the second crucial convention on which the parliamentary accountability of the executive is founded – collective responsibility.[28] This doctrine ensures that ministers share culpability for the policies of the government, and thus provides parliament with the means of holding government accountable as a whole.

Woodhouse argues that collective responsibility really provides public accountability only when a government resigns following the loss of a vote of confidence. Otherwise, she claims, the doctrine serves the interests of government cohesion, especially in coalition governments, rather than parliamentary accountability, as was its intention.[29] However, as coalition government is now the norm in Ireland, collective responsibility gives opposition parties wider scope for attacking the executive, as they attempt to exploit ideological and political differences between the governing parties.

As Silkin[30] observes, these doctrines combined ensure that, firstly, the departmental minister cannot have a policy that diverges from that of cabinet and, secondly, as the head of his or her department the minister must publicly support the policy. It follows, therefore, that once cabinet has made a decision, the actions and policy statements of departmental civil servants must conform to those of the minister and the government as a whole. For these reasons, ministerial and collective responsibility have been the defining features of Westminster-type parliamentary systems, and have been adopted by most former British colonies, Ireland included. As with so many other constitutional provisions, however, the theory behind the concept is some way from the reality of its execution.

The founders of the Irish Free State adopted the principle of ministerial responsibility at the time of independence in 1922. Along with the concept of collective responsibility, it is to be found enshrined in both the 1922 and 1937 Constitutions. The common purpose was to ensure that all members of the executive retain the confidence of the Dáil. However, if viewed as a method of dislodging ineffectual ministers or governments, ministerial responsibility is a weakly enforced doctrine and is often used by ministers to shield themselves from scrutiny. No minister in the history of the Irish State

---

[28] Jordan, G. (1994) *The British Administrative System: Principles versus Practice.* London: Routledge, p. 191.

[29] Woodhouse, D. (1994) *Ministers and Parliament.* Oxford: Clarendon Press.

[30] Silkin, A. (1989) 'The "Agreement to Differ" of 1975' in G. Marshall (ed.) *Ministerial Responsibility.* Oxford: Oxford University Press, p. 55.

has resigned for failure to uphold the doctrine. Therefore, while the executive state has expanded, the convention of ministerial responsibility has been used to deflect parliamentary scrutiny and to prevent challenges to the increased power of government. This trend has led to a weakening of parliamentary accountability and its replacement with extra-parliamentary forms of oversight. Before considering this phenomenon, it is necessary to develop further the meaning of the term 'accountability'.

Defining 'accountability'

'Accountability' has its roots in the idea of monitoring state finances or accounts. It became a key concept in administrative law before appearing more recently as a substitute for the concept of political responsibility. As Deleon indicates, students of public administration have long distinguished between accountability and responsibility:[31] the former is regarded as a form of external control on behaviour, while the latter refers to internal controls inspired by personal ethics. Nonetheless, the two concepts are intertwined; calling someone to account may or may not mean that they are also personally responsible. Mulgan notes that the use of the term 'accountability' has expanded significantly in tandem with the growing body of literature surrounding new concepts of 'governance' and 'public management',[32] and argues that 'accountability' is now used to denote issues of control and responsiveness as well as responsibility.

Since Romzek and Dubnik's[33] seminal work on accountability mechanisms, we can identify an increasing trend towards identifying dichotomies in modern states with respect to accountability. As Thomas points out, distinctions are now made between political and administrative accountability, external and internal accountability, centralised and devolved accountability, and procedural and

31 Deleon, L. (2003) 'On Acting Responsibly in a Disorderly World: Individual Ethics and Administrative Responsibility' in B. G. Peters and J. Pierre (eds) *Handbook of Public Administration*. London: Sage, p. 569.

32 Mulgan, R. (2000) 'Accountability: an Ever-Expanding Concept?', *Public Administration* Vol. 78(3), 556; Mulgan, R. (2003) *Holding Power to Account: Accountability in Modern Democracies*. London: Macmillan, pp. 15–22.

33 Romzek, B. S. and Dubnik, M. J. (1987) 'Accountability in the Public Sector: Lessons from the Challenger Tragedy', *Public Administration Review* Vol. 47, 227–38.

performance accountability, to name but a few.[34] Accountability can be sought by and from either an individual or a collective. What all interpretations of accountability have in common, however, is that they depend on their context. The principal difficulty with the term is that the more widespread its use, the looser is its meaning.

Within the Irish public service, increasing 'accountability' has become a key justification for significant reforms at local and national levels,[35] in line with the international trend whereby governments accept new modes of accountability, including investigative agencies, in response to growing public scepticism towards public representatives and institutions.[36] The achievement of accountability is offered as a social and political panacea, often without adequate assessment of the consequences of creating myriad channels of oversight and responsibility.

At central government level, accountability via the institution of ministerial responsibility is relatively easily understood in theory. It implies a formal relationship whereby an actor (a minister) is called 'to account' for his or her actions by a body external to him or her (parliament), and accepting that that body has the authority to impose sanctions on him or her for failure to act in the principal's interest. The threat of being called to account ensures that it is in the actor's interest to comply. Indeed, all accountability relationships involve a mutual understanding between two sets of actors concerning responsibilities and potential sanctions. Difficulties arise when these relationships are subject to competing interpretations. For accountability to function properly, it must be grounded in formal and accepted rules or procedures such as parliamentary standing orders.

In many legislatures the formal methods of accountability are weak and are used by the government to deflect lines of enquiry. In Ireland, members of the Dáil find that they must step outside the formal boundaries of enquiry in order to pursue greater oversight of the executive. For example, opposition parties have increasingly

---

[34] Thomas, P. G. (2003) 'Accountability' in B. G. Peters and J. Pierre (eds) *Handbook of Public Administration.* London: Sage, p. 552.

[35] In particular, improving accountability was a principle of the public sector's Strategic Management Initiative (later called the Public Service Modernisation Programme) launched in 1994, and is central to its offshoot reform programmes, *Delivering Better Government* for the civil service and *Better Local Government* for local government, both initiated in 1996.

[36] Mulgan, R (2003) *Holding Power to Account: Accountability in Modern Democracies.* London: Macmillan.

called for greater powers for parliamentary committees to question civil servants. Parliamentary committees are considered in more detail in Chapter 5, but it is important to note here that they have evolved in many jurisdictions as a response by MPs to the inadequate information passed from government to parliament. In the Oireachtas (as in Westminster), whether or not committees create a comprehensive new mechanism by which government can be held to account remains open to debate. Comparative studies across legislatures suggest that where committees are strong (and party discipline weak) they can help reduce the imbalance in policy expertise between the legislature and the executive.[37]

The appearance of civil servants before parliamentary committees to answer questions concerning their role or to provide explanations for particular decisions causes particular difficulties given the principle of 'corporation sole'. As discussed above, under this principle the minister is theoretically responsible for all decisions made in the department under his or her aegis. This convention reinforces the political neutrality and anonymity of the civil service, and preserves the doctrine of ministerial responsibility as the most crucial link in the delegation (and therefore accountability) chain.

In response to this dilemma, the Committees of the Houses of the Oireachtas (Compellability, Privileges and Immunities) Act, 1997 established new parameters for public servants asked to give evidence before a parliamentary committee. Section 15 of the Act precludes public servants from expressing an opinion on the merits or objectives of any policy of the government or a government minister. Nonetheless, allowing non-government TDs[38] to question civil servants directly represents a significant break from the traditional chain of accountability. Similar developments have occurred in Britain, where, for example, the Franks Report on the origins of the Falklands War, which exposed serious inefficiency in the Foreign and Commonwealth Office, involved extensive questioning of civil servants.[39]

---

[37] Saalfeld, T. (2000) 'Members of Parliament and Governments in Western Europe: Agency Relations and Problems of Oversight', *European Journal of Political Research* Vol. 37(3), 367.

[38] 'TD' is an abbreviation of Teachta Dála: a member of Dáil Éireann. A literal translation is 'Messenger of the House'.

[39] Marshall, G. (1991) 'The Evolving Practice of Parliamentary Accountability: Writing Down the Rules', *Parliamentary Affairs* Vol. 44(4), 464.

Such methods of inquiry remove the buffer of ministerial protection from the public administration. At the same time, new external mechanisms of executive oversight in Ireland, such as the Freedom of Information Act, effectively bypass parliament. Quasi-judicial forms of scrutiny have become a prominent feature of Irish politics since the early 1990s, and include the judicial tribunals of inquiry that are currently investigating abuses in public life.

Accountability has many different faces and applications, but the focus of this study is on parliamentary accountability, i.e. the ability of Dáil Éireann – and particularly its non-government party members – to elicit information from government, and to sanction government as necessary. It also considers how parliamentary accountability has shaped, and been shaped by, alternative mechanisms of executive oversight in recent years. The principal challenges to the traditional methods of parliamentary accountability come from two sources, which can be categorised for our purposes as 'judicial' and 'public' accountability. While these have assumed independent identities in recent years, they are in many respects connected, with judicial accountability having a controlling influence over both parliamentary and public accountability.

Competing accountabilities in Ireland

The difficulties that parliament faces in holding a powerful executive to account are common to almost all parliamentary systems – recent work on Westminster by Flinders[40] in many ways reflects the challenges experienced by the modern Irish legislature. This study argues that in Ireland, the problem of inadequate executive scrutiny has been augmented by the introduction of extra-parliamentary mechanisms of oversight, and also by some new internal institutional arrangements. These mechanisms, as set out in Table 1.2, are briefly sketched below and discussed in detail in later chapters.

Traditional mechanisms of parliamentary accountability

The parliamentary question is the principal oversight tool available to parliamentarians in most parliamentary democracies, and in its oral (as opposed to written) format is used to probe individual ministers or the government collectively, as well as to check on the

---

[40] Flinders, M. (2001) *The Politics of Accountability in the Modern State.* Aldershot: Ashgate.

Table 1.2: Parliamentary, judicial and public mechanisms of accountability

		Mechanism	Used to hold whom to account?	Accountable to what institution?
Parliamentary accountability	Old	Parliamentary questions, debate	Executive (including the public administration), individual ministers and members	Dáil Éireann
	New	Parliamentary committees*	Executive (including the public administration), individual ministers and members	Houses of the Oireachtas
Judicial accountability		Tribunals of inquiry, statutory/non-statutory inquiries, Commissions of Inquiry	Public representatives, public administration, private citizens	Government
Public accountability	Old	Ombudsman	Public administration	–**
		Comptroller & Auditor-General	Public administration	Independent office by virtue of constitutional guarantee
	New	Freedom of Information Commissioner	Executive (including the public administration)	–**
		Electoral Acts, Standards in Public Office Commission	Political parties, public representatives	Houses of the Oireachtas

* The *Report of the Public Accounts Committee Sub-Committee on Certain Revenue Matters* ('DIRT Inquiry') was presented to Dáil Éireann, not to both Houses of the Oireachtas. Reports by select committees (i.e. committees consisting of members from one House only) also go to Dáil Éireann only. Reports by joint committees are presented to both Houses.
** While the Ombudsman and Freedom of Information Commissioner are appointed by the Houses of the Oireachtas and present reports to both Houses, they are in fact independent of those Houses and not accountable to them.

actions of the administration. Apart from questions, members engage in various forms of adversarial debate over legislation and policy with the government, and attempt to expose deficiencies in the actions or proposed actions of the executive. Dissent and approval on motions are expressed by voting.

While questions and debate form the bedrock of parliamentary accountability, a significant recent development for the Irish parliament has been the creation of a comprehensive and departmentally aligned committee system. At a minimum, committees provide members with an alternative forum for debate and questioning, although, as argued below, how effective committees can expect to be will depend on institutional and party political circumstances. While the committees are now an established feature of Irish parliamentary politics, in the light of a recent Supreme Court case some confusion remains as to how far their oversight remit extends.[41]

Judicial accountability

The ineffectiveness of parliamentary mechanisms of accountability, and parliamentary questions in particular, has resulted in Dáil Éireann deferring to judicial mechanisms of accountability. The principal and most obvious example of such 'judicial' accountability in Ireland has been the creation of several tribunals of inquiry, as well as statutory and non-statutory inquiries, each chaired by an independent judicial figure. Our focus will be on tribunals of inquiry.

While the Oireachtas appoints tribunals, experience has shown that they assume a life of their own and their progress remains free of political interference. They have been called on to investigate, among other things, corrupt payments to public representatives, weak accountability mechanisms within sectors of the administration, and political favouritism in the decision-making process. They have also been responsible for the establishment of several new regulatory bodies and legislation aimed at controlling the financing of politics in the state.

While tribunals of inquiry were used in previous decades to investigate matters such as specific public disasters, this study argues that since 1991 their use is directly attributable to the failure of parliamentary accountability. They have also acted as a

---

[41] The Supreme Court is the final court of appeal in Ireland. The case in question is the Abbeylara case, which is discussed in Chapter 5.

catalyst for the creation of other extra-parliamentary institutions of oversight, either as part of the tribunals' recommendations or by governments anxious to reduce the need for them in the future. Public accountability has thus been shaped not just by parliamentary but also by judicial accountability. Commissions of inquiry have recently been created which offer an alternative to tribunals.

Public accountability

By 'public' accountability, we mean the mechanisms of executive oversight that have allowed for greater public access to information without the use of parliament or public representatives. The Office of the Comptroller and Auditor-General, and since the early 1980s the Office of the Ombudsman, are examples of this form of accountability.[42] The tribunals of inquiry have given rise to further public mechanisms of accountability that have created a complex, and sometimes confusing, new layer of regulation in the governing and political processes. Examples of such institutions include the Standards in Public Office Commission, which monitors election expenditure and the fund-raising activities of the political parties, and the Office of the Freedom of Information Commissioner, which has overseen a sea change in the relationship of the public administration and the public. Like judicial forms of accountability, public accountability mechanisms pose challenges for parliament and, as Chapter 8 details, have stimulated internal parliamentary reform.

Judicial and public accountability has changed the political and parliamentary environment in contemporary Irish politics. With alternative routes of redress or information available to the public, the focus on parliament and parliamentary accountability is reduced. When parliament cannot fulfil its role of holding government to account, the value of its existence and the democratic legitimacy of its decisions may be called into question. Furthermore, accountability of the executive to the legislature cannot be delegated to extra- and non-parliamentary institutions.

Parliamentary accountability has emerged as a contested concept in Irish democracy. More successful and efficient forms of executive

---

[42] Of course parliamentary accountability can be considered a form of public accountability, as one of the principal purposes of any legislature is to give effect to public accountability in government.

scrutiny challenge the adherence to traditional parliamentary devices. In response, successive governments in the 1990s introduced institutional mechanisms for increasing the accountability not just of government, but also of individual members of parliament and even members of the bureaucracy. However, this study demonstrates that attempts at parliamentary reform must address the core problems *within* parliament that resulted in the need for alternative mechanisms of oversight, rather than simply responding to the unfolding demands of these mechanisms.

PART II

The Irish parliament in comparative institutional perspective

CHAPTER 2

Parliaments as institutions

Institutionalism in legislative studies

In their classic treatise on social construction, Berger and Luckman state that institutions play an essential role in the control of human conduct.[1] Legislative studies have a long tradition of applying institutional analysis to explain why, despite the potential for constant volatility, so much stability is found in parliaments.[2] To some extent, interest in institutions and constitutions moved away from the centre of research in political science in the mid-twentieth century. From the 1950s to the 1970s, behavioural, cultural and rationalist approaches, with roots in conflict theory and particularly Marxist class theory, made inroads into all sub-disciplines of political science, including the study of legislatures. Nonetheless, it may be argued that institutional analysis has always been a core methodology in legislative studies. In the 1960s, Polsby's seminal work on the US House of Representatives argued that:

> It is hard – indeed for the contemporary observer impossible – to shake the conviction that the House's institutional structure does matter greatly in the production of political outcomes.[3]

Legislative studies today are dominated by work on the US Congress, and particularly the House of Representatives, which has led the way for many new approaches to legislative studies.[4] Early twentieth-century comparative legislative work concentrated on appraisal of the differences between US presidential and Westminster parliamentary

---

[1] Berger, P. and Luckman, T. (1966) *The Social Construction of Reality*. London: Penguin Books.

[2] Döring, H. (1995) 'Institutions and Policies: Why We Need Cross-national Analysis', in H. Döring (ed.) *Parliaments and Majority Rule in Western Europe*. New York: St Martin's Press, p. 33.

[3] Polsby, N. W. (1968) 'The Institutionalization of the US House of Representatives', *American Political Science Review* Vol. 62, 165.

[4] Gamm, G. and Huber, J. (2002) 'Legislatures as Political Institutions: Beyond the Contemporary Congress' in I. Katznelson and H. V. Milner (eds) *Political Science: State of the Discipline*. New York: W. W. Norton, p. 314.

forms of government, as well as the variations in party structure and influence; by the late twentieth century institutional analysis had become much more sophisticated and involved detailed analysis of how rules and procedures within parliamentary chambers influence outcomes.[5] This reappraisal of institutions, or 'neo-institutionalism', in legislative studies put a new emphasis on the explanatory power of structures, rules and procedures such as those regulating the relationship between the executive and legislative branches.[6]

Actors in institutional context

Institutions such as parliaments do not appear by accident: actors with different motivations and desired outcomes inform their design. Institutions typically become embedded in a wider structural context and will often influence actors in unanticipated ways. Some distinct schools of thought have emerged concerning how best we can understand the origins and purposes of institutions, and the extent to which we can look to them for an explanation of political outcomes and policy changes.

It has been argued that institutionalist approaches may be taken from rational choice, sociological or historical viewpoints.[7] However, most scholarly work tends to 'border-cross' or combine the central tenets of each approach, all of which agree that we cannot understand the motivations of actors without considering the institutional context in which they are embedded. This is particularly true of parliamentarians.

Rational choice institutionalism

Rational choice theory is one of the more contested methodologies in political science, and its use in legislative studies reflects this. Its conceptual origins lie in parallels between market competition for

---

[5] See for example Krehbiel, K. (1991) *Information and Legislative Organization*. Ann Arbor: University of Michigan Press; Döring, H. (ed.) (1995) *Parliaments and Majority Rule in Western Europe*. New York: St Martin's Press; Döring, H. and Hallerberg, M. (eds) (2004) *Patterns of Parliamentary Behaviour*. Aldershot: Ashgate.

[6] Strøm, K. (1995) 'Parliamentary Government and Legislative Organisation' in H. Döring (ed.) *Parliaments and Majority Rule in Western Europe*. New York: St Martin's Press, p. 59.

[7] Hall, P. A. and Taylor, R. (1996) 'Political Science and the Three New Institutionalisms', *Political Studies* Vol. 44(5), 936–57.

goods and political competition for the fruits of power.[8] Among the best-known early rational choice theorists are Arrow,[9] Downs[10] and Olson.[11] Indeed, Olson's work on collective action problems has informed much of rational choice institutionalism.

Advocates of the institutional approach argue that we can understand institutions as tools designed by actors for the purpose of solving collective action dilemmas. Depending on the problem to be solved, rational choice institutionalists argue that actors choose certain institutions over others in the search for a solution, and that by examining these institutions we can make more accurate predictions of future outcomes.[12]

Rational choice institutionalism can also examine the outcomes of political deliberation with a view to understanding the impact of institutions on actors' choices in the decision-making process. For example, Immergut's comparison of health insurance politics in France, Switzerland and Sweden adopts a rational choice approach to help explain divergence in policy outcomes.[13] In short, applying rational choice theory to institutionalism has proved a useful methodological approach and has yielded new explanatory frameworks, particularly in the field of comparative legislative studies.

Fenno's work on legislative organisation and the motivations of legislators is among the first contributions of rational choice institutionalism to legislative studies.[14] Building on it, Shepsle and Weingast link the processes of building stable party majorities to the institutional and organisational characteristics of the US Congress.[15] In more recent years, as Kieweit *et al.* describe, rational choice approaches to the US Congress and, increasingly, to European

[8] Green, D. and Shapiro, I. (1994) *Pathologies of Rational Choice Theory*. New Haven, CT: Yale University Press.
[9] Arrow, K. J. (1963 [1951]) *Social Choice and Individual Values*. New York: Wiley.
[10] Downs, A. (1957) *An Economic Theory of Democracy*. New York: Harper & Row.
[11] Olson, M. (1965) *The Logic of Collective Action: Public Goods and the Theory of Groups*. Cambridge, MA: Harvard University Press.
[12] Laver, M. (1997) *Private Desires, Political Action*. London: Sage.
[13] Immergut, E. M. (1992) 'The Rules of the Game: the Logic of Health Policymaking in France, Switzerland and Sweden' in S. Steinmo, K. Thelen and F. Longstreth (eds) *Structuring Politics: Historical Institutionalism in Comparative Analysis*. Cambridge: Cambridge University Press, pp. 57–89.
[14] Fenno, R. F. (1973) *Congressmen in Committees*. Boston: Little, Brown.
[15] Shepsle, K. A. and Weingast, B. R. (1982) 'Institutionalising Majority Rule: a Social Choice Theory with Policy Implications', *American Economic Review* Vol. 72, 367–73.

legislatures and their functions have become commonplace.[16] As Weingast points out, one of the main reasons for this is the ability of rational choice institutional analysis to demonstrate 'how microlevel details imply macropolitical differences'.[17] Indeed, practitioners of rational choice find political settings such as legislatures ideal as subjects of study, as they tend to be stable and discrete, with clearly identifiable boundaries. For example, Kiewiet and McCubbins,[18] and more recently Cameron,[19] used rational choice institutionalism to explain how legislative outcomes in Congress were influenced by the presidential veto. Similarly, Cox and McCubbins[20] adopt a rational choice approach to develop a model of Congress based on political party organisation, and Tsebelis and Money[21] examine the nature and impact of bicameralism.

In European parliamentary systems, and particularly those based on the Westminster model, rational choice institutional work is less developed but has influenced legislative analysis in a number of ways. Rational choice theorists have, for example, compared ideal-type Westminster parliamentary systems (see below) to firms where the executive attempts to maintain a monopoly on the production of legislation. With this in mind, any changes to the rules and procedures of parliament will be expected to underpin or enhance the government's dominance of the chamber. However, since government members realise that they might soon be in opposition themselves, such reforms will not be excessive, and so a form of equilibrium exists in an otherwise adversarial environment.

---

[16]   Kiewiet, D. R., Loewenberg, G. and Squire, P. (2002) 'The Implications of the Study of the US Congress for Comparative Legislative Research' in G. Loewenberg, P. Squire and D. R. Kiewiet (eds) *Legislatures: Comparative Perspectives on Representative Assemblies.* Ann Arbor: University of Michigan Press, p. 5.

[17]   Weingast, B. R. (2002) 'Rational-Choice Institutionalism' in I. Katznelson and H. V. Milner (eds) *Political Science: the State of the Discipline.* New York: W. W. Norton, p. 662.

[18]   Kiewiet, D. R. and McCubbins, M. D. (1988) 'Presidential Influence on Congressional Appropriation Decisions', *American Journal of Political Science* Vol. 32 (August), 713–36.

[19]   Cameron, C. M. (2000) *Veto Bargaining: Presidents and the Politics of Negative Power.* Cambridge: Cambridge University Press.

[20]   Cox, G. W. and McCubbins, M. D. (1993) *Legislative Leviathan.* Berkeley: University of California Press.

[21]   Tsebilis, G. and Money, J. (1997) *Bicameralism.* Cambridge: Cambridge University Press.

Veto players

Rational choice institutionalism provides useful concepts for understanding why some institutions are chosen over others. Chief among
these is the concept of 'veto players', which are checks on the development of an institution. The term originates in Tsebelis' study of how
the number of parties in government in a parliamentary system
influences policy choices. He defines veto players as 'institutional or
partisan actors whose agreement is necessary for a change in policy'.[22]
In other words, a veto player's approval is necessary for a change in the
status quo. Any change to the status quo must benefit all veto players.[23]

Veto players are particularly important to our understanding of
the myriad ways in which the executive can prevent parliament from
acting as a check on its work. Indeed, rational choice institutional
approaches to parliaments shift the focus of analysis away from
comparative typologies based on the roles and functions of legislatures, and onto the micro-institutions of rules and procedures. As
Gamm and Huber note, rational choice studies of Congress have inspired and provided the theoretical framework for many similar legislative studies elsewhere;[24] systematic comparative rational choice
studies of European legislatures have appeared in the past few years.
Among the most comprehensive are the research projects co-ordinat-
ed by Döring[25] and, more recently, Döring and Hallerberg.[26]

The contributors to Döring's work identified and compared the
institutional veto players common to the diverse range of European
parliaments. They argued that issues such as the ability to raise a
parliamentary question and to establish committees, and even
whether or not voting is secret in the chamber, will influence legislation and executive strategy. Ignoring the cultural or historical
contexts of parliaments and focusing on particular veto players allows

---

[22] Tsebelis, G. (1995) 'Veto Players and Law Production in Parliamentary
Democracies' in H. Döring (ed.) *Parliaments and Majority Rule in Western
Europe*. New York: St Martin's Press, p. 88.

[23] Magaloni, B. (2002) 'Horizontal Accountability, the Rule of Law and the Judiciary: Mexico in Comparative Perspective' in S. Mainwaring and C. Welna (eds)
Democratic Accountability in Latin America. Oxford: Oxford University Press, p. 4.

[24] Gamm, G. and Huber, J. (2002) 'Legislatures as Political Institutions: Beyond
the Contemporary Congress' in I. Katznelson and H. V. Milner (eds) *Political
Science: State of the Discipline*. New York: W. W. Norton, p. 325.

[25] Döring, H. (ed.) (1995) *Parliaments and Majority Rule in Western Europe*. New
York: St Martin's Press.

[26] Döring, H. and Hallerberg, M. (eds) (2004) *Patterns of Parliamentary Behaviour*. Aldershot: Ashgate.

rational choice institutionalists to create models of behaviour and thus attempt to predict institutional outcomes.

Critical junctures

According to Pierson and Skocpol, rational choice institutional analysis provides another important concept – that of 'critical junctures'.[27] Collier and Collier define critical junctures as major events that 'establish certain directions of change and foreclose others in a way that shapes politics for years to come'.[28] Critical junctures are points in time at which decisions are made and alternatives ignored, and after which a return to the prior status quo becomes difficult and often undesirable. Examples of critical junctures might include new constitutions, new procedural rules or new internal institutions such as parliamentary committees.

Critical junctures are not just significant changes in the configuration of institutions such as parliaments; they also include decisions with later implications for how the institutions work. For example, as Chapter 3 will demonstrate, when political parties change their government formation preferences from single party to coalition government, this has consequences for the 'rules of the game' in the parliamentary arena. For this reason we must consider closely the actors and their changing motivations, by engaging in a more historical analysis of the relationship between actors and institutions. Therefore, critical junctures have come to be a core postulate of historical institutional theory, which considers the development of institutions over time rather than simply as responses to short-term problems.

Rational choice institutionalism provides an interesting framework, but its advocates have difficulty in explaining 'non-rational' behaviour or why actors choose actions that do not appear to benefit them directly. Cameron argues that the rational choice approach in legislative studies does not help us understand the decision-making process, and instead has resulted in 'empty propositions about the uninteresting'.[29] The principal criticism of rational choice accounts

[27] Pierson, P. and Skocpol, T. (2002) 'Historical Institutionalism in Contemporary Political Science' in I. Katznelson and H. V. Milner (eds), *Political Science: State of the Discipline*. New York: W.W. Norton.

[28] Collier, R. B. and Collier, D. (1991) *Shaping the Political Arena: Critical Junctures, the Labor Movement, and Regime Dynamics in Latin America*. Princeton, NJ: Princeton University Press, p. 27.

[29] Cameron, C. M. (2000) *Veto Bargaining: Presidents and the Politics of Negative Power*. Cambridge: Cambridge University Press, p. 265.

of institutions and legislative organisation is that they are ahistorical and, in Lane and Ersson's view, 'thin' compared to more holistic explanations.[30]

In fact, Cox and McCubbins's[31] contribution notwithstanding, most rational choice work on the US Congress focuses on individual legislator behaviour and how institutions are established to provide incentives or disincentives to certain courses of action. This would be more difficult in European parliamentary systems, where strong party discipline and cohesion must be factored into any study of preference formation and voting habits. Also, much Congressional research is predicated on a fixed institutional context that does not allow for local or cultural factors. For example, rational choice theorists view the development of committees in Congress as a decision taken for reasons of information acquisition or 'economies of operation'.[32] Such a view would not adequately explain the belated development of committees in the Irish parliament, which was a consequence of, among other things, the dynamics of the party system.

Sociological institutionalism

Among the most vocal critics of rational choice approaches to institutional theory are advocates of a more 'sociological' approach. With its roots in organisation theory, sociological institutionalism is heavily influenced by Durkheim and his ideas concerning institutions as patterns of behaviour.[33] It defines institutions not just as rules and procedures but also as the symbol systems, cognitive scripts and moral templates that guide human action. Unlike the atomising principles of rational choice institutionalism, the sociological approach emphasises the influence of 'macro' factors in determining 'micro' institutions. Sociological institutionalists see outcomes as the products of interaction among various groups, interests, ideas and

---

[30] Lane, J. E. and Ersson, S. (2000) *The New Institutional Politics. Performance and Outcomes.* London: Routledge, p. 4.

[31] Cox, G. W. and McCubbins, M. D. (1993) *Legislative Leviathan.* Berkeley: University of Californias Press.

[32] Mattson, I. and Strøm, K. (1995) 'Parliamentary Committees' in H. Döring (ed.) *Parliaments and Majority Rule in Western Europe.* New York: St Martin's Press, pp. 249–307.

[33] Hall, P. A. and Taylor, R. (1996) 'Political Science and the Three New Institutionalisms', *Political Studies* Vol. 44(5), 946.

institutional structures. Powell and DiMaggio[34] are prominent advocates of this approach and identify the 'embeddedness' of individuals in cultural and social norms as the principal motivator for their actions.

However, for institutionalists from the sociological school of thought, individual and rational actions are largely unimportant in explaining macro-level phenomena. Instead, what matters is the contest between different views of large-scale institutions such as the state; what occurs thereafter can only be understood with reference to the outcome of that contest.[35] Conflict theories such as Marxism, for example, focus on broad structures such as socio-economic class. They argue that what happens at the intermediate level, such as the design of legislatures, the dynamics of party competition, or union organisation is of secondary importance in terms of political outcomes. Hall and Taylor regard sociological institutionalist approaches as 'curiously bloodless',[36] as they tend not to appreciate the clashes of power that often occur at a time of institutional change, especially at this intermediate level.

The sociological approach is probably the least developed of the three theoretical strands in institutional studies, and is not a common methodological tool in legislative studies. While sociological institutionalists can explain institutional stability and inertia, they have difficulty in explaining institutional change. Instead, along with critical junctures and veto players, an appreciation of historical factors has come to be accepted as a key part of contemporary institutional theory. These factors offer a potentially richer methodological framework for studying the development of legislatures, and the oversight capability of Dáil Éireann.

Historical institutionalism

The distinguishing feature of historical institutionalism is its appreciation of the influence of long-term processes and historical context on the development of institutions. For example, March and Olsen's seminal work comparing administrative reform in the US and Britain

---

[34] Powell, W. and DiMaggio, P. J. (eds) (1991) *The New Institutionalism in Organisational Analysis*. Chicago: University of Chicago Press.

[35] Lane, J. E. (1993) *The Public Sector: Concepts, Models and Approaches*. London: Sage, p. 174.

[36] Hall, P. A. and Taylor, R. (1996) 'Political Science and the Three New Institutionalisms', *Political Studies* Vol. 44(5), 954.

emphasises not only the institutional but also the historical differences between the two states.[37] They argue that administrative reform in Britain became a policy tool for the Prime Minister precisely because responsible administrative authority was located within the cabinet. In contrast, American administrative reform was enmeshed in the political struggle between Congress and the presidency.

Defining institutions in the broadest sense, Berger and Luckman argued that 'it is impossible to understand an institution adequately without an understanding of the historical process in which it was produced.'[38] The historical institutionalist approach has been adopted across many sub-fields of political science, from the role of the state[39] to social identities in politics.[40] More importantly for the purposes of this study, it has also been a very productive method of research in parliamentary studies.[41] As Gamm and Huber point out, by examining legislatures from a historical viewpoint, we can see how various internal institutions emerge and change.[42]

Historical institutionalists define institutions as 'the formal or informal procedures, routines, norms and conventions embedded in the organizational structure of the polity or political economy'.[43] They emphasise the role of institutional choices made early in the development of policy areas, or even of political systems, and argue that these initial choices will have a pervasive effect on subsequent

[37] March, J. G. and Olsen, J. (1989) *Rediscovering Institutions: the Organizational Basis of Politics.* London: Free Press.

[38] Berger, P. and Luckman, T. (1966) *The Social Construction of Reality.* London: Penguin Books, p. 72.

[39] Skocpol, T. (1985) 'Bringing the State Back In: Strategies of Analysis in Current Research' in P. B. Evans, D. Rueschemeyer and T. Skocpol (eds.) *Bringing the State Back In.* Cambridge: Cambridge University Press, pp. 3–37.

[40] Lustik, I. (1993) *Unsettled States, Disputed Lands: Britain and Ireland, France and Algeria, Israel and the West Bank–Gaza.* Ithaca, NY: Cornell University Press.

[41] See for example Damgaard, E. (ed.) (1992) *Parliamentary Change in the Nordic Countries.* Oslo: Scandinavian University Press; Copeland, G. W. and Patterson, S. C. (eds) (1994) *Parliaments in the Modern World: Changing Institutions.* Ann Arbor: University of Michigan Press; Olson, D. M. and Norton, P. (eds) (1996) *The New Parliaments of Central and Eastern Europe.* London: Frank Cass; Norton, P. (ed.) (1998) *Parliaments and Governments in Western Europe.* London: Frank Cass.

[42] Gamm, G. and Huber, J. (2002) 'Legislatures as Political Institutions: Beyond the Contemporary Congress' in I. Katznelson and H. V. Milner (eds) *Political Science: State of the Discipline.* New York: W. W. Norton, p. 336.

[43] Hall, P. A. and Taylor, R. (1996) 'Political Science and the Three New Institutionalisms', *Political Studies* Vol. 44(5), 938.

policy changes.[44] In other words, once they have been developed, institutions shape goals and define means. Furthermore, historical institutionalists tend to attach importance to the static and enduring features of institutions. Episodes of change, or critical junctures, expose the underlying pressures for change that otherwise are not immediately apparent. Often these junctures occur after a long period of relative stability. Change is precipitated by a key actor or actors, but something must also have changed in the preference ordering of the actor or actors, and perhaps too in the context that makes it possible for them to give effect to those altered preferences. Historical institutionalism offers a very useful explanatory framework for the shifting dynamics in party politics and how they can influence and be influenced by the modus operandi of parliament.

Path-dependency

Decisions made at critical junctures shape and create the developmental trajectory of institutions. This self-reinforcing process has come to be known as 'path-dependency'. It posits that once chosen, political institutions (or dynamics) will repeat themselves and prove difficult to dismantle. Path-dependency is crucial to historical institutionalists, who argue that institutions are enduring, slow to reform, and not easily abandoned when circumstances change. For example, path-dependency may help us understand why the broad institutional make-up of the Irish parliament remained largely unchanged despite the many changes in government since 1922.

As noted above, critical junctures often occur not just as a result of rational decision-making but also following a long period of relative stability. Thelen argues that when studying institutions, we must consider not only the outcome of institutional change but also the processes by which actors in previous institutions moved towards the creation of new ones.[45] In legislative studies, changes in the dynamics of the party system can provide clues as to the motivation of actors in instigating particular institutional reforms. This is in sharp contrast to the rational choice approach, which tends to emphasise facets of institution-building that are purely goal-driven and cost-reducing.

---

[44] Peters, B. G. (1996) 'Political Institutions, Old and New' in R. E. Goodin and H. D. Klingemann (eds) *A New Handbook of Political Science.* Oxford: Oxford University Press, p. 210.

[45] Thelen, K. (1999) 'Historical Institutionalism in Comparative Politics', *Annual Review of Political Science* Vol. 2, 369–404.

For example, political parties in a typical Westminster-style system will have different views on the need for parliamentary reform depending on whether or not they are in government. The institutional logic of single-party government means that the party in power will be reluctant to concede any advantage to the opposition. Empowering the opposition may leave the government vulnerable to attack. This makes the explanation of parliamentary reform in such systems even more intriguing, and lends weight to historical institutionalists' emphasis on wider factors than those permitted by rational choice approaches.

Institutional change and unintended consequences

A final concept to consider here is the idea that institutional change might produce future benefits or costs not anticipated at the moment of change. Indeed, it is often because of a fear of 'unintended consequences' that political actors do not make reforms that might in theory improve their position. For example, governments change the electoral system less frequently than might be expected on the basis on their rational self-interest alone. They know that any change that would entrench their position in power would also make it more difficult for them to regain power were they to lose it. Unintended consequences are discussed in later chapters in the context of how successive periods of coalition government have resulted in significant institutional reform in Dáil Éireann.

Combining institutional approaches

Hay and Wincott argue that the rational choice, historical and sociological approaches to institutionalism should exist as separate methodological canons.[46] However, most social scientists would not agree that they are exclusive domains; the most productive work moves between the various institutional approaches in order to explain social or structural phenomena.[47] Authors such as Hall and Taylor,[48]

---

[46] Hay, C. and Wincott, D. (1998) 'Structure, Agency and Historical Institutionalism', *Political Studies* Vol. 46(5), 951–7.

[47] Thelen, K. (1999) 'Historical Institutionalism in Comparative Politics', *Annual Review of Political Science* Vol. 2, 370.

[48] Hall, P. A. and Taylor, R. (1996) 'Political Science and the Three New Institutionalisms', *Political Studies* Vol. 44(5), 936–57; Hall, P. A. and Taylor, R. (1998) 'The Potential of Historical Institutionalism', *Political Studies* Vol. 46(5), 958–62.

Hall,[49] and Pierson and Skocpol[50] argue that the most productive work using institutional theory draws on elements of all three approaches.

Legislative studies benefit significantly from the synthesis of approaches, particularly the rational choice and historical approaches outlined above. This facilitates rigorous comparative analysis while acknowledging the unique historical setting in which each elected parliament finds itself. Institutional reform frequently produces unintended consequences; later chapters demonstrate that this is particularly true of actors in parliamentary settings.

Parliaments in comparative perspective

Legislative studies is one of the oldest sub-fields of political science, and comparative case studies of parliamentary systems abound.[51] These texts have introduced a variety of methodologies and variables with which to compare legislatures, particularly in Western democracies. Cross-national studies of parliaments over time, however, are scarce,[52] and the variables under comparison are mixed. For example,

---

[49] Hall, P. A. (1997) 'The Role of Interests, Institutions and Ideas in the Comparative Political Economy of Industrialised Nations' in M. I. Lichbach and A. S. Zuckermann (eds) *Comparative Politics: Rationality, Culture and Structure.* Cambridge: Cambridge University Press, pp. 174–207.

[50] Pierson, P. and Skocpol, T. (2002) 'Historical Institutionalism in Contemporary Political Science' in I. Katznelson and H. V. Milner (eds) *Political Science: State of the Discipline.* New York: W. W. Norton, p. 721.

[51] Wheare, K. C. (1963) *Legislatures.* London: Oxford University Press; Blondel, J. (1973) *Comparative Legislatures.* London: Prentice Hall; Mezey, M. (1979) *Comparative Legislatures.* Durham, NC: Duke University Press; Lijphart, A. (1984) *Democracies.* New Haven, CT: Yale University Press; Laundy, P. (1989) *Parliaments in the Modern World.* Aldershot: Dartmouth; Norton, P. (ed.) (1990) *Legislatures.* Oxford: Oxford University Press; Olson, D. M. and Mezey, M. L. (eds) (1991) *Parliaments and Public Policy.* Cambridge: Cambridge University Press; Copeland, G. W. and Patterson, S. C. (eds) (1994) *Parliaments in the Modern World: Changing Institutions.* Ann Arbor: University of Michigan Press; Döring, H. (ed.) (1995) *Parliaments and Majority Rule in Western Europe.* New York: St Martin's Press; Norton, P. (ed.) (1998) *Parliaments and Governments in Western Europe.* London: Frank Cass; Lijphart, A. (1999) *Patterns of Democracy: Government Forms and Performance in Thirty-Six Countries.* New Haven, CT: Yale University Press; Maurer, A. and Wessels, W. (eds) (2001) *National Parliaments on Their Ways to Europe: Losers or Latecomers?* Baden-Baden, Germany: Nomos.

[52] Blondel, J. (1973) *Comparative Legislatures.* London: Prentice Hall; Mezey, M. (1979) *Comparative Legislatures.* Durham, NC: Duke University Press; Shugart, M. S. and Carey, J. M. (1992) *Presidents and Assemblies: Constitutional Design and Electoral Dynamics.* Cambridge: Cambridge University Press.

Norton argues that the most efficient way to compare legislatures cross-nationally is by looking at the procedures for passing legislation.[53] Tsebelis believes that the most used mode of distinguishing between legislatures is based on the number of parties in parliament, and points to the work of Duverger and Sartori in this area.[54] There are also many theoretical approaches to comparative legislative studies. In particular, as noted above, much has been made of the recent use of institutional theory, especially from a rational choice perspective.[55]

Nonetheless, there is now near-universal agreement that the institutional make-up of legislatures has a substantial impact on their functioning and output. Examining the institutional infrastructure of parliaments, and its historical development, elucidates the motivations of the actors within it. Only then is it possible to investigate how parliamentary accountability operates, and to assess the effectiveness of the mechanisms designed to ensure scrutiny of the executive.

The Lijphart typology

Perhaps the most influential study of how the arrangement of government structures in democracies affects their performance and the activities of the actors within them is the work of Arend Lijphart. Contemporary comparative politics has found particularly useful his dichotomous classification of governments as operating under either a 'majoritarian' or a 'consensus' institutional configuration[56] (Figure 2.1). Indeed, Lane and Ersson refer to this as 'the most influential institutionalist text in political science during the post-war period'.[57] While these two forms of democratic government are ideal types, they allow us to establish how the broad institutions of state affect the dynamics of parliamentary accountability.

[53] Norton, P. (ed.) (1990) *Legislatures*. Oxford: Oxford University Press.

[54] Tsebelis, G. (1995) 'Veto Players and Law Production in Parliamentary Democracies' in H. Döring (ed.) *Parliaments and Majority Rule in Western Europe*. New York: St Martin's Press, p. 83.

[55] Cox, G. W. and McCubbins, M. D. (1993) *Legislative Leviathan*. Oxford, University of California Press; Döring, H. (ed.) (1995) *Parliaments and Majority Rule in Western Europe*. New York: St Martin's Press.

[56] Lijphart, A. (1984) *Democracies*. New Haven, CT: Yale University Press; Lijphart, A. (1999) *Patterns of Democracy: Government Forms and Performance in Thirty-Six Countries*. New Haven, CT: Yale University Press.

[57] Lane, J. E. and Ersson, S. (2000) *The New Institutional Politics. Performance and Outcomes*. London: Routledge, p. 205.

As Table 2.1 demonstrates, Lijphart proposes ten variables, which, he argues, operate differently depending on the type of government. He groups them into two broad dimensions: the executive–parties dimension concerns the concentration or dispersion of power within the government itself; the federal–unitary dimension concerns the territorial concentration or dispersion of power. Combining these dimensions, he identifies two clusters of governmental types. The majoritarian or Westminster style represents parliaments that adopted the principal features of the British parliament at Westminster; this model is referred to in Chapter 1. The consensus model applies to parliamentary systems and activities that are most commonly found in continental European political systems. It is worth considering in some detail the aspects of these models relevant to this study.

Westminster-type systems

On the executive–parties dimension, the most significant feature of Westminster systems is the dominance of the executive over the legislature. This is possible as a single party holds a majority of seats in the parliament, and elects from its ranks a committee to assume cabinet or executive control. At the apex of this system will be a powerful premier, and strong party discipline will ensure that the executive can pursue its agenda largely unhindered by the chamber that elects it. Also, a majoritarian electoral law is used, which has a centripetal effect on the two main parties that compete for the levers of power. As Mulgan points out, this type of system can offer greater public accountability, as an adversarial opposition party will be eager to reveal government malpractices to the public.[58] However, this is only possible if the governing party or parties do not dominate the legislature, and adequate mechanisms are in place for the opposition to enquire into the activity of government.

Moving to the federal–unitary dimension, we also find several institutional features that distinguish majoritarian systems from consensus systems. The primary characteristic here is the unitary and centralised nature of government, with a great deal of power in the hands of the executive. Furthermore, the second chamber of parliament (if there is one) will be of a different size and created using a different electoral system from the more powerful lower chamber. It will also contain a government majority, and its ability to act as a

---

[58] Mulgan, R. (2003) *Holding Power to Account: Accountability in Modern Democracies.* London: Macmillan, p. 60.

Table 2.1: Lijphart's two models of democracy

Majoritarian	Consensus
Executive–parties dimension	
• Single-party majority cabinets	• Multiparty executive coalitions
• Executive dominance	• Executive–legislative power balance
• Two-party system	• Multiparty system
• Majoritarian electoral law	• Proportional electoral law
• Pluralist interest group system	• Corporatist interest group system
Federal–unitary dimension	
• Unitary and centralised government	• Federal and decentralised government
• Asymmetrical bicameralism	• Symmetrical bicameralism
• Flexible or 'unwritten' constitution	• Rigid constitution
• Legislative sovereignty	• Judicial review
• Central bank dependent on executive	• Independent central bank

Source: Lijphart (1994), 3–4

check on the executive's prerogative will be weak. Finally, in Lijphart's majoritarian system there will be relatively weak constitutional checks on government.

In such an environment, parliamentary politics will tend to be adversarial. Mechanisms for allowing the opposition parties to probe the intentions of government may exist in the Lower House, but the majority party will consistently (and successfully) frustrate attempts to use them. The result is that parliamentary politics takes on a zero-sum format, whereby a gain by the opposition is a loss for government, and vice versa. Government will be inclined to disclose as little information as possible about its operations. Westminster-type parliaments are therefore associated with strong executives, and the institutions of government make it difficult for the opposition to involve itself in government work. These broad structural factors fundamentally affect the degree to which parliament can act as a check on the executive. In short, the closer a parliament is to the ideal-type Westminster parliament, the less effective we can expect its structures of parliamentary oversight to be.

Consensual systems

The institutional arrangement of the Westminster-style system contrasts with that of the consensual or 'continental' systems. Consensual government entails considerably more dispersal of power because of institutional arrangements on both the executive–parties and federal–unitary dimensions. On the former dimension, the principal feature of consensus systems is the balance of power between the executive and legislature. Lijphart argues that in a typical consensual parliamentary democracy, a proportional electoral system returns a multiparty parliament, which ensures that coalition government is the norm. Coalition government will be more responsive to the legislature, partly because of the more frequent turnover of multiparty coalitions, but also because of the institutional and constitutional arrangements that facilitate direct involvement of the opposition in shaping and amending legislation, as well as deliberating on government policy.

On the federal–unitary dimension, the principal institutions of state are designed to provide for separation of power and for multiple checks and balances. For example, the existence of a powerful second chamber, which acts as a veto player over the first, is a defining feature of ideal-type consensual systems. Power is also frequently dispersed through federal and decentralised government. Furthermore, a written constitution prevents government from too easily altering the institutional configuration of the state and obviates the concentration of power in any one institution.

Parliamentary politics is more co-operative in consensual than in majoritarian systems. The frequency of coalition and minority governments ensures that the opposition parties are not institutionally removed from the decision-making process, and the internal structures of parliament provide for opposition checks on government. Indeed, Lijphart argues that consensual governments are generally more accountable and less corrupt than majoritarian ones.[59] One of the principal reasons for this is that in consensual parliamentary systems, the institutional arrangement is such that the government is more responsive to parliament's right to scrutinise its actions. Conversely, in Westminster systems the structures of parliamentary oversight are weaker and mean that parliament is less able to exert a restraining and accountability-enforcing influence on government.

The institutional variation in the political systems of Western Europe makes a simple dichotomy such as Lijphart's difficult to sustain. Indeed, Lijphart himself recognised the distance between his *de jure* Westminster and the *de facto* Westminster of the 1990s.[60]

---

[59] Lijphart, A. (1999) *Patterns of Democracy: Government Forms and Performance in Thirty-Six Countries.* New Haven, CT: Yale University Press, pp. 288–9.
[60] Ibid., p. 10.

Norton has argued that even the British parliament is not an exact fit for the ideal/typical Westminster model.[61] Lane and Ersson[62] recognise that Lijphart's dichotomy is an oversimplification and that in Europe only the United Kingdom and Switzerland come close to either ideal type. Nonetheless, Lijphart's emphasis on institutional variation in the performance of government is now common currency in comparative politics. Rather than attempting to force the variety of experience into two categories, it is more useful to consider the diversity of country experiences as clustered or dispersed, in greater or lesser proximity to one or other ideal type.

Comparing the powers of parliament

Giving a weighting to Lijphart's criteria for the two models of government, and comparing them along his two dimensions, Lane and Ersson (1998: 236) depict parliamentary legislatures spatially. Their classification, quite plausibly in my view, places the Irish legislature close to other majoritarian and centralised systems such as those of France, Greece and Luxembourg (Figure 2.1). Unlike in Britain, these countries use some form of proportional electoral system, which has produced multiparty systems and subsequent coalition governments. This results in their being situated some distance from Britain, but, as Figure 2.1 shows, they operate in an adversarial manner similar to the 'Westminster' model described above. These parliaments are associated with strong centralised governments, weak committee systems and little opposition input into government work.

Using Lijphart's criteria, Lane and Ersson[63] argue that the Irish, British and French executives are among the most powerful in Europe, controlling the parliamentary agenda and the right to dissolve parliament and even call elections. They also identify the role of parliamentary committees in redressing a power imbalance in favour of the government. In consensual parliaments such as the German Bundestag and Swedish Riksdag, committees play a strong role in the initiation and amending of legislation. Indeed, the German parliamentary committees are essential to the functioning of

---

[61] Norton, P. (1983) 'The Norton View' in D. Judge (ed.) *The Politics of Parliamentary Reform*. London: Heinemann Educational Books, p. 59.
[62] Lane, J. E. and Ersson, S. (1998) *Politics and Society in Western Europe*. London: Sage, p. 235.
[63] Ibid., pp. 216–17.

Figure 2.1: Spatial analysis of European legislatures (x-axis, executive–parties dimension; y-axis, federal–unitary dimension)

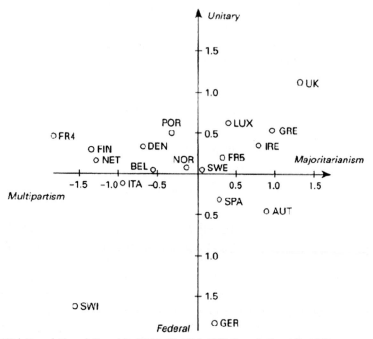

FR4, Fourth French Republic 1946–58; FR5, Fifth French Republic 1958–present
Source: Lane and Ersson (1998), p. 236

the parliamentary system, which combines federal institutions (principally the Bundesrat) with a parliamentary cabinet system in which the premier occupies a prominent position. Similarly, the bicameral legislature uses committees to facilitate agreement between the Houses.

Norton also emphasises the importance of the institutions of governing.[64] He presents a typology of parliaments based on how they perform in one of the principal functions of parliament – deliberating over policy. Taking this as the dependent variable, he distinguishes between legislatures that make policy, those that influence policy and those with little or no policy effect, in which the

---

[64] Norton, P. (1994) 'The Legislative Powers of Parliament' in L. Flintermann, A. W. Heringa and L. Waddington (eds) *The Evolving Role of Parliaments in Europe.* Antwerp: Maklu, p. 18.

Table 2.2: Policy deliberation in European legislatures

Category	Legislature
Policy-making	United States
Policy influencing	Italy
	Denmark
	Netherlands
	Germany
	United Kingdom
	Ireland
	France
Legislatures with little or no policy effect	

Source: Adapted from Norton (1994), p. 20

executive has complete control over policy-making. Once again, a comparative classification of the principal features of the Irish parliamentary system indicates that it features an unusually strong executive and unusually weak parliamentary powers (Table 2.2).

The United States Congress is the only legislature that fits into the first category of 'policy-making', as the institutional separation of powers allows Congress to modify, reject and replace government proposals without fear of dissolution. In the second category of 'policy-influencing', this typology again demonstrates a distinction between the performance of consensual and majoritarian-style parliaments. At the upper end are the consensual European parliaments. These have more influence on policy than those at the lower end, all of which are legislatures with majoritarian institutions of government.

The Irish parliament features in the lower end of the 'policy-influencing' category, close to the French legislature, and perilously close to the borderline with the category of legislatures with 'little or no policy effect'. It must be noted that unlike the Irish constitution, the French constitution confers strong formal powers on the executive (divided between parliament and the president) at the expense of the legislature.[65] As Chapter 3 will discuss, the reason why the Irish legislature has so little influence on the policy-making process has to do with the accumulated actions of the political parties within the institutions of government.

---

[65] Tsebelis, G. (1995) 'Veto Players and Law Production in Parliamentary Democracies' in H. Döring (ed.) *Parliaments and Majority Rule in Western Europe*. New York: St Martin's Press, p. 101.

Table 2.3: Authority to determine the plenary agenda

I	II	III	IV	V	VI	VII
IRE	FRA	LUX	AUT	DEN	ITA	NET
UK	GRE	POR	BEL	FIN		
		SWI	GER	ICE		
			NOR	SWE		
			SPA			

◄───►

more government control   **less government control**

(I) The government alone determines the plenary agenda; (II) in a president's conference the government commands a majority larger than its share of seats in the chamber; (III) decision by majority rule in a president's conference where party groups are proportionally represented; (IV) consensual agreement of party groups sought in president's conference but right of the plenary majority to overturn the proposal; (V) president's decision after consultation of party groups cannot be challenged by the chamber; (VI) fragmentation of agenda-setting centres if unanimous vote of party leaders cannot be reached; (VII) the chamber itself determines the agenda.

Source: Döring (1995) 'Time as a Scarce Resource: Government Control of the Agenda' in H. Döring (ed.) *Parliaments and Majority Rule in Western Europe.* New York: St Martin's Press, p. 225; see also Döring (2001) and Döring in Döring and Hallerberg (2004), p. 149

Döring identifies the internal rules and structures of parliament as key to the success of its performance.[66] He considers the work timetable (or plenary agenda) of the legislature to be one of the principal factors, and identifies which actors are responsible for setting it. The authority to determine the plenary agenda is the most basic form of government dominance of parliament. In institutionalist terms, Döring seeks to recognise the 'veto players' whose decision on what work parliament will undertake is final (Table 2.3).

As Table 2.3 shows, the survey of eighteen legislatures in contemporary Western Europe produces some interesting results. It is clear that the parliaments more closely aligned with the Westminster model hold greater influence over the parliamentary agenda than those

---

[66] Döring, H. (ed.) (1995) *Parliaments and Majority Rule in Western Europe.* New York: St Martin's Press.

displaying features of the consensual model. The UK and Ireland appear as the most government-dominated legislatures in Europe. Once again, this reveals how the executive in the Westminster system of government is 'power-hungry'.[67] This is in stark contrast with the Dutch legislature, for example, where the Tweede Kamer (Lower House) has sole authority to decide the legislative agenda.

The Oireachtas as a Westminster-type parliament

It is now clear that whether a parliament is closer to a Westminster or a consensus style of government will have an important bearing on its performance and will influence the behaviour of the actors that seek to exert power through influencing the policy-making process or controlling the plenary agenda. As we have seen, the principal features of the Irish legislature align it quite closely with Lijphart's Westminster-style government; this is crucial for understanding the (in)ability of parliament to hold the executive to account.

Broadly speaking, consensus-style parliaments are more conducive to effective executive oversight than Westminster-style ones. As we shall see in later chapters, this is facilitated by internal institutions such as parliamentary committees that provide for better information flows and cross-party co-operation. The adversarial Westminster system encourages the party or parties in power to keep the opposition parties removed from the decision- and policy-making process. Indeed, as Crossman[68] noted in his celebrated introduction to Bagehot's *The English Constitution*, the real opposition to government in Westminster itself frequently comes not from across the parliamentary chamber but from dissenting backbenchers of the governing party.

In a similar vein, Gallagher[69] argues that the executive–parliament dichotomy does not provide a useful template for the range of activities undertaken in Dáil Éireann. Drawing on work by King[70]

---

[67] Webb, M. and O'Brien, P. (1991) 'The Ghost in the System', in P. O'Brien and M. Webb (eds) *The Executive State: WA Inc. and the Constitution*. Perth, Australia: Constitutional Press, p. 343.

[68] Crossman, R. H. S. (1964) 'Introduction' in W. Bagehot, *The English Constitution*. London: C. A. Watts, p. 44.

[69] Gallagher, M. (2000) *Parliamentary Control of the Executive in Ireland: Non-Party, Inter-Party, Cross-Party and Intra-Party*. Workshop on Parliamentary Control of the Executive, European Consortium of Political Research Joint Sessions, Copenhagen, 14–19 April.

[70] King, A. (1976) 'Modes of Executive–Legislative Relations: Great Britain, France and West Germany', *Legislative Studies Quarterly* Vol. 1(1), 11–34.

and Andeweg and Nijzink,[71] he identifies the web of interactions between government and opposition parliamentary parties, and frontbenchers and backbenchers within these opposing blocs. However, while there is indeed a range of informal and formal relationships within the lower chamber, the dominant feature of Dáil Éireann is the zero-sum approach adopted by the parliamentary parties on policy issues, which produces a classic Westminster-style adversarial governing process. This style of parliamentary politics does not encourage members to 'break ranks' or to engage in activity that might cause difficulty for their party or (in most cases) the parties with which they share either the opposition or government benches.

Of course, the Oireachtas is not an exact fit for Lijphart's Westminster model (Table 2.1). On the federal–unitary dimension, many Westminster-type systems are unicameral, or asymmetrically bicameral[72] in a federal context. Interestingly, Ireland is unique in Lijphart's typology as it is the only unitary *small* country to be bicameral.[73] The Upper House, Seanad Éireann, is smaller than Dáil Éireann and is indirectly elected. Most important to the present study, however, is the fact that the Seanad has only a legislative function, i.e. it does not have a role in financial matters, or the election and dismissal of government. The absence of the need for a federal system and the high degree of centralisation in the Irish parliamentary system are among the reasons (institutional history and population size being the significant others) that the Upper House has been deprived of influence. As in Britain, the Irish government is elected from and 'fused' with the Lower House.[74] The constitution ensures a government majority in the Seanad, and therefore the government effectively holds power over the Upper House as well. Ireland also has a written constitution, with provision in it for judicial review.[75]

On the executive–parties dimension, the Oireachtas does not correspond fully to an ideal-type Westminster system. The proportional electoral system has produced a multiparty system and, as later

---

[71] Andeweg, R. B. and Nijzink, L. (1995) 'Beyond the Two-Body Image: Relations Between Ministers and MPs' in H. Döring (ed.) *Parliaments and Majority Rule in Western Europe*. New York: St Martin's Press, pp. 152–78.

[72] Asymmetrical bicameralism occurs where there is an unequal balance of power between the two chambers in the legislature.

[73] Lijphart, A. (1984) *Democracies*. New Haven, CT: Yale University Press, p. 94.

[74] Article 28.7.2 of the 1937 Constitution allows for the appointment of up to two Senators to the Cabinet.

[75] Article 26.

chapters will show, coalition government is increasingly the norm. However, notwithstanding Duverger's thesis concerning the fragmenting effect of proportional electoral systems, there have also been extensive periods of single-party government and this has produced a two-bloc effect, typical of Westminster systems, in Irish politics.

In short, although it deviates from the classic majoritarian model, Irish parliamentary politics exhibits features resembling the classic Westminster model. This demonstrates the powerful institutional logic of the Westminster model of government and its resilience in the face of practices more typically associated with consensual democratic systems. However, as the institutional theory discussed above informs us, while institutions have a strong influence on the courses of action open to actors, we must also consider the preferences of the actors. Chapter 3 will examine both the development of the Irish parliament and the motivations of the political parties that have successively maintained the zero-sum environment of Irish parliamentary politics.

The political parties, critical junctures and the development of parliamentary accountability

Political parties and parliament

As Ostrow points out, members of a legislature may organise themselves into subunits along the lines of either parliamentary parties or parliamentary committees.[1] In Ireland, the pre-independence experience of party politics in Westminster was the main reason for the use of parliamentary parties as the unit of organisation in Dáil Éireann in 1922. Despite attempts at institutional design for the purpose of avoiding large, disciplined parties, the circumstances of the post-independence 1922–23 Civil War ensured that Dáil Éireann came to be dominated by a relatively small number of well-organised political parties. In fact, the two factions that crystallised during the Civil War were eventually to organise into the two political parties that still dominate Irish politics today.

The relationship between the political parties and parliament is fundamental to the development of legislative–executive relations in Ireland. Sartori recognised this as a universal phenomenon when he drew attention to the ability of political parties to manipulate their environments.[2] More recently, Norton concluded that the party system is the most fundamental constraint on legislatures in the parliamentary regimes of Western Europe.[3] However, neither the 1922 nor the 1937 Constitution recognised the existence of political parties in Ireland; indeed, party labels did not appear on election ballot papers until the Electoral Act of 1963 permitted it.[4]

---

[1] Ostrow, J. M. (2000) *Comparing Post-Soviet Legislatures.* Columbus: Ohio State University Press, p. 5.

[2] Sartori, G. (1976) *Parties and Party Systems.* London: Cambridge University Press.

[3] Norton, P. (1998) 'Conclusion: Do Parliaments Make a Difference?' in P. Norton (ed.) *Parliaments and Governments in Western Europe.* London: Frank Cass, p. 192.

[4] FitzGerald, G. (2003) *Reflections on the Irish State.* Dublin: Irish Academic Press, p. 75.

This relationship with parliament has been surprisingly under-appreciated or ignored by analysts of the complex Irish party system. The most recent comprehensive works on the Irish party system[5] display little interest in the role of the main parties in changing the parliamentary system. Earlier writings such as Manning's[6] provide useful surveys of the situation at a particular point in time, but give little insight into the dynamics of parliamentary politics. The same is true of more recent detailed studies on individual parties, such as those by Dunphy[7] and Collins[8] on Fianna Fáil; by Gallagher and Marsh[9] on Fine Gael; and by Gallagher[10] on the Labour Party. All deal with the significance of the Dáil in shaping party strategy, but none shows much interest in the ways in which party strategy and the dynamics of party competition contribute to shaping or reshaping the structures and practices of the Dáil.

The lack of literature examining the impact of political parties on legislatures is not unique to Ireland. As Wiberg argues, older legal and formal understandings of parliament and parliamentary control still prevail in most European states, despite the changes brought about by the growth of the modern party system.[11] Also, the constitutional context is understood as invariant or immutable, when it is better seen as a fluid and dynamic process.

In his work on Westminster, Cox identifies this two-way relationship between disciplined parliamentary parties and parliament, and notes how the parties contribute to the importance of the cabinet.[12] No legislature can be properly understood without reference to the

---

[5] Gallagher, M. (1985) *Political Parties in the Republic of Ireland.* Manchester: Manchester University Press; Mair, P. (1987) *The Changing Irish Party System.* London: Pinter.

[6] Manning, M. (1972) *Irish Political Parties: an Introduction.* Dublin: Gill & Macmillan.

[7] Dunphy, R. (1995) *The Making of Fianna Fáil Power in Ireland: 1923–48.* Oxford: Clarendon Press.

[8] Collins, S. (2000) *The Power Game: Fianna Fail since Lemass.* Dublin: O'Brien Press.

[9] Gallagher, M. and Marsh, M. (2002) *Days of Blue Loyalty: the Politics of Membership of the Fine Gael Party.* Dublin: PSAI Press.

[10] Gallagher, M. (1982) *The Irish Labour Party in Transition 1957–82.* Manchester: Manchester University Press.

[11] Wiberg, M. (1995) 'Parliamentary Questioning: Control by Communication?' in H. Döring (ed.) *Parliaments and Majority Rule in Western Europe.* New York: St Martin's Press, p. 218.

[12] Cox, G. W. (1987) *The Efficient Secret.* Cambridge: Cambridge University Press.

political parties that compete to be represented there. To understand the development of parliamentary accountability in Dáil Éireann, therefore, we must consider the dynamics of party competition in Ireland.

As Table 3.1 shows, Mezey proposed a simple negative correlation between large and disciplined parties and the independence of legislatures. He argued that where a majority party controls the executive, the legislature's freedom to act will be constrained. In contrast, a legislature composed of undisciplined parties will usually facilitate a strong parliamentary influence on government.

The drafters of the 1922 Irish Free State Constitution were conscious of the relationship between parties and the legislatures in which they operate. They envisaged the creation of a strong legislature to elect coalition governments.[13] Such governments were believed to be an inevitable product of an electoral system based on proportional representation by the single transferable vote (PR-STV). However, this was not to be the case, and for most of its existence since 1922 Dáil Éireann has more closely resembled the model of a weak legislature dominated by a majority party.

By 1927, the Dáil was being shaped by the confrontation between large and disciplined parties that competed for political power. Unlike many other European legislatures, such as those of the Nordic states and Germany, parliamentary committees did not emerge in Ireland to offer members an alternative mode of organisation and participation.[14] The reluctance of successive governments in Ireland to facilitate the development of mechanisms of executive oversight reveals the changing preferences of the larger parties depending on whether or not they were in power. Also, the parliamentary parties in Ireland were too small to allow specialised committees and groups to develop within them as occurs at Westminster.[15]

The development of strong and disciplined parliamentary parties with external organisational support should not necessarily be seen as

---

[13] Chubb, B. (1982) *Cabinet Government in Ireland.* Dublin: IPA, p. 23.

[14] In fact proposals for the introduction of a committee system along the lines of the US model did emerge during the early years of the Dáil's foundation, but the matter was postponed and not returned to. A motion was proposed by J. J. Walsh (*Dáil Debates,* 17 September 1920, Vol. 1, Cols 213–14).

[15] Fianna Fáil experimented with such committees in the party's early years (O'Halpin, E. (1997) 'Parliamentary Party Discipline and Tactics: the Fianna Fáil Archives, 1926–32', *Irish Historical Studies* Vol. XXX(120), 587), but apart from ad hoc committees there has been no organised party committee system among the political parties in Ireland.

Table 3.1: Classification of legislatures by Mezey (1979)

Party system	Legislature's and legislators' independence		
	Strong	**Moderate**	**Weak**
Majority party			X
Multiparty coalition		X	
Undisciplined parties	X		

Source: Suleiman (1986), p. 6

a negative development in the Irish Free State. There are substantial benefits to political parties. As the rational choice tradition in legislative studies points out, they reduce transaction costs and solve collective action problems.[16] They offer parliamentarians and ministers the means to obtain what they wish. Parliament's ability to perform its work would be severely hampered by the competition between individuals in a non-party environment. Parties allow a large number of decisions to be taken in a limited time and with large volumes of information. Sartori also emphasises the functional role of parties, and in particular their value as channels of representation through expression of public opinion.[17]

Olson notes that collective goods are underprovided unless personal incentives are aligned to such goods;[18] similarly, the internal procedures of parliament are crucial to maintaining party discipline. In other words, the legislature must be organised in order to advance the party agenda of otherwise individualised members. For example, party leaders use positive inducements such as committee chairs as rewards for consistent loyalty and as an example to other members of the benefits of cohesion within the legislature. Indeed, in a polity such as Ireland's, with a personalistic electoral system, the emphasis on party cohesion within parliament becomes even more important.

---

[16] Cox, G. W. and McCubbins, M. D. (1993) *Legislative Leviathan*. Berkeley: University of California Press; Müller, W. (2000) 'Political Parties in Parliamentary Democracies: Making Delegation and Accountability Work', *European Journal of Political Research*, Vol. 37(3), 312.

[17] Sartori, G. (1976) *Parties and Party Systems*. Cambridge: Cambridge University Press, pp. 24–9.

[18] Olson, M. (1965) *The Logic of Collective Action: Public Goods and the Theory of Groups*. Cambridge, MA: Harvard University Press.

While the influence of parties on modern legislatures is unquestioned, there is a paucity of literature on parliamentary party groupings or party caucuses. As Bowler *et al.* recognise, the maintenance of a cohesive voting bloc inside a legislative body (such as the Dáil) is an essential feature of parliamentary life.[19] However, the adversarial and often secretive political arena in Ireland makes it difficult to assess the levels of party cohesion. Flinders recognises the importance of ministers' accountability to their own parliamentary party, and refers to it as the 'informal' mode of accountability in Westminster-type parliaments.[20]

Two views of government

In Dáil Éireann, where ministerial responsibility is a keystone in the process of accountable government, two views emerge as to how government should perform its duties and what its responsibilities to parliament are. Farrell identifies this dichotomy in terms of a 'Whitehall' and a 'Liberal' view of parliamentary government in the Westminster model.[21] Beattie identifies 'Peelite' and 'Whig' interpretations of Westminster-style government.[22] As Table 3.2 shows, the 'Peelite' view emphasises strong and centralised government, where strict party discipline ensures a government majority in parliament. Such a view also emphasises the 'insulation' of ministers from opposition attempts to scrutinise executive work.

The alternative 'Whig' view is closer to Lijphart's consensual model, and emphasises the accountability of the executive to parliament. Ministers are subject to increased parliamentary oversight, therefore there are incentives for increasing the involvement of the opposition parties in policy- and decision-making. Representative rather than

---

[19] Bowler, S., Farrell, D. M. and Katz, R. S. (1999) 'Party Cohesion, Party Discipline, and Parliaments' in S. Bowler, D. M. Farrell and R. S. Katz (eds) *Party Discipline and Parliamentary Government.* Columbus: Ohio State University Press, p. 3.

[20] Flinders, M. (2001) *The Politics of Accountability in the Modern State.* Aldershot: Ashgate, p. 14.

[21] Farrell, B. (1973) 'The First Dáil and After' in B. Farrell (ed.) *The Irish Parliamentary Tradition.* Dublin: Gill & Macmillan, pp. 208–20; cited also in Kissane, B. (2002) *Explaining Irish Democracy.* Dublin: UCD Press, p. 207.

[22] Beattie, A. (1995) 'Ministerial Responsibility and the Theory of the British State' in R. Rhodes and P. Dunleavy (eds) *Prime Minister, Cabinet and Core Executive.* London: Macmillan, pp. 158–81.

Table 3.2: Two views of government

Peelite/Adversarial	Whig/Co-operative
Strong government	Parliamentary/representative government
Executive decision-making	Control of government
Exclusion	Inclusion
Stability	Participation
Realism	Accountability
Insulation of ministers	Scrutiny of ministers

Source: Beattie (1995), *passim*; Flinders (2002), p. 26; Kissane (2002), p. 207

strong government is advocated in this inclusive model, in contrast to the exclusivist tendencies of the 'Peelite' form of government.

The 'Peelite' view implies a minimum of opposition input into the governing process, while the 'Whig' view envisages a less adversarial parliamentary environment. This typology is central to understanding how the political parties interpret ministerial responsibility, and more importantly parliamentary accountability, in Ireland. While the 'Peelite' view will be referred to as 'adversarial' and the 'Whig' view as 'co-operative' throughout this volume, the salient point is that the convention of ministerial responsibility permits these competing interpretations to exist simultaneously.

In Ireland, the institutions for governing traditionally encouraged the party or parties in government to adopt an adversarial attitude, while opposition parties typically advocated a more co-operative form of inclusive government. Typically, the power imbalance between the executive and legislature is not one that governments are prepared to address, principally because they wish to pursue their work programme with as few obstacles as possible. This is easiest when the government is composed of members of one party only, i.e. a single-party majority. A co-operative style of government involving more consensual parliamentary practices is more likely to occur when coalition government is the norm, as has been the case in Ireland since the early 1990s. In order to appreciate this development, it is necessary to consider a chronology of the three main political parties' electoral fortunes from 1922 until 2005 and to identify how these have influenced their government formation preferences. This prejudges the analysis of the critical junctures in the latter part of this chapter, but provides an enhanced framework for understanding the motivations of the parties.

The Irish political parties

Political analysts (and indeed the parties themselves) fail to agree as to how best Irish political parties should be understood. In Rose's influential collection of country-specific studies, Ireland ranked bottom of fifteen countries in terms of the capacity of social structure to explain variations in party support.[23] In the same volume, John Whyte referred to political parties in Ireland as being 'without social bases'.[24] Carty argued that 'social characteristics do not structure voting behaviour in Ireland'.[25] Indeed, the Irish party system may be considered *sui generis*, defying a comfortable fit into the more accepted comparative socio-economic models. Laver contests this view, arguing that social structural position does produce some identifiable trends in Irish voting patterns.[26] However, a clear case remains that Irish parties do not comfortably compare with conventional left–right European party typologies.

The principal actors in the institutional development of the Oireachtas have been the Labour Party, Fianna Fáil and Fine Gael. The Labour Party was formed in 1912 as a vehicle for parliamentary representation organised by the trade union movement.[27] It has historically attracted an average of 14 per cent of the popular vote, far below the European Social Democrat average of approximately 40 per cent. Fianna Fáil and Fine Gael represent two wings of the former Sinn Féin party that negotiated the Anglo-Irish Treaty of 1921 before it split over certain provisions in that Treaty. The pro-Treaty faction of Sinn Féin became known as Cumann na nGaedheal in

---

[23] Rose, R. (1974) 'Comparability in Electoral Studies' in R. Rose (ed.) *Electoral Behaviour: a Comparative Handbook*. London: Collier Macmillan, p. 17.

[24] Whyte, J. (1974) 'Politics without Social Bases' in R. Rose (ed.) *Electoral Behaviour: a Comparative Handbook*. London: Collier Macmillan, pp. 619–51.

[25] Carty, R. K. (1981) *Party and Parish Pump: Electoral Politics in Ireland*. Waterloo, Ontario: Wilfred Laurier Press, p. 74.

[26] Laver, M. (1986) 'Ireland: Politics with Some Social Bases: an Interpretation Based on Survey Data', *Economic and Social Review* Vol. 17(3), 193–213.

[27] Gallagher argues that the party merely existed on paper until the 1920s, but Sinnott contests this, arguing that manifestos were drawn up and plans put forward for candidates to contest seats in the 1918 election, although the party subsequently stood aside in that election (Gallagher (1985) *Political Parties in the Republic of Ireland*. Manchester: Manchester University Press, p. 68; Sinnott (1995) *Irish Voters Decide*. Manchester: Manchester University Press, p. 53).

1923 and was to hold power in the new Irish Free State parliament until 1932. In 1933 it joined with two small groups, the militant Army Comrades Association and the agrarian Centre Party, to form Fine Gael (United Ireland Party).

Anti-Treaty Sinn Féin split in 1926, with the larger faction calling itself Fianna Fáil (Soldiers of Destiny). This new party entered Dáil Éireann in 1927 and took over power from Cumann na nGaedheal following its successful election campaign in 1932. Since then it has consistently been the most electorally successful party in the State, while the fortunes of Fine Gael and Labour have been mixed (Figure 3.1).

The political parties that emerged in Ireland during and after the Civil War of 1922–23 did not align themselves along any of the familiar cleavages identified by Lipset and Rokkan that still dominate much of the comparative literature on political parties.[28] Indeed, it is frequently noted that Fine Gael and Fianna Fáil, despite never coalescing to form a government, occupy similar ideological positions on many issues. Their main founding aims were almost identical, namely the creation of a self-sufficient, united Ireland and the restoration of the Irish language, and both managed to attract a broad spectrum of electoral appeal.

Despite significant changes in Irish society, these two parties and the Labour Party continue to dominate the political landscape at national, local and European levels. While this study does not attempt to provide an alternative mode of distinction between the parties, it does emphasise their different government formation preferences and how these have influenced parliamentary reform in Ireland.

A snapshot of the self-image of the three parties taken by Garvin in his ground-breaking study of a Dublin electoral constituency some thirty years ago should be noted here.[29] Following a survey of party workers, he argued that these self-images appeared to be:

- 'a national movement' (Fianna Fáil)
- 'clean government' (Fine Gael)
- 'socialist justice' (Labour Party).

---

[28] Lipset, S. M. and Rokkan, S. (1967) 'Cleavage Structures, Party Systems, and Voter Alignments: an Introduction' in S. M. Lipset and S. Rokkan (eds) *Party Systems and Voter Alignments: Cross-National Perspectives*. London: Collier Macmillan, pp. 1–64.

[29] Garvin, T. (1974) *Political Parties in a Dublin Constituency* (unpublished PhD thesis). Department of Political Science, University of Georgia, Athens, p. 194.

Figure 3.1: First preference general election results for the three main political parties, 1922–2002 (%)

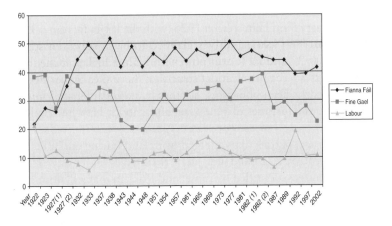

Note: Fianna Fáil includes anti-Treaty Sinn Féin (1922–3); Fine Gael includes pro-Treaty Sinn Féin (1922) and Cumann na nGaedheal (1923–32).
Source: Coakley (2005), p. 466

While there is now considerable agreement among the parties on major policy areas such as the economy and Northern Ireland, these self-images are still recognisable in the rhetoric used both inside and outside parliament.

Government formation preferences of the main parties

The government formation preferences of the three large parties have been remarkably consistent since 1932 and must be considered individually. Once in power, Fianna Fáil saw that its future hold on government required the maintenance of majoritarian parliamentary structures (indeed, this remains the case). With reference to Lijphart's typology of government (Table 2.1), Fianna Fáil's government formation preferences can be considered in decreasing order as:

1   single-party majoritarian government (including single-party minority government)
2   coalition majoritarian government
3   single-party consensus government
4   coalition consensus government.

As we shall see, Fianna Fáil did not partake in government in any form other than its first preference until the late 1980s, when it agreed to form a coalition majoritarian government. For Fine Gael, however, the achievement of an overall majority has not been a realistic possibility since Fianna Fáil's ascension in the late 1920s, and the party has rarely publicly claimed to be in search of such a mandate. Its adversarial relationship with Fianna Fáil, and the institutional logic of the government structures, have meant that despite advocating consensus politics while in opposition, it has traditionally resorted to majoritarian-style government when in power. The party's preferences, therefore, have traditionally been limited to:

1   coalition majoritarian government
2   coalition consensual government.

Furthermore, as the party was unlikely to coalesce with Fianna Fáil, its fortunes have traditionally been tied to those of the Labour Party. In this respect, the Labour Party has often been the 'maker or breaker' for Fine Gael's attempts to form a government. On many occasions since 1932, Fianna Fáil has formed a government as a result of the inability of Fine Gael and the Labour Party to coalesce.

The Labour Party's government formation preferences are influenced by the fact that it has traditionally been a junior partner in any government it helps form. With Fianna Fáil and Fine Gael adopting majoritarian practices, the party has had difficulty in pursuing a more consensual form of parliamentary politics, which would ultimately allow it to have more influence in parliament. Historically, when it has decided to 'go it alone', particularly in relation to pre-election voting transfer pacts, it has prevented Fine Gael from being in government. Also, Fianna Fáil's entry to power in 1932 was possible only with Labour Party acquiescence, as the party could form only a minority government. Labour agreed to give its support on condition that Fianna Fáil implement some of its policies.[30]

Like Fine Gael, the Labour Party has only ever been in coalition governments; within those governments it has never been the senior partner. As we shall see, when its bargaining power increased in the government formation process in the 1990s, this resulted in the introduction of reforms associated with consensual parliamentary politics. Therefore, we can argue that its preferences have been:

1   coalition consensual government
2   coalition majoritarian government.

---

[30] Kissane, B. (2002) *Explaining Irish Democracy*. Dublin: UCD Press, p. 180.

With these preferences in mind, Table 3.3 sets out the periods in power that the main parties have enjoyed since 1922. As discussed below, the most striking features are how long Fianna Fáil governments have been in power, and how from 1932 to 1989 the party alternated with coalition governments. This presented the electorate with a choice of either a Fianna Fáil single-party government or a coalition containing, at the very least, both Fine Gael and Labour. After 1989, we can see that this pattern changed dramatically.

While the government formation preferences of the main parties illuminate their actions while in opposition, it is clear that the institutions of government have traditionally left little room for consensual politics. This is partly explained by the adversarial nature of the 'Fianna Fáil versus the rest' dynamic that has characterised Irish politics since independence.

As opportunities arose for variations in the government formation preferences of the parties, there have been consequences for the

Table 3.3: The parties in power 1922–2005 (Fianna Fáil-led governments in grey)

1922–32	Cumann na nGaedheal (later Fine Gael)
1932–48	Fianna Fáil
1948–51	First inter-party government (all non-Fianna Fáil parties)
1951–54	Fianna Fáil
1954–57	Second inter-party government (all non-Fianna Fáil parties)
1957–73	Fianna Fáil
1973–77	Fine Gael/Labour Party
1977–81	Fianna Fáil
1981–82	Fine Gael/Labour Party
1982–82	Fianna Fáil
1982–87	Fine Gael/Labour Party
1987–89	Fianna Fáil
1989–92	Fianna Fáil/Progressive Democrats
1992–94	Fianna Fáil/Labour Party
1994–97	Fine Gael/Labour Party/Democratic Left
1997–2005	Fianna Fáil/Progressive Democrats

operation of parliamentary accountability. However, as institutional theory informs us, it is not enough to consider the actions of the parties alone. To understand fully the development of parliamentary accountability, we must also consider the institutions and the critical junctures in their progress.

The first critical juncture: the 1922 Constitution and the consolidation of adversarial parliamentary politics

Despite the political mood in 1922, which was to distance the state from all things British, it was never in doubt that the Irish Free State would adopt a form of representative parliamentary government rather than a US-style presidential system.[31] There was a strong conservative strain in the Irish revolutionary leadership and the experience of Westminster politics and administration had deep roots in Ireland.[32] The structures within which the new political regime would operate were clearly shaped around the familiar Westminster model.

The 1922 Constitution was created by agreement between London and Dublin following the Treaty granting 26 counties of Ireland dominion status within the Commonwealth. It provided for an asymmetrical bicameral parliament to coexist with a weak Head of State in the form of the Crown's representative in Ireland, the Governor-General, who had minimal input into the process of government. The Constitution's Irish coauthors wished to ensure that a form of 'responsible' government was established; with this in mind, it contained elements of republican idealism. In line with French and Swiss ideas of direct democracy, the sovereignty of the people as opposed to the legislature was emphasised through the provision for referendums and popular initiative.[33] To avoid parliament being dominated by one or two large party groupings (as well as to ensure representation for the protestant minority), the Constitution did not change the PR-STV system for parliamentary elections,[34] which had been introduced for national elections[35] under the Government of

---

[31] Ward, A. J. (1994) *The Irish Constitutional Tradition: Responsible Government and Modern Ireland, 1782–1992.* Dublin: Irish Academic Press, p. 168.

[32] Farrell, B. (1988) 'From First Dáil through Irish Free State' in B. Farrell (ed.) *De Valera's Constitution and Ours.* Dublin: Gill & Macmillan, pp. 18–32.

[33] McCracken, J. L. (1958) *Representative Government in Ireland.* London: Oxford University Press, p. 161.

[34] Article 26 of the Irish Free State Constitution.

[35] PR-STV was first used at local level in 1918.

Ireland Act 1920 and was used in the 1922 election. It was envisaged that this electoral system, combined with the provision for referendums and popular initiative, would encourage a strong culture of parliamentary and public accountability.

As Chubb argues, the political and legal elite recognised the imperfections of the British cabinet system, especially control of government by strong parties and the domination of parliament by the cabinet.[36] With a view to avoiding these flaws, the position of the legislature as opposed to the executive was emphasised in the Constitution, and opportunities for executive oversight were created that were not available even in Westminster during this period. An Executive Council of not fewer than five or more than seven ministers, all members of the Dáil and responsible collectively, was to be elected by that House, along with several 'extern' ministers. These extern ministers were to be chosen by, and individually responsible to, the Dáil rather than the Executive Council.

In further attempts to curb the power of the government and to increase that of the Dáil (as well as to reduce the functions of the Governor-General), provision was made for the election of the President of the Executive Council of the Dáil, and for express approval by the Dáil of his nominations to the Executive Council. An extremely important power also given to the Dáil was its ability to govern its time of assembly and dissolution. This gave the Dáil extensive agenda-setting powers and allowed it to exercise an unusual degree of control over the government. Furthermore, the President of the Executive Council was apparently not intended to have the position of a British Prime Minister. Indeed, the wording of the Constitution suggested a desire to give him a lesser status. He was not granted a free hand in choosing his colleagues and was required to resign if defeated; he did not have the right to obtain dissolution of the Dáil in circumstances in which his government remained undefeated, since this power was entrusted to the Executive Council as a whole. These were significant departures from the existing practice at Westminster.

The 1922 Constitution was a critical juncture in the development of parliamentary accountability in the Irish parliament, as it established the framework within which party politics could operate. Within the Dáil, the institutional infrastructure was designed to provide for as much equilibrium as possible between government and opposition, while also allowing the government enough room to

---

[36]   Chubb, B. (1982) *Cabinet Government in Ireland.* Dublin: IPA.

govern effectively. In institutionalist terms, the Dáil was given significant scope to act as a 'veto player' on the proposals of the government. However, the subsequent development of relations between the government and the Dáil was heavily influenced by external factors that cannot be explained by institutional analysis alone, which contrived to reduce parliamentary power over the executive. Indeed, despite the constitutional provisions, from an early stage the Executive Council sought to consolidate and centralise its power at the expense of parliamentary oversight.

As noted above, the Civil War over the Anglo-Irish Treaty ultimately created two large political parties, Fianna Fáil and Fine Gael, that were to dominate Irish politics. This resulted in the adversarial parliamentary politics that the authors of the 1922 Constitution had attempted to avoid through institutional design. Under the Constitution, parliament could amend the Constitution for a period of eight years after its enactment without submitting its proposals to a referendum. Between 1923 and 1927 this procedure was used to eliminate the constitutional mechanisms designed to facilitate parliamentary oversight of the executive and prevent the growth of disciplined parties. As an unintended consequence of the constitutional amendment process, the government swiftly moved towards institutionalising an adversarial view of Westminster-style government – strong, majoritarian, cabinet government.

With the formation of Fianna Fáil in 1926 and its entry into Dáil Éireann in 1927, the Cumann na nGaedheal party sought to exclude the opposition parties from acting as a check on government work. Through the removal of consensual parliamentary institutions, Dáil Éireann became as adversarial a chamber as the House of Commons, with two large parliamentary parties representing opposing sides from the recent Civil War. Recently available evidence from the Fianna Fáil archives points to the existence of high levels of discipline and involvement in legislative matters among its members from the period of the party's entrance to the Dáil in 1927.[37] Thus, it is clear that from the earliest years of the state's existence, both Fianna Fáil and Cumann na nGaedheal/Fine Gael sought to assume control of the Dáil with a view to establishing an adversarial mode of governance.

It was not long, therefore, before the procedures designed to provide for more equilibrium between parliament and government were abandoned to the advantage of the latter. The extern ministers were

---

[37] O'Halpin, E. (1997) 'Parliamentary Party Discipline and Tactics: the Fianna Fáil Archives, 1926–32', *Irish Historical Studies* Vol. XXX(120), 581–90.

no longer appointed after 1927 and the provision for popular initiative was removed from the Constitution, thus eliminating an important provision for both parliamentary and public accountability of the executive. Also, the possibility for legislative referendum was abolished and this accelerated the transformation of the Dáil into a government-dominated body. By 1928, the only consensual measure to remain intact was the proportional electoral system. Arguably, the principal reason for this was that it successfully delivered one of the principal prerequisites of Westminster-style legislatures as described by Lijphart – single-party government.

As Kissane indicates, the first two Presidents of the Executive Council, W. T. Cosgrave (1922–32) and Eamon de Valera (1932–7), participated in the gradual acceleration towards the 'efficient secret' of the British parliamentary system, the fusion of the government and the legislature.[38] Just as in Britain, party rather than parliamentary government became the norm in Ireland. Indeed, by the 1930s the two large parties that opposed each other in the Dáil had 'progressively stripped their constitution of anything that limited executive power'.[39]

By the time Fianna Fáil assumed power as a minority government (with Labour Party support) in 1932, it had built up strong support across all levels of Irish society, from trade unions to building and farming interests. The party has successfully managed to maintain its 'catch-all'[40] or 'cross-class'[41] appeal to this day, and this has contributed to its being in government for fifty-five of the seventy-three years since 1932. This long duration in power has cultivated the public perception of Fianna Fáil as the traditional party of government and Fine Gael and the Labour Party as parties of opposition.

Apart from the institutional resilience of the Westminster model of government, the electoral success of Fianna Fáil is one of the principal factors in the lack of experimentation in terms of parliamentary reform. It has always been the party with most to lose from any move towards a more consensual type of politics, and has traditionally conducted parliamentary government in an adversarial manner. Fianna Fáil stayed in government for a sixteen-year period from 1932

---

[38] Kissane, B. (2002) *Explaining Irish Democracy*. Dublin: UCD Press, p. 200.
[39] Ibid., p. 207.
[40] Laver, M. (1986) 'Ireland: Politics with Some Social Bases: an Interpretation Based on Survey Data', *Economic and Social Review* Vol. 17(3), 193–213.
[41] Dunphy, R. (1995) *The Making of Fianna Fáil Power in Ireland: 1923–48*. Oxford: Clarendon Press, p. 3.

to 1948, during which time Fine Gael frequently accused it of 'unparliamentary' practices. Members of the opposition became increasingly irritated by the government's tendency to legislate through ministerial order and statutory instrument.[42] Fianna Fáil showed no desire to reform parliament or to adopt more consensual institutional mechanisms in Dáil Éireann to allow opposition involvement in the decision-making process. In a revealing speech by the eminent Fine Gael parliamentarian and later party leader, James Dillon, Fianna Fáil's strict enforcement of its adversarial view of government was roundly criticised:

> the Fianna Fáil Party's theory of democratic government is that if they get a majority in this House it is part of their prerogative to jump on everybody else's face so long as they have power to do so.

He added that:

> Since this Parliament came into being last July, this House has sat only on one day each week because the Government would not let it sit on more than one day.[43]

Majoritarian parliamentary politics and the lack of a professional and full-time parliamentary opposition meant that Fianna Fáil effectively governed in a 'rubber-stamp' parliament. For example, Private Members' Time, when the opposition could control the Dáil for a number of hours per week, was persistently usurped by the government for financial estimates debates. Executive decisions – which, due to the lack of a committee system, barely involved even government backbenchers – were taken with minimal parliamentary involvement. Dunphy argues that this reflected a tightening of party control within Fianna Fáil.[44] In September 1937 the party rules were changed in response to the perceived threat from the deterioration in international relations as well as internal dissent caused by the party's shifting economic policy. The party executive could now add or de-select candidates to and from constituency lists as well as dissolve *cumainn* (the smallest, parish-based units of the party's organisation) as deemed necessary, further increasing its power.

---

[42] Manning, M. (2000) *James Dillon: a Biography.* Dublin: Wolfhound Press, p. 59.

[43] Dáil Debates, 3 December 1937, Vol. 69, Col. 1669. Interestingly, in 2002 (an election year) the Dáil sat for only fifty-four days, an average of just over once a week – a similar situation to that of sixty-five years previously.

[44] Dunphy, R. (1995) *The Making of Fianna Fáil Power in Ireland: 1923–48.* Oxford: Clarendon Press, p. 212.

The second critical juncture: the 1937 Constitution

As we have seen, the consensual institutional mechanisms included in the original 1922 Constitution did not withstand the adversarial parliamentary politics that emerged during the state's formative years. Indeed, the Westminster-style parliamentary system provided an ideal template for the continuation of Civil War politics within the confines of a democratically elected chamber. With the Upper House increasingly marginalised,[45] Dáil Éireann moved even closer to (if not beyond) its Westminster origins, and became a chamber in which the opposition had few parliamentary rights and little opportunity for input into policy-making. By 1936, the President of the Executive Council reigned supreme as head of a single-party government in a unicameral legislature, with freedom to amend the Constitution simply by statute.

However, by this time the Constitution had been amended so many times that the government deemed a new one necessary. This reaffirmed the Free State's *de facto* independence and facilitated the later severance of most of the remaining links with the British Commonwealth. The new Constitution was referred to as Bunreacht na hÉireann[46] and was heavily influenced by the Fianna Fáil leader and President of the Executive Council, Eamon de Valera. His decision to create a new Constitution marks the second critical juncture in the development of parliamentary accountability.

De Valera was a strong proponent of single-party government and often expressed the view that coalitions were inherently weak. Article 28.4.1 of the new Constitution envisaged that Dáil Éireann would appoint and dismiss the government, which would be (collectively) 'responsible to it'. In this respect the Constitution, like its predecessor, continued to support the classic liberal theory of power separation. Also, like the 1922 Constitution, it did not provide formal constitutional status to political parties. More importantly, it implicitly facilitated government dominance of parliament.

The size of Dáil Éireann remained the same but the Upper House, Seanad Éireann, was re-established. Each House was given the power to make its own rules and standing orders,[47] but the reality of party government meant that in effect power to decide the legislative agenda, including times of assembly, moved firmly away from Dáil Éireann

---

[45] The Seanad was eventually abolished in 1936.
[46] A literal translation is 'the Basic Law of Ireland'.
[47] Article 15.10.

and into the executive's hands. The reconstituted Seanad could merely delay, not permanently veto, legislation. This power remains largely intact today and leaves Britain and Ireland as the only two countries in Western Europe in which the government has exclusive power to determine the plenary agenda for the Lower House (Table 2.3).

This centralisation of authority is best seen in the transformation of the office of President of the Executive Council to that of Prime Minister or Taoiseach under Bunreacht na hÉireann.[48] The new office substantially increased the powers of the Irish premier, giving him,[49] for example, the power (subject to his command of a majority in the chamber) to dismiss ministers. This was a significant departure from the Free State Constitution, whereby to exercise such power the President would have had to resign, form a new cabinet of ministers, and present it to the Dáil for approval. As Gwynn Morgan points out, it is also unusual given that all other important official functions are given to the government as a whole to perform.[50]

The institutional arrangement of the Westminster-type parliament facilitated this centralising of power in the Taoiseach's office. While consensus-style parliaments involve a more diffuse concentration of power, and governments frequently consist of coalitions, the Westminster-style legislature allows a single-party majority to concentrate power in a small minority of its members. In Dáil Éireann, the Taoiseach acquired the power to control the appointment of the cabinet, the agenda of the executive and even the order in which business in the Dáil would be taken. The Taoiseach was also empowered to appoint eleven of the sixty Senators in Seanad Éireann, which guaranteed a government majority in the Upper House. This gave the governing party complete 'veto power' over parliament and the ability of parliamentarians in either House to scrutinise government work. No mechanisms for the Dáil's involvement in the government agenda, such as had existed with the extern minister idea in the original 1922 Constitution, were provided for in this Constitution. The provision for popular referendum was reintroduced, but the initiative for this rested with the government rather than the people, as had been the case previously.

---

[48] The term was derived from the title given to the chieftain of Gaelic Irish clans during the medieval period.

[49] The 1937 Constitution referred to all state office holders in the masculine.

[50] Gwynn Morgan, D. (1990) *The Constitutional Law of Ireland.* Dublin: Round Hall Press, p. 56.

The 1937 Constitution, therefore, did not attempt to restore any of the consensual parliamentary practices or public accountability mechanisms of the original 1922 Constitution. In many respects, the Oireachtas became more like an ideal-type Westminster system than Westminster itself. Although the government at Westminster dominated the Commons, formal (and traditional) rights for the opposition had always existed; similar procedures were not introduced into the Dáil subsequent to the 1937 Constitution. Irish parliamentary culture until the 1970s was conservative in this regard, and reflected the majoritarian view that government should be allowed to govern and not be hindered by parliament. In particular, Fianna Fáil and Fine Gael continued to support an adversarial conception of governing for decades after the Constitution was ratified by referendum. When in opposition, however, they tended to sing a different tune.

The 1937 Constitution formalised an adversarial form of government that already existed in practice, and institutionalised the zero-sum format of parliamentary politics. From this period until the mid-1980s, successive governments gave very little concession in their dominance of the Dáil. However, as Fine Gael and the Labour Party's time on the opposition benches increased, they became increasingly vocal in calling for parliamentary reform.

'Fianna Fáil versus the rest'

As noted above, Fianna Fáil's hold on government from 1932 until 1948 entrenched the majoritarian nature of government. With little opportunity for the opposition parties to involve themselves in, or veto, government work, both Fine Gael and the Labour Party[51] became desperate to remove Fianna Fáil from office. Along with several independents and two small radical parties, the agrarian Clann na Talmhan and the republican Clann na Poblachta, they formed the first inter-party government of 1948–51 (Table 3.3).

This coalition was an unusual mix of ideologies, held together by a collective desire to keep Fianna Fáil out of office. Indeed, so determined was the coalition to break from Fianna Fáil that it refused to reappoint the incumbent Secretary to the Government under suspicion that he had sympathies with that party, having served under Fianna Fáil governments for so long. However, as McCullagh points out, lax cabinet discipline weakened the inter-party government's

---

[51] The Labour Party split in 1944 over ideological differences but the two factions reunited in 1950.

effectiveness.[52] So too, he argues, did the coalition's strained relationship with the non-partisan civil service, which had become used to Fianna Fáil's modus operandi and, expecting to return to it, saw little point in changing its work practices significantly. The coalition frequently lost parliamentary votes through weak discipline, and opportunities repeatedly arose for the Fianna Fáil opposition to block government proposals.

The coalition's fragile nature contributed to the desire of government to exercise, as Fianna Fáil had done, a restricted form of government. Notwithstanding Fine Gael's earlier criticisms of Fianna Fáil's attitude towards parliament, no proposals for parliamentary reform materialised during the inter-party government. Instead, the party system now firmly revolved around the axis of 'Fianna Fáil versus the rest', with both sides viewing government in exclusive rather than inclusive terms.

Fianna Fáil returned to government for three years, and in 1954–57 a second inter-party coalition held power. In 1951–54, the same Fianna Fáil ministers that had been in government from 1932 to 1948 were reappointed. The lack of new front-bench members led to further institutional inertia, as these members were reluctant to re-appraise a system that had previously kept them in power for so long. Notwithstanding two three-year periods in government between 1948 and 1957, the main opposition parties failed to give Dáil Éireann the means to hold future governments and political parties successfully to account. Indeed, it appears that the inter-party coalitions were so eager to keep Fianna Fáil out of government that they engaged in the very thing they criticised it for – closed and unaccountable government.

Fianna Fáil began a second sixteen-year period in power beginning in 1957, when the party returned to government with a majority of Dáil seats. This second lengthy period in government allowed Fianna Fáil to consolidate its image as the party most closely identified with government and stability, and to reinforce the perception that majoritarian government was preferable to weak and potentially volatile coalitions.

From this period, at election time voters were effectively given a choice of a Fianna Fáil single-party government or a coalition of the other parties. For Fine Gael, leading a government was made more unlikely by the Labour Party's decision not to enter into pre-election

---

[52] McCullagh, D. (1998) *A Makeshift Majority.* Dublin: IPA, p. 254.

pacts with it and instead adopting a 'go-it-alone' strategy during the 1957–73 period. Former Labour Party TD Barry Desmond argues that, by the early 1970s if not before:

> there were many members of the Opposition parties in Leinster House who in the inner recesses of their minds felt that Fianna Fáil was the natural and permanent ruler of the Republic.[53]

This attitude helped Fianna Fáil to maintain control over the levers of power both within parliament and outside it. As Bartholomew's pioneering work discovered, Fianna Fáil's continued success even allowed it to influence the composition of the judiciary.[54] Bartholomew found that a favourable relationship with the government significantly enhanced a barrister or judge's chances of appointment to a more senior judicial position.

The apparent omnipresence of the Fianna Fáil party in Irish public life causes frustration for the other major parties. In March 2002, the then Fine Gael leader Michael Noonan TD voiced this frustration on a popular television show when he claimed that even when Fianna Fáil were not in power they were 'half in power'.

Fianna Fáil's domination of parliamentary politics was aided by the fact that until the early 1960s many senior opposition deputies, particularly those from Fine Gael, were part-time parliamentarians. Fine Gael attempted to reverse this tendency and encouraged its members to become more fully involved in parliamentary affairs. As Manning points out, meetings that had been irregular were now more formalised, proper records were kept, and the party's front-bench members were instructed to give a lead in policy development and attendance in parliament.[55] However, Fine Gael failed to capitalise at the polls and Fianna Fáil remained in government following elections in 1961, 1965 and 1969.

Parliamentary reform and the political parties

From the late 1960s onwards, the pressure for parliamentary reform and increased scrutiny of government grew substantially, as reflected not just in proposals for reform published by Fine Gael and the Labour Party but also in the support for these proposals in the print

---

[53] Desmond, B. (2000) *Finally and in Conclusion*. Dublin: New Island, p. 56.
[54] Bartholomew, P. C. (1971) *The Irish Judiciary*. Dublin: IPA, pp. 32–6, 42.
[55] Manning, M. (2000) *James Dillon: a Biography*. Dublin: Wolfhound Press, p. 331.

media and among academics. Of course, the desire for parliamentary reform mirrored the demands for social change in Ireland during this period. Traditional institutions of authority such as the Catholic Church began to be challenged, the role of women began to change dramatically, and Ireland prepared itself for entry to the European Economic Community (EEC).

Given the tendency of incumbent administrations to maintain the institutional status quo, issues of how and why reforms in the Irish parliament occur require close examination and explanation. External political factors play an important part in the government's willingness to concede rights of time and influence to the opposition. Parliamentary reforms in Ireland have mostly tended to come about many years after they were first proposed: indeed, proposals for reform that originated in the 1960s did not come to fruition until the mid-1990s.

The first real opportunity for a review of parliament and the role of the Dáil came under Seán Lemass. Following his accession to power in 1959, the new Fianna Fáil leader and Taoiseach proposed that the Constitution be reviewed every twenty-five years.[56] With this in mind, in 1966 he established and later chaired an Oireachtas Committee on the Constitution to consider whether amendments to Bunreacht na hÉireann were necessary. The committee's report the following year made no recommendations on parliamentary reform, save that a provision be inserted to make it clear that a Dáil vote was necessary to remove a government.[57] No action was taken on this recommendation. The report also recommended that the electoral system be changed from PR to a plurality ('first-past-the-post') system, a development that would have brought Ireland closer to the ideal-type Westminster model. However, a referendum proposing the introduction of such a system was defeated in 1968.[58]

In 1968, the momentum for reform increased following the publication of a set of proposals by the Labour Party under two broad headings – increasing the involvement of TDs in legislation and the number of sitting hours.[59] More specifically, the party wanted:

- a Dáil Standing Committee to debate the committee stages of Bills and Estimates

---

[56] Gwynn Morgan, D. (1990) *The Constitutional Law of Ireland.* Dublin: Round Hall Press, p. 30.

[57] Oireachtas Committee on the Constitution (1967) *Report of the Committee on the Constitution.* Dublin: Oireachtas Éireann, p. 153.

[58] The result was 39.2 per cent in favour and 60.8 per cent against.

[59] 'Is the Dáil inefficient?' *Public Affairs* (1969) Vol. 1(4), 5. See also Appendix A.

- a permanent committee to examine and report on the activities of the semi-state bodies
- an increase in weekly sitting hours (from 21.5 to 35 hours) and a decrease in the length of the summer recess period
- greater facilitation of private members (i.e. the opposition) in the business of the Dáil.[60]

These proposals were not acted on prior to the general election the following year. In the event, Fianna Fáil's success in this election (helped greatly by Labour's decision to adopt a 'go-it-alone' policy) reaffirmed its dominance in parliamentary politics. However, by this stage pressure for parliamentary reform was coming not only from the opposition parties but also from the media and wider community, particularly in the light of a rapidly expanding public sector that needed to be subject to parliamentary oversight. An influential think-tank of the period, Tuairim ('Opinion'), provides evidence of the concerns surrounding the ineffectiveness of the Dáil and parliamentarians. This civic-minded liberal group was composed of parliamentarians and academics who 'believe in a democratic society and are anxious that it realise itself more completely'.[61]

Tuairim established a 'Study Group on Parliamentary Democracy' in October 1970. The group, which included several prominent parliamentarians from the three main political parties, devoted much of its energy to investigating methods for improving the efficiency of the Dáil. It provided a non-adversarial forum for the discussion of problems and the finding of common ground on the need for reform. The minutes of Tuairim meetings reveal that the extended use of parliamentary committees was among the recommendations made most forcefully. It also questioned the efficacy of the nine stages through which legislation passed in the two Houses of the Oireachtas, and voiced several other recommendations that were similar to those in the Labour Party's 1968 proposals,[62] including:

- broadcasting of Dáil and Seanad proceedings
- more scope for opposition initiatives and Private Members' Bills
- a list system for those who wish to take part in debates
- better facilities and information services for TDs and Senators

---

[60] The Labour Party (1968) *Proposals for the Reform of Parliamentary Procedure in Dail Eireann.* Leinster House, Dublin: Parliamentary Labour Party.

[61] Barrington, T. J. (1970) *Discussion Paper – Parliamentary Study Group.* Dublin: Tuairim.

[62] Many prominent Labour Party members were also members of Tuairim.

- Dáil and Seanad salaries to be tied to a public service rank
- sitting hours to be extended and recess periods reduced.[63]

While these proposals did not receive real debate in parliament, the momentum for a review of parliamentary procedures continued and led to the establishment of a committee to investigate the matter a few years later.

1971/2 Informal Committee on Reform of Dáil Procedure

Gwynn Morgan, in his work on constitutional law in Ireland, argues that:

> the impact which [parliamentary] reforms make, depends ultimately upon a fundamental political question – the effect which the reforms have on the balance of power between the Government and the legislature.[64]

Given the institutional resilience of the Westminster system of government, it is not surprising that successive governments did not prioritise parliamentary reform for several decades after the 1937 Constitution. The issue of parliamentary procedure, and the dominant position of the government over parliament, was not properly addressed by an incumbent government until 1971, thirty-four years after the Constitution had given each House the power to make its own rules and standing orders. The Taoiseach at the time, Jack Lynch, reluctantly conceded the need for such an examination, and criticised:

> references in newspapers and other media to the degradation of the parliamentary system with the inference that the Government are to blame.[65]

In an interview with this author, the chair of the informal committee, Desmond O'Malley, noted that its establishment represented the fact that:

> There was a beginning of a feeling that became stronger afterwards that the Dáil procedures were somewhat stultified [and that] the Dáil was becoming less responsive to current events.[66]

---

[63] The Labour Party (1968) *Proposals for the Reform of Parliamentary Procedure in Dail Eireann*. Leinster House, Dublin: Parliamentary Labour Party; Tuairim (1968) *Minutes of meetings of Dublin Branch*. Dublin.

[64] Gwynn Morgan, D. (1990) *The Constitutional Law of Ireland*. Dublin: Round Hall Press, p. 144.

[65] *Dáil Debates*, 17 December 1970, Vol. 250, Col. 1598.

[66] Interview with Desmond O'Malley, 20 June 2003.

The report of this committee was significant as it represented the first time since the establishment of the parliament that its procedures had been given detailed attention. However, the committee interpreted its terms of reference rather narrowly and O'Malley noted that there were 'unwritten terms of reference that the general framework of what was there was to be maintained'.[67]

The informal committee presented its proposals to the Dáil Committee on Procedure and Privileges in December 1972 (shortly before the general election). These were far from a thorough examination of Dáil procedure. They proposed amendments to standing orders covering issues such as timetabling of the parliamentary day, private members' rights and government Bills. However, the report also recommended:

> a wide-ranging examination … to establish how effectively the Houses of the Oireachtas are discharging their functions in present day circumstances.[68]

In effect, this allowed the informal committee to ignore the issue of executive oversight, a function of parliament that by this stage had been acutely undermined. The amendments eventually introduced as a result of the committee's work also included recommendations added afterwards by the Ceann Comhairle (Speaker of Dáil Éireann) and his staff.

The informal committee recommended thirty-five changes to the Dáil standing orders, almost all of which were implemented by the incoming Fine Gael/Labour Party administration (the 'National Coalition') in 1973. While some of the amendments actually 'copper-fastened the dominance of government',[69] most reflected a consensus among the main parties that government was entitled to expedite its business as efficiently as possible. Indeed, many of the amendments to the procedures were intended to reduce time-wasting and the length of contributions during various forms of debate.

During the period that the informal committee was conducting its work, correspondence between Labour Party deputies reveals that Fianna Fáil and Fine Gael:

> were of the view that all was generally well with the procedures of the Houses of the Oireachtas and that only relatively minor reforms were contemplated.[70]

---

[67] Ibid.

[68] Informal Committee on Reform of Dail Procedure (1972) *Final Report*. Dublin: Stationery Office, p. 6.

[69] Interview with Kieran Coughlan, 30 April 2002.

[70] Desmond, B. (1971) *Report to Parliamentary Party of Meeting on Reform of Dail Eireann Procedures on 29th January, 1971*. Leinster House, Dublin: Parliamentary Labour Party.

This memo seems to hint that the Labour Party, as the smaller of the two main opposition parties, was more concerned than Fine Gael that the opposition's rights be protected. Fine Gael, despite its anti-Fianna Fáil rhetoric, also saw the role of government and parliament in an adversarial manner, with a view to one day assuming control of the executive function.

The 1973–77 'National Coalition' Proposals for Dáil Reform

The consensus among the large parties that some parliamentary procedures needed to be tightened was reflected in the fact that, as we have seen, the National Coalition implemented most of the informal committee's recommendations. Of the thirty-five recommendations of the Sub-Committee on Reform of Dáil Procedure, the new coalition government eventually implemented thirty-three, including reforms that were the antithesis of the consensus-style government advocated by the parties while in opposition. This again reflected the institutional logic of Westminster-style government.

Given the extraordinary periods of time that Fine Gael and the Labour Party spent in opposition, in a chamber that afforded little opportunity to be involved in the decision-making process, the lack of initiative in creating a more consensual parliament is interesting. One explanation is that Fine Gael believed it could win a second term in office, and therefore did not want to alter the structures of government in which it now found itself. It was also determined to keep Fianna Fáil out of power. In addition, external events of the time encouraged the government to strengthen its position in the Dáil. The acute civil unrest in Northern Ireland threatened the stability of the rest of the island, and forced the government to reject any challenges to its authority. Also, Ireland's entry to the EEC in 1973 demanded firm government control of the political agenda. However, the Labour Party managed to convince Fine Gael to agree to some reforms, reflecting its preference for a more co-operative parliamentary regime.

The Labour Party's Barry Desmond TD, as assistant government chief whip, along with the Fine Gael chief whip John Kelly TD, established five ad hoc parliamentary committees to consider legislation of major importance. Although the appearance of committees was a welcome development, their powers were weak and their temporary existence meant that they did not challenge the government on any major issue. Desmond was a vocal advocate of

Oireachtas reform, and was dissatisfied with the recommendations of the informal committee, which he saw as failing to address the 'more serious defects' of Dáil procedure in favour of short-term solutions. He was also unhappy with the performance of his government in addressing Dáil reform. Presenting his arguments, he built on previous Labour proposals with his 1975 publication *The Houses of the Oireachtas – a Plea for Reform.*[71]

The document accused the Dáil of being a 'sanctuary of conservatism' and argued that without much-needed reform it would 'ossify into a permanent state of preservation'. The launch of the document received much media publicity even though it criticised parliamentary reporters for their inadequate coverage of Oireachtas business. Perhaps most significantly, Desmond's proposals represent the only time in the history of Dáil Éireann that an incumbent member of government has so comprehensively criticised the modus operandi of the Dáil.

Not only was Desmond the Government assistant whip, he was also the parliamentary Labour Party whip and a member of the Dáil Committee on Procedure and Privileges, a body charged with ensuring that the chamber operates efficiently. In the document he gave voice to the concerns of backbenchers from all parties concerning the perceived increasing irrelevance of the Oireachtas in decision-making. Furthermore, he bluntly accused Fine Gael and the Labour Party of adopting what he considered to be a Fianna Fáil attitude to government, i.e. that the government govern with minimal input or interference from parliament.

He also accused Fianna Fail, during its time in government from 1957 to 1973, of having:

> conceded only minor reforms and [using] their control of the Committee on Procedure and Privileges and their Government's prerogative to order Dáil business to effectively stifle any proposed changes.[72]

Unlike the Labour Party's 1968 proposals, he did not call for an increase in the weekly sitting hours of the Dáil, recognising that this would not be supported by many *de facto* part-time TDs, but he did call for shorter recesses. His recommendations went further than any before, and included:

- the development and greater use of a committee system
- better oversight of semi-state bodies via an Oireachtas committee

---

[71] See Appendix A for the main proposals.
[72] Desmond, B. (1975) *The Houses of the Oireachtas – a Plea for Reform.* Leinster House, Dublin: Parliamentary Labour Party, p. 8.

- the practice whereby debate on departmental estimates was taken in the House to be ended, and that it be taken in a Standing committee instead
- a list of speakers to be created for each debate
- a review of the Question Time format
- the length of debates and contributions to be cut
- TV and radio broadcasts of the Dáil and Seanad to be allowed
- state assistance to parties for work outside parliament
- declaration of members' interests
- better resources for deputies and parliamentary parties
- Citizens Advice Bureaux to combat brokerage in politics
- abolition of university seats and Taoiseach's eleven nominees to Seanad.[73]

However, Desmond's document, while comprehensive and informed, failed to inspire a radical overhaul of the parliamentary infrastructure, again showing the reluctance of incumbent governments to cede decision-making power to the Dáil. Indeed, Fine Gael was confident of winning a successive term in office and therefore saw little need to move from the status quo. Manning noted that:

> The case for parliamentary reform has been made and made forcefully over the past number of years without apparently making the slightest impact on those who are in a position to make the changes – the politicians and their leaders.[74]

A progress report by Desmond following his proposals showed that the situation remained unchanged in spite of his efforts. In an interview with this author, he commented that during the National Coalition's period in office 'constitutional reform was a bigger issue than parliamentary reform'.[75] As noted above, some ad hoc committees were introduced and a Committee on State-Sponsored Bodies was eventually established, but Fianna Fáil refused to participate in committees established to deal with Bills of a technical nature. The party clearly did not want to encourage changes in parliamentary practice that might make the task of government (which it was likely to return to) more difficult. In the event, many of the suggestions common to the Labour proposals of 1968 and 1975, such as a permanent and extensive committee system, were eventually to come about, but only after a further two decades had elapsed.

---

[73] Ibid.

[74] Manning, M. (1975) 'Making Dail and Seanad more democratic and effective', *The Irish Press*, 6 March, 9.

[75] Interview with Barry Desmond, 9 June 2003.

One significant development with respect to the committee system during this government's tenure was the establishment in July 1973 of the Joint Committee on the Secondary Legislation of the European Communities. This committee served to educate Irish parliamentarians about the developing European project and Ireland's obligations within it, as well as to encourage the activity of legislative scrutiny (albeit of the non-domestic variety). Its role was to expand gradually over the next two decades.

Fianna Fáil's return to power in 1977 with an overall majority perpetuated and strengthened the adversarial nature of government in Dáil Éireann. Fine Gael's disappointment at the scale of the Fianna Fáil victory in 1977 saw the party begin to embrace the need for parliamentary reforms that had not concerned it while in government. It was from this period onwards, therefore, that Fine Gael adopted the Labour Party's mantle of most vocal party in calls for parliamentary reform, as evidenced by the party's production of proposals in 1980, 1990 and 2000, while the Labour Party did not produce a further set of proposals until 2003. However, the Labour Party continued its calls for reform; indeed, the party has played a large part in initiating many of the recent reforms in the Irish parliament, as later chapters will describe.

The introduction of parliamentary committees

In 1980 Fine Gael produced its first detailed and comprehensive proposals for changing the institutional make-up of the Lower House. Titled *Reform of the Dáil*, the document was principally the work of John Bruton TD, and had parallels with proposals in Desmond's 1975 document.[76] In it, the party pledged to implement a range of proposals if elected to government. The main points were:

- greater and more effective use of parliamentary committees
- better scrutiny of government estimates and the Capital Budget
- longer hours for parliamentary questions and ministers to answer questions related to semi-state bodies
- establishment of a committee on delegated legislation
- greater flexibility for Private Members' Bills
- better resources for deputies including induction courses
- code of practice for opening government files to public scrutiny.[77]

---

[76] See Appendix A.
[77] Fine Gael (1980) *Reform of the Dail: Fine Gael Policy on Reform of the Dail.* Leinster House, Dublin: Fine Gael Parliamentary Party.

Fine Gael and Labour formed a coalition in 1981, which lasted for only nine months and did not allow Fine Gael time to implement any substantial Dáil reform. In December 1982, following an even shorter Fianna Fáil administration, the two parties again coalesced and this government lasted until 1987. In keeping with Fine Gael's new-found commitment to parliamentary reform, John Bruton was appointed to the new position of 'Leader of the House with special responsibility for Dáil reform'. Among proposed reforms he outlined to the Dáil in early 1983 were:

- a review of procedures for parliamentary questions, speeches and Private Members' Time
- broadcasting of parliamentary business
- extending and widening the scope of committees, including their use to take evidence from the public.[78]

In an interview with this author, Bruton revealed that he found it difficult to convince the chief whip to push forward rapidly some of the proposals outlined in the 1980 document, because the whip's priority was getting opposition co-operation on daily business, and the opposition was not interested in some of the proposed reforms.[79] Nonetheless, during this government's term of office reforms were made to the format of question time, including a new 'priority question' facility that allowed the opposition to address topical issues with relatively short notice. While Fine Gael displayed elements of both adversarial and consensual views of government during its period in power, the consensual view was to become more prominent as it spent increasing time in opposition post-1987.

The introduction of a comprehensive select committee system in 1983 was a significant event in the development of parliamentary accountability. It was made possible by the fact that Fine Gael, realising it was no longer in its interest to act as Fianna Fáil had done in excluding the opposition from government work, changed its government formation preference to align it with that of the Labour Party. This is not to say that the coalition was harmonious; there was constant tension between the two parties over economic issues. Nonetheless, the government introduced eight new committees, significantly expanding the old and underdeveloped committee

---

[78] *Dáil Debates*, 8 February 1983, Vol. 339, Cols 1258–76.
[79] Interview with John Bruton, 12 February 2002.

system to seventeen.[80] This was a positive development for the Irish parliament, as committees were widely regarded as fora where discussion could take place in a non-partisan manner and contribute to a more co-operative parliamentary culture. The new committees did not shadow government departments, as they were created for the purpose of pursuing issues that cut across several government departments, e.g. the Committee on Small Businesses and the Committee on Crime, Lawlessness and Vandalism. At the end of the coalition government's period in power in 1987, sixteen committees were still in operation.[81] They represented a major departure for the Oireachtas and the coalition, and were a precursor of similar developments in the early 1990s.

Consensus government and the Tallaght Strategy

Given Fianna Fáil's preference for single-party majoritarian administration, it is not surprising that when it returned to power in 1987 it did not re-establish these committees. The party leader, Charles Haughey TD argued that government's role was to govern and that it would be inappropriate that committees could challenge the work of parliament.[82] On the question of parliamentary reform and whether or not a member of the cabinet with responsibility for Dáil reform would be reappointed, he stated that:

> It is my personal opinion, reinforced by a long number of years in the House, that responsibility for these matters should be vested in one single parliamentary person.[83]

In other words, parliamentary reform would be under the control of the chief whip, who would in turn be directly accountable to the Taoiseach, thus ensuring that the Dáil would not act as an obstacle to government work. Haughey also sidestepped opposition calls for reform of the House by arguing that 'responsibility for parliamentary reform is a matter for the Dáil'.[84]

---

[80] O'Halpin, E. (1998) 'A Changing Relationship? Parliament and Government in Ireland' in P. Norton (ed.) *Parliaments and Governments in Western Europe*. London: Frank Cass, p. 135. The other nine committees were standing committees and were automatically established when a new government entered office.

[81] O'Halpin, E. (1987) 'Oireachtas Committees: Experience and Prospects', *Seirbhís Phoibli* Vol. 7(2), 3.

[82] The same justification was given by the Fianna Fáil/Progressive Democrat government in March 2003 when it sought to reduce the powers of the Freedom of Information Act (see Chapter 7).

[83] *Dáil Debates*, 24 March 1987, Vol. 371, Col. 131.

[84] Ibid., Col. 129.

However, Fianna Fáil's return to power coincided with a period of great economic difficulty in Ireland, and the party began to make expenditure cuts that it had previously criticised the Fine Gael/ Labour coalition for making. In response, and reflecting its acceptance of a more consensual style of politics, Fine Gael announced that it would pledge support for the government 'as long as it stayed on the economic straight and narrow'.[85] Known as the 'Tallaght Strategy',[86] this was an unprecedented step in Irish politics given the traditional zero-sum relationship between the two larger parties. It reflected Fine Gael's conversion to more co-operative government but did not benefit it electorally, and it was some time before the party returned to government.

The economic crisis of this period also resulted in a new development known as 'social partnership', a corporatist-style arrangement between the government, farmers, employers' organisations and trade unions. Its goal was to resurrect the failing economy, and such was its success in doing so that agreements have been formed between these groups every three years since.[87] However, questions have been raised concerning the democratic nature of the social partnership process, given that parliamentary approval of such agreements is neither sought nor given. It has also been suggested that the structures that have been built to support this process further erode the Dáil's position as the centre of debate on public policy.

In 1990 Fine Gael produced a second comprehensive set of proposals for reform of the Oireachtas. Titled *Dáil Reform*, the document noted that the Irish parliament's procedures and practices 'have failed to respond adequately to the enormous changes in Irish society' and that the 'Oireachtas has shown itself to be more resistant to change than most of the E.C. member state parliaments.'[88] The reforms it proposed were not drastic – a point picked up by an *Irish Times* editorial that saw the reforms as involving 'the smallest degree of disruption and a minimum of innovative effort', and somewhat

---

[85] Collins, S. (2000) *The Power Game: Fianna Fail since Lemass*. Dublin: O'Brien Press, p. 173.

[86] Named after the Dublin suburb where the policy was announced by the Fine Gael leader, Alan Dukes TD.

[87] In recent years, a coalition of organisations representing the unemployed, women's groups, and bodies addressing social exclusion and disadvantage, known collectively as the Community and Voluntary Pillar, has also been involved in the process.

[88] Fine Gael (1990) *Dáil Reform*. Fine Gael Parliamentary Party, Leinster House, Dublin, p. 4; see also Appendix A.

prophetically noted that 'a feeble parliament is an invitation to corruption'.[89] Among the proposals for reform, the main points were:

- three new business committees – economic, social affairs and general affairs – to deal with the committee stage of all Bills
- private members to be allowed to propose amendments to estimates of government expenditure
- a new Dáil timetable, with the House sitting five days a week (instead of three)
- remuneration for committee chairpersons
- witnesses before committees to receive parliamentary privilege
- increasing public awareness of parliament's work
- powers of the Public Accounts Committee and the Comptroller and Auditor-General to be enhanced
- provision for Private Members' Bills to be introduced by lottery
- an increase in Question Time
- improved links between the Oireachtas and European institutions
- additional staffing for the Oireachtas and Parliamentary Draftsman's Office.[90]

Despite considerable media coverage, the government did not act on these and the other reforms in the document. However, it was at this point that the third critical juncture in the development of parliamentary accountability occurred, as Fianna Fáil abandoned its traditional reluctance to form a coalition government. An unintended consequence of this decision was to open up the opportunity for new institutional arrangements within Dáil Éireann, including the formal mechanisms of parliamentary accountability.

The third critical juncture: the 1989 coalition government

The 'Fianna Fáil versus the rest' dynamic of Irish politics after 1937 ensured a continuum of adversarial-type governments, all of which resisted opposition involvement in the governing process and therefore parliamentary accountability. However, in 1989 the Fianna Fáil Taoiseach, Charles Haughey TD, called a snap election in the hope of winning an overall majority for his party – something that had eluded him in four previous elections. In the event, Fianna Fáil lost

---

[89] *Irish Times*, 19 July 1990, 13.
[90] Fine Gael (1990) *Dáil Reform*. Fine Gael Parliamentary Party, Leinster House, Dublin.

seats and Haughey's only hope for remaining in government was to form a minority coalition with a small liberal party that, ironically, had formed out of a split in Fianna Fáil over his leadership.[91] This was the Progressive Democrat party.

The Progressive Democrats radically altered the dynamics of the Irish party system, not least because it initiated a more open electoral market that now offered government options in addition to a Fianna Fáil/Labour Party or a Fine Gael/Labour Party coalition. Desmond O'Malley, whose clashes with Haughey had caused great divisions within Fianna Fáil, led the party.[92] It was on the right in relation to fiscal and economic matters, liberal on divorce and contraception, and, more importantly for this study, very vocal in its demands for more transparency and accountability in politics. In this policy, as in many others, the party most challenged by it was Fine Gael. The Progressive Democrats won fourteen of the 166 Dáil seats in the 1987 election but retained only six after 1989.

As it transpired, the decision to coalesce ended the 'Fianna Fáil versus the rest' axis around which political and parliamentary life had revolved since the mid-1920s. The acceptance by Fianna Fáil of its second government formation preference, majoritarian *coalition* government, did not immediately result in a reconfiguration of the adversarial nature of Dáil politics, but, as Mair points out:

> In entering coalition and declaring itself coalitionable, Fianna Fáil effectively undermined the foundation on which the post-war party system had been structured. From 1989 onwards it was no longer Fianna Fáil versus the rest. From then on ... Fianna Fáil became just another party.[93]

Indeed, from this period forward, a number of developments challenged the traditional institutional environment of Dáil Éireann. It is curious that the books looking at various aspects of elections since this period have not considered the issue of the Dáil/political party relationship. Institutional design, particularly of committee systems within parliament, has become an important feature in

---

[91] The new party's founder, Desmond O'Malley, had been expelled from Fianna Fáil.

[92] Collins, S. (2000) *The Power Game: Fianna Fail since Lemass*. Dublin: O'Brien Press, pp. 152–64.

[93] Mair, P. (1993) 'Fianna Fáil, Labour and the Irish Party System' in M. Gallagher and M. Laver (eds) *How Ireland Voted 1992*. Dublin: Folens/PSAI Press, p. 171.

coalition negotiations, yet remains under-appreciated by commentators on recent Irish elections.[94]

In the terminology of institutional theory, coalition governments in parliamentary systems have the effect of introducing a new veto player into the political and delegation process. Furthermore, the greater the ideological distance between the coalition partners, the more important the institutional arrangements between them become. Indeed, in parliamentary systems, committee chairs or junior ministries are often given to one coalition member as a check on ministries headed by a member of the other party. Previous Fianna Fáil governments had operated in a manner whereby the party controlled all the vetoes in both Houses of parliament, and the decision to enter a coalition necessitated a new system of delegation and oversight. The introduction of multiple veto players moved the Irish parliament further away from Lijphart's Westminster model and closer to the consensual one, in which there is more opportunity for executive oversight.

In his analysis of government formation in European parliamentary democracies, De Winter found that where the policy agenda is set prior to the creation of a new coalition government, there are trade-offs in respect of government oversight.[95] In order that problems be avoided in translating policy programmes into legislation, the coalition partners will want adequate veto mechanisms. The importance of programmes for government in post-election negotiations in Ireland corroborates this thesis, and helps explain the introduction of several new institutions of oversight during the 1990s within the executive and outside it.

As an unintended consequence of the decision to coalesce with the Progressive Democrats, a party committed to increasing transparency in the political process, Fianna Fáil was forced to agree the establishment of a quasi-judicial tribunal of inquiry into the actions of former Fianna Fáil ministers (see Chapter 6). Another unintended consequence was that when this government fell in 1992, Fianna Fáil had government formation options other than simply 'going it alone'.

---

[94] The issue receives little treatment in Gallagher, M. and Laver, M. (eds) (1993) *How Ireland Voted 1992*. Dublin: Folens/PSAI Press; Marsh, M. and Mitchell, P. (eds) (1999) *How Ireland Voted 1997*. Oxford: Westview/PSAI Press; Gallagher, M., Marsh, M. and Mitchell, P. (eds) (2003) *How Ireland Voted 2002*. Basingstoke: Palgrave.

[95] De Winter, L. (1995) 'The Role of Parliament in Government Formation and Resignation' in H. Döring (ed.) *Parliaments and Majority Rule in Western Europe*. New York: St Martin's Press, pp. 115–51.

This was to prove most detrimental to Fine Gael. Furthermore, subsequent coalition governments were to contribute to the erosion of the majoritarian nature of governing that had characterised Irish politics. For all these reasons, the creation of the 1989 coalition must be seen as the third critical juncture in the development of parliamentary accountability.

The Fianna Fáil/Labour Party coalition

Fianna Fáil's decision to form a coalition with the Labour Party in 1992 following the collapse of its coalition with the Progressive Democrats was another milestone in Irish politics. Within Fianna Fáil a strong desire remained to return to single-party government – indeed, one prominent party member referred to the 1989–92 coalition with the Progressive Democrats as 'a temporary little arrangement'[96] – but this was not to be. In early 1992, with its highest ever first preference vote share (19.3 per cent), the Labour Party sought a return to government but could not agree a programme with its traditional coalition partner, Fine Gael. Fianna Fáil had had a poor election and was prepared to concede the Labour Party's demands in order to return to office.[97] This combination of events was to have an unprecedented impact on the shape of the Irish parliament.

This changing pattern of government formation preferences is crucial to understanding the development of more consensual government in the years after 1992. In particular, the Labour Party's ability to demand more co-operative government in its negotiations with Fianna Fáil is of great importance. Fine Gael's acceptance of more consensual parliamentary practices also became a feature when the Fianna Fáil/Labour Party government ended in 1994. This constellation of changes in government formation preferences engendered a significant period of change in parliamentary and public accountability in Ireland.

By this stage a tribunal of inquiry had been established (on the Progressive Democrats' insistence) to investigate the actions of senior Fianna Fáil figures and their relationship to certain business interests during the 1980s. Furthermore, the Progressive Democrats complained that when in government it had been left in the

---

[96] See Girvin, B. (1993) 'The Road to the General Election' in M. Gallagher and M. Laver. (eds) *How Ireland Voted 1992*. Dublin: Folens/PSAI Press, p. 1.
[97] Girvin, B. (1999) 'Political Competition, 1992–1997' in M. Marsh and P. Mitchell (eds) *How Ireland Voted 1997*. Oxford: Westview/PSAI Press, p. 3.

dark regarding important government decisions, and this had played a part in the coalition's breakdown. The Labour Party needed to ensure that it could monitor the actions of its partner in government, and therefore sought to restructure the cabinet system.

As Farrell indicates, this desire for reform was not related solely to suspicions of Fianna Fáil but also to Labour's unsatisfactory experiences of being a 'junior' partner in government with Fine Gael during 1973–77 and 1983–87.[98] The Labour Party had not been able to pursue its agenda of a more consensual parliamentary environment without Fine Gael support. The size of the Labour vote in 1992 enabled it to push for a more co-operative style of government.

Indeed, from this period onwards it is possible to identify significant developments in the processes of parliamentary accountability, as well as the introduction of regulations and codes of ethics for those holding public office. The Labour Party's demands for adequate checks on its coalition partner necessitated the creation of a more open style of government. Institutional devices were created to provide for better transparency and information flows within both government and the Oireachtas. The Labour Party's demand to be seen as an equal in government is reflected in the title of the agreed *Programme for a Partnership Government*. Under the document's sub-title, *Broadening our Democracy*, a range of reforms to parliament and local government was envisaged, as well as ethics and freedom of information legislation. There was also significant realignment of activities within the civil service, with some government departments being merged and new ones being created. Interestingly, this practice has been repeated with each new government since 1992.

As part of its plan to implement the programme for government, the Labour Party introduced 'programme managers' whose role was to co-ordinate activities between government departments.[99] They operated within the civil service but had a political role. The new coalition also agreed on the use of 'special advisers' whose function was to provide advice or any other assistance to the minister, and who were to be directly accountable to him or her. Also, the position of deputy Prime Minister or Tánaiste, which had previously carried nominal political weight, was significantly augmented within a new

---

[98] Farrell, B. (1993) 'The Formation of the Partnership Government' in M. Gallagher and M. Laver (eds) *How Ireland Voted 1992*. Dublin: Folens/PSAI Press, p. 155.

[99] O'Halpin, E. (1997) 'Partnership Programme Managers in the Reynolds/Spring Coalition, 1993–4: An Assessment', *Irish Political Studies* Vol. 12, 78–91.

Office of the Tánaiste, with the incumbent expecting to be consulted on all government matters. Furthermore, the Labour Party sought to re-establish the committee system that had been abolished in 1987. However, the former leader of Fine Gael, John Bruton TD, claims that the committee system introduced following these negotiations:

> was a direct lift from the FG manifesto of the 1992 election … Labour more or less took our material and used it as something that they would negotiate with Fianna Fail for.[100]

Unlike the committees created during the 1983–87 Fine Gael/ Labour coalition, the new committee system was departmentally aligned and contained members from both Houses (Joint Committees). For example, a new Joint Committee on Finance and General Affairs, as well as a Joint Committee on Foreign Affairs, coexisted with joint committees on cross-departmental issues such as women's rights and sustainable development. Also, thanks to the Labour Party's efforts, the issues of parliamentary reform and executive accountability were brought to the centre of government business. Indeed, many of its proposals, particularly on freedom of information and ethics in public office, subsequently became law.

This coalition ended in 1994 when the Labour Party withdrew, accusing Fianna Fáil of misleading it on several occasions and, in a final instance, misleading the Dáil.[101] A significant phenomenon then occurred – the Dáil approved a new government without an intervening election. The fact that a government had been replaced because a Taoiseach was found to have misled the Lower House was an unprecedented departure for the Dáil, and in many respects an example of effective parliamentary accountability. The Dáil has only ever dismissed two governments in its history – in 1982 and 1992 – and general elections immediately followed. A government change between elections had never occurred before, and is an event more associated with jurisdictions that practise consensus-style politics. It also demonstrated the influence of coalition arrangements on executive accountability.

The 'Rainbow' Coalition and the opening up of government

As the Taoiseach had lost his parliamentary majority, constitutionally he could not dissolve parliament or call an election and so Fine Gael,

---

[100] Interview with John Bruton, 12 February 2002.

[101] Girvin, B. (1999) 'Political Competition, 1992–1997' in M. Marsh and P. Mitchell (eds) *How Ireland Voted 1997*. Oxford: Westview/PSAI Press, pp. 13–16.

the Labour Party and the small socialist Democratic Left party proceeded to form the 'Rainbow' Coalition of 1994–97 without a direct
popular mandate. It continued with both the joint committee system
and the use of programme managers to monitor the implementation
of policy. Furthermore, as part of the coalition's programme, titled
A Government of Renewal, a commitment was given to establish a
Constitution Review Group to consider the issue of constitutional
reform.

However, as with the 1971/2 Informal Committee on Reform of
Dáil Procedure, this committee failed to consider seriously the lack
of parliamentary accountability in the Oireachtas. An all-party
Oireachtas Committee on the Constitution was established on
recommendation of the review group, and in 2002 this committee
produced a report concerning parliament. Like the all-party Informal
Committee on Reform of Dáil Procedure in 1972, however, the
committee chose to ignore the nature of parliamentary accountability
in Ireland, saying:

> It is not the task of the All-Party Committee to conduct an exhaustive analysis
> of the standing and functioning of the Houses of the Oireachtas, although we
> believe that these questions are important and urgent enough to form the
> subject of a dedicated and comprehensive examination.[102]

The Rainbow Coalition government made significant strides in
increasing accountability and transparency in the political and
administrative spheres. It succeeded in passing the ethics in public
office and freedom of information legislation that had been initiated
under the previous administration, and instigated a wide-ranging
Dáil debate on Dáil reform and parliamentary accountability in
October 1996 that lasted for several days and involved considered
contributions from all sides of the House. Furthermore, the
coalition government was responsible for establishing within the
Dáil Committee on Procedure and Privileges a 'Sub-Committee on
Dáil Reform'. This sub-committee was responsible for the introduction of the Houses of the Oireachtas Commission in 2004, which
enabled the Oireachtas to plan its finances independently of the
Department of Finance. These developments will be considered in
greater detail in Chapter 8.

The number of programme managers appointed decreased after
the Rainbow Coalition's term ended; the new Fianna Fáil/Progressive

---

[102] Informal Committee on Reform of Dail Procedure (1972) *Final Report*.
Dublin: Stationery Office, p. 10.

Democrat government that came to power after the 1997 election delegated many of their functions to ministers of state.[103] However, as of 2005 there were still programme managers in the Departments of the Taoiseach, Health and Transport, and the use of special advisers has continued. Their role was legislated for in the 1997 Public Service Management Act.[104] Ministers have also begun employing 'press advisers'.[105] Important questions have emerged in recent years over the accountability of both ministers of state and special advisers for activities in their respective departments, as well as their relationship with the minister.[106]

While there has been a significant amount of institutional change in Dáil Éireann since 1993, the outgoing Fianna Fail/Progressive Democrat administration that returned to government in 2002 has been slow to keep up the momentum. For example, the Sub-Committee on Dáil Reform has not made substantial progress since the election of 2002, and the Freedom of Information Act has been revised and its scope significantly curtailed. Furthermore, the number and size of committees have been reduced.

During the Fianna Fáil/Progressive Democrat governments, the two main opposition parties have published new proposals for parliamentary reform. Fine Gael's most recent set of proposals reflects again its desire for more consensual parliamentary practices. Published in September 2000 and titled *A Democratic Revolution*, the document called for more wide-reaching reforms than its forerunners. In terms of parliament, the authors criticised the inability of the Dáil to scrutinise government, and complained that:

---

[103] The 1924 Ministers and Secretaries Act allowed for the appointment of not more than seven 'parliamentary secretaries' or deputy ministers to assist ministers, who did not have cabinet rank. Under the Ministers and Secretaries (Amendment) (No. 2) Act, 1977, the title of parliamentary secretary was changed to 'minister of state', and the number of such appointments increased from seven to ten. Subsequent legislation in 1980 and 1995 raised the number of such appointments to fifteen and seventeen respectively. It is common for the Taoiseach to appoint a full quota of ministers of state.

[104] Section 11 (2) (a) (i–iii) of the Act states that the role of special advisers includes 'providing advice, monitoring, facilitating and securing the achievement of Government objectives that relate to the Department'.

[105] A parliamentary question in 2005 revealed that the annual salaries of programme managers, special advisers and press officers were estimated at 5 million.

[106] This issue emerged as part of an investigation in 2005 by the Oireachtas Joint Committee on Health and Children concerning a report into illegal charges levied on people in public long-stay care institutions.

The difference between the Legislative Branch and the Executive Branch has been fudged and obscured resulting in essentially political questions being referred to the Judicial Branch in either Courts or Tribunal for resolution.[107]

The proposals for parliamentary reform were very detailed. In relation to parliament and parliamentary oversight, the main concerns were:

- financial independence (from the Department of Finance) for the Oireachtas through the establishment of an Oireachtas Commission
- better recognition of the rights of the opposition and better resourcing for them
- to regularise the role of the whips
- better staffing for parliamentarians
- provision for the expulsion of deputies who breach ethical guidelines
- reducing the number of committees and improving their resources and powers
- longer Dáil sittings and shorter recesses
- improvement in the effectiveness of parliamentary questions
- new facilities to raise issues of urgent public importance
- provision for the initiation of a parliamentary inquiry.

To date, there has been progress with regard to some of these proposals, including the financial independence of parliament through the creation of the Houses of the Oireachtas Commission, and an increase in research facilities for parliamentarians and committees.

In October 2003 the Labour Party also produced a new package for Dáil reform. Titled *Putting our House in Order*, the proposals were detailed and covered a range of issues, from reform of Dáil standing orders to the relationship of civil servants with the Houses of the Oireachtas. Some of the proposals mirrored those made by the party in the 1970s, including longer Dáil sittings, reduced recess periods and more parliamentary time for the opposition. Indeed, the document went so far as to call for a complete redrafting of the Dáil standing orders. Many of the Labour Party's proposals are consistent with those of Fine Gael, including better opportunities for raising topical issues in the chamber. However, new and innovative ideas were also proposed, notably a new 'Committee of Investigations, Oversight and Petitions' whose role would involve the initiation of investigations into matters of public concern, and supervision of a new 'Office of Parliamentary Investigator'. This office was envisaged

---

[107] Fine Gael (2000) *A Democratic Revolution*. Leinster House, Dublin: Fine Gael Parliamentary Party. See also Appendix A.

as adopting a role akin to that of the Comptroller and Auditor-General, with powers to conduct specific investigations, take evidence and prepare reports.[108] The document also proposed a reappraisal of the concept of ministerial accountability to reflect more accurately the changes brought about by the devolution of responsibility within the public service as part of the Strategic Management Initiative (see above).

In February 2004, a Dáil debate on the issue of Dáil reform took place during Private Members' Business, and government chief whip Mary Hanafin proposed several changes to the parliamentary timetable that corresponded to those proposed by the Labour Party publication. These included extending the sitting hours during the Dáil week, the publication of a monthly schedule of second stage legislation, a weekly opportunity for committee chairmen to address the Dáil, and an hour per week to be made available for debate on committee reports. The chief whip also proposed that the adjournment debate be replaced with a form of 'commencement' debate, to take place in the mornings and to allow discussion of topical issues.[109] While these were progressive proposals in terms of improving parliamentary accountability, at the time of writing there has only been some progress with regard to a dedicated TV channel for parliamentary proceedings. The Sub-Committee on Dáil Reform meets sporadically but has produced no further reports.

---

[108] Labour Party (2003) *Putting Our House in Order: Dáil Reform, Parliamentary Oversight and Government Accountability.* Leinster House, Dublin: Parliamentary Labour Party. See also Appendix A.

[109] *Dáil Debates*, 10 February 2004, Vol. 579, Cols 1031–62.

PART III

Mechanisms of parliamentary accountability in Ireland

CHAPTER 4

How parliamentary accountability functions in Dáil Éireann

Procedures in Dáil Éireann

Tsebilis reminds us that constitutions often bestow institutional advantage on the government by giving them extensive agenda-setting powers.[1] For example, Article 45 of the Constitution of the Fifth French Republic permits the government to declare a Bill to be urgent, thus reducing the number of rounds through which it will shuttle between chambers. Article 68 of the German Basic Law grants the Federal Chancellor the discretion to propose to the Bundestag a question of confidence in government, which if lost may result in the Federal President dissolving that chamber. No analogous constitutional powers are granted to the government in Ireland.

While account must be taken of the passage of Money Bills, debates on estimates and the role of the Public Accounts Committee, the complex budgetary process and vagaries of financial procedures cannot be dealt with fully here. It suffices to note that, as the annual Finance Act is one of the most important pieces of legislation in the parliamentary year, the executive tightly controls its passage through parliament. Indeed, a government that fails to pass its Budget will normally resign, as happened in 1982 with the Fine Gael/Labour Party minority government.

There are several sources for the procedures of Dáil Éireann.[2]

1   Article 15.10 of Bunreacht na hÉireann gives each House the right to 'make its own rules and standing orders'.
2   In a few areas, statute law can have a bearing on procedure but the constitutional protection given to each House to create its own rules has primacy.

---

[1]   Tsebelis, G. (1995) 'Veto Players and Law Production in Parliamentary Democracies' in H. Döring (ed.) *Parliaments and Majority Rule in Western Europe*. New York: St Martin's Press, p. 101.
[2]   See also Gwynn Morgan, D. (1990) *The Constitutional Law of Ireland*. Dublin: Round Hall Press, pp. 133–5.

3   The day-to-day procedure of parliament takes place within the parameters of a set of rules titled 'Standing Orders relative to Public Business'.

4   Sessional orders, which are distinct from standing orders in that they terminate with the life of a parliamentary session (usually the length of a government's term in office), may be used. Sessional orders are often used to experiment with potential new standing orders.

5   On each sitting day, the order of the day can temporarily set aside standing orders and provide for time limits to items of business.

6   The Speaker of Dáil Éireann, the Ceann Comhairle, has the authority to interpret the 171 Dáil standing orders, and to rule on matters not covered in the standing orders for Dáil Éireann. For this the Ceann Comhairle has a book of rulings that is based on precedent and updated as new circumstances arise.

The third source, Dáil Standing Orders relative to Public Business (DSO), provides detailed insights as to why parliament is incapable of detailed scrutiny of the executive. Dáil Éireann adopted its standing orders, based on the House of Commons, on its second sitting day in 1922. These were amended in 1926, and again following the new Constitution in 1937. A major revision of Dáil procedures took place in 1974 following the recommendations of the Informal Oireachtas Committee on Reform of Dáil procedure in 1972, as discussed in the previous chapter. There have been minor periodic revisions since then, such as in 1996 when the Rainbow Coalition made some amendments. While an exhaustive analysis of the 171 standing orders that currently exist is neither possible nor desirable here, in order to understand how parliamentary accountability operates in Dáil Éireann we must identify the specific rules that act as veto points over the ability of individual (usually opposition) members and parliamentary parties to scrutinise the executive.

Formal mechanisms of parliamentary accountability

The principal mechanisms at the disposal of the parliamentary opposition for the purposes of overseeing and questioning government work are derived from Westminster. These are: debate during the various stages of the legislative process; various forms of parliamentary questions (PQs); and deliberation over motions and resolutions. The principal sources of information on the Irish legislature recognise these basic mechanisms, and the more recent editions add the development of parliamentary committees as a further tool at the disposal of the Dáil membership.[3] However, as in Westminster, what undermines the effectiveness of these formal mechanisms is that they are embroiled in the party political warfare of the House.[4]

Debate on legislation

One of the principal tasks of any parliament is the production of legislation. As noted in Chapter 3, the adversarial nature of Irish parliamentary politics influences the method by which this is done. In terms of legislative production, the original Irish Free State Constitution favoured parliament (as opposed to government) more than Bunreacht na hÉireann does. For example, it gave the opposition the power to refer back financial estimates that it found unsatisfactory. The legislative process in Ireland today, however, bears witness to the idea of the governing party or parties operating a 'legislative cartel', maintaining a monopoly in the production of law.[5]

Like most other parliaments, the Oireachtas devotes most of its time to legislative matters. The processing of legislation in both Houses provides the opposition with opportunities to probe the intentions of government and bring them to public attention. As Wheare argued, legislatures 'are asked to consider Bills and, in the course of doing this, they look into administration'.[6] The development of a more professional and better-resourced Oireachtas, with full-time parliamentarians, has not produced a huge rise in the number of Bills enacted each year. However, the complexity of drafting increasingly intricate Acts of parliament, as well as the necessity to guard such legislation against future litigation, takes up a growing share of the parliamentary timetable. Another defining trend has been the increase in the number of amendments proposed by the opposition parties.[7] These factors contribute to explaining why the

---

[3] McCracken, J. L. (1958) *Representative Government in Ireland*. London: Oxford University Press; McGowan Smyth, J. (1973) *The Houses of the Oireachtas*. Dublin: IPA; Chubb, B. (1982) *Cabinet Government in Ireland*. Dublin: IPA; Chubb, B. (1992) *The Government and Politics of Ireland*. London: Longman; Dooney, S. and O'Toole, J. (1998) *Irish Government Today*. Dublin: Gill & Macmillan; Gallagher, M. (2005) 'Parliament' in J. Coakley and M. Gallagher (eds) *Politics in the Republic of Ireland*. London: Routledge/PSAI, pp. 211–41.

[4] Flinders, M. (2001) *The Politics of Accountability in the Modern State*. Aldershot: Ashgate, p. 14.

[5] Cox, G. W. and McCubbins, M. D. (1993) *Legislative Leviathan*. Berkeley: University of California Press.

[6] Wheare, K. C. (1968) *Legislatures*. London: Oxford University Press, p. 90.

[7] Interview with Kieran Coughlan, 30 April 2002.

number of Acts promulgated each year since the 1970s remains largely similar, as a survey of non-election years in Table 4.1 demonstrates. An exception to this is 2001, where there is a significant increase on the previous year. Of course, TDs may still meet in committee when the House is not in session and so facilitate the legislative process. However, there is rarely enough parliamentary time to consider all Bills adequately; in the week before the 2004 summer recess twelve substantive Bills were rushed to completion in parliament with rigorous use of the guillotine.[8]

It would be misleading to base the effectiveness or efficiency of parliament on how many statutes it passes each year. However, as noted above, Norton identifies the procedures by which parliaments pass legislation as a suitable feature for cross-national comparisons.[9] What is important for this study is how the legislative process in Ireland reveals the difficulties faced by the non-governing parties in Dáil Éireann in properly scrutinising government and being involved in the legislative process.

The Constitution (Article 15.2.1) provides the Oireachtas with exclusive law-making powers but, as with most other European parliaments, the government has developed a dominant position over the legislative function. Robinson believed that the main contribution of the Oireachtas was not legislative but 'one of providing publicity and education through debate'.[10] Chubb developed this theme by arguing that, like the House of Commons in Britain, the Dáil came to accept its subservient role to the government and has been slow in developing procedures or giving itself the resources to act as an effective policy critic.[11] Ward recognised some time ago that:

> Dáil Éireann, as any other legislature, has a duty to scrutinise the government's day-to-day conduct of public affairs and to discuss public policies in general, non-legislative terms. However, the Dáil is not encouraged to perform this task effectively.[12]

---

[8]   The guillotine is a time limit, proposed at the outset of debate on legislation, after which any outstanding opposition amendments will be considered to have fallen.

[9]   Norton, P. (ed.) (1990) *Legislatures*. Oxford: Oxford University Press.

[10]   Robinson, M. T. W. (1974) 'The Role of the Irish Parliament', *Administration* Vol. 22(1), 6.

[11]   Chubb, B. (1982) *Cabinet Government in Ireland*. Dublin: IPA, p. 75.

[12]   Ward, A. J. (1974) 'Parliamentary Procedures and the Machinery of Government in Ireland', *Irish University Review* Vol. 4(2), 226.

Table 4.1: Quantity of legislation passed by the Oireachtas in non-election years (excluding Acts to amend the Constitution)

Year	Number of Bills enacted	Number of sittings (days)
2004	44	101
2003	46	97
2001	55	94
2000	43	90
1999	34	88
1998	54	89
1996	44	99
1995	36	100
1993	40	102
1991	32	99
1990	38	93
1988	35	89
1986	39	103
1985	24	97
1984	28	98
1983	43	90
1980	44	85
1979	43	85
1978	35	87
1976	39	94
1975	29	110
1974	35	89
1972	35	87
1971	37	99
1970	25	89

Source: 'Returns relating to Sittings and Business of the Nineteenth, Twentieth, Twenty-First, Twenty-Fourth and Twenty-Fifth Dáil', *Parliamentary Bulletin*, 2002; www.oireachtas.ie

Legislation occurs in the form of either Public Bills, which become Acts of parliament applicable to the general body of citizens, or Private Bills, which apply to individuals or individual institutions. Private Bills are rare and are dealt with under extraneous procedures; as such they do not form part of this study. Public Bills may be sub-divided into (a) Bills initiated by the government and (b) those initiated by a member of the opposition or government representing a group of not fewer than seven members (DSO 114); the latter are known as Private Members' Bills (PMBs). Government Bills are by far the most common form of legislation and are sponsored by a minister (or minister of state if the minister is absent). The passage of legislation provides TDs with opportunities to challenge and question the relevant minister (and, by virtue of collective responsibility, the government as a whole) as to his or her intentions and the rationale for the legislation.

The path through which all legislation must pass mirrors the process in Westminster. However, a chasm has opened up between the traditional understanding and the reality of lawmaking in an altered political and social environment. As Chubb pointed out over two decades ago, the public or parliamentary stages occur *after* the government has evolved a policy that has received broad parliamentary party approval.[13]

Government Bills

The path for a Public Bill introduced by the government in the Dáil is as follows.

- *Stage 1* – The Ceann Comhairle must first approve the text of the Bill in terms of its compliance with standing orders, as well as its purpose (this is known as 'the long title'). One of two procedures then occurs: (1) the Bill may be presented to the chamber by a minister, minister of state or member of a recognised group of members (this does not require the leave of the House); (2) otherwise, any member is entitled to request permission to introduce a Bill to the House. If permission is granted, the Bill is published and circulated. Normally, government-sponsored Bills proceed to publication without prior approval.
- *Stage 2* – The broad outline and principle of the Bill are discussed and there is some debate, but not on the finer points of the proposed legislation. Dáil Standing Order 119 (3) limits the speeches of the opposition leaders to thirty minutes, and those of any other members to twenty minutes. There is no debate on the detail of the Bill at this stage, but amendments to delay its introduction may be proposed.
- *Stage 3* – The 'committee stage' is when the Bill is considered in detail. It is at this stage that the opposition has its best opportunity to alter sections of the Bill it disagrees with and to question the minister or minister of state promoting the legislation as to their and the legislation's intentions. Up to 1983, the vast majority of government-sponsored Bills had their committee stage in the whole House rather than an actual committee of the House.[14] Today, select committees, which consist of members

---

[13] Chubb, B. (1982) *Cabinet Government in Ireland*. Dublin: IPA, p. 72.

[14] Gwynn Morgan, D. (1990) *The Constitutional Law of Ireland*. Dublin: Round Hall Press, p. 100.

of the Dáil only, are used for almost all Bills, but the procedures and organisation of the committee stage ensures that the government does not have to accept opposition proposals. In fact, outright acceptance of opposition amendments is rare. Nevertheless, the use of select committees in the passage of legislation has become an important feature of Irish politics in recent years and will be dealt with more fully below.

- *Stage 4* – At this, the 'report stage', the Bill is reported back to the House as a whole and only the amendments arising from the committee stage are debated. The Ceann Comhairle may disallow proposals by the opposition for any new amendments. No amendment may be made here that is similar to an amendment defeated at the committee stage (DSOs 129, 130).

- *Stage 5* – This is the final reading of the Bill, where no amendments, apart from those that are 'merely verbal' (DSO 132), are accepted. The Bill then goes to the Seanad where it begins at the second stage or, if it began its life in the Upper House, it is presented to the President to be signed into law.

While this study focuses on the Dáil, in legislative terms it is worth noting the role of the Seanad. Tsebilis and Money argue that in most bicameral legislatures, the Upper House will play an important role in legislative outcomes, regardless of formal powers.[15] Virtually no analysis has been conducted on this in Ireland. The Constitution (Articles 21.2.1, 23.1.2) states that the Seanad has the power to delay a Bill for ninety days (or twenty-one days in the case of a money Bill). A non-money legislative Bill may also begin in the Seanad, which, through institutional design, will normally have a government majority. However, if a Bill that originates in the Seanad is amended in the Dáil, under Article 20.2.2 of the Constitution the Bill is treated as if it began in the Dáil. As with most other bicameral parliaments, a navette or 'shuttle' system (whereby the Bill moves between the two Houses until agreement is reached) is used to solve intercameral difference, but with the Lower House having the final and decisive say. Like other Westminster-style legislatures such as that of Canada, the Oireachtas also has the facility to use a 'conference committee' (a special joint committee) to overcome differences between the chambers,[16] but the use of this facility is rare given the primacy of the Dáil in such matters.

---

[15] Tsebilis, G. and Money, J. (1997) *Bicameralism*. Cambridge: Cambridge University Press.

[16] Tsebilis, G. and Rasch, B. (1995) 'Patterns of Bicameralism' in H. Döring (ed.) *Parliaments and Majority Rule in Western Europe*. New York: St Martin's Press, p. 369; Tsebilis, G. and Money, J. (1997) *Bicameralism*. Cambridge: Cambridge University Press, p. 63.

The government retains a distinct advantage over the opposition in the formation of legislation. Most fundamentally, it can schedule the time and length of debate and set conditions that are favourable to itself. The most critical phase in this process is arguably Stages 2 and 3, when the shape and scope of the Bill are largely decided on. When a draft Bill reaches Stage 3, its principle and broad outline have already been voted on and the committee is therefore constrained in what it may amend. This veto point gives a huge advantage to the government and ensures that it can deliver on its legislative programme more easily.

Norton also argues that the stage at which a committee receives Bills is crucial in deciding whether or not it will develop independence from government.[17] Döring refers to the practice of deciding the parameters for discussion as an 'ingenious agenda-setting device'.[18] The Irish parliament is one of only three European legislatures of eighteen that restrict the committee stage in this way (Table 4.2). Most European legislatures allow committees to alter the shape and scope of legislation significantly before it reaches the House.

As Strøm notes, the rights or authorities given to the structures through which legislation passes have an important impact in determining the eventual outcome.[19] In Ireland, the government maintains a parliamentary majority at all stages of the legislative process in both chambers and maintains swingeing powers to guillotine Dáil business (see below). The fact that ministers reply 'I do not accept this amendment', or, more rarely, 'I accept this amendment' shows how legislation is treated as if it were the preserve of government ministers rather than the House. As previous chapters have shown, the dynamics of the party system combined with the institutional design of the House results in government reluctance to facilitate cross-bench co-operation in this process, despite the ideological similarities between the two largest parties in the State.

The proliferation of secondary legislation (also known as delegated legislation or statutory instruments) to manage the business of the government has also raised questions concerning parliamentary accountability. Such legislation is provided for under primary Acts of

---

[17] Norton, P. (ed.) (1990) *Legislatures*. Oxford: Oxford University Press, *passim*.

[18] Döring, H. (1995) 'Time as a Scarce Resource: Government Control of the Agenda' in H. Döring (ed.) *Parliaments and Majority Rule in Western Europe*. New York: St Martin's Press, p. 233.

[19] Strøm, K. (1995) 'Parliamentary Government and Legislative Organisation' in H. Döring (ed.) *Parliaments and Majority Rule in Western Europe*. New York: St Martin's Press, p. 69.

Table 4.2: Is the committee stage of a Bill restricted by a preceding plenary decision?

I	II	III
Ireland	Denmark	Austria
Spain		Belgium
United Kingdom		Finland
		France
		Germany
		Greece
		Iceland
		Italy
		Luxembourg
		Norway
		Netherlands
		Portugal
		Sweden
		Switzerland

◀━━━━━━━━━━━━━━━━━━━━━━━━━━━━━▶

more government control   **less government control**

(I) Plenary decides on principles before committee and leaves little room for substantial changes; (II) plenary decision usually before committee but not strictly binding; (III) committee stage before consideration in plenary presents final solution.

Source: Döring, H. (1995) 'Time as a Scarce Resource: Government Control of the Agenda' in H. Döring (ed.) *Parliaments and Majority Rule in Western Europe.* New York: St Martin's Press, p. 234; see also Döring (2001)

the Oireachtas, and grants ministers[20] considerable flexibility to determine how aspects of legislation can be implemented. However, providing for secondary legislation in order to avoid debating details during the parliamentary stages of a Bill is not uncommon, and in recent years has caused difficulties when challenged in the courts. For example, in 1999 a High Court judge found a section of the 1999 Immigration Act unconstitutional as it contained a ministerial order that had been given the same status as a piece of primary legislation.[21]

---

[20] Local authorities and other designated bodies are also allowed to create certain types of secondary legislation such as by-laws.

[21] Collins, S. (2004) 'Politics', *The Sunday Tribune*, 25 January, 12.

In 2004, a regulation from 1976 concerning charges for patients in long-stay care institutions was found to be unconstitutional; this has resulted in a huge financial loss to the State.

Money Bills and estimates debates

Bills dealing with money and taxation are even more firmly under the control of government than routine legislation. As noted above, the Seanad is constitutionally precluded from introducing motions, Bills or amendments to Bills that may impose a charge on the Exchequer. The Constitution (Article 17.1.2) gives the Dáil the sole right to introduce legislation involving taxation and spending. If a private member wishes to propose legislation involving expenditure (as most Bills do), they must receive a resolution from the government allowing them access to funds. This is similar to the practice in the French Assemblée Nationale, where all Private Members' Bills are referred to the Bureau of the Assembly, which decides whether they can proceed on the basis of Article 40 of the French Constitution, which places restrictions on non-government Bills that may cause a reduction in public funds or an increase in public expenditure.[22]

Furthermore, no amendments to legislation that involves a charge either on the people or on State revenue can be proposed by a member of the Dáil, except for a member of the government or a minister of state (DSOs 148, 149 (3)). These standing orders were inserted into the Standing Orders relative to Public Business in 1974 following the recommendation of the Informal Committee on Reform of Dáil Procedure. The informal committee went so far as to recommend the abolition of money resolutions for legislative Bills, which, it argued, were never debated anyway. These resolutions authorised the cost that would accrue to the State as a result of the implementation of an Act, and although replaced by a 'money message' from the government, their removal from the debating process, as eventually happened in 1974, was a regressive step.[23] The informal committee also recommended that the procedure whereby estimates, financial (tax) and money resolutions go through a committee of the whole House be abolished, leaving one stage for the opposition to challenge the government. Limits were put on the speeches in debates on

---

[22] Mattson, I. (1995) 'Private Members' Initiative and Amendments' in H. Döring (ed.) *Parliaments and Majority Rule in Western Europe.* New York: St Martin's Press, p. 465.

[23] Interview with Kieran Coughlan, 16 May 2002.

estimates and financial resolutions. Once implemented, these recommendations significantly restrained the ability of the Dáil to keep the government's handling of financial affairs under control.

Debates on estimates provide another opportunity for the opposition to probe a minister's agenda or to discuss policy. However, they are automatically moved to the relevant select committee where, by virtue of the plenary powers of government (under Article 28.4.3 of the Constitution) reflected in standing orders, they can only be considered and not amended, thus prohibiting the opposition from making recommendations. This may, however, lead to a debate on many areas of the department in question, though it is primarily designed to achieve parliamentary approval for that department's budget. Again, the best an opposition member can hope for out of these various forms of debate is that sufficient publicity will bring pressure to bear on the government or minister involved.

Guillotine of debate

The opposition faces substantial difficulties in getting its proposed amendments accepted during the legislative process. Apart from the structural difficulty of overcoming a government majority, the standing orders permit the executive to push through its proposals easily. The principal tool at the disposal of the government for defeating opposition amendments is the 'guillotine'.[24] It differs from the guillotine in the French Assemblée Nationale, which is enshrined in the Constitution (Art. 49.3) and was created for the purpose of protecting government legislation. The guillotine in this case permits a government to attach a vote of censure to the proposed Bill, i.e. the government can attach its fate to that of the Bill under consideration.[25] However, like the French guillotine, the guillotine used in the Oireachtas can negate all opposition attempts to obstruct the passage of legislation.[26] As Table 4.3 shows, curtailing debate in this manner most frequently occurs in majoritarian-style parliaments such as those in Greece, France and Ireland, while most other European

---

[24] Both the 'guillotine' and rules for 'closure' have their origins in rules of procedure introduced to the House of Commons in 1877, designed to curtail the lengthy speeches and obstructionist tactics of the Irish Home Rule Party.

[25] Huber, J. D. (1992) 'Restrictive Legislative Procedures in France and the United States', *American Political Science Review* Vol. 86(3), 676.

[26] Humphreys, R. F. (1991) 'Legislative Obstruction: How to Do It', *Administration* Vol. 39(1), 55–69.

Table 4.3: Curtailing of debate before the final vote of a Bill in the plenary

I	II	III
Ireland	Denmark	Finland
Greece	Austria	Netherlands
United Kingdom	Belgium	Sweden
France	Germany	
	Iceland	
	Italy	
	Luxembourg	
	Norway	
	Portugal	
	Spain	
	Switzerland	

◀─────────────────────────────────▶

more government control   **less government control**

(I) Limitation in advance by majority vote; (II) advance organisation of debate by mutual agreement between the parties; (III) neither advance limitation nor closure.

Source: Döring, H. (1995) 'Time as a Scarce Resource: Government Control of the Agenda' in H. Döring (ed.) *Parliaments and Majority Rule in Western Europe.* New York: St Martin's Press, p. 240

parliaments decide the legislative timetable by mutual agreement between the parties.

The result is that in the committee stage, there is pressure on the opposition to avoid repetition in its criticisms of proposed legislation, as this wastes the time available for other amendments. In Westminster, standing orders allow the chair to select amendments to be discussed in order to save time and limit repetition. If a proposed amendment is rejected, amendments designated by the chair to be similar to it also fall. In Ireland, the amendments are similarly 'grouped' so that when a proposed amendment is met the first time, all the amendments that the Chair considers to be similar or related to that subject matter are taken for debate with it. However, in voting on the sections of a Bill, the proposed amendments are considered seriatim; this time-consuming practice usually contributes to a guillotine of the debate.

It is very difficult to assess the impact of opposition amendments to legislation, as the minister sponsoring the legislation will prefer to co-opt a good amendment into the Bill for the report stage rather than concede the point in committee. Interviews suggest, however, that the number of opposition amendments accepted is higher than generally acknowledged.[27] For the opposition successfully to halt the passage of a Bill or question the motivations of the government in proposing a new law, it must successfully engage with extra-parliamentary forces such as the media, public opinion or even the courts. Formal external methods also exist, such as the constitutional provision that allows the President to refer a Bill to the Supreme Court to test its constitutionality (Article 26.1), but this rarely occurs. When drafting legislation, the government will want a Bill to pass through the Houses as smoothly as possible and so will be careful not to provide room for the opposition to attack its proposals. In this way the opposition has an indirect influence on legislation. It is also possible for non-government members to introduce legislation of their own, known as Private Members' Bills (PMBs).

Private Members' Bills

In the mid-nineteenth century Westminster House of Commons, much time was devoted to the debate of Bills proposed not by government but by individual members. Modern party government does not provide a suitable environment for such activity and without proper procedures to facilitate them, the chances of a PMB making its way to promulgation are extremely small in parliaments based on this model. However, while the individual member's influence on legislative matters is constrained by political parties, it is also through the party that a member may hope to have the greatest impact.[28] In all European states, parliament's right to introduce laws is shared with the government; in the case of Britain, Ireland and France it is very much subservient to it.

The greater part of the Dáil timetable is given to the passage of government proposals and motions for the implementation of government policies. If the government is to achieve its goals, it must use the sitting time of the Dáil to its full potential and any delays caused by the opposition must be minimised. Thus, at no stage in the passage of legislation can the government be outvoted; the most the opposition can hope for is that the government will co-opt its ideas

---

27 Interview with Kieran Coughlan, 16 May 2002.
28 Mattson, I. (1995) 'Private Members' Initiative and Amendments' in H. Döring (ed.) *Parliaments and Majority Rule in Western Europe*. New York: St Martin's Press, p. 449.

and incorporate them into the Bill as a government-sponsored amendment. So strong is the government's prerogative in passing its legislative programme in Ireland that it will usually step down following defeat on a major Bill or a Budget (even though it is not constitutionally obliged to). Humphreys argues that attempts to obstruct the passage of legislation can draw public attention to it, embarrass the government and provide a focus for mobilising public opposition.[29] However, this highlights the opposition's reliance on external methods of control over the government agenda, as opposed to internal formal mechanisms.

As Table 4.4 shows, the successful passage of a PMB is rare in Ireland and only fifteen have reached promulgation since 1937, showing the historically dominant position of the executive in parliament. Former Fine Gael TD Alan Shatter was one of the most successful deputies in his attempts to bring PMBs into law. The 1989

Table 4.4: Private Members' Bills enacted 1923–2002

Year	Number of PMBs
2002	1
2001	0
2000	1
1999	0
1998	1
1997	0
1996	3
1995	0
1994	1
1993	0
1992	0
1991	1
1990	0
1989	1
1937–88*	6
1923–37	6

* These PMBs were enacted in 1951 (2), 1952, 1953 (2) and 1958.
Source: Gwynn Morgan (1990), p. 103; Gallagher (1999), p. 188; personal communication with Bills Office, Leinster House

---

[29] Humphreys, R. F. (1991) 'Legislative Obstruction: How to Do It', *Administration* Vol. 39(1), 56.

Judicial Separation and Family Law Act, which he initiated, was the first successful PMB in thirty years. Shatter noted that when he first entered the Dáil in 1981, 'there was no tradition of PMBs ever going anywhere' and that:

> most Ministers resent individual TDs producing legislation. It's not seen as a constructive way of addressing an issue; it's seen as a mechanism for politically embarrassing a Minister. Most civil servants are pissed off by members of the Dáil drafting legislation because they see it as their prerogative. You're standing on the toes of both the bureaucracy and the Minister when you produce legislation. And if you produce legislation when your own party is in government – that is deemed treacherous.[30]

Shatter succeeded in having four PMBs enacted, principally in the area of family law, and was helped greatly by the fact that he was by profession a lawyer, given the meagre resources provided for such Bills. In all, six PMBs were passed between 1937 and 1988, five of them during the unstable 1951–54 period, when a multiparty coalition government traded places with a Fianna Fáil minority government. The number of PMBs signed into law since then is nine, three of which occurred in 1996 during the Rainbow Coalition's period in government. In Westminster, PMBs are more frequently assented into law; 268 were successfully sponsored by backbenchers from both sides of the House between 1979 and 1997.[31] However, as Mattson points out, many of these are uncontroversial and proceed through parliament largely uncontested.[32]

For the opposition to successfully introduce and steer a Bill through the legislature in majoritarian parliaments, it requires some of the limited annual parliamentary time. In fact, lack of parliamentary time is probably the biggest obstacle to a PMB becoming law, especially when the executive controls this so tightly. For such a Bill to make it beyond even the first committee stage depends on the government's willingness to allocate time, and even then the Bill is likely to encounter general hostility.

Döring's cross-national work finds that special time is allocated for opposition or private members in Greece, Portugal, Britain and

---

[30] Interview with Alan Shatter, 24 June 2003.
[31] Silk, P. and Walters, R. (1998) *How Parliament Works*. London: Longman, p. 113.
[32] Mattson, I. (1995) 'Private Members' Initiative and Amendments' in H. Döring (ed.) *Parliaments and Majority Rule in Western Europe*. New York: St Martin's Press, p. 479.

Ireland.[33] In fact the Greek constitution specifically provides for monthly opposition time to discuss Bills. In Westminster, thirteen Fridays per session are set aside for private members' time,[34] which is substantially more than the three hours per week allocated to Private Members' Business in the Oireachtas.[35] Indeed, Norton finds that in Westminster, less than 5 per cent of time in each session is spent on PMBs and that 'it is time that is generally well spent [which] allows for some quite productive legislation to get onto the statute book'.[36]

Private Members' Business

Private Members' Business can be used by the opposition to debate its own PMBs or to discuss motions (see below). The provision for Private Members' Business in the Dáil is between 7 p.m. and 8.30 p.m. on Tuesdays and Wednesdays when the Dáil is in session.[37] Prior to the recommendation by the 1972 Informal Committee on Reform of Dáil Procedure that the practice end, both McCracken[38] and Ward[39] noted that the government pre-empted the three hours per week for financial business for most of the year. Indeed, the informal committee itself noted that from 1951 to 1971, never more than 5 per cent of the total number of hours' sitting was devoted to private members' legislation, with 1970 being exceptionally low at one and a half hours, or 0.2 per cent.[40] This was partly due to the fact that there was not a full-time parliamentary opposition for many of these years.[41]

---

[33] Döring, H. (1995) 'Time as a Scarce Resource: Government Control of the Agenda' in H. Döring (ed.) *Parliaments and Majority Rule in Western Europe.* New York: St Martin's Press, p. 226.

[34] Silk, P. and Walters, R. (1998) *How Parliament Works.* London: Longman, p. 111.

[35] Interestingly, only opposition groups are entitled to use private members' time, i.e. government backbenchers are excluded.

[36] Norton, P. (1997) *The Provision of Government Time for Private Members' Bills in the House of Commons.* Centre for Legislative Studies, University of Hull, p. 22.

[37] The Labour Party proposals for Dáil reform published in 2003 noted that in the 1920s, four hours per week was allocated to Private Members' Business (p. 12).

[38] McCracken, J. L. (1958) *Representative Government in Ireland.* London: Oxford University Press, pp. 124–5.

[39] Ward, A. J. (1974) 'Parliamentary Procedures and the Machinery of Government in Ireland', *Irish University Review* Vol. 4(2), 225.

[40] Informal Committee on Reform of Dail Procedure (1972) *Final Report.* Dublin: Stationery Office, p. 71.

[41] Manning, M. (2000) *James Dillon: a Biography.* Dublin: Wolfhound Press, pp. 318–42.

The informal committee did not go so far as to ensure that Private Members' Business be guaranteed for non-government business. Instead, it half-heartedly suggested that the whips try to minimise 'those periods when no time can be given for private Members' business'.[42] Even this was nullified by its recommendation that the government be allowed to appropriate this time without prior notice, showing yet again that the government was not prepared to guarantee the opposition any parliamentary time if it did not have to. It remains the case today that the government may co-opt Private Members' Business for its own business if it deems it necessary (DSO 111).

Under Dáil standing orders, there are several constraints to the use of parliamentary time by private members. To propose a PMB, a member must be part of a parliamentary 'group' (party) of not fewer than seven members (DSO 114 (1)). Furthermore, no group can have more than one Bill before the House at any one time (DSO 114 (4)). This rule was also introduced in 1974 on the recommendation of the abovementioned informal committee, which recognised that the government could defeat all PMBs at the first stage and therefore the draft Bill would never be circulated as normally happens between the first and second stages of a government-sponsored Bill. Therefore the informal committee recommended that some PMBs should automatically be circulated, suggesting that this be limited to one per group in order to prevent a potential flood of private members' legislation.

If a PMB passes the first stage, there is a time limit of six hours on debate at the second stage (DSO 115 (2)), after which the Bill must go to a special or select committee for the third stage (DSO 112). From here it cannot proceed without the government giving it some of its parliamentary time. Before the recent development of a select committee system, PMBs had to be referred to special committees that were established specifically to consider the Bill in question.[43] Unlike a select committee, a special committee does not have the power to send for 'persons, papers, records'.

If PMBs rarely become law, why do members of the opposition propose them? In fact, most PMBs are used to gain publicity for an issue or to embarrass the government into introducing its own legislation on the issue. For example, following revelations at a tribunal

---

[42] Informal Committee on Reform of Dail Procedure (1972) *Final Report.* Dublin: Stationery Office, p. 17.

[43] Malone, S. (1947) *Oireachtas Procedure.* Dublin: Stationery Office, p. 44.

of inquiry that public representatives were lobbied to ignore official planning advice, the Labour Party proposed two PMBs in 1999 and 2000 to provide for a register of lobbyists. The government managed to avoid introducing this, but the Bills increased the opposition's opportunities to attack the government on the issue.

In the past, most PMBs never made it beyond the first or second stage in the Lower House, as they were voted down. Indeed, the tacit acceptance by the opposition that PMBs will not proceed to detailed debate in committee has meant that most of them consist of only a long and a short title. However, in recent years the development of the select committee system has resulted in such Bills proceeding to the committee stage, where they suffer what is referred to in other parliaments as 'committee killings'.[44] This occurs when a PMB at committee stage remains unselected by the committee chair – in most cases a supporter of the government. Shatter argued that this device was increasingly used because governments wanted:

> to adopt the pretence that they were dealing with legislation in a reasonable way. What they did was, they wouldn't oppose them on second stage so as to avoid controversy and then they just languish in committee.[45]

He also notes that:

> For the Bill to be taken at committee stage it required arrangements to be agreed with the minister and his department as to when the minister is available. So simply the minister would never be available.[46]

An example of such a committee killing was the Whistleblower's Protection Bill, a Private Member's Bill proposed by the Labour Party that was referred to committee stage in June 1999. The nature of the Bill was such that it would be difficult for the government to be seen to oppose it, and it advanced to committee for deliberation. However, an actual debate on the legislation at committee stage was never initiated, and though it was restored to the order paper by the Fianna Fáil/Progressive Democrat government following the 2002 election, its position remained unaltered six years later.

It is clear, therefore, that the government's control of the parliamentary agenda, which is reflected in standing orders, severely

---

[44] Mattson, I. (1995) 'Private Members' Initiative and Amendments' in H. Döring (ed.) *Parliaments and Majority Rule in Western Europe.* New York: St Martin's Press, p. 465.

[45] Interview with Alan Shatter, 24 June 2003.

[46] Ibid.

restricts PMBs in Ireland. This in turn sustains the adversarial dynamic of Irish parliamentary politics, as unless a TD is in government, his or her ability to change or create legislation is severely restricted. If a TD is in opposition and not a member of a recognised 'group', it is even more unlikely that he or she will have any power to initiate law. In this respect the Irish parliament is grouped with those of Greece, France and Luxembourg, as Table 4.5 demonstrates. The countries least likely to impose restrictions on PMBs are those closest to Lijphart's consensual model of parliament (see Table 2.1).

Table 4.5: Inhibition of individual member's right to submit law initiative

		Yes		No
Numerical requirement	Ballot	Government controls agenda	Council controls agenda	
Austria	UK	France	Luxembourg	Belgium
Germany		Greece		Denmark
Italy		Ireland		Finland
Spain				Iceland
				Netherlands
				Norway
				Portugal
				Sweden
				Switzerland

Source: Mattson (1995), p. 469

Parliamentary questions

While oversight of government legislation requires concerted action, parliamentary questions (PQs) facilitate oversight by individual members of parliament. The PQ, if used correctly, is theoretically the most potent facility at the disposal of the opposition in order to obtain information and to hold ministers (and therefore government) to account. It also gives the Dáil its most immediate tool in the control of public administration. In some countries, such as Austria and Finland, the procedure for asking questions is even enshrined in the constitution.[47] Wiberg argues that parliamentary questioning provides an outlet for tensions to be released in the political system, which in turn contributes to the legitimacy of that system.[48] In the Dáil[49] there are two types of parliamentary question, those for written and oral reply, although even oral questions in all parliaments must be submitted in writing in advance.

Question Time

Parliamentary Question Time was originally instituted to give backbench TDs on both sides of the House a chance to probe and press ministers on government policy, and to elicit information hidden between the lines of ministerial speeches. However, the reality of parliamentary party politics means that the vast majority of (if not all) the PQs in any year are put by members of the opposition, normally the party front benches. Indeed, there is a strong argument to be made that the least influential position to occupy in Dáil Éireann is on the government back benches, where speaking out of turn is regarded as treacherous. Parliamentary questions are conducted in the adversarial format that pervades politics in Dáil Éireann, and are regulated by both standing orders and precedent.

When it is in session, Question Time in the Dáil, which was slightly rearranged in October 2002, takes place on:

• Tuesdays, 2.30–4.15 p.m.
• Wednesdays, 2.30–3.45 p.m.
• Thursdays, 2.30–3.50 p.m. (although by agreement this has tended to take place from 3.30 to 4.45 p.m.).

Prior to the reforms recommended by the informal committee in 1972, only one hour was set aside for PQs on Tuesdays and Wednesdays, and over two hours on Thursdays. The practice grew up of postponing questions that were not answered, and this led to a backlog in the system. The informal committee recommended that the standing orders be amended so as to allow government to extend the time for the taking of PQs; this was approved in 1974. Within

---

[47] Norton, P. (1993) 'Introduction: Parliament since 1960' in M. Franklin and P. Norton (eds) *Parliamentary Questions.* Oxford: Clarendon Press, p. 2.

[48] Wiberg, M. (1994) 'To Keep the Government on its Toes: Behavioural Trends in Parliamentary Questioning in Finland 1945–1990' in M. Wiberg (ed.) *Parliamentary Control in the Nordic Countries.* Jyväskylä, Finland: Gummerus Printing, p. 188.

[49] There is no provision for PQs in the Seanad.

the allocated Question Time, there is a division between questions to the Taoiseach and questions to other members of the government.

Taoiseach's questions

DSO 36 (1) permits questions to be asked of the Taoiseach on Tuesdays and Wednesdays at the beginning of Question Time for forty-five minutes. Prior to the Rainbow Coalition's decision in 1996 to extend the time for Taoiseach's questions, only twenty-five minutes on each day had been set aside for them.[50] Other members of the government answer questions in turn on an agreed daily rotation for the remainder of the question time. This rotation of ministers repeats itself every five weeks or so, thus providing some regularity with which deputies can question a minister. Before reforms introduced following recommendations by the 1972 informal committee, if ministers did not reach a question put to them within the time specified, the questioner would have to wait for some weeks before the minister would return to give a reply. The reforms allowed ministers to supply a written response to the question. Questions to the Taoiseach require at least four days' notice.

In October 2002, the Fianna Fáil/Progressive Democrat government secured a change to the Taoiseach's questions. Instead of answering questions in the afternoon on Wednesdays, an amendment to DSO 35 (1) allowed him to answer questions in the morning following leaders' questions (see below). As the Tánaiste or chief whip usually took the Taoiseach's questions on Thursday afternoons, this new rule effectively allows the Taoiseach to finish his weekly interaction with the House by Wednesday morning. Nonetheless, the aggregate amount of time spent by the Taoiseach answering questions in the Dáil compares favourably with the thirty minutes per week to which the British Prime Minister is committed.

Questions to ministers

A criticism of Question Time in the Dáil by a former Taoiseach (and long-time advocate of parliamentary reform) is that it has become less of an inquisitorial process designed to pursue accountability, and more of a process whereby the parties state their positions.[51] However, this is not just an Irish phenomenon, as

---

[50]   *Dáil Debates*, 9 October 1996, Vol. 469, Col. 1705.
[51]   Interview with John Bruton, 12 February 2002.

Wiberg notes.[52] He argues that PQs are used not only to receive information, but also to *give* information to actors both inside and outside parliament. In Ireland this is evidenced by TDs using the opportunity of a PQ to engage in partisanship and to let their constituents know that they are working on their behalf. PQs are also used variously to help a member of parliament build up a reputation in some matters, to encourage opposition unity, and even on occasion to create elements of excitement or drama.

Oral PQs in Ireland must be submitted at least four days in advance (three for written questions) in order to allow the relevant minister's (or Taoiseach's) department to prepare a response. Before a question can appear on the Dáil Order Paper, it is examined to make sure that it is in accordance with standing orders. For example, questions must not seek information already provided to the Dáil within the previous four months, or contain 'argument or personal imputation' (DSO 34 (3) and (5)). However, as former minister Desmond O'Malley pointed out in an interview, government departments attempt to use standing orders to reduce the number of questions they have to answer:

> When say fifty questions come in in a particular week in a particular department, they're all faxed across to the department and the first job of some official there is to go through the fifty of them, ring back the Questions Office in Leinster House an hour or two later when he has studied all the questions, and object to perhaps half or three quarters of them on kind of recognised grounds that they're argumentative or that they're repeats or vexatious.[53]

With the permission of the Ceann Comhairle, when a question is put and a response given, the questioner may put a second and in some cases a third supplementary question. This supplementary will usually attempt to 'catch out' the minister, who may not be able to answer the question sufficiently and therefore appear incompetent. There was an example of a supplementary question being used in this manner during Taoiseach's questions in October 2002. The Fine Gael leader, Enda Kenny TD, as leader of the opposition, attempted to use a supplementary question on tourism to get the Taoiseach to comment on Northern Ireland. The Ceann

---

52 Wiberg, M. (1995) 'Parliamentary Questioning: Control by Communication?' in H. Döring (ed.) *Parliaments and Majority Rule in Western Europe.* New York: St Martin's Press, p. 180.
53 Interview with Desmond O'Malley, 20 June 2003.

Comhairle's decision to disallow it shows how the government's position is insulated not just by weak answers but also by the rules of the House:

> **Enda Kenny** asked the Taoiseach his Department's legislative programme for the remainder of 2002; and if he will make a statement on the matter.
>
> **The Taoiseach:** My Department has three Bills awaiting Second Stage. These are the Interpretation Bill, 2000, the National Economic and Social Development Office Bill, 2002, and the Statute Law Restatement Bill, 2000. I have no plans to introduce further legislation at this time.
>
> **Mr Kenny:** I notice that the legislative programme includes a national tourism development authority Bill. In view of the looming crisis in the Northern Ireland peace process and the possible suspension of the institutions, how will that impact in the context of this Bill?
>
> **An Ceann Comhairle:** That matter does not arise now.[54]

Most ministers quickly learn to be evasive and to cope with difficult supplementaries without losing face. So many PQs are currently tabled for oral answer that it is impossible for each to be responded to orally during the time allocated for them. Figures for 2001 show that 31,514 questions were submitted during the year, of which only 1,736 – approximately 6 per cent – were answered orally.[55] Ireland follows a similar trend to other European states, whereby increasing complexity and the expansion of the public sector have led to a huge increase in the number of parliamentary questions submitted (see Table 4.6). As Wiberg argues, another factor in explaining the significant increase in questions is the increased availability to parliamentarians of resources and people with the necessary skills for drafting them.

Expressing the statistics in Table 4.6 graphically, we see more clearly how between 1968 and 2004 the number of questions put to the government has multiplied by a factor of almost five (Figure 4.1). The amount of parliamentary time allocated to replies to these questions has increased only slightly, and the overwhelming majority of questions now receive a written answer.

Traditionally, PQs were short and received specific answers. It was not uncommon to have the order paper of questions for the day cleared. For example, of 5,470 PQs put to the government in 1969,

---

54 *Dáil Debates*, 9 October 2002, Vol. 554, Col. 461.
55 *Parliamentary Bulletin* (2002) Issue 1, January to December 2001. Dublin: Leinster House, 22.

all except 331 were answered orally.[56] This was achieved by having a two-and-a-half-hour question period on Thursdays, during which virtually all ministers and the deputies who wished to pursue their questions were present.[57] It must also be noted that written questions were less frequent then, due partly to the lack of expertise and resources available to TDs who wished to ask them.

Recent developments, particularly in relation to the Hamilton Inquiry into the Beef Processing Industry (Beef Tribunal), where ministers were alleged to have been evasive with answers to questions, show that the efficacy of the PQ has been somewhat blunted. The memoirs of a former civil servant in the Department of Foreign Affairs reveal that PQs 'threw everyone into a sort of panic' and that 'the idea was to say as little as possible'. He went on to say that 'We had to protect the state from overly inquisitive TDs and there was no point in being garrulous and volunteering information.'[58] A PQ will rarely cause a change in government policy or procedure. If it does, it is more likely to be as a result of publicity generated about an issue than of the question itself – a situation that has existed for many decades.[59] Indeed, while in opposition, Progressive Democrat TD Liz O'Donnell argued during a debate on a Bill to grant new powers to parliamentary committees that:

> If the Taoiseach and the Cabinet are serious about learning the lessons of the past about real accountability, the parliamentary questions system should be examined in a comprehensive way. If necessary, the Civil Service will have to be retrained in how to answer such questions. At present, the Government can hide successfully and mislead the Dáil through the many obstacles which are there specifically to confuse Deputies or to keep them in the dark. That is well known by Ministers, the Opposition and civil servants.[60]

A typical reply to an oral PQ involves the preparation of a usually bland written reply by the relevant minister's department, with further responses to possible supplementaries and a 'background note' tucked in behind them in the minister's folder. These folders are well guarded by the minister's department, as 'ambitious (and troublesome) backbenchers have made productive inroads by finding the

[56] McGowan Smyth, J. (1973) *The Houses of the Oireachtas*. Dublin: IPA, p. 55.
[57] Interview with John Bruton, 12 February 2002.
[58] Delaney, E. (2001) *An Accidental Diplomat*. Dublin: New Island, p. 61.
[59] See for example Troy, T. (1959) 'Some Aspects of Parliamentary Questions', *Administration* Vol. 7(3), 258.
[60] *Dáil Debates*, 21 November 1995, Vol. 458, Col. 1094.

Table 4.6: Number of parliamentary questions (PQs) put in non-election years (excluding Private Notice Questions)

Year	PQs permitted*	PQs answered orally	PQs answered in writing
2004	27,568	1,875 (7%)	25,693
2003	25,906	1,894 (7%)	24,012
2001	24,990	1,736 (6%)	23,254
2000	23,719	1,874 (8%)	21,845
1999	21,054	1,774 (8%)	19,280
1998	21,771	1,597 (7%)	20,174
1996	19,138	1,714 (9%)	17,424
1995	12,838	1,895 (15%)	10,943
1993	14,291	2,317 (16%)	11,974
1991	11,269	2,063 (18%)	9,206
1990	11,282	2,070 (19%)	9,212
1988	11,037	3,454 (31%)	7,583
1986	11,456	1,647 (14%)	9,809
1985	10,923	1,499 (14%)	9,424
1984	10,763	1,632 (15%)	9,131
1983	14,268	1,934 (14%)	12,334
1980	6,529	2,241 (34%)	4,288
1979	5,406	2,174 (40%)	3,232
1978	5,852	2,438 (42%)	3,414
1976	3,664	2,192 (60%)	1,472
1975	5,187	4,317 (83%)	870
1974	5,220	4,707 (90%)	513
1972	5,619	4,996 (89%)	623
1971	6,459	5,969 (92%)	490
1970	5,567	5,270 (95%)	297
1968	4,931	4,717 (96%)	214

* PQs may be disallowed for being too general, outside a minister's remit or in contravention of standing orders.
Sources: Returns relating to Sittings and Business of the Nineteenth, Twentieth, Twenty-First, Twenty-Fourth and Twenty-Fifth Dáils; *Parliamentary Bulletin* (2001); McGowan Smyth (1973), p. 55; personal communication

"real replies" inside a mislaid folder.'[61] The natural instinct of a civil servant is to protect his or her department and minister, and as a consequence replies tend to be minimalist. As Wiberg and Koura argue,

---

[61] Delaney, E. (2001) *An Accidental Diplomat*. Dublin: New Island, p. 63.

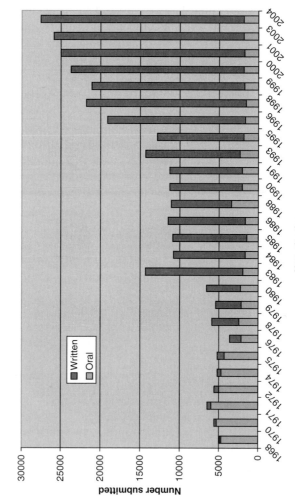

Figure 4.1: Parliamentary questions 1968–2004

it is no surprise that ministers rely on ambiguity in their responses to PQs – they do not want to tie their hands for the future with precise statements.[62] In Ireland, as in the UK, Switzerland, Spain, Norway and Iceland, written questions may not be put to ministers when the parliament is in adjournment.[63]

Questions are chosen by lottery and a TD is restricted to two oral questions on any sitting day. Due to the limits of parliamentary Question Time, there is much competition among members of the opposition front benches for the opportunity to get questions in. It is now common for frontbenchers to nominate questions for oral reply in the name of party backbenchers.[64] The reality, therefore, is that ordinary backbenchers have very little chance of their own questions being answered, as the needs of the parliamentary party front bench dictate matters. Interestingly, the informal committee report of 1972 recommended that no limit be put on the number of questions a TD may ask,[65] but the rapid increase in the number of PQs soon made this aspiration unsustainable.

Preparing replies to parliamentary questions takes up a lot of time within government departments, but the final responses to questions as delivered by ministers will give very little of the detail supplied by the department. Furthermore, when drafting replies to PQs, civil servants naturally tend to argue their case rather than admit error or seek compromise.[66] In the Dáil, debates or statements on a minister's reply are not permitted. Also, the Ceann Comhairle has no power to ensure the questioner receives a satisfactory response. Interviews by this author suggest that answers to PQs have deteriorated in recent years as ministers wished to avoid future accusations on a particular issue.

The introduction of the Freedom of Information Act, 1997 has further undermined the parliamentary question, as it has become the 'poor relation in the information stakes'.[67] Coughlan argued that

---

[62] Wiberg, M. and Koura, A. (1994) 'The Logic of Parliamentary Questioning' in M. Wiberg (ed.) *Parliamentary Control in the Nordic Countries.* Jyväskylä, Finland: Gummerus Printing, p. 27.

[63] Wiberg, M. (1995) 'Parliamentary Questioning: Control by Communication?' in H. Döring (ed.) *Parliaments and Majority Rule in Western Europe.* New York: St Martin's Press, p. 205.

[64] Interview with Kieran Coughlan, 30 April 2002.

[65] Informal Committee on Reform of Dail Procedure (1972) *Final Report.* Dublin: Stationery Office, p. 8.

[66] Dooney, S. and O'Toole, J. (1998) *Irish Government Today.* Dublin: Gill & Macmillan, p. 239.

[67] Interview with Kieran Coughlan, 16 May 2002.

TDs feel that their position as public representatives has been eroded by the new regulations. Opposition members have demanded that responses to parliamentary questions be as comprehensive as replies to requests under the Act. This is unlikely to happen, as the Act allows four months for a reply whereas a PQ can be submitted as late as four days in advance. Dissatisfaction with the response to a PQ can result in a deputy appealing for the matter to be readdressed during the adjournment debate (see below), or (s)he may repeat the question at a later date, but this cannot be less than four months from the time of the original reply (DSO 34 (3)). The limit for written questions is two weeks.

Apart from Question Time, there are other opportunities for TDs to ask questions in the Dáil. Since McCracken's[68] brief attempt to explain comprehensively the procedures around which the parliamentary day is organised, these opportunities have been largely ignored or reduced to footnotes in studies involving the Oireachtas. They include leaders' questions, questions on the Order of Business, priority questions and private notice questions.

Leaders' questions

The introduction of leaders' questions has been the most significant development in the parliamentary timetable in terms of increasing the opposition's opportunities to raise matters of immediate concern in the Dáil. Since 2001 opposition party leaders have been allowed to raise questions relevant to the business of the day, such as the timetable for promised legislation. Normally the opportunity is used to raise a topical matter concerning an incident or event of public importance that might embarrass the government.

The origins of leaders' questions lay in a tradition that developed in the Dáil of allowing opposition party leaders to ask questions related to Northern Ireland outside the normal Question Time period. In 2001, with the Taoiseach's consent, it was agreed that the practice would be formalised in the standing orders and expanded. Following further amendments in October 2002, under DSO 26 a total of twenty-one minutes is now allowed on Tuesdays and Wednesdays prior to Public Business for three party leaders to ask the Taoiseach questions. The format for each leader is as follows:

1   the opposition leader asks a brief question not exceeding two minutes
2   the Taoiseach replies for no more than three minutes

---

[68]   McCracken, J. L. (1958) *Representative Government in Ireland.* London: Oxford University Press.

3   the opposition leader who asked the question may put a supplementary
    question for one minute
4   the Taoiseach may reply for one minute.

While the introduction of leaders' questions is interesting, not least
because the Taoiseach allowed himself to be questioned for longer in
the House, it was not opposition pressure that led to its being formalised. Interviews suggest that the then Ceann Comhairle, Seamus
Pattison, recognised the sterile nature of many PQs and provided for
this new mechanism to be introduced. In June 2005 the chief whip,
Tom Kitt TD, proposed reforms to standing orders that would
oblige the opposition to give prior notice of what they planned to ask
the Taoiseach during leaders' questions. The opposition parties were
strenuously opposed to this and other proposed changes to the Order
of Business (see below).[69]

Questions on the Order of Business

Opposition TDs' next opportunity for questions occurs at the Order
of Business, when the programme of work for the sitting is
announced. These questions are largely concerned with procedural
matters and are usually a protest at the ability of the Taoiseach to
conduct business as suits the government rather than the Dáil. As
Elgie and Stapleton point out, opposition parties' use of the Order of
Business to press their agenda and harry the government is a comparatively recent development, and has become one of the more common methods of trying to embarrass the government.[70] When the
Taoiseach presents the timetable (the Order) in which the government is going to take the Dáil business for the day, the opposition
will usually raise objections and call for a vote on his proposals. Technically, opposition members can only ask questions on proposed
legislation, but normally they break this rule in order to raise other
issues. An amendment to standing orders in October 2002 allows the
Ceann Comhairle to ask the Taoiseach questions concerning the
matters related to the order paper, including promised legislation, if
he so requires.

---

[69]   Reid, L. (2005) 'Plan to cut time Ahern must spend facing Dáil questions', *Irish
       Times*, 27 June, 1.
[70]   Elgie, R. and Stapleton, J. (2004) 'The Parliamentary Activity of the Head of
       Government in Ireland (1923–2002) in Comparative Perspective', *Journal of
       Legislative Studies* Vol. 10(2, 3), 170.

The Taoiseach presents the Order of Business on Tuesdays, Wednesdays and Thursdays and, as detailed above, answers questions on Tuesdays and Wednesdays. However, following the 2002 general election the government proposed changes that would allow the Taoiseach to absent himself from the Dáil, and therefore both leaders' questions and the Order of Business, on Thursdays. This followed a deal by the government with the Labour Party, which was concerned that a new 'technical group' of smaller parties and independent members would be entitled to more parliamentary time than it, given that this group was larger (see below). While the reality was that the Taoiseach was often not present on Thursdays and was replaced by the Tánaiste, this has proved to be a retrograde step for the Dáil and government oversight, and was roundly criticised in the media.[71] Interestingly, in their examination of the Taoiseach's level of activity in the Dáil since 1923, Elgie and Stapleton argue that it has increased over time. However, they concede that this increase is from a very low base, and is partly due to an increased number of annual set-piece roles such as briefing the House on the outcome of European Council meetings and presenting budget resolutions.[72] As part of the standing order reform package announced by the government in June 2005 (see above), it was proposed that the Order of Business on Tuesdays and Thursdays be taken by the government whips and be confined to legislative matters. Following vociferous and public opposition criticism of this proposal and those concerning leaders' questions, however, the reforms were withdrawn a few months later in September.

Priority questions

Introduced by the Fine Gael/Labour Party government in 1986 and subject to the permission of the Ceann Comhairle, DSO 38 permits up to five questions to be asked during a period of thirty minutes before ministerial question time on a sitting day. These are allocated to the parties on the basis of party strength, and only recognised parliamentary groups (see above) may ask them. Priority questions

---

[71] 'The government has engaged in a shoddy, backstairs deal', *Irish Times* (editorial), 24 October 2002; 'Unholy alliances help maintain the balance of power', *Sunday Tribune*, 27 October 2002.

[72] Elgie, R. and Stapleton, J. (2004) 'The Parliamentary Activity of the Head of Government in Ireland (1923–2002) in Comparative Perspective', *Journal of Legislative Studies* Vol. 10(2, 3), 154–73.

are usually asked by the opposition parties' front-bench spokespersons, further restricting the ability of backbenchers and independent members to question the government. Unlike normal PQs, which are 'cleared' by Assistant Secretaries[73] in civil service departments, priority questions are normally cleared by Secretaries-General.

Private notice questions

Private notice questions (PNQs), as Gwynn Morgan points out, were introduced to cater for urgent matters that could not afford to join the queue for normal PQs.[74] They are asked without prior notification (but must be submitted by 2.30 p.m. on the day that they are to be answered) and usually relate to a matter of urgent public importance. Whether or not a deputy (usually an opposition party leader) may ask the question is at the discretion of the Ceann Comhairle, and a time is designated for the question if permitted.[75] In 2001, of 357 PNQs tabled, only 22 were allowed to be asked.[76] Table 4.7 gives the numbers permitted in the non-election years since 1970.

Despite these various opportunities to ask questions in parliament, the PQ is fast becoming too weak a method of probing and investigating the actions of government. As Wiberg and Koura argue, adversarial parliamentary politics inhibits the usefulness of PQs.[77] It allows partisan debate rather than examination of policy, and questions are often directed at an audience outside the Dáil as TDs attempt to publicise themselves to their constituents. The complexity of the modern state and its bureaucracy means that a narrowly defined question is unlikely to elicit much information or to undermine the government seriously. Standing orders also favour the

---

[73] The Assistant Secretary position is the second-highest ranking position in the civil service.

[74] Gwynn Morgan, D. (1990) *The Constitutional Law of Ireland*. Dublin: Round Hall Press, p. 154.

[75] The discretionary powers of the Ceann Comhairle frequently provoke heated exchanges with the opposition, as the tendency is to favour the government's prerogative to carry out its work rather than the opposition's right to enquire. Indeed, it may be argued that the office of the Ceann Comhairle is inherently partisan, given that the parliamentary parties compete for the position.

[76] *Parliamentary Bulletin* (2002) Issue 1: January to December 2001. Dublin: Leinster House, 22.

[77] Wiberg, M. and Koura, A. (1994) 'The Logic of Parliamentary Questioning' in M. Wiberg (ed.) *Parliamentary Control in the Nordic Countries*. Jyväskylä, Finland: Gummerus Printing, p. 38.

Table 4.7: Number of private notice questions asked during non-election years 1970–2004

Year	Number of PNQs
2004	19
2003	26
2001	22
2000	17
1999	7
1998	34
1996	18
1995	36
1993	39
1991	47
1990	43
1988	48
1986	34
1985	23
1984	43
1983	56
1980	18
1979	22
1978	10
1976	7
1975	7
1974	1
1972	4
1971	17
1970	19

government by facilitating bland replies, scant on detail and often adding little to the knowledge of the House.

Debates on the adjournment

A device for scrutinising the executive not found in Ireland but common in many European parliaments is the procedure of interpellation. This is a question, often accompanied by a statement, the answer to which can be debated and may, in some parliaments, result in a vote. PQs differ from interpellations in some obvious respects: they do not require a prefatory explanation, the debate is very short and confined to the questioner and the relevant government member, and there is no vote on the question. Interpellations allow other members to participate.

Although the interpellation device does not formally exist in Ireland, there are methods by which a similar result can be achieved. At the discretion of the Ceann Comhairle, a debate on the adjournment of the House allows a TD who put a parliamentary question that (s)he believes was not satisfactorily answered to initiate a short debate on the matter. Up to four deputies may be selected to make a speech, each one of which can be no longer than five minutes. This is followed by a ministerial reply whose quality the Chair has no power over, usually consisting of the relevant minister reading from a prepared script. Unlike interpellation, no vote is taken at the end of the adjournment debate and however diverse the issues raised, normally only one member of government will respond to all of them. Again, the best the opposition deputy can hope for is to gain publicity for his or her cause, as the debate is usually poorly attended and the reply may be unsatisfactory.

Debate on matters of 'urgent public importance'

As with most Westminster-style parliaments, there exists in Ireland (under DSO 31) the facility for an adjournment debate to consider a matter of 'urgent public importance', with the permission of the Speaker. The debate can last up to ninety minutes but, again, rarely takes place. Such a debate occurred only thirteen times from 1922 to 1974, and only once after 1947 in this period.[78] Since 1974 only eleven debates have been permitted under this rule. On almost every day that the Dáil sits, however, a number of opposition deputies will call for a debate using this device. While rejection is almost guaranteed, it provides the deputy with the opportunity to publicise an issue, which may range from concern regarding unemployment following a factory closure in the deputy's constituency to the government's position on a looming international war.

The following is an example of parliamentarians using this procedure to bring attention to several diverse issues, and being frustrated by the inability to have them debated.

> **An Ceann Comhairle:** Before coming to the Order of Business I propose to deal with a number of topics under Standing Order 31 and I will call on the Deputies in the order in which they submitted their notices to my office.

---

[78] Ward, A. J. (1974) 'Parliamentary Procedures and the Machinery of Government in Ireland', *Irish University Review* Vol. 4(2), 228.

Aengus Ó Snodaigh: I seek leave to move the Adjournment of the Dáil on the following specific and important matter of public interest requiring urgent consideration, the decision by FÁS to issue a directive freezing all social economy schemes throughout the State.

Mr Crowe: I seek to move the Adjournment of the Dáil under Standing Order 31 to raise a matter of national importance, the ongoing disagreement between two Departments, the Department of the Environment and Local Government and the Department of Arts, Sports and Tourism, in relation to the excavations at Carrickmines Castle where the National Museum of Ireland has objected to an excavation licence issued by Dúchas.

Mr Hayes: I seek to move the Adjournment of the Dáil under Standing Order 31 to discuss a matter of national importance, the need for the Minister for Health and Children, Deputy Martin, to clarify proposed plans for the withdrawal of maternity services from St Joseph's Hospital Clonmel in County Tipperary. This long-standing service is vital for the people of south Tipperary who have relied on it for so many years and it is difficult to comprehend that at a time of huge development at the said hospital, such a move could be considered.

Mr Allen: I seek to interrupt the business of the House to discuss the ongoing row between the Department of the Environment and Local Government and the IFA in relation to the placing of conservation restrictions on large tracts of farmland in the west and today's escalation of that dispute where the IFA is extending its campaign by preventing Dúchas officials from going on to land along the River Moy in County Mayo.

Mr Cuffe: Under Standing Order 31, I seek leave to move the Adjournment of the Dáil on a specific and important matter of public interest requiring urgent consideration in regard to Carrickmines Castle. Can the Taoiseach clarify whether procedures for the issuing of an archaeological licence for the removal of the medieval wall at the Carrickmines site were correctly followed by Dúchas; will he request that work on the removal of this wall be suspended pending the outcome of an appeal to the Supreme Court on this important issue; and will he consider making changes to the route of the M50 motorway so that damage to this important and historical monument is averted?

Mr Sargent: I seek leave to adjourn the Dáil under Standing Order 31 to raise a matter of national and international importance: That Irish taxpayers have been faced with a multimillion euro bill due to the US Government's refusal to pay for its military over-flying of this neutral country and the Irish people have shown in a massive demonstration by 100,000 people in Dublin last Saturday and in recent public opinion polls that they are totally opposed to such military over-flights and to a war against Iraq.

An Ceann Comhairle: Having considered all the matters raised, I do not consider them to be in order under Standing Order 31.

Mr Rabbitte: On a point of order, do you see any point, a Cheann Comhairle, in retaining this Standing Order? Are there any circumstances under which you think its use would be contemplated?

An Ceann Comhairle: There are precedents for its use, Deputy Rabbitte, but if the members of the Dáil reform committee wish to do away with the Standing Order, the Chair will implement whatever decision they take.[79]

Seasonal adjournments

Finally, seasonal adjournments, which occur during a motion to adjourn the House for seasonal holidays, can also lead to debates that range across the gamut of government work. However, these debates have traditionally been unstructured and tend to have little impact on the overall thrust of government policy.[80] As with all the other devices outlined above, seasonal adjournment debates are conducted in an adversarial manner. It is worth noting Mattson's argument that all parliamentary conflict has a 'symbolic–expressive' or legitimising function.[81] In other words, it allows politicians to present themselves to the people as champions of government accountability and effective policy-making.

Motions and resolutions

After the legislative process and the answering of various forms of parliamentary question, the other main type of debate is that concerned with government motions. These may be substantive motions, where the House is asked to approve or take note of some action or proposal, or they may take the form of adjournment motions, which allow the House to discuss a topic without having to take a vote or reach a particular decision on it. These adjournment debates are different from the questions on the adjournment referred to above. Most of the substantive motions tabled by the government in an adjournment debate will tend to be related to procedural or 'domestic' matters, for example proposing the establishment of a new select committee.

The Dáil debates motions proposed by itself or by the opposition (during Private Members' Business). Motions of censure or 'no confidence' in the government or Taoiseach are used to attack the policies of the government and result in a vote. The motion of no

---

[79] *Dáil Debates*, 18 February 2003, Vol. 561, Cols 948–9.

[80] Ward, A. J. (1974) 'Parliamentary Procedures and the Machinery of Government in Ireland', *Irish University Review* Vol. 4(2), 228.

[81] Mattson, I. (1994) 'Parliamentary Questions in the Swedish Riksdag' in M. Wiberg (ed.) *Parliamentary Control in the Nordic Countries*. Jyväskylä, Finland: Gummerus Printing, p. 352.

confidence is a fundamental form of parliamentary control, and is based on the premise that the government must retain the confidence of a majority in the legislature. However, as Ward recognised, raising a motion of no confidence or censure in a government is 'too blunt a weapon to be used more than infrequently'.[82] Rasch concurs with this view and argues that overuse of such motions would call into question the credibility of parliament itself.[83] Nonetheless, motions of no confidence in the government have twice been directly responsible for the dissolution of the Dáil.[84]

More pressing issues in the Dáil are dealt with as ad hoc motions. There are also motions to have a debate on the adjournment of the House, which again see the opposition attempt to gain public support for its campaign against the government. Private members may propose motions for debate, which lead to expressions of opinion on matters, but they do not take precedence over government business. As noted above, the time allowed for debate on a private member's motion, but not any stage of a Private Member's Bill, is restricted to three hours in the Dáil (DSO 115 (1)). However, low attendance, coupled with a lack of media and public interest in day-to-day parliamentary activities, means that parliamentarians largely pay lip service to the use of debate on such motions as a method of holding government accountable.

Parliamentary time

Wiberg argues that parliamentary politics in Western Europe is principally about attempting to control the parliamentary agenda.[85] If this is true, then it is clear from the above that the executive in Ireland maintains a significant advantage over the opposition in deciding what will constitute parliamentary business. In Westminster, the

---

[82] Ward, A. J. (1974) 'Parliamentary Procedures and the Machinery of Government in Ireland', *Irish University Review* Vol. 4(2), 227.

[83] Rasch, B. E. (1994) 'Question Time in the Norwegian Storting' in M. Wiberg (ed.) *Parliamentary Control in the Nordic Countries.* Jyväskylä, Finland: Gummerus Printing, p. 248.

[84] The first occasion was in 1982 when the Fianna Fáil government found itself in a minority situation and was subsequently defeated in the no-confidence motion. In 1992, the Progressive Democrat Party withdrew from its coalition government with Fianna Fáil and the latter party again lost a no-confidence motion.

[85] Wiberg, M. (1995) 'Parliamentary Questioning: Control by Communication?' in H. Döring (ed.) *Parliaments and Majority Rule in Western Europe.* New York: St Martin's Press, p. 179.

parliamentary opposition is allotted twenty days in the year in which it may choose the subject for debate. In Ireland, the ability of the opposition to instigate parliamentary debate on a topic is severely constrained. DSO 26 (2) gives the Taoiseach the power to decide the sequence of parliamentary business for the day on the Order Paper, prepared under the direction of the Ceann Comhairle.

Nonetheless, there are regular businesslike meetings between the whips from all parties in which the order of business is discussed so as to facilitate TDs who cannot be present at all sittings. Debates on non-legislative matters during Private Members' Business (see above), which takes place on Tuesdays and Wednesdays for an hour and a half, are arguably the most effective method of government scrutiny after the parliamentary question. Ministers are required to defend their position on a particular subject and a vote is normally taken on the matter under debate on the Wednesday evening. As with the parliamentary question, there is a limit on repetition of subjects for debate in the Dáil. If the Dáil has debated a matter, it cannot be debated again for six months, even if it was debated during Private Members' time. However, the government cannot ignore a crisis by insisting that it has already debated the matter, and the Chair will usually be flexible about such matters.

As Humphreys indicates, in order to oppose the government, the parliamentary opposition attempts to postpone, interrupt and prolong debate.[86] By attempting to clog up the Order of Business at the start of a sitting with requests for adjournment debates, the opposition hopes to hinder the ability of government to introduce legislation. The principal method of interrupting debate is to call for a quorum – under DSO 19 at least twenty members are required for a debate to take place. Use of the guillotine renders other methods of obstruction largely ineffective. If a Bill has a timetable or guillotine attached, the opposition wishes to maximise the time available to it to attempt to amend the Bill and therefore it is against its interest to delay debate. The guillotine also renders lengthy opposition speeches or numerous amendments largely ineffectual.

Since 1997, the standing orders have provided increased incentives for TDs to be part of parliamentary groups of not fewer than seven members, in order to achieve better participation in debates and questions (DSO 114). As noted above, following the 2002 election a technical group was formed composed of small (and

---

[86] Humphreys, R. F. (1991) 'Legislative Obstruction: How to Do It', *Administration* Vol. 39(1), *passim*.

ideologically diverse) parties and independent members for the purposes of securing parliamentary privileges not otherwise available to
them.[87] Without this coalition of junior opposition members, the
two larger opposition parties, Fine Gael and the Labour Party, could
practically monopolise speaking time and question rights. As this
group was larger than the Labour Party, the latter struck a deal with
Fianna Fáil to maintain its position as second after Fine Gael in order
of speaking slots to government Bills, priority questions, the Private
Members' Business rota and PMBs (DSOs 38, 114, 119). In return
Fianna Fáil received the Labour Party's support for allowing the
Taoiseach to absent himself from Question Time in the Dáil on
Thursdays, a situation that Fianna Fáil argued existed anyway as
the Tánaiste frequently seconded for him. This episode serves to
highlight the influence and dominance of the main political parties
on the chamber, as well as the fact that the parties do consider parliament to be an important forum for debate, despite the inferior
position of the opposition.

The Dáil that was returned following the 2002 general election
is markedly different in composition from previous Dáileanna.
Several small parties and independents now join the Labour Party
and Fine Gael in the competition for resources, speaking time and
the right to ask questions during the various parts of the parliamentary day. This has had two effects on the chamber. Firstly,
many of these new TDs do not see any point in gaining experience
in using and reforming parliamentary procedures, and instead
tend to complain about the existing rules. Secondly, because of the
fragmented nature of the opposition, the government is not being
scrutinised as effectively as possible. The loss of several experienced parliamentarians from Fine Gael following the 2002 general
election also diminished the potency of the Dáil opposition.

Seanad Éireann

While the focus of this study is on accountability within Dáil
Éireann, it is appropriate that the work of the Upper House, Seanad
Éireann, be considered here. The sixty seats in the Seanad are filled
through a combination of Taoiseach's appointment (eleven seats),
direct election by graduates from select third-level institutions
(six seats), and indirect election by city and county councillors and

---

[87] A technical group consisting of the Workers Party, the Green Party and
Independents also existed during the 1992–97 governments.

TDs (forty-three seats). A government majority in the Upper House guarantees that the Seanad rarely overturns its agenda, although on rare occasions a Bill has been amended or even abandoned due to Seanad opposition.[88] Such cases usually require significant media publicity.

As with Dáil Éireann, procedures in the Seanad are governed by Article 15.10 of the Constitution, statute law as appropriate, standing orders, sessional orders, rulings by the Chair[89] and precedence. The Cathaoirleach does not normally enter the chamber until a quorum of twelve deputies is present. The day then opens with the Order of Business when the issues before the Seanad and the time to be spent debating them are presented. The Order of Business contains items of government business, Private Members' Business and any associated proposals that the House needs to make a decision on. As in the Dáil, members often use the Order of Business to raise objections or other issues of concern, but speeches are not allowed. If a member ignores the Chair's rulings, (s)he may be 'named', i.e. suspended from the House. All the issues before the House are published on the Order Paper. Motions for debate must be signed by two Senators to be permitted. Non-government motions are debated for a maximum of two hours, from 6 to 8 p.m. on Wednesdays.

Due to the constitutional provision that the government is responsible only to the Dáil, the Taoiseach and ministers do not take questions in the Seanad. However, there are methods of raising matters of concern to Senators. Under Seanad Standing Order 28, Senators may raise a matter related to administration of a minister's department on the adjournment of the day's proceedings. Three such matters may be raised on a sitting day, but notice must be given by the previous day at the latest. A minister, or more frequently a minister of state, may address these concerns. Seanad Standing Order 30 allows Senators to raise matters of concern on a Thursday. They may be raised via a two-minute statement. The Cathaoirleach may select up to six matters, but they must be submitted no later than 10 a.m. on Thursday.

---

[88] A celebrated example of this was independent Senator Shane Ross's amendment to the 2001 Electoral Amendment Bill. The Bill had proposed to ban opinion polls the week before an election or referendum, but Ross spotted that the legislation allowed for them to be produced on the day of the poll itself, causing the government withdraw the Bill.

[89] In the Seanad, the chair is known as the Cathaoirleach.

Also, Seanad Standing Order 29 allows the Seanad to debate a 'specific and important matter of public interest which has arisen suddenly'. Any member may seek to raise a matter in this way by informing the Cathaoirleach in writing not later than 2.30 on a day when the Seanad meets before noon and not later than 4.30 when it meets at noon or after. One hour after time of notice, the Chair calls on the Senator to request the debate and, after he or she reads the notice, a decision is given on whether or not the debate can take place. If allowed, the debate will last for a maximum of one and a half hours.

As noted above, the Seanad's principal role is in processing legislation, and this takes up the vast bulk of its time. When the legislation comes before the House, the sponsoring minister or minister of state will attend the debate to defend the proposed new law. The stages are similar to those in Dáil Éireann (see above), and include a committee stage. Due to the small number of Senators, the committee stage is taken in the House as a whole. Divisions are taken when a question is put and the response given to the Cathaoirleach challenged. Eight minutes is given between the vote being called and the vote being taken. If a division follows a previous one, then only four minutes is given. If the Bill originates in the Dáil, the first stage in the Seanad is waived. If the Seanad passes it without amendment, it goes to the President to be signed into law. If the Seanad amends it, it goes back to the Dáil for consideration; the Dáil can overrule any Seanad amendments and send it to the President. If a Bill begins in the Seanad, when it goes to the Dáil for consideration it is treated as if it has begun in the Dáil, thus allowing the Lower House to control its content.

As with the Dáil, the Seanad has various standing committees. These include the Committee of Selection (which nominates Senators to sit on committees) and the Committee on Procedure and Privileges. There are also select and special committees, consisting of Senators only. In addition, Senators sit on joint committees, which consist of members of both Houses, as will be explained below.

Parliamentary committees

Although the above devices and procedures are complex and seem to provide plenty of opportunity for a government to be 'caught out', in the face of government obduracy the impotence of the House is indisputable. Partisan party politics predetermines the operation of the Dáil, including the formal mechanisms of executive oversight.

Standing orders also favour the government, and the neutrality of the Ceann Comhairle tends towards the preservation of the status quo rather than enforcing the Dáil's right to act as a check on government. Therefore, the development of select committees (composed of members of one House only) becomes all the more significant.

Lane and Ersson see a dichotomy in European legislatures between those that operate a form of 'cabinet parliamentarism' and those that exhibit 'committee parliamentarism'.[90] The former is applicable to Westminster-style parliaments such as Ireland, where government is stronger than parliament and where any committees that do exist are microcosms of the larger legislature. In such systems, committee members often have no particular expertise in the policy area of the committee they sit on. Decision-making occurs in a more centralised arena, namely the cabinet, and the legislature and committees perform largely consultative roles. Committee parliamentarism applies to parliamentary systems where committees that allow substantial opposition input can significantly alter government proposals. These committees will be expected to develop a level of expertise and so increase the knowledge of expected policy outcomes.

Apart from the Public Accounts Committee (see below), the experience of Dáil Éireann with committees prior to the early 1990s was scanty. In fact the only committees that were re-established automatically after elections (permanent or 'standing' committees) were those concerned with 'housekeeping' and procedural matters, such as the Dáil Committee on Members' Services or the Committee on Procedure and Privileges. In 1972, in anticipation of Ireland's accession to the EEC, a committee consisting of members from both Houses (joint committee) was established to examine and report on European legislative proposals. This committee was hampered by a lack of technical expertise (and in some cases interest) among members, as well as poor financing and resourcing.[91] Also, as Manning pointed out, the frequent difficulty in getting a quorum revealed an ambivalence among TDs towards such a development.[92]

---

[90] Lane, J. E. and Ersson, S. (1998) *Politics and Society in Western Europe*. London: Sage, p. 209.

[91] Keatinge, P. and Laffan, B. (1999) 'Ireland: a Small Open Polity' in J. Coakley and M. Gallagher (eds) *Politics in the Republic of Ireland*. London: Routledge/ PSAI, p. 340.

[92] Manning, M. (1975) 'Making Dail and Seanad more democratic and effective', *Irish Press*, 6 March, 9.

As discussed in Chapter 3, attempts to introduce committees by the Fine Gael/Labour coalition of 1973–77 failed as the efforts of the government to set them up 'were frustrated by the unwillingness of deputies to give the necessary time to an activity which received no public notice'.[93] However, cross-party consensus resulted in the establishment of the Joint Committee on Commercial State Sponsored Bodies in 1976. These bodies received substantial state funding but their accountability to parliament was weak if not non-existent in some cases. Parliamentarians, journalists and academics had advocated the establishment of a parliamentary committee to bridge this accountability gap for some time previously.[94] Barry Desmond, former Labour Party TD and a member of the first such Committee on State Sponsored Bodies, noted that the committee was 'regarded as a prize committee and a lot of very senior deputies fought to get onto it'. He also noted how the localised nature of Irish politics resulted in traditionally low levels of oversight of the semi-state sector by public representatives, recalling that:

> we travelled around the country in a very interesting way because lots of deputies had never seen a sugar factory and lots of deputies had never seen how Aer Lingus [the national air carrier] worked … because a great many deputies were from local constituencies and they were either schoolteachers or publicans or farmers or business people but they never travelled around the country.[95]

Following pre-election promises, the Fine Gael/Labour coalition of 1982–87 introduced an extensive increase in the number of Oireachtas committees in 1983, from seven at the dissolution of the previous government in the autumn of 1982 to sixteen. The impetus for establishing this committee system was related to the growing volume of legislation emanating from the institutions of the European Union, and the need to process it by others means than the plenary. Furthermore, the strong committee system of the European Parliament provided a useful template for the Irish parliament in its search for a new mode of organisation.

The terms of reference of the new committees were designed to avoid party politics as they prohibited the committees from issuing recommendations on a subject, allowing instead only findings. This was an attempt to avoid committees becoming weakened by

---

[93] O'Halpin, E. (1987) 'Oireachtas Committees: Experience and Prospects', *Seirbhís Phoiblí* Vol. 7(2), 6.

[94] Arkins, A. (1988) 'The Committees of the 24th Oireachtas', *Irish Political Studies* Vol. 3, 93.

[95] Desmond, B. (2000) *Finally and in Conclusion.* Dublin: New Island.

partisan politics. Zimmerman notes that this was successful, and the absence of party divisions in the committees was facilitated in part by the selection of non-contentious issues by the chairs.[96] However, as detailed above, the committees were not re-established in 1987.

Since 1993, committees have become a permanent feature of the House and have been credited with several important developments. Perhaps most significantly, they facilitate greater backbench participation in the legislative process and in parliamentary life generally, the lack of which was historically criticised constantly by the media and parliamentarians themselves. For governments, anxious to deliver on promised legislation, they allow for better 'economy of operation'[97] – in other words, the parallel production of laws that otherwise would cause a backlog in the House.

The committees also allow members to build up expertise in certain areas that they can bring to bear on future legislation. Committee chairs, vice-chairs and convenors are entitled to remuneration, and are frequently used as a reward for party loyalty or as a bargaining chip during coalition arrangements.[98] Indeed, the rationale behind the allocation of committee chairs and vice-chairs can be interpreted very negatively on this basis. Former Fine Gael TD Alan Shatter has argued that they basically 'provide sinecures for disgruntled members of government parties who have not been elevated to ministerial status'.[99] It has been claimed that minor committees are occasionally established purely to provide recognition for certain senior party members. Attention was drawn to the former Joint Committee on the Strategic Management Initiative (SMI) as an example of this, which disappeared after the 2002 election even though the SMI is still developing within the public administration. Governments can also establish special committees to consider legislation or

---

[96] Zimmerman, J. F. (1988) 'An Oireachtas Innovation: Backbench Committees', *Administration* Vol. 36(3), 271.

[97] Strøm, K. (1998) 'Parliamentary Committees in European Democracies' in L. D. Longley and R. H. Davidson (eds) *The New Roles of Parliamentary Committees*. London: Frank Cass, p. 24.

[98] Interestingly, only two TDs in the current (29th) Dáil are not earning extra payment for work such as that mentioned here. One of the only parliamentary positions for which no form of remuneration is available is as a substitute for the Ceann Comhairle when the Leas-Cheann Comhairle (Deputy Speaker) is unavailable.

[99] Interview with Alan Shatter, 24 June 2003.

perform other activities such as an inquiry or recommendation of action (see below).

It is considered that the use of parliamentary committees in Western European legislatures reduces the highly centralised and partisan mode of decision-making associated with many legislatures. Indeed, as Shaw notes, there is general consensus among students of legislatures that the impact of a legislature (on the executive) depends crucially on its committee arrangements.[100] Norton also regards the degree to which committees are used by parliament as a useful indicator of how specialised a parliament is.[101] Committees are considered successful in this regard if they facilitate increased opposition involvement in legislative work and encourage non-party politics.[102] Also, a developed committee system will be able to oversee the executive more effectively than the House as a collective. However, the select committees in Ireland (and the ad hoc 'standing committees' of Westminster) do not necessarily conform to this format. In fact, as with the Dáil, the Irish committee system has a built-in system of veto players that prevents committee work from upsetting the executive agenda.

In the first instance, the government will always maintain a majority of seats in the committees. Furthermore, the main political parties in the Oireachtas appoint 'convenors' as a form of party whip in order to ensure that discipline is maintained. The committee chairs (with few exceptions, members of the governing party or parties) have extensive agenda control or 'gatekeeping' powers that prevent non-government legislation from proceeding. Indeed, the Director of Committees in the Oireachtas noted that 'it's very rare that a member would challenge a chair in relation to procedures or an administrative issue.'[103] In the majoritarian parliamentary system of the Oireachtas, the timetables of the committees are largely

[100] Shaw, M. (1998) 'Parliamentary Committees: a Global Perspective' in L. D. Longley and R. H. Davidson (eds) *The New Roles of Parliamentary Committees*. London: Frank Cass, p. 229.

[101] Norton, P. (1998) 'Introduction: the Institution of Parliaments' in P. Norton (ed.) *Parliaments and Governments in Western Europe*. London: Frank Cass, p. 9.

[102] Longley, L. D. and Ágh, A. (1997) 'On the Changing Nature of Parliamentary Committees' in L. D. Longley and A. Ágh (eds) *The Changing Roles of Parliamentary Committees*. Lawrence University, Appleton, WI, Research Committee of Legislative Specialists. Working Papers II, 3–13; Longley, L. D. and Davidson, R. H. (eds) (1998) *The New Roles of Parliamentary Committees*. London: Frank Cass.

[103] Interview with Art O'Leary, 17 July 2003.

Table 4.8: Committee powers 1998–2005

Power	Procedure and Privileges	Public Accounts	Members' Interests (Dáil)	Members' Interests (Seanad)	House Services	Consolidation Bills	Departmentally aligned joint committees
Standing sub-committees	Yes	No	No	No	Yes	No	No
Appoint sub-committees	Yes	No	No	No	Yes	No	No
Engage consultants	Yes	Yes	Yes	Yes	Yes	No	Yes
Travel	Yes	Yes	No	No	Yes	No	Yes
Publish reports	Yes	Yes	No	No	No	Yes	Yes
Send for persons, papers, records	No	Yes	No	No	No	Yes	No
Take oral/written submissions	No	Yes	No	No	No	Yes	Yes
Invite/accept submissions	No	No	No	No	No	No	Yes
Draft legislation	No	No	No	No	No	No	Yes
Meet ministers re policy/ legislation	No	No	No	No	No	No	Yes
Meet office holders in state bodies	No	No	No	No	No	No	Yes

Source: Houses of the Oireachtas website

controlled by the government through the office of the chief whip (see below). This correlates with Laver and Shepsle's argument that control of the timetable is a way to determine what will be decided.[104]

As mentioned above, the committees have become an important part of the legislative process, but they also perform other functions. Table 4.8 shows that since 1998 the joint committees in particular have had the potential to use substantial powers, but these are always subject to Dáil (and therefore government) permission. If granted these powers, such as the ability to hire consultants or call a minister to appear before them, these committees should, in theory, contribute to parliamentary oversight of government work. Furthermore, the ability to produce legislation, normally the preserve of government, is an important potential power at the disposal of joint committees. However, the reality is that many of these committees rarely meet, and those that do tend not to pursue detailed investigations of the department they are mirroring.

Often the attraction of media attention rather than the obligation of democratic accountability will be a motivating factor in committee work. In terms of better scrutiny of the executive and its bureaucracy, the joint committee experiment to date leaves much to be desired. If the committees used all their powers to look at such issues as secondary legislation, departmental strategy statements or the work of state agencies under the aegis of various departments, they could contribute significantly to a culture of parliamentary accountability. However, many TDs (and Senators) protest that they do not have the time to engage in detailed study of the administration, and question the electoral return for such work.

Committee chairpersons tend to pursue matters that are of interest to the committee membership, and an examination of recent committee reports shows that scrutiny of departmental financial estimates is practically non-existent. Also, there is no statutory provision for committee reports to be debated by the House, which makes it less likely for TDs to pursue committee rather than constituency work. There are occasional upsets in the committees, however. For example, in October 2004 the government-dominated European Affairs Committee passed a motion condemning Israeli treatment of Palestinians despite pleas from the Department of Foreign Affairs not to do so.

---

[104]   Laver, M. and Shepsle, K. A. (eds) (1994) *Cabinet Ministers and Parliamentary Government.* Cambridge: Cambridge University Press.

By and large, the committees do not escape the party politics of the Dáil or the watchful eye of the whips. In the Oireachtas, the committees have not superseded the parties, which continue to be the unit of parliamentary organisation and dominate parliamentary business. The eleven-member Committee of Selection[105] was in effect a rubber stamp in terms of choosing personnel for committees. As former Taoiseach John Bruton points out, it is the party leaderships (in consultation with the chief whip) that effectively allocate people to committees, as part of good 'party management'.[106] Of course, a TD who expresses an interest in a particular committee will be likely to achieve a place on that committee, but only with the blessing of the party leadership. Appointments are based on several factors, the most common being rewards for loyalty, policy expertise and also a form of consolation prize for TDs who missed out on a place in government or as a minister of state. There are now over seventy paid positions in the committee system. As of October 2002, committee chairpersons receive €15,413.35 and vice-chairpersons €7,882.53 annually. Sub-committee chairpersons receive €4,912.62 per annum. Parties also have convenors in each committee, who are entitled to a payment of €4,912.62 per annum. In addition, a budget is available to the committees for the appointment of rapporteurs.

Committees and the EU

Ireland's continued process of integration into the European Union has presented challenges and opportunities for the committee system. Following the defeat of a referendum to permit the government to ratify the Nice Treaty in 2001,[107] new measures were introduced to assuage public concerns over issues of European governance.[108] Apart from establishing a 'Forum on Europe' to act as a medium for the public to air their concerns, the government decided to establish within the Joint Committee on European Affairs a 'Sub-Committee

---

[105] This committee was abolished and a motion of the Dáil now decides committee membership. In reality this places it further under the control of the party whips.

[106] Interview with John Bruton, 12 February 2002.

[107] A second referendum on the matter in 2002 saw a reversal of this result, and the Treaty was subsequently ratified.

[108] One of the findings of the Forum of Europe was that two issues dominated public concerns over the Nice Treaty – the issue of Ireland's neutrality in respect of the EU Common Foreign and Security Policy, and the ability of the Oireachtas to scrutinise EU legislation.

on European Scrutiny'.[109] This sub-committee is unique in that it has been created by statute rather than by standing orders.[110] As the first report by the sub-committee notes, its role was to 'help address the growing awareness that a democratic deficit exists in relation to European Union issues' and that:

> The very limited role, to date, for the Oireachtas in the examination of European Union matters has arguably been one of the reasons for the development of an information gap in Ireland in relation to the European Union.[111]

The sub-committee's role is to present the Oireachtas with objective information on EU affairs and forthcoming legislation, and to sift through such legislation before forwarding it to the respective joint committees as appropriate. It represents a new departure for the national parliament in overcoming the traditionally centralised decision-making process in relation to EU affairs.[112] However, the sub-committee's role is not as comprehensive as it might be. For example, by the time it receives documents, it is very late in the policy process and its ability to alter a policy is limited. Also, the sub-committee is not usually informed of what happens to information once it has passed it on to the relevant sectoral committee.

The fact that the sub-committee's establishment was an initiative of the government rather than the Oireachtas demonstrates again that the institutional arrangement of the Irish legislature is subject to the government's prerogative. Also, the strong role given to the sub-committee contrasts with the lack of similar powers of scrutiny given to other committees and sub-committees. However, as with most national parliaments in EU member states, the *sui generis* nature of EU legislation has required innovative methods of oversight, often different from those used for domestic legislation.[113]

---

[109] This was by virtue of the European Union Scrutiny Act, 2002.

[110] It has been argued that as it was not technically necessary to use primary legislation to establish the sub-committee, the principal reason for the legislation was to provide publicity for the government's new-found commitment to parliamentary scrutiny of EU affairs.

[111] Committee on Foreign Affairs Sub-Committee on European Scrutiny (2002) *First Report*. Dublin: Stationery Office.

[112] Laffan, B. and O'Mahony, J. (2003) *Managing Europe from Home: the Europeanisation of the Irish Core Executive*. Dublin: Dublin European Institute.

[113] For more on this, see Maurer, A. and Wessels, W. (eds) (2001) *National Parliaments on Their Ways to Europe: Losers or Latecomers?* Baden-Baden, Germany: Nomos.

A new document tracking system for EU matters relevant to Ireland and from central government departments on EU matters has been introduced in order to allow committees to monitor European affairs more closely. The Director of Committees noted that systematic scrutiny of EU legislation is increasingly becoming a feature of the committee system as members engage more with it, and that it is now the norm that the Minister and Minister of State for Foreign Affairs appear before the Joint Committee on European Affairs in advance of meetings of the Council of Ministers.[114]

Ministers are asked to 'have regard to' the position of the relevant parliamentary committee when adopting a position in the Council of Ministers. While this provides at least a notional role for the committees in EU affairs, they cannot bind a minister to policy positions in the manner that the Danish Folketing can. However, ministers are unlikely to adopt a position in Brussels that is contrary to that of their parliamentary party, whatever about the committees. It is still more common for officials rather than ministers to come before the committees to explain Ireland's position on EU matters.

Amending legislation at committee stage

At the committee stage of a legislative Bill, the Senators on a joint committee leave, and the committee becomes a select committee for the purpose of debating the Bill. As Table 4.9 shows, the ability of committees in Ireland to alter government legislation substantially is quite restricted compared to that of other legislatures. While the more consensual parliaments such as those in Switzerland and Sweden give committees wide-ranging powers to rewrite legislation, the majoritarian parliaments such as in Ireland, France and the UK do not. It may be surprising that Denmark and the Netherlands are also included in this group – it must be remembered that parliaments in these states are given strong powers to decide the plenary agenda and control the early stages of the passage of legislation (Table 2.3).

The dominance of the government in law-making is such that even in a non-partisan committee environment, the opposition will rarely have the opportunity to derail its agenda. Indeed, when asked how often a committee had convinced a minister to change his mind on a significant matter, the Director of Committees noted that he could 'count it on one hand'.[115] Nonetheless, he

---

[114] Interview with Art O'Leary, 17 July 2003.
[115] Ibid.

Table 4.9: Authority of committees to rewrite government Bills

I	II	III	IV
Denmark	Greece	Austria	Belgium
France		Luxembourg	Finland
Ireland		Portugal	Germany
Netherlands			Iceland
United Kingdom			Italy
			Norway
			Spain
			Sweden
			Switzerland

◄━━━━━━━━━━━━━━━━━━━━━━━━━━━━━━━━━━━━━►

more government control   **less government control**

(I) House considers original government Bill with amendments added; (II) if redrafted text is not accepted by the relevant minister, chamber considers the original Bill; (III) committees may present substitute texts that are considered against the original text; (IV) committees are free to rewrite government text.

Source: Döring (1995),'Time as a Scarce Resource: Government Control of the Agenda' in H. Döring (ed.) *Parliaments and Majority Rule in Western Europe.* New York: St Martin's Press, p. 236.

said that it was increasingly common for ministers to appear before committees, and that even the Taoiseach had recently presented his departmental estimates to the Committee on Finance and Public Service.[116] This can be regarded as a small but significant step in improving the potential oversight capacity of ordinary members.

The oldest non-housekeeping committee in Dáil Éireann is the Committee of Public Accounts – commonly referred to as the Public Accounts Committee (PAC). It is charged with overseeing the expenditure of the executive and in this it is significantly helped by the work of the Comptroller and Auditor-General, a constitutional officer of state.[117] It is essentially concerned with

---

[116] The Taoiseach also appeared before the Joint Committee on European Affairs in April 2004 to answer questions concerning the accession of new member states to the EU.

[117] Article 33 of Bunreacht na hÉireann.

'the parliamentary scrutiny and oversight of the Public Financial Procedures in Ireland'[118] and therefore its enquiries are technically financial rather than political. As with its counterpart in Westminster, it is by tradition chaired by a member of the opposition and none of its members may be a member of the government or a minister of state. It is a select committee in that no Senators are members. The PAC has built up a tradition of non-partisan work and for this reason, as the next chapter will detail, it has been called upon twice in the recent history of the state to examine issues of public and political concern. However, most of the committee's work is involved with government expenditure that has already occurred, and as such its ability to prevent or veto government spending plans is limited. The committee is unusual in that its role is described in standing orders (DSO 156), and because the minister must reply to its recommendations if he or she disagrees with them. In practice such disagreement is rare. Because of its special status (as well as the fact that it is one of the oldest standing committees in the Oireachtas), the PAC is pre-eminent among the committees and its work contributes significantly to financial and administrative probity.

The office of the chief whip

While all the above procedures and structures govern the daily modus operandi of Dáil Éireann, the institution that exists at the interface of the Dáil and government is the system of parliamentary party whips. It is through the whips (referred to in Westminster as 'the usual channels')[119] that the government party or parties negotiate with the opposition parties. In many other legislatures, formal 'business committees' are used to negotiate and decide on the organisation of parliamentary business but the whip system as used in Ireland is one of the key features of Westminster-style parliaments. In Ireland, the government whip is known as the chief whip and also holds the position of minister

---

[118] Public Accounts Committee (2001) *Sub-Committee on Certain Revenue Matters: Parliamentary Inquiry into D.I.R.T. – Final Report Vol. 1.* Dublin: PAC, p. 86.

[119] Rush, M. and Ettinghausen, C. (2002) *Opening Up the Usual Channels.* London: Hansard Society.

of state at the Department of the Taoiseach, in order to ensure close co-operation between the two offices.[120]

As noted above, the initiative for organising the work of parliament lies exclusively with the government. More than in Westminster, the government's ability to secure passage of its legislation and to arrange the parliamentary timetable is very strong in the Dáil. The opposition whips usually concede the government's right to pursue its agenda, and will try to agree a programme rather than refuse to co-operate and risk no concessions from government on matters of concern to them. However, there is an element of gamesmanship to such meetings, as the chief whip will not want the opposition parties to make life difficult for government by breaking informal practices such as pairing agreements (see below) and being generally obstructive. These weekly Wednesday meetings of the party whips are private and unrecorded, and, as Humphreys points out, have evolved informally.[121] Proposals have been made to register these meetings on standing orders as business meetings, but this had not been formalised at the time of writing. While no minutes would be taken, the purpose would be to have a record that such meetings took place.

One of the principal functions of the whip's office in each party is to draw the attention of members to forthcoming debates by circulating notes – confusingly, also known as whips – that indicate the importance of the occasion by variations in the degree of underlining. A debate underlined once is one in which no division (vote) is expected; one underlined twice is one in which there will be a division (TDs are expected to attend unless they have arranged a 'pair' with a member of another party); a three-line whip states that a division is of particular importance and all members must attend.

The office of the chief whip has several other tasks to perform, including:

- arranging parliamentary business on behalf of the government
- meeting informally with opposition frontbenchers to resolve difficulties over legislation and parliamentary timetabling

---

[120] The chief whip was known as the Parliamentary Secretary to the President of the Executive Council from 1922 to 1938, and as Parliamentary Secretary to the Taoiseach from 1938 to 1978. The changes in the title were brought about by amendments to the 1924 Ministers and Secretaries Act, which, until the Public Service Management Act, 1997, was the legal origin for all ministerial functions.

[121] Humphreys, R. F. (1991) 'Legislative Obstruction: How to Do It', *Administration* Vol. 39(1), 59.

- organising 'pairing' arrangements that allow a member of the governing party or parties to be absent from a vote if a member of the opposition is likewise absent
- organising committee memberships
- providing a conduit between government and the party back benches over difficulties that may arise.

To facilitate the chief whip's work, as well as underlining the importance of the position, his or her office is situated in government buildings beside that of the Taoiseach. Also, the chief whip attends the weekly cabinet meetings, and the chief whip's office produces weekly reports on the progress of legislation for the Taoiseach's attention. The office of the chief whip has increased in importance as the range of parliamentary (and executive) activity has grown. From an institutionalist perspective the position may be considered as chief agenda setter, largely controlling what will be decided on in parliament. The opposition party whips have no power to make the chief whip do their bidding, and are reliant on his or her goodwill to allow them to pursue their agenda.

It has been argued that the power of the whips to control the day-to-day business of parliament undermines the ability of the parliament to function as an oversight body. As Zimmerman points out, the backbencher's role is to vote according to the party whip's bidding.[122] The committee system established in 1983 was intended to give these backbenchers an opportunity to participate in policy-making, but the legislative committees are very much the 'creatures of the whips' as, via the convenors mentioned above, the whips exert their influence on the progress of legislation.[123] The abolition of the Committee of Selection in 1997 enhanced the power of the whips to control committees. As noted above, following a meeting of the whips, a Dáil motion now decides committee membership based on expediency rather than expertise or suitability.

The chief whip is also involved in less public but nonetheless important roles in Leinster House. He or she chairs a body known as the Legislation Committee. Officials from the Office of Parliamentary Counsel to the Government, the Bills Office in the Oireachtas and the Department of the Taoiseach, as well as legal advisers from the Attorney-General's office and the Leader of the Seanad, are involved in the work of this committee. Its principal function is to

---

[122] Zimmerman, J. F. (1988) 'An Oireachtas Innovation: Backbench Committees', *Administration* Vol. 36(3), 265.

[123] Interview with John Bruton, 12 February 2002.

co-ordinate and monitor progress in the drafting of legislation approved by government. The committee also prioritises work, monitors progress and considers resource issues.[124] Each week, the chief whip's office produces reports on the progress of legislation for the Taoiseach. The Taoiseach depends on the chief whip to detect discontent in his own party over policy or regional issues. These can then be addressed at the parliamentary party meetings, which prevents any internal party dissension from becoming public.

While those who work in the Oireachtas accept the necessity for whips for the effective running of the business of the Dáil, the whips are frequently criticised for their negative impact on parliamentary independence. John Bruton referred to the effect of whips on the Dáil as 'stultifying'.[125] The large parties in the Oireachtas, and in particular Fianna Fáil, support strict whipping of their members and this discourages the voicing of dissent among government backbenchers. As Robinson argued, in the Oireachtas 'there are numerous examples of disciplining which are enough to curtail any members who might wish to vote by conscience rather than by party line'.[126] It is clear, therefore, that the chief whip plays a pivotal role in ensuring that it is the executive that controls the Dáil, and not the other way round.

Committee on Procedure and Privileges

The chief whip plays a central role in deciding the distribution of personnel among, and the composition of, many parliamentary institutions. Perhaps most significantly, the chief whip will always be a member of the Committee on Procedure and Privileges (CPP), which is traditionally chaired by the Ceann Comhairle and provided for under DSO 97. This committee is centrally involved in the consideration of the rules and standing orders of the House, and hence in the infrastructure through which the government must operate in order to fulfil its objectives. As the primary role of the chief whip is to ensure that parliamentary procedure and business operate as smoothly as possible, any attempt at reform in parliamentary procedure would affect the chief whip's office. The Fianna Fáil/Progressive Democrats government of 1997–2002 established two

---

Murray, F. (1997) 'The Irish Political and Policy-making System and the Current Programme of Change', *Administration* Vol. 45(4), 43.
125 Interview with John Bruton, 12 February 2002.
126 Robinson, M. T. W. (1974) 'The Role of the Irish Parliament', *Administration* Vol. 22(1), 9.

sub-committees of the CPP to examine the crucial issues of compel-lability (i.e. whether or not a joint committee could compel a witness to appear) and Dáil reform. Significantly, the chief whip chairs both of these sub-committees and ensures that no changes occur that would jeopardise the government's dominant position.

Oireachtas staffing

As a final note on how Dáil Éireann works, attention must be drawn to the permanent staff that facilitate the work of parliamentarians. As Dooney and O'Toole point out, there is an important difference between civil servants under the direction of government ministers and under the direction of the chairpersons of the Dáil and Seanad.[127] Those in the latter category may be more correctly defined as *public* servants, and are appointed under the Staff of the Houses of the Oireachtas Act, 1959. The loyalties of such staff should technically be with the state rather than government. However, while a distinction is frequently made between government and parliament, there is a blurring of the lines in terms of distinguishing between public and civil servants in the Oireachtas, and this has consequences for parliamentary accountability.

Many of the Oireachtas public servants begin their careers in government departments and, for most, promotional opportunities lie in those departments rather than in the small Oireachtas work-force. It has been suggested that because of this, the Oireachtas staff are less likely to 'take on' departments. The problem is particularly acute in the committee system, which does not have an internal career structure. Departments will typically send their representatives to ensure that decisions taken or views aired in committees are mon-itored, and do not cause difficulties for departmental objectives. The administrative staff of the committees will not usually challenge members of the departmental civil service. This, it is argued, contrib-utes to 'the downgrading of the significance and influence of parlia-ment because its own servants are not committed to it'. Alan Shatter has argued that such 'cross-fertilisation' resulted in a clear 'conflict of interest' among staff in Leinster House.[128]

We can conclude, therefore, that there is merit in Döring's assertion that parliamentary procedures that restrict the rights of the individual member and provide special prerogatives to government and the party

---

[127] Dooney, S. and O'Toole, J. (1998) *Irish Government Today*. Dublin: Gill & Macmillan.
[128] Interview with Alan Shatter, 24 June 2003.

leaderships are 'skilful devices to exploit the advantages of majority rule'.[129] O'Halpin argues that this dynamic may be in the process of change due to recent institutional realignments such as the creation of the committee system and the introduction of outside actors such as the Ombudsman.[130] However, as this chapter has shown, the evidence indicates that the fundamental dynamic of 'strong government, weak parliament' is sustained through a variety of subtle yet significant methods. In particular, the Dáil standing orders allow the incumbent government a range of vetos over opposition initiatives and lines of enquiry that are crucial to effective parliamentary accountability.

O'Halloran makes the point that there is excessive emphasis on the issue of internal procedures and rules in literature concerning the issue of Dáil reform, and that this is to the detriment of the more fundamental issue of Dáil Éireann's role in contemporary Irish life.[131] However, as the institutionalist school of thought argues, micro-level details can have macro-level implications, and this chapter reveals how Dáil procedures can influence enormously the choices made across the spectrum of public policy. In order for the Lower House to develop itself in the context of significant social and economic realignment, it must have the capacity to allow parliamentarians of all sides to play a more fulfilling role in the formation and oversight of such policy.

At the first sitting of the Dáil in 2003, the new Labour Party leader, Pat Rabbitte, reflected this when he criticised the government's unenthusiastic approach to parliamentary reform, claiming that:

> Unfortunately, the Government seems intent on continuing as it started. Piecemeal, minimal reforms of Dáil procedure are gradually introduced depending on whether they are judged to be to the advantage of the Government. The settled policy is to sanitise Dáil procedures to the extent that all spontaneity is stifled and Government backbenchers do not even have to show up for the Order of Business nowadays. Public confidence in Dáil Éireann will continue to diminish if it is not seen as a functioning, relevant forum where the Government makes itself amenable and the procedures are such that it can be held to account by the Opposition.[132]

---

[129] Döring, H. (1995) 'Institutions and Policies: Why We Need Cross-National Analysis' in H. Döring (ed.) *Parliaments and Majority Rule in Western Europe.* New York: St Martin's Press, p. 31.

[130] O'Halpin, E. (1998) 'A Changing Relationship? Parliament and Government in Ireland' in P. Norton (ed.) *Parliaments and Governments in Western Europe.* London: Frank Cass, pp. 123–41.

[131] O'Halloran, A. (2005) 'Transformation in Contemporary Ireland's Society, Economy and Polity: an Era of Post-Parliamentary Governance?' *Administration* Vol. 53(1), 54–79.

[132] *Dáil Debates,* 29 January 2003, Vol. 560, Cols 73–4.

—————————— CHAPTER 5 ——————————

Alternative mechanisms of parliamentary accountability: committees of inquiry

Parliamentary committees in Ireland

The establishment, development and effectiveness of parliamentary committees in Western European parliaments has been well documented,[1] and the previous chapter has demonstrated the importance of committees in the Oireachtas for processing legislation. For parliamentary scholars, the development of a strong committee system is the hallmark of an effective legislature. As with most political institutions, however, there is wide variation in the design and functioning of parliamentary committees.[2]

While active parliamentary committees have become an integral part of many European parliaments, they sit uneasily with the classical Westminster model, particularly with the emphasis in such systems on cabinet control of the legislature.[3] Indeed, a notable feature of consensus-type parliaments is the 'embeddedness' of committees in the work of parliament, as opposed to the scepticism towards them shown by governments in Westminster-style legislatures. This correlates with Mezey's thesis that for a legislature to have strong

---

[1] Lees, J. D. and Shaw, M. (eds) (1979) *Committees in Legislatures: a Comparative Analysis.* Durham, NC: Duke University Press; Mattson, I. and Strøm, K. (1995) 'Parliamentary Committees' in H. Döring (ed.) *Parliaments and Majority Rule in Western Europe.* New York: St Martin's Press, pp. 249–307; Longley, L. D. and Ágh, A. (1997) 'On the Changing Nature of Parliamentary Committees' in L. D. Longley and A. Ágh (eds) *The Changing Roles of Parliamentary Committees.* Lawrence University, Appleton, WI, Research Committee of Legislative Specialists. Working Papers II, pp. 3–13; Longley, L. D. and Davidson, R. H. (eds) (1998) *The New Roles of Parliamentary Committees.* London: Frank Cass.

[2] Strøm, K. (1995) 'Parliamentary Government and Legislative Organisation' in H. Döring (ed.) *Parliaments and Majority Rule in Western Europe.* New York: St Martin's Press, pp. 51–82; Strøm, K. (1998) 'Parliamentary Committees in European Democracies' in L. D. Longley and R. H. Davidson (eds) *The New Roles of Parliamentary Committees.* London: Frank Cass, pp. 21–59.

[3] Longley, L. D. and Davidson, R. H. (1998) 'Parliamentary Committees: Changing Perspectives on Changing Institutions' in L. D. Longley and R. H. Davidson (eds) *The New Roles of Parliamentary Committees.* London: Frank Cass, p. 2.

policy-making power, it requires a highly developed committee system.[4] Inspired by work on the US Congress, rational choice institutional theory identifies four functions for which committees are used by legislatures, as follows.[5]

1 *Economy of operation.* Committees working in parallel can process parliamentary work more efficiently than the chamber sitting in plenary.
2 *Partisan co-ordination.* Committees provide party leaders with structures to control their parliamentarians. Thus parties can have an influence on the work of committees.
3 *Gains from trade.* Different committees will influence legislation in different ways and will therefore expect other committees to defer to their decisions. Also, committees help overcome collective action problems.
4 *Information acquisition.* Through specialisation, committee members will gain expertise about the consequences of a Bill and therefore the legislature can trust the committee to perform better than the chamber as a whole.

It is worth considering here how each of these generic functions applies to the contemporary Irish committee system. Firstly, in terms of economy of operation, we note that all the joint committees in the Oireachtas during the 29th Dáil can sit as select committees for the third stage of government Bills. In fact the biggest constraint to committee work is often the availability of only four committee rooms in Leinster House at any one time.[6] In processing legislation, committees free up parliamentary time for the chamber to discuss other issues. Indeed, the original purpose of committees in Dáil Éireann was to create greater opportunity for processing work. Former Fine Gael Taoiseach Garret FitzGerald noted in an interview with this author that one of his prime motivations for establishing a committee

---

[4] Mezey, M. (1979) *Comparative Legislatures.* Durham, NC: Duke University Press, p. 64.
[5] Cox, G. W. and McCubbins, M. D. (1993) *Legislative Leviathan.* Berkeley: University of California Press; Mattson, I. and Strøm, K. (1995) 'Parliamentary Committees' in H. Döring (ed.) *Parliaments and Majority Rule in Western Europe.* New York: St Martin's Press, pp. 251–4; Longley, L. D. and Davidson, R. H. (eds) (1998) *The New Roles of Parliamentary Committees.* London: Frank Cass, pp. 25–7; Strøm, K. (1998) 'Parliamentary Committees in European Democracies' in L. D. Longley and R. H. Davidson (eds) *The New Roles of Parliamentary Committees.* London: Frank Cass, p. 24.
[6] An extension to Leinster House, where the Oireachtas sits, was completed in 2000. It provides extra office space for members and administrators, and the lower floor of the complex is given over to committee chambers.

system in 1983 was 'because things were not happening as there was not enough time in the Dáil'.[7]

In terms of partisan co-ordination, the Oireachtas committees have also been successful. The joint committees have provided the Fianna Fáil/Progressive Democrat government with structures to allow backbenchers (and Senators) to move beyond their role of 'lobby fodder' and to become involved in more fulfilling legislative work. This in turn provides a legitimacy function as parliamentarians increasingly view their role as that of national legislators rather than simply ambassadors for their constituency. However, as shown in the previous chapter, party discipline in committees is maintained through the appointment of convenors.

The third and fourth functions identified above – gains from trade and information acquisition – are not easily identifiable in the Irish parliamentary system. While little research has been conducted in this field, interviews suggest that committee chairs and vice-chairs in particular are not awarded on the basis of expertise.[8] While TDs with a particular interest in a subject may be successful in attaining a seat in a relevant committee, the allocation to each committee is at the discretion of the Taoiseach and the chief whip. In many cases, TDs are appointed simply to maintain a government majority, and some committees in fact rarely meet.

Calls for better use of the committee system have appeared from various quarters. In 1996, the body charged with overseeing the implementation of the SMI, the Co-ordinating Group of Secretaries-General, proposed that:

> The process of Oireachtas reform, in particular of the Committee System, be continued in support of the change to greater openness and transparency in public administration. In this regard also, the need for greater clarity in relation to the role and remit of individual committees is essential.[9]

A consultancy report prepared for the Houses of the Oireachtas the following year found that the committees were weakly embedded in the parliamentary infrastructure, and that parliamentarians found 'a lack of clarity about the overall purpose of the committee system'.[10]

---

[7] Interview with Garret FitzGerald, 8 August 2003.
[8] Interview with John Bruton, 12 February 2002; interview with Alan Shatter, 24 June 2003.
[9] Co-ordinating Group of Secretaries (1996) *Delivering Better Government*. Dublin: Department of the Taoiseach, p. 17.
[10] Gallagher, M., Laver, M. and Marsh, M. (1997) *The Oireachtas Committee System*. The Policy Institute, Trinity College Dublin, p. 5.

It also recommended that committees should not contain more than eleven members, of whom four would be Senators. However, the Fianna Fáil/Progressive Democrat government that assumed power in 1997 with a minority coalition largely ignored the report.

Many of the committees established by the government were very large, as the government had to appoint extra members in order to ensure they had a majority on each. This led to many TDs being members of two or three committees at any one time – a workload many did not appreciate. Furthermore, little attempt was made to co-ordinate their activities. The success of the outgoing government in the 2002 election saw it return to power without the need for independent members. Subsequently, the number of seats on select committees was capped at eleven rather than fourteen, as had been the case previously, with at least six government members on each.

Table 5.1: Committee procedures in nine European parliaments

Country	Selection of chair	Allocation of chair	Minority reports
Austria	Committee	Mainly majority party	Right exists
Sweden	Committee	Proportional	Right exists
Denmark	Committee	Proportional	Right does not exist
Finland	Committee	Proportional	Right exists
France	Committee	Mainly majority party	Right does not exist
Germany	Committee	Proportional	Right exists
Greece	Committee	Majority party only	Right exists
Ireland	Decided by chief whip and Taoiseach followed by motion of Dáil Éireann	Government parties only*	Right does not exist
UK (standing committees)	House/Speaker	Mainly majority party	Right does not exist

* With the exception of the Public Accounts Committee.
Source: Strøm (1998), pp. 43–4[11]

---

[11]   The information for both Ireland and the UK in Strøm's dataset is inaccurate and/or outdated; I have altered it accordingly. The data for the other countries may therefore also be oversimplified and subject to correction.

Nonetheless, it would be reasonable to assume that as members serve on successive committees, their ability to gain superior knowledge on certain issues will play a role in the development of policies. Interviews suggest that chairs who are reappointed have familiarity with the issues under the committee's remit, and this helps the committee to be more productive. It also contributes to better relationships and communications between parliament and the bureaucracy.

Table 5.1 shows that while the appointment and allocation of committee chairs in most European legislatures are based on agreement and proportionality, in Ireland the procedure is completely in the domain of the government. Similarly, the right to submit a dissenting or minority report to the chamber does not exist in Ireland, although this is a feature of other committee systems. It is clear, therefore, that the dominant position of the government in the Lower House is reflected in the committees, and this plays a significant part in preventing committees from acting as a check on the executive.

While committees may find it difficult to challenge the government directly, they perform other important functions, including considering:

1   public affairs administered by the department as it may select
2   matters of policy for which the minister is responsible
3   the strategy statement of the relevant department
4   certain annual reports and accounts of bodies under the aegis of the departments.[12]

However, comparison of the powers of the Irish joint committees with their counterparts in other legislatures shows that they are relatively underdeveloped. As Table 5.2 demonstrates, in the range of powers common to committees in many European parliaments, the Irish committee system has little ability to take independent action. For example, its powers of compellability and demanding documents are subject to control by a special sub-committee of the Dáil Committee on Procedure and Privileges, chaired by the chief whip. Indeed, Alan Shatter has argued that the lack of real power in Oireachtas committees renders them in many respects 'parliamentary eunuchs'.[13]

---

[12]   *Parliamentary Bulletin* (2002) Issue 1: January to December 2001. Dublin: Leinster House, 32–3.
[13]   Interview with Alan Shatter, 24 June 2003.

Table 5.2: Powers of committees in nine European parliaments

Country	Initiate bills	Compel witnesses	Demand documents from government
Austria	Restricted	Can compel	Can demand
Sweden	Have right	Can invite but not compel	Can demand
Denmark	No right	Can compel	Cannot demand
Finland	Right to consolidate or split only	Can invite but not compel	Can demand
France	No right	Can compel	Can demand
Germany	Right to consolidate or split only	Can invite but not compel	Cannot demand
Greece	Right to consolidate or split only	Can invite but not compel	Cannot demand
Ireland	No right	Special compellability committee grants power	Special compellability committee grants power
UK (standing committees)	No right (as their existence is coterminous with the Bill in question)	No right	Cannot demand

Source: Strøm (1998), pp. 49–51[14]

In the government-dominated and tightly disciplined Irish parliamentary system, a situation whereby committees significantly challenge executive hegemony of the chamber has not been fully realised. The principal functions of the permanent committee system in Ireland that has operated since 1993 are concerned with legislation (select committees), taking evidence from interest groups, and aspects of administrative oversight. Even these functions, however, are constrained by the reality of party political considerations.

While some joint committees may be very active, others are poorly attended and perform little work during the year. For example, during 2001 the Joint Committee on Agriculture, Food and Marine met only seventeen times and published no reports. During the same period, the Joint Committee on European Affairs met forty-four

---

[14]   As in Table 5.1, the data for Ireland and the UK has been corrected.

times and produced three reports. The scope for improving the efficiency and functions of these committees would appear to be vast, but the logic of Westminster-style power centralisation prevents devolution of significant responsibilities to them.

Furthermore, Irish parliamentarians themselves do not seem interested in adapting committees to make the Oireachtas more efficient or effective. In 1996, the Rainbow Coalition's chief whip, Fine Gael's Jim Higgins, noted that while working on the issue of parliamentary reform:

> I wrote … to the chairperson of each committee asking for suggestions from Members on reform. In doing so, I was conscious that I might be accused of interfering in their operations but I felt it was appropriate to allow Members to indicate their wishes. I invited them to convey any proposals for reform to me either directly … or otherwise. I regret to say I did not receive a single reply.[15]

Strøm identifies the power to establish sub-committees as an important structural feature of committees in Europe.[16] While sub-committees are a common feature of many European parliaments, their establishment in the Oireachtas is strictly controlled. There is no provision in standing orders to allow committees to establish sub-committees. To do so requires approval from the Dáil. The few occasions when they have been appointed were for the purpose of conducting specific tasks such as an inquiry, and are dealt with more fully below.

With such narrowly defined and strictly controlled terms of reference, any use of committees by the government to conduct activities outside their limited remit deserves further attention. Indeed, the use of committees for certain tasks that may potentially lead to adverse results for the executive increases both the standing of committees and the ability of parliament to perform its oversight function. The occasions when this has occurred in Ireland can be thematically categorised under two headings: the use of committees for the acquisition of specific information and subsequent recommendation of action on an issue; and the use of committees as mechanisms of inquiry.

---

[15] *Dáil Debates*, 9 October 1996, Vol. 469.

[16] Strøm, K. (1998) 'Parliamentary Committees in European Democracies' in L. D. Longley and R. H. Davidson (eds) *The New Roles of Parliamentary Committees*. London: Frank Cass, pp. 21–59.

Acquisition of information and
recommendation of action

The use of committees for the purposes of information acquisition or identifying efficient courses of action has become more common in the Oireachtas in recent years as committees are accepted as a permanent feature of the parliamentary infrastructure. The establishment of a Committee on the Constitution in 1966, composed of members from the three main political parties, is an earlier example of the use of committees in this manner. As noted in Chapter 3, this committee was asked to examine the 1937 Constitution and to make recommendations on aspects of it that the committee believed required amendment. The committee's work was mainly uncontentious and its report concluded that little needed to be adjusted in the Constitution.

The 1972 Informal Committee on Reform of Dáil Procedure, which was established to improve the efficiency of parliament in processing its work, is also discussed above. The committee presented thirty-five recommendations for reform of Dáil Éireann and resulted in a series of proposals being presented to parliament, most of which were subsequently adopted. The 1982–87 Fine Gael/Labour government also used committees to develop recommendations on issues that fell between the remits of government departments, for example the Joint Committees on Marriage Breakdown, Small Businesses and Women's Rights. More recently, in 1997 an all-party Oireachtas Committee on the Constitution was created for the purpose of recommending possible amendments to the Constitution. In 2001, the Joint Committee on Health and Children created a Sub-Committee on Health and Smoking to investigate the possibility of legal action by the state against tobacco companies.

Indeed, since the foundation of the state, governments have periodically taken advantage of the legal, technical or informational expertise of some parliamentarians to provide recommendations on certain matters. These matters were delegated to committees as the most efficient method of proceeding. In almost all cases, party discipline was relaxed as the government's position was not challenged by the work or outcome of the committees' deliberations.

The development of committees as mechanisms for inquiry

While the use of committees to acquire information and to identify preferable options for the government is regarded as productive and non-adversarial parliamentary work, the use of committees to investigate matters of public concern is fraught with difficulties, mainly because such investigations raise issues concerning the extent of committee independence, party discipline and the strength of the government. They also provide insights into the ability of parliament to oversee the executive.

A precedent for the use of a committee for the purpose of inquiry was established very early in the State's existence. In 1935 Fine Gael TD Patrick McGilligan accused the Minister for Industry and Commerce of making a decision concerning mining rights in Co. Wicklow that favoured two of his party colleagues. The minister established a committee, chaired by Labour Party leader William Norton, which subsequently found that the allegations were unfounded.[17]

This was a minor affair, though, compared to the first significant inquiry by a parliamentary committee in 1970. The 'Arms Crisis' inquiry is the first of five committee inquiries in Ireland to be considered here. Each has had an important bearing on the development of parliamentary accountability outside the traditional process of ministerial responsibility (Table 5.3). They are best understood as building on, and being influenced by, the previous committee investigation.

The Arms Crisis

As established in the previous chapter, the PAC is unique in that it is a permanent committee, composed only of TDs, and is not concerned with housekeeping or procedural issues. Furthermore, it is traditionally chaired by a member of the opposition and draws on the work of the Comptroller and Auditor-General in the examination of executive expenditure. Unlike for most other committees, the Dáil standing orders detail the powers and procedures of the PAC, and it has built up a reputation in Irish parliamentary politics for impartiality and objectivity in its work. This places it in an ideal position for conducting an inquiry into potentially sensitive matters.

---

[17] O'Flaherty, H. (1975) 'Tribunals and tribulations', *Irish Press*, 18 July, 9.

Table 5.3: Committee inquiries 1970–2001

Name	Period	Subject under investigation	Outcome	How issue came to light
Arms Crisis	1970–71	Misappropriation of funds	Collapse of inquiry after High Court judgment	Garda investigation
Legislation and Security	1994	Circumstances surrounding collapse of Fianna Fail/Labour coalition in 1994	Findings of fact on subject under investigation, no recommendations	Collapse of coalition government
DIRT	1999–2000	Tax evasion, failure of executive agency	Establishment of new regulatory agencies	Media investigation
Abbeylara	2001–02	Potentially 'unlawful' shooting	Collapse of inquiry after Supreme Court judgment	Public concern over fatal police shooting, parliamentary questions
Mini-CTC	2000–02	Cost overruns in state-owned body	Collapse due to Abbeylara judgment	Budgeting deficit

In December 1970, a motion of the Dáil was passed requesting that the PAC investigate whether grant-in-aid money allocated for humanitarian relief in Northern Ireland was instead used to purchase armaments for a paramilitary group (the emerging Provisional IRA). During the debate on the Fianna Fáil government's motion, the opposition highlighted the limitations of the committee's ability to investigate the matter. The Fine Gael leader, Liam Cosgrave, who was concerned that the committee could not conduct a proper inquiry, pointed out that it had no power to compel a witness to attend, and that the motion requesting the investigation did not provide power to send for persons, papers or records.[18]

---

[18] *Dáil Debates*, 1 December 1970, Vol. 250, Cols 46–52.

When the committee sat, Cosgrave's concerns were borne out, as it found that it could not subpoena witnesses or grant them privilege. In its first interim report of December 1970, the PAC reported to the Dáil that it had encountered difficulties in the application of constitutional privilege to witnesses and members of the committee, as well as to documents placed before the committee.[19] In response, the government initiated, and the Oireachtas passed, the Dáil Éireann (Privilege and Procedure) Bill, 1970. This Act provided that if any witness refused to attend or answer a question to which the committee might legally require an answer, the Chairman might certify the offence to the High Court, which was then free to punish the person as if he had been in contempt of the High Court itself.[20] This was a significant development, as it was the first time that a parliamentary committee had been granted such powers.

However, omissions in the Act relating to the issue of privilege were challenged in the courts not long after its enactment. The committee's work began to unravel when Padraic 'Jock' Haughey[21] was requested to appear before it to be questioned concerning his alleged role as an intermediary in the purchase of the arms. He attended and gave a statement but refused to answer the committee's questions, and the matter was referred to the High Court, which sentenced him to six months in prison for contempt.[22] On appeal to the Supreme Court, the sentence was quashed on the grounds that his constitutional rights to natural justice had been infringed and that the portion of the 1970 Act relating to privilege was unconstitutional.[23] In its judgment, the Court found that the Oireachtas had no constitutional right to extend parliamentary privilege to those whom it called to give evidence. Interestingly, the witness in question did not challenge the right of the PAC to hold an inquiry in the first place, something that was to become a major issue in the Abbeylara Inquiry (see below).

---

[19] Public Accounts Committee (1970) *Interim Report – December 1970*. Dublin: Stationery Office.

[20] Public Accounts Committee (2001) *Sub-Committee on Certain Revenue Matters: Parliamentary Inquiry into D.I.R.T. – Final Report Vol. 1*. Dublin: PAC, p. 101.

[21] Haughey was a brother of the then Minister for Finance and later Taoiseach, Charles Haughey.

[22] *In re Haughey* [1971] 217, 231.

[23] Ibid., pp. 217, 255, see also Law Reform Commission (2005) *Report on Public Inquiries including Tribunals of Inquiry*. Dublin, p. 71.

Strengthening the committees I: the Houses of the Oireachtas
(Privilege and Procedure) Bill, 1976

The Supreme Court ruling destroyed the capacity of the committee to pursue its investigation effectively, and a number of key witnesses were not called to present evidence.[24] Indeed, it was not until the mid-1990s that committees were used in this capacity again. Given the turmoil that the Arms Crisis had caused within Fianna Fáil, it was no surprise that the party was not anxious to provide committees with stronger powers of oversight. However, in 1976, during the Fine Gael/Labour 'National Coalition' government, the Committee on Procedure and Privileges requested the Dáil that legislation be introduced to provide absolute privilege in relation to the proceedings and deliberations of the committee. The result was the introduction by the government of the Houses of the Oireachtas (Privilege and Procedure) Bill, 1976, which was opposed by Fianna Fáil.

When initiated, this Bill contained a section that conferred absolute privilege on a witness before a committee and on a person sending a document to a committee. However, during the committee stage of the legislation in the Dáil, the Fianna Fáil leader, Jack Lynch, objected to the inclusion of this section, arguing that it would give the committee 'judicial status'.[25] The Taoiseach, Liam Cosgrave, stated that the matter of privilege was before the Committee on Procedure and Privileges, which was investigating the issue of privilege in the Oireachtas. Therefore, he was prepared to omit the section if the opposition did not agree with it, as he wanted to pass the rest of the Bill as soon as possible.[26] The section was removed and the subject was not returned to for another twenty years, when it appeared as part of the Oireachtas (Compellability, Privileges and Immunities) Act, 1997 (see below).

The Select Committee on Legislation and Security

Following the PAC's 'Arms Crisis' Inquiry, it was not until 1994 that a committee was again called on to perform an investigation. Unlike the previous committee inquiry, which had been established by Fianna Fáil to investigate its own members, this inquiry was created by the incoming Rainbow Coalition government of Fine Gael, the Labour

---

[24] Gwynn Morgan, D. (1990) *The Constitutional Law of Ireland.* Dublin: Round Hall Press, p. 162.

[25] *Dáil Debates,* 25 March 1976, Vol. 289, Col. 313.

[26] Ibid., Col. 318.

Party and Democratic Left. In fact the Labour Party was the prime mover for the Select Committee on Legislation and Security. The committee's role was to investigate the circumstances surrounding the fall of the previous Fianna Fáil/Labour Party administration, which the Labour Party felt had been due to the actions of the senior coalition partner. The two parties had disagreed and ultimately parted ways in 1994 over the appointment of a High Court judge as well as a controversy over the extradition of a priest from Northern Ireland on child abuse charges. The select committee in turn appointed a sub-committee to pursue the inquiry.

In order to conduct its work, the sub-committee needed to be able to provide witnesses to the committee with immunity from prosecution and full privilege regarding evidence produced. This resulted in the passing of the Select Committee on Legislation and Security of Dáil Éireann (Privilege and Immunity) Act, 1994. Like the 1976 Houses of the Oireachtas (Privilege and Procedure) Bill, this new Act was promulgated by a non-Fianna Fáil government, and represented an important step in the development of the Oireachtas committee system, although it was created to support the Sub-Committee on Legislation and Security and was not of general application, i.e. it did not empower other committees. Nonetheless, the Act was indicative of the attempts by Fine Gael and the Labour Party (as discussed above) to increase the profile and powers of committees and, by proxy, parliament.

This new legislation permitted witnesses to be granted privilege during evidence but, as stated in the sub-committee's report, it did not provide for witnesses to be compelled. Indeed the report noted that while it did not encounter difficulties in this regard, 'it cannot be assumed that such a degree of dependence on voluntary attendance by witnesses would be satisfactory for future inquiries by Committees.'[27] This issue was to be revisited in a later committee inquiry.

The work of the sub-committee was significant as it was the first time since the 1935 inquiry that such a body had considered a series of political events.[28] The parliamentary debates subsequent to the sub-committee's report drew attention to the fact that it did not reach conclusions, and that it was 'not given specific powers to make findings [or recommendations] based on the evidence given to it',[29]

---

[27] Sub-Committee of the Select Committee on Legislation and Security (1995) *Report of the Sub-Committee*. Dublin: Stationery Office, p. 6.

[28] The PAC's 1970–71 inquiry had been based solely within its remit of ensuring financial rather than political accountability.

[29] *Dáil Debates*, 4 April 1995, Vol. 451, Col. 1071.

but concentrated solely on findings of fact. The expeditious nature of the sub-committee's work was contrasted with the expensive and lengthy process of a tribunal of inquiry, and was ascribed to the absence of legal representatives from the hearings. After three years of investigation, a tribunal of inquiry into the beef processing industry had produced its final report some months previous to that of the sub-committee.

In his foreword to the report, the chair of the sub-committee, Fianna Fáil's Dan Wallace TD, criticised the preclusion of the sub-committee from making findings or judgments. The report made several recommendations, which he hoped would:

> be acted on immediately so that the full potential of Oireachtas Committees to conduct effective inquiries at reasonable cost to the taxpayer and to make findings of fact, can be realised.[30]

However, many in Dáil Éireann were concerned about what they regarded as the increased devolution of responsibility to committees and sub-committees, and viewed this trend as a threat to government control. Reflecting this majoritarian view, the new Fianna Fáil leader, Bertie Ahern, stated during the debate on the findings of the sub-committee that:

> It would be a very unhappy state of affairs if a committee of the House were to take it upon itself to act in a quasi-judicial manner, delivering verdicts and distributing blame.[31]

In the two years following this report, several new tribunals of inquiry were established to investigate allegations of political corruption and the nature of the relationship between certain political and financial interests in Ireland. As the spiralling costs and slow pace of the tribunals became apparent, pressure grew both inside and outside Leinster House for the Oireachtas to provide a more efficient means of inquiry (see Chapter 6). Again, committees were seen as the optimal institutional arrangement. But for any committee to pursue an inquiry successfully, it was necessary to introduce new legislation to provide for the powers to compel the attendance of witnesses and to grant them privilege. This led to the Oireachtas (Compellability, Privileges and Immunities) Act, 1997.

---

[30] Sub-Committee of the Select Committee on Legislation and Security (1995) *Report of the Sub-Committee*. Dublin: Stationery Office, p. ix.
[31] *Dáil Debates*, 4 April 1995, Vol. 451, Col. 1079.

Strengthening the committees II: Committees of the Houses of the Oireachtas (Compellability, Privileges and Immunities) Act, 1997

As with the two other Acts discussed above, this piece of legislation was initiated by a non-Fianna Fáil government. The Labour Party sponsored the Bill, which it saw as forming part of its attempt to improve 'transparency [in] the process of governance and in the accountability of office holders and public servants'.[32] The party also saw it as supplementing the Ethics in Public Office Act, which had recently been enacted. That Act provided for increased over-sight of public representatives and senior administrators, and took the Rainbow Coalition government almost two years to bring into law.

The Compellability Act (as it subsequently became known) built on the Select Committee on Legislation and Security of Dáil Éireann (Privilege and Immunity) Act of 1994, which had granted that par-ticular sub-committee certain powers. The fact that a multiparty coalition government introduced it emphasised the importance of multiple veto players within the executive for the development of more consensual parliamentary procedures. The new Act extended rights of privilege and evidence collection to all Oireachtas commit-tees as required and, significantly, added to the powers of compella-bility. This permitted a committee with such powers to demand the attendance of persons, including civil servants, on pain of legal action for refusal.[33]

By virtue of the Act, when appearing before a committee civil serv-ants are precluded from questioning or expressing an opinion on the merits of any policy of the government or Attorney-General or on the objectives of such policy.[34] This does not prevent them from explaining particular policies but is evidence of the continued impor-tance of 'corporation sole' as the underlying dynamic in the relationship between ministers and the public service. These new powers were a significant departure for the committee system, and presented a new forum for political action and possible publicity for members of the parliamentary opposition. They also presented parliament with a mechanism for investigating the public administration without going through the appropriate minister.

---

[32] Ibid., 21 November 1995, Vol. 458, Col. 1071.
[33] An amending Act in 2004 provided for the appearance of a judge before such a committee.
[34] A similar practice exists in Westminster under the 'Osmotherly rules'.

The Act finally allowed the Oireachtas to overcome the effects of the Supreme Court judgment in the Arms Crisis[35] and the failure of the 1976 Act to facilitate the granting of privilege. Furthermore, unlike the PAC's 1970 Privilege and Procedure Act, and the Committee on Legislation and Security's 1994 (Privilege and Immunity) Act, this legislation was of general application, meaning that any committee could apply for the powers. However, under an amendment proposed by Fianna Fáil's Dermot Ahern TD at committee stage, the new powers of compellability were not automatically granted to committees. Instead, a sub-committee of the Committee on Procedure and Privileges was established, to which individual committees would apply for compellability. The sub-committee is now known as the 'Compellability Committee' and, significantly, is chaired by the chief whip.

The role of the Compellability Committee is to provide committees appropriately with the power to compel the attendance of witnesses and the discovery of evidence. It also establishes the rights of witnesses and of those identified in the course of a committee's proceedings.[36] Ultimately the Dáil, and therefore the government, must approve the granting of these powers.

The Public Accounts Committee Sub-Committee on Certain Revenue Matters

Deposit Interest Retention Tax (DIRT) was introduced under the 1986 Finance Act as a levy on interest paid by financial institutions to their customers. In October 1998, a report in the current affairs journal *Magill* revealed widespread evasion of the tax through the use of fake 'non-resident' accounts, with the collusion of several of the state's largest financial institutions and the Office of the Revenue Commissioners. The resultant public outcry prompted the newly installed Fianna Fáil/Progressive Democrat government to investigate the matter. However, with several tribunals of inquiry already under way, politicians from all sides of the Dáil were reluctant to establish another investigation by this method, and instead approved referral of the matter to the Public Accounts Committee. This inquiry became popularly known as the DIRT Inquiry, and its work

---

[35]   Collins, S. (2000) *The Power Game: Fianna Fail since Lemass.* Dublin: O'Brien Press, p. 90.

[36]   Public Accounts Committee (2001) *Sub-Committee on Certain Revenue Matters: Parliamentary Inquiry into D.I.R.T. – Final Report Vol. 3.* Dublin: PAC, p. 2.

represented a radical departure for parliamentary committees in the Irish parliament.

The PAC established a sub-committee of its members to pursue the matter, which was the first committee to apply for compellability powers under the 1997 Compellability Act. As described in Chapter 4, the PAC is in an exceptional position as the office of the Comptroller and Auditor-General supports its principal role of scrutinising executive expenditure. The Comptroller and Auditor-General's involvement was crucial, as most of the PAC's membership did not have the technical knowledge necessary to investigate the web of financial impropriety involved in the inquiry. The Dáil therefore requested the Comptroller and Auditor-General to prepare a report for the committee. In order for him to do so, the remit of the office had to be widened and this resulted in the promulgation of the Comptroller and Auditor General and Committees of the Houses of the Oireachtas (Special Provisions) Act, 1998.

Strengthening the committees III: Comptroller and Auditor General and Committees of the Houses of the Oireachtas (Special Provisions) Act, 1998

As noted above, the legislation that had permitted committees to develop to the point where they could feasibly conduct an inquiry was enacted under non-Fianna Fáil administrations. This new Act occurred under the Fianna Fáil/Progressive Democrat coalition government, again demonstrating how the former party's decision to drop its first government formation preference (single-party majoritarian government – see Chapter 3) had opened up opportunities for more institutional innovation in parliament. In this case, the Progressive Democrats insisted on an investigation into the affair, and the media publicity surrounding the issue made it a political imperative for the government to agree to an inquiry.[37]

One of the more significant features of the DIRT Inquiry and related legislative requirements was the speed with which its investigation proceeded. During the second stage of the Comptroller and Auditor General and Committees of the Houses of the Oireachtas (Special Provisions) Bill, the Minister for Finance, Charlie McCreevy, noted that 'The fact that this is not a party political matter strengthens

---

[37] It later transpired that two Fianna Fáil TDs, Beverley Cooper-Flynn and Micheál Collins, and former Fianna Fáil Senator Vivian O'Callaghan had been involved with tax evasion. Cooper-Flynn became the first Fianna Fáil TD to be expelled from the party since Desmond O'Malley.

the basis for the investigation.'[38] Indeed, the non-political nature of the inquiry was crucial to its final outcome and underlined Shaw's maxim that where political parties (and therefore divisions) are strongest, committees and their influence will be weak.[39]

The Act allowed the Comptroller and Auditor-General and his staff to investigate more fully the circumstances and details surrounding the tax evasion and to draw up a report for the PAC. Without this statutory power, the Comptroller and Auditor-General's work might have been subject to legal challenge and the PAC Inquiry would have taken much longer to conclude. From April to June 1999, the Comptroller and Auditor-General's office held fifty-nine hearings and took evidence from seventy-six witnesses before preparing a report for the PAC.[40] A subsequent study by the Office of the Attorney-General found that the work of the Comptroller and Auditor-General, as aided by the 1998 Act, was critical to the successful outcome of the DIRT Inquiry.[41]

The sub-committee's proceedings generated widespread public interest due to the introduction of television cameras into the hearings. The daily hearings and witness statements were also re-enacted on radio in the evenings. The inquiry produced several weighty reports that were wide-ranging and particularly critical of the failure of the Oireachtas to deal with the transgressions by the financial institutions.[42] The chairman of the sub-committee, Fine Gael's Jim Mitchell TD, was a strong advocate of parliamentary reform and many of his views on the role of committees were contained in proposals for parliamentary reform produced by Fine Gael during this period.[43] Building on previous Fine Gael proposals, he used the investigation as a platform to pursue the issue of Dáil reform and parliamentary accountability.

---

[38] *Dáil Debates*, 15 December 1998, Vol. 498, Col. 820.
[39] Shaw, M. (1979) 'Conclusion' in J. D. Lees and M. Shaw (eds) *Committees in Legislatures: a Comparative Analysis*. Durham, NC: Duke University Press, p. 396.
[40] Law Reform Commission (2003) *Consultation Paper on Public Inquiries including Tribunals of Inquiry*. Dublin, p. 75.
[41] Office of the Attorney General (2000) *Comparative Study of Tribunals of Inquiry and Parliamentary Inquiries*. Dublin: Stationery Office, p. 34.
[42] Public Accounts Committee (1999) *Sub-Committee on Certain Revenue Matters: Parliamentary Inquiry into D.I.R.T. – First Report*. Dublin; Public Accounts Committee (2001) *Sub-Committee on Certain Revenue Matters: Parliamentary Inquiry into D.I.R.T. – Final Report Vol. 1*. Dublin.
[43] Fine Gael (2000) *A Democratic Revolution*. Leinster House, Dublin: Fine Gael Parliamentary Party.

First report

The DIRT Inquiry's first report was released in December 1999. It praised the:

> enhanced powers of the Committee of Public Accounts, examination under oath, live broadcasting and rapid publication of the proceedings [as representing] a major advance and modernisation of the parliamentary process and parliamentary scrutiny.[44]

Taking the opportunity to raise the matter of Dáil reform, the report argued that:

> Many of the issues which have been under inquiry could have been examined and dealt with earlier if the Oireachtas had been better organised and resourced

and noted further that:

> Oireachtas procedures, practices and resources have not kept pace with the expansion of our economy and the modernisation of our society.[45]

This report considered the role of the Houses of the Oireachtas in some detail. Indeed, it strayed somewhat from the details of the inquiry in its conclusions, which contained a series of recommendations for the improvement of parliamentary accountability in the Oireachtas. The main recommendations were that:

- an Oireachtas Commission (similar to the British House of Commons Commission) be established, which would oversee the running of the Oireachtas
- the committee system be funded from a separate Vote
- this Vote should increase substantially and be independent of the Department of Finance
- an Oireachtas legal adviser be appointed
- provision be made in law for the appointment of Parliamentary Inspectors with powers similar to High Court Inspectors under the Companies Acts
- a parliamentary inspection be initiated only by the Houses of the Oireachtas, with its remit clearly defined and that it be designated to a committee to which it reports
- the committees of the Oireachtas be granted the right of initiative in proposing an inquiry.[46]

---

[44] Public Accounts Committee (1999) *Sub-Committee on Certain Revenue Matters: Parliamentary Inquiry into D.I.R.T. – First Report*. Dublin, p. 3.

[45] Ibid., p. 180.

[46] Ibid., p. 199.

Furthermore, it made several recommendations for the improvement of parliamentary procedures to facilitate increased levels of legislative scrutiny, including:

- that the role of committees in the passage of legislation be reviewed
- consideration of allowing committees to take oral questions not answered in the Dáil
- that the chairmen and chief executives of state-sponsored companies be responsible to the appropriate committee for operational decisions
- that a *Handbook of Parliamentary Inquiries* be prepared for reference by future committees and sub-committees
- that a comparative study be undertaken by the Department of Finance and the Attorney-General's Office into parliamentary inquiries and tribunals of inquiry in light of this inquiry.

During 2000, the committee heard evidence from the financial institutions involved in the controversy and also from members and staff of the Oireachtas. The Clerk of the Dáil and the chief whip were called to give evidence concerning the issue of parliamentary reform. For the Clerk of the Dáil in particular, the inquiry provided an opportunity to voice concerns about the under-resourcing and staffing problems in the Oireachtas.[47]

During the taking of evidence into the issue of parliamentary reform, the sub-committee called for the chief whip to give evidence. The Chair used his presence to state that:

> there needs to be a great deal more urgency among the Whips in all the parties in addressing the question of how we in the Oireachtas do our business. There is an obvious area where action is needed, in view of the need for tribunals and inquiries over the past few years, all of which, in part at least, went back to a lack of accountability, a lack of success by the Oireachtas in getting accountability or preventing bad habits developing in a number of places.[48]

Unsurprisingly, the chief whip disagreed on this point, arguing that parliamentary reform was a slow process, and fraught with difficulties. He pointed out that the 'process of Dáil reform has been bedevilled for years by political wrangling'.[49]

Furthermore, he argued that the emergence of tribunals and parliamentary inquiries could not be regarded as a direct result of the failure of parliamentary tools designed to hold government to

---

[47]   Interview with Kieran Coughlan, 30 April 2002.
[48]   Public Accounts Committee (2001) *Sub-Committee on Certain Revenue Matters: Parliamentary Inquiry into D.I.R.T. – Final Report, Vol. 3*. Dublin, p. 10.
[49]   Ibid.

account. Nonetheless, in its third (and final) report, the sub-committee repeated the necessity for substantial progress in legislative reform in order to increase the ability of the Oireachtas to hold executive agencies (in this case the Revenue Commissioners) to account.

Third report

The third report of the sub-committee returned to the issue of Oireachtas reform and the establishment of an Oireachtas Commission. It repeated the view that the issues exposed by the inquiry could, in part, be blamed on a breakdown in parliamentary scrutiny of the executive. It welcomed the fact that many of its recommendations from the first report (see above) had been taken up by the government. In particular, the announcement by the chief whip that the government had decided to proceed with the establishment of an Oireachtas Commission was warmly received. The sub-committee envisaged that this commission would oversee funding, staffing and the organisation of the Oireachtas, while emphasising the role of the Lower House *vis-à-vis* the government.

It was also announced that the government had agreed to the appointment of a Parliamentary Inspector as needs required.[50] In addition, the sub-committee noted that its wish for a Parliamentary Law Officer to advise the Houses and their committees had been agreed to and that as of June 2000, the position had been created. Finally, the sub-committee reported that external consultants had been appointed 'to allow objective benchmarking of the funding and staffing of the Houses of the Oireachtas'.[51]

The financial institutions involved agreed to pay the amount of tax outstanding, and the matter was considered closed. The PAC's DIRT Inquiry was regarded as a watershed in Irish parliamentary history as it was the first successfully completed committee inquiry of its type. Furthermore, it appeared to present an opportunity for the development of the committee system beyond its original remit of considering legislation and/or taking evidence from interest groups or bodies. Indeed, within a year of the DIRT Inquiry's final report, two further inquiries had been established that attempted to repeat the successful performance of the PAC. These were the investigations by a sub-committee of the Joint Committee on Justice, Equality,

---

[50] Public Accounts Committee (2001) *Sub-Committee on Certain Revenue Matters: Parliamentary Inquiry into D.I.R.T. – Final Report, Vol. 1*. Dublin: PAC, p. 89.

[51] Ibid., p. 92.

Defence and Women's Rights into a controversial shooting incident, and by a sub-committee of the Oireachtas Joint Committee on Public Enterprise and Transport into cost overruns on a project.

The limits to parliamentary committees: the Abbeylara Inquiry

Following a fatal shooting by the Gardaí at Abbeylara, Co. Longford in April 2000, the Commissioner of the Garda Síochána launched an investigation into the incident. A report was submitted to the Minister for Justice, Equality and Law Reform in June and, following a motion of both Houses of the Oireachtas, was forwarded for consideration to the Joint Committee on Justice, Equality, Defence and Women's Rights in October 2000. Over the following months, the joint committee invited submissions and observations from the persons referred to in the report and other interested parties. On 8 March 2001, the joint committee established a sub-committee to be known as the Sub-Committee on the Abbeylara Incident to consider the Commissioner's report.

The sub-committee was encouraged by the recent success of the DIRT Inquiry; indeed, its chairman, Fianna Fáil's Seán Ardagh TD, had also been a member of that sub-committee. However, this new sub-committee was lax in its procedures. On 10 April, the joint committee changed its terms of reference to allow the sub-committee to take evidence in relation to the incident and to report back with findings. To facilitate its investigation, the sub-committee applied to the Committee on Procedure and Privileges for powers provided for under the Committees of the Houses of the Oireachtas (Compellability, Privileges and Immunities) Act, 1997. A motion of both Houses granted it this power in April 2001.

By this stage, however, the Houses of the Oireachtas, the joint committee and the sub-committee had already made a number of procedural mistakes. In part this was due to the relative inexperience of TDs in such inquiries, but a member of the sub-committee, Fine Gael's Alan Shatter, noted that there were also administrative errors in relation to the sub-committee's documentation that were not the fault of its members.[52] In the first instance, the Dáil had simply referred the Commissioner's report to the joint committee with no instructions or authorisation to conduct an inquiry into it. The Seanad had also

---

[52] Interview with Alan Shatter, 24 June 2003.

referred it to the joint committee, but under the wrong order of reference. Subsequently, the joint committee's order to change its terms of reference on 10 April could not be located.[53] For these reasons, the sub-committee applied for compellability powers under the wrong terms of reference.

The sub-committee proceeded to take evidence despite not receiving powers to do so until 30 April, having changed its terms of reference for a third time. The inquiry attracted much media attention, especially when its members visited the scene of the shooting. However, its investigations came to an abrupt halt when the Gardaí involved in the case refused to appear before it to give evidence and appealed their case to the High Court. The case was also appealed in the Supreme Court and both hearings saw a wide-ranging debate concerning the extent of the powers of the Oireachtas and its committees to perform non-legislative functions.

High Court ruling

The case taken by the thirty-six Gardaí ranged from the procedural flaws in the establishment and empowerment of the sub-committee (see above) to the power of the Oireachtas to establish inquiries 'which are likely to lead to findings of fact or expressions of opinion adverse to the good name of people who are not members of the Oireachtas'.[54] They also argued that there was a 'structural bias' in the sub-committee's work as the inherent nature of being an elected representative undermined the concept of independence, and therefore impartiality.

The court upheld the appeal and, adopting a particularly positivist interpretation, found that neither the 1922 nor the 1937 Constitution granted such powers of inquiry as envisaged by the sub-committee's members. It also found that the sub-committee had breached fair procedure by not allowing the Gardaí involved an opportunity to cross-examine witnesses until the last day of public hearings. It did not, however, comment on whether or not there was indeed a 'structural bias' in an inquiry of this type being conducted by elected representatives. This matter was returned to in the subsequent Supreme Court appeal.

---

[53] Browne, V. (2001) 'Politicians must take blame for inquiry fiasco', *Irish Times*, 28 November, 16.

[54] *Maguire* v. *Ardagh* [2001] H.C. (2002) *Irish Reports*. High Court, Dublin. Vol. 1, Part II, p. 407.

The High Court ruling went further than the sub-committee's investigation, and ruled out all Oireachtas inquiries, except those into the actions of politicians. It ruled that no Dáil committee could investigate major issues if such an investigation would affect the livelihood or reputation of anyone outside the Oireachtas. This was similar to the judgment given by the High Court during the Arms Crisis (see above), when it found that the procedures followed by the Oireachtas were not adequate in protecting the rights of the individual. It highlighted the disparity between the well-protected rights of the individual and the weak definition of the powers ascribed to the Irish legislature in the Constitution.

While the sub-committee's disorganised approach to the inquiry led many politicians to express reservations about it and its work, this ruling took many by surprise. In effect, the courts were preventing the Oireachtas from investigating part of the executive apparatus, and this created a constitutional difficulty that the sub-committee decided to challenge in the Supreme Court. It was considered by members of the sub-committee and sections of the media to have created a 'constitutional crisis', which possibly necessitated a referendum on the powers of the Oireachtas. The sub-committee proceeded to appeal its case to the Supreme Court.

Supreme Court ruling

Counsel for the Gardaí argued that the Minister for Justice, Equality and Law Reform was accountable to Dáil Éireann for the Gardaí via the Garda Commissioner, and that it was outside the remit of the sub-committee to ask questions of individual Gardaí. They also pointed out that no individual was accountable to the Oireachtas and that the sub-committee had overstepped its remit in pursuing its inquiry. Agreeing with this position in his ruling, Justice Hardiman found that not only citizens but also the Garda Commissioner are 'not directly or personally responsible to the Dáil or the Oireachtas'.[55]

This finding embodies one of the core difficulties for the development of alternative methods of parliamentary accountability. The constitutional emphasis on the doctrine of ministerial responsibility prevents parliament from bypassing the government in attempts to attain accountability from state agencies such as the police. The judicial emphasis in the Abbeylara case on maintaining ministerial

---

[55] *Maguire* v. *Ardagh* [2002] S.C. (2002) *Irish Reports.* Supreme Court, Dublin. Vol. 1, Part II, 701.

accountability at the core of parliamentary accountability arguably represents the biggest obstacle to the development of parliamentary committees.

On behalf of the sub-committee, Fine Gael's Alan Shatter TD argued in the Supreme Court that the High Court decision had not given 'proper regard to the constitutional role and rights of parliament and the role of the government'.[56] He, along with the Attorney-General and the sub-committee's legal representation, used the example of the United States Congress to demonstrate how legislative power included the ability to establish committees and use powers of compellability as deemed necessary. However, Justice Denham rejected this comparison as she indicated that the United States Constitution clearly gives inherent powers of inquiry and compellability to Congress to facilitate its legislative functions.[57]

Furthermore, she pointed out that the clear constitutional separation of powers precluded the sub-committee from arguing that it could perform such an inquisitorial or adjudicative function as may occur in Westminster. In this respect the Abbeylara Inquiry set a precedent, as it was 'not a system utilised by the legislature previously'.[58] She contrasted the right of Westminster to inquire into matters with that of the Irish parliament, which was limited by the Constitution.

By a majority of five to two, the Supreme Court ruled that the sub-committee had 'no explicit, implicit or inherent power to conduct an inquiry' into the fatal shooting incident. Significantly, the Supreme Court rolled back the High Court decision that the Oireachtas could not perform any inquiries, leaving the door open for an alternative form of investigation to be created. Each individual Justice gave a lengthy explanation for his or her decision but there was a consensus on the central themes of the five who ruled in favour of the High Court decision. These were that:

- the sub-committee did not uphold fair procedure and citizens' constitutional rights in its work
- its scope and power went far beyond any powers existing in statute or implied in the Constitution
- it had been negligent in the way it followed procedures in its work.

---

56 Carolan, M. (2001) 'Court ruling called "attack on democracy"', *Irish Times*, 19 January, 6.
57 *Maguire* v. *Ardagh* [2002] S.C. (2002) *Irish Reports*. Supreme Court, Dublin. Vol. 1, Part II, p. 560.
58 Ibid., p. 561.

Similarly, a subsequent consultation paper by the Law Reform Commission on the issue of inquiries identified the principal difficulties common to the majority judges as, firstly, that the committee aimed to be 'adjudicatory' and, secondly, that it was investigating ordinary citizens, albeit public servants.[59] The two judges who upheld the appeal also had some reservations as to the future ability of such inquiries to maintain requirements of natural justice and fair procedures. Interestingly, one of them, the Chief Justice, argued in his dissenting judgment that he saw no reason why politicians should not be able to participate in such committees unaffected by pressures from their constituents or parties.[60] This was a rejection of the claim by the Gardaí that there was a 'structural bias' to the inquiry, given that the sub-committee members were elected on certain platforms that meant they could not be impartial in their approach to the issue.

Chief Justice Keane's judgment in favour of the appellants noted that the Committee of Public Accounts of Dáil Éireann (Privilege and Procedure) Act, 1970 (see above) empowered the committee to summon and examine witnesses for the PAC's inquiry of 1970–71. However, it did not authorise the holding of the inquiry itself, because the legislation had been enacted on the assumption that the Oireachtas had such power inherently.[61] He also noted that the Arms Crisis case did not consider whether the power to conduct such an inquiry was questionable. He concluded that, in his opinion, the challenge to the inherent power of the Oireachtas to establish committees of inquiry should fail. However, the majority decision decided the matter.

The above mentioned consultation report by the Law Reform Commission in 2003 noted that while the Abbeylara judgment was clear in disallowing an Oireachtas Committee to investigate private individuals, it did not disallow tribunals of inquiry from doing so.[62] It identified the examples of businessman Larry Goodman in the Beef Tribunal, and former Fianna Fáil Taoiseach Charles Haughey in the Moriarty Tribunal (Chapter 6). The report concluded that the Supreme Court must believe that there was indeed a 'structural bias'

---

[59] Law Reform Commission (2003) *Consultation Paper on Public Inquiries including Tribunals of Inquiry*. Dublin, p. 79.

[60] *Maguire* v. *Ardagh* [2002] S.C. (2002) *Irish Reports*. Supreme Court, Dublin. Vol. 1, Part II, p. 530.

[61] Ibid., pp. 519–21.

[62] Law Reform Commission (2003) *Consultation Paper on Public Inquiries including Tribunals of Inquiry*. Dublin, p. 89.

to inquiries held by elected representatives. It also found that legislation would probably not be sufficient to define the limits of such inquiries and, while not explicitly recommending it, hinted that a constitutional amendment might well be necessary to do so.[63]

The Supreme Court's decision, coupled with public unease over the circumstances surrounding the shooting at Abbeylara, forced the government into creating an alternative form of inquiry for the incident. A tribunal of inquiry with a judge as sole chairman was established a week later, but it did not begin its investigation until over a year later and is ongoing at time of writing.[64] The 'Abbeylara judgment', as it is now known, has raised serious long-term difficulties for the ability of committees, and by proxy parliament, to extend their scope for providing accountability.

The Abbeylara case contributed to accusations that the judicial pillar of state was increasingly encroaching on the work of the legislative and executive pillars. Commenting on the judgment, Shatter argued that not only has the committee system 'been castrated by the government approach to it, the committee system has now been castrated by the courts'. He continued:

> when it comes to the Supreme Court dealing with the political arena across a broad range of areas, including the committee system, the Supreme Court is fundamentally wrong and doing real damage to democracy in this country.[65]

However, the judiciary could with justification argue that its decision ensured that the legislature did not engage in matters reserved solely for the courts, and that judicial restraint has been a defining feature of the Irish Supreme Court. Supreme Court Judge Adrian Hardiman has argued that:

> Anything which constitutes an 'administration of justice' is within the exclusive domain of the Courts and cannot be undertaken by any other body such as a parliamentary committee (as in the Abbeylara case), the Oireachtas by the passage of legislation, or a public inquiry.[66]

In terms of parliamentary accountability, the Abbeylara judgment has severely retarded what progress had been made since the mid-1990s

---

[63] Ibid., pp. 89–90.
[64] This inquiry is known as the Barr Tribunal.
[65] Interview with Alan Shatter, 24 June 2003.
[66] Hardiman, A. (2004) 'The Role of the Supreme Court in Our Democracy' in J. Mulholland (ed.) *Political Choice and Democratic Freedom in Ireland*. Dublin: Transcripts of 2004 McGill Summer School, Glenties, Co. Donegal, pp. 32–44.

in increasing the profile and power of committees. Furthermore, the Supreme Court decision, with its emphasis on the separation of powers, has drawn attention to the narrow parameters within which parliament can develop its oversight function. More immediately, the judgment in the Abbeylara case resulted in the collapse of a parallel inquiry into a significant cost overrun by the national rail company, Coras Iompar Éireann (CIÉ).

CIÉ/Mini-CTC Signalling Project

The final case of the use of committees as a mechanism of inquiry was the establishment of a sub-committee by the Oireachtas Joint Committee on Public Enterprise and Transport in November 2000 to investigate a matter of public concern. This was the cost overrun on the Mini-CTC signalling system established along part of the national rail network by Coras Iompar Éireann (CIE). During its proceedings, and similarly to the Abbeylara Inquiry, the sub-committee compelled executives of CIÉ, as well as some prominent business figures, to attend and give evidence; it was issued with a stay and challenged in the High Court by the widow of the former CIÉ chief executive who had been involved in the contract.

In the High Court, her counsel argued that the establishment of Oireachtas committees to carry out investigations that had an impact on the good name and reputation of citizens marked the ascension of 'a parallel system of justice in Ireland'.[67] However, the High Court overturned the stay and allowed the sub-committee to continue its hearings. The sub-committee's work was subsequently suspended following the Abbeylara High Court decision and never recommenced, as a question hung over the power of such committees to conduct inquiries. The ending of the parliamentary session meant that the subject could not be returned to.

At its final sitting before suspension, the sub-committee's chairman voiced his frustration and that of Oireachtas members more generally:

> The High Court in the Abbeylara decision appears to have removed, in an important aspect, the ability of the Oireachtas to properly discharge [its legislative] function. In so doing the High Court appears to have employed a narrow and limiting view of the role of the national parliament. At the same time, the courts have reserved to themselves an organic view of their own power

---

[67]   O'Doherty, C. (2001) 'Court rules Oireachtas rail inquiry can proceed', *Irish Times*, 16 October, 4.

… The issue for this sub-committee is no longer what happened to the tax-payer's money but the extent to which the Oireachtas can be permitted to exercise its legislative function.[68]

The Abbeylara judgment has had serious implications for the role of parliamentary committees and for parliamentary accountability. The Supreme Court's narrow view of the functions of committees has retarded their ability to develop into alternative arenas for parliamentary work. The judgment also raises questions concerning the DIRT Inquiry and whether or not its work would have been possible had the Supreme Court decision already been taken.

Reasons why the DIRT Inquiry was successful

The PAC's work in bringing the DIRT Inquiry to a conclusion was regarded as a significant breakthrough for parliamentary committees and the development of the role of the legislature in oversight activity.[69] However, several extraneous reasons why the sub-committee reached such a quick and successful conclusion become apparent in the light of the failure of subsequent committee inquiries. First, the PAC is in a unique position in that it does not question government policy as such, instead concentrating its efforts on examining the effectiveness of executive expenditure. The sub-committee itself recognised this, stating that its cohesion and non-partisan approach were due 'to the non-involvement of the Committee of Public Accounts in policy assessment'.[70]

Secondly, the PAC has a strong relationship with the Office of the Comptroller and Auditor-General, which had already prepared and investigated much of the material that was subsequently used by the sub-committee. The work of the Comptroller and Auditor-General in preparing the case for the DIRT Inquiry took seven months, and allowed the sub-committee to complete the taking of evidence from all parties in less than six weeks. This was in sharp contrast to tribunals of inquiry (particularly the Beef Tribunal – see below), where much of the time was spent collecting and searching for evidence before hearings could get under way.

---

[68] Joint Committee on Public Enterprise and Transport (2001) *Transcript of the Sub-Committee on the Mini-CTC Signalling Project.* Dublin: Stationery Office.

[69] The DIRT Inquiry also resulted in the establishment of the Irish Financial Services Regulatory Body in 2003.

[70] Public Accounts Committee (2001) *Sub-Committee on Certain Revenue Matters: Parliamentary Inquiry into D.I.R.T. – Final Report, Vol. 1.* Dublin, pp. 109–11.

Thirdly, as will be demonstrated below, unlike the Flood and Moriarty Tribunals the subjects under investigation (in this case the banks) did not challenge the legality or constitutionality of the committee's work. A report by the Office of the Attorney General pointed out that unlike some of the tribunals in the 1990s:

> The recent DIRT inquiry benefited from precisely drawn terms of reference which must have contributed to the speed in which it completed its task.[71]

Fourthly, for TDs to be seen publicly questioning the banks and Revenue Commissioners and exposing flaws in their work was a big political success and provided significant media coverage for members of the sub-committee. However, the search for such publicity may have contributed to members of the Dáil attempting to establish further inquiries without proper preparation and assessment of the nature of the investigation. Fifthly, the sub-committee recognised that it had been able to take advantage of an extended parliamentary recess that allowed its members to concentrate solely on the inquiry.[72]

The first report of the DIRT Inquiry noted that the sub-committee's work was possible subject to the agreement of the Department of Finance to provide extra staffing and resources.[73] In preparing for the inquiry, the sub-committee spent a great deal of time considering legal issues that had involved heavy use of scarce resources. As these resources came from a central fund, other committees were deprived of funding for their work. As shown above, this was a factor in its recommendation that resources be increased and that a Parliamentary Legal Adviser be appointed to the Oireachtas to assist with future investigations. The sub-committee's chairman also noted that the Oireachtas had functioned without a Parliamentary Legal Adviser for eighty years and that this had contributed to a lack of effectiveness in achieving accountability. He argued that such an office would 'open up the possibilities of further hearings for Dáil committees and better accountability'.[74]

---

[71]   Office of the Attorney General (2000) *Comparative Study of Tribunals of Inquiry and Parliamentary Inquiries*. Dublin: Stationery Office, p. 27.

[72]   Public Accounts Committee (2001) *Sub-Committee on Certain Revenue Matters: Parliamentary Inquiry into D.I.R.T. – Final Report, Vol. 1*. Dublin, pp. 107–8.

[73]   Public Accounts Committee (1999) *Sub-Committee on Certain Revenue Matters: Parliamentary Inquiry into D.I.R.T. – First Report*. Dublin, p. 181.

[74]   Public Accounts Committee (2001) *Sub-Committee on Certain Revenue Matters: Parliamentary Inquiry into D.I.R.T. – Final Report, Vol. 3*. Dublin, p. 19.

As noted above, these forays into wider issues of parliamentary reform were related to the chair's long-standing interest in the subject. The ongoing tribunals of inquiry that paralleled the work of the PAC's sub-committee were directly related to the failure of formal parliamentary mechanisms of accountability, as presented in Chapter 4. The issue of Dáil and wider legislative reform, therefore, was politically prominent during the sub-committee's inquiry and it was opportune of the sub-committee to pressurise the government to address the matter.

Thus, the DIRT Inquiry's success and recommendations were possible due to a range of factors not available to the Abbeylara investigation. The legal challenge to the committee's work in this inquiry exposed the limits of the non-legislative role of parliamentary committees, as well as of Dáil Éireann's ability to circumvent the key doctrine of ministerial responsibility. However, since the Supreme Court's 2002 judgment several other committee inquiries have been initiated in the Oireachtas, including the following.

- An investigation by the Joint Committee on Health and Children based on a report into illegal charges levied on people in public long-stay care institutions.[75]
- Investigations into the Dublin and Monaghan bombings of 1974, and the Dublin bombings of 1972 and 1973, by two sub-committees of the Joint Committee on Justice, Equality and Law Reform.[76]
- An investigation by a special committee concerning the removal of a Circuit Court judge from office under Article 35.4.1 of the Constitution. The committee's work was challenged in the High Court but, significantly, that Court found that it could proceed on the basis that as the Constitution provided for the removal of judges from their positions, the committee's work was a legitimate means of doing this, provided it did not act in an adjudicatory manner. In his judgment on the issue, Mr Justice Smyth stressed the duty of the Oireachtas in ensuring public confidence in the judicial system.

Nonetheless, as committees elsewhere are credited with reversing the 'decline of parliament' and become embedded in the infrastructure of representative institutions, the development of the committee

---

[75] This was the *Report on Certain Issues of Management and Administration in the Department of Health & Children associated with the Practice of Charges for Persons in Long-Stay Care in Health Board Institutions and Related Matters,* also known as the Travers Report after its author, John Travers.

[76] Reports on both of these investigations have since been published and a new commission of investigation is now considering the matters.

system in Ireland is currently in a state of limbo. While the re-establishment of joint committees by successive governments since 1993 points to their increased institutionalisation in parliamentary life, their ability to move beyond narrow and strictly defined roles has been limited. As Norton indicates, committees face this difficulty in other Westminster-style parliaments such as Canada and India, as well as Westminster itself.[77] In particular, their ability to act as alternative loci for executive oversight has been delivered a sharp blow by the judgment in the Abbeylara case, and future committee inquiries will tread carefully around issues of a judicial nature.

Despite its theoretical potential for putting TDs and Senators at the centre of public issues and increasing their role as legislators, the experiment with parliamentary committees of inquiry has not been encouraging for parliamentarians in the Oireachtas. The 2002 general election saw two of the leading figures in the DIRT Inquiry lose their Dáil seats: Jim Mitchell (Fine Gael) and Derek McDowell (Labour Party) had a poor electoral return for their work, reinforcing the view that committees do not offer an alternative career path to party for ambitious TDs. One of the Abbeylara Inquiry's leading figures, Alan Shatter (Fine Gael), also failed to retain his seat despite much publicity during the Abbeylara Supreme Court appeal in the run-up to the election.

Subject to further legal challenges, it is clear that Oireachtas committees will continue to test the limits of their remit and to establish their place in the governing infrastructure. As noted above, it may take a constitutional referendum to secure some of the gains made thus far, particularly in the light of the Abbeylara judgment.[78] However, political party affiliation rather than committee member-ship remains the key organising principle in the Houses of the Oireachtas and, apart from constituency work, offers the best guarantee of re-election. Members will think twice before breaking the party whip in a committee.

---

[77] Norton, P. (1998) 'Nascent Institutionalisation: Committees in the British Parliament' in L. D. Longley and R. H. Davidson (eds) *The New Roles of Parliamentary Committees.* London: Frank Cass, pp. 143–4.

[78] A 2005 report on public inquiries by the Law Reform Commission suggested that analysis of this issue comes within the remit of the Oireachtas Committee on the Constitution.

PART IV

Extra-parliamentary accountability and its impact on Dáil Éireann

CHAPTER 6

Tribunals of inquiry and judicial accountability

The development of tribunals of inquiry

The inadequacy of formal mechanisms of parliamentary accountability, combined with the arrested development of parliamentary committees, has increased the focus on judicial mechanisms of executive and administrative oversight. Since the early 1990s the use of tribunals of inquiry to investigate matters of public concern has become a prominent feature of Irish political life, but one that has not yet received much academic attention.[1] It is noteworthy that in other Westminster-style parliamentary democracies such as Australia, Canada, New Zealand and Britain, such extra-parliamentary judicial mechanisms of oversight have also appeared as alternatives to formal structures of executive and administrative oversight.[2]

The principal reason for the use of judicial methods of oversight is that because they are extra-parliamentary, they are free of party political constraints that hinder parliamentary mechanisms of scrutiny. The fact that tribunals are chaired by an independent judicial figure eliminates the partisan bias that may diminish parliamentary committees' effectiveness. What is significant for this study is that almost all the allegations of maladministration and improper conduct among public representatives, as later revealed by the tribunals, originated in the Dáil during Question Time and debates. However, the ease with which ministers could insulate themselves, their departments and their political parties from probing questions points to a structural imbalance in Dáil–government relations. Indeed, a recurring theme of recent tribunals of inquiry has been that parliamentary procedures such as Question Time and adjournment debates have failed in their role of overseeing the executive.

---

[1] The Law Reform Commission's 2005 report on the issue of public inquiries considers the difficulties encountered with tribunals as a form of investigation.

[2] Ward, A. J. (1996) 'The Constitution Review Group and the "Executive State" in Ireland', *Administration* Vol. 44(4), 42–63; The Law Reform Commission (2005) *Report on Public Inquiries including Tribunals of Inquiry*. Dublin.

At time of writing, tribunals of inquiry have encountered much criticism over costs, delays and bureaucracy but, as we shall see, the proposed alternatives do not envisage any reinforcement of the powers of the legislature. In this chapter, we examine six tribunals of inquiry conducted since 1991. In order to elucidate the variety of issues before them, we categorise the tribunals into two themes – those concerned with (a) administrative oversight and (b) the activities of political actors.

A precedent for the modern tribunal of inquiry is the appointment of Royal Commissions in Westminster at the discretion of the government to investigate political issues or provide non-partisan recommendations. For example, the Parnell Commission of 1888 exonerated the Irish Parliamentary Party and its leader, Charles Stuart Parnell, of involvement in murder and forgery. The independence from both executive and parliament of such commissions holds the key to understanding the modern tribunal of inquiry.[3]

The legal basis for tribunals of inquiry

The statutory basis for contemporary tribunals of inquiry in Ireland lies in the Tribunals of Inquiry (Evidence) Act, 1921, which predates the official creation of the Irish Free State by some eight months.[4] Although amended several times since its promulgation, this Act provides the foundation for tribunals in Ireland, and until 2005 in Britain as well.[5] Its creation was deemed necessary as until then the only method of investigating matters of public concern was via ad hoc select committees of parliament or Royal Commissions of Inquiry.

In 1912, one such ad hoc committee of the House of Commons appointed to investigate the 'Marconi Scandal'[6] returned a blatantly

---

[3]   Keeton, G. W. (1960) *Trial by Tribunal.* London: Museum Press, p. 225.

[4]   O'Neill, B. (2000) 'Political and Legal Issues Arising out of Recent Tribunals of Inquiry', *Irish Political Studies* Vol. 15, 201.

[5]   In Britain the Inquiries Act, 2005 has replaced the 1921 Tribunals of Inquiry (Evidence) Act.

[6]   The Postmaster-General in a Liberal government accepted a tender by the English Marconi Company for the construction of a chain of state-owned wireless telegraph stations throughout the British Empire. Rumours abounded that the government had favoured the Marconi Company and that certain members of it had benefited from the transaction.

partisan verdict on the conduct of government ministers. The result was that public faith in such committees as tools of investigation was nullified. When allegations were made in 1921 against another minister, the government at Westminster decided that a new form of investigation was required.[7] A tribunal of inquiry was created under the new Tribunals of Inquiry (Evidence) Act, 1921. Under this Act, Tribunals are initiated not by the legislature but by the government.[8] Typically, the assent of both Houses of the Oireachtas is required for the establishment of a tribunal in Ireland, and though the Oireachtas may further empower it via statutory law, it is *de jure* rather than *de facto* an agent of parliament.

The Act gave tribunals powers similar to the High Court in respect of the production of documents and the attendance of witnesses. Surprisingly, there were some glaring omissions from the Act, such as the qualifications of the members of the tribunal or the procedure to be followed.[9] Indeed, Sir Richard Scott, whose non-statutory inquiry into the sale of arms to Iraq proved a watershed in British politics[10] similar to the Beef Tribunal in Ireland (see below), commented:

> In England, the Tribunals of Inquiry (Evidence) 1921 Act is hardly ever used because it is thoroughly inconvenient to use it.[11]

The Act does not specify who should chair proceedings but traditionally, members of the judiciary have been appointed – their constitutional independence theoretically providing a safeguard against partisanship. Procedural details such as this have evolved in practice over time in both jurisdictions. However, the existence of a written constitution in Ireland has caused difficulties in recent times as the powers of tribunals have been subject to several legal and constitutional challenges.

---

[7] The Law Reform Commission (2005) *Report on Public Inquiries including Tribunals of Inquiry*. Dublin, p. 17.

[8] An original draft of the Act would have given the power to establish a tribunal to a minister, but the need for parliamentary approval was accepted and the Act amended to reflect this.

[9] Salmon, C. (1967) 'Tribunals of Inquiry', *The Hebrew University of Jerusalem Lionel Cohen Lectures*. Jerusalem, p. 7.

[10] The Scott Inquiry bears many similarities to the Beef Tribunal (see below) in terms of the role of parliamentary oversight and the subsequent establishment of new oversight mechanisms.

[11] Law Reform Commission (2003) *Consultation Paper on Public Inquiries including Tribunals of Inquiry*. Dublin, p. 11.

Under Section 1(1) of the 1921 Act, the purpose of tribunals was 'for inquiring into a definite matter ... of urgent public importance' or an event that causes 'public disquiet'. They are tools of inquiry and interrogation but, unlike judicial courts, are not adversarial and do not determine rights, duties or obligations.[12] Tribunals were given powers equivalent to those of the High Court to compel the attendance of witnesses and the production of documents. Since the 1921 Act there have been several amendments to increase their versatility and powers of inquiry, for example the Tribunals of Inquiry (Evidence) (Amendment) Act of 1979, which borrowed from the work of a British Royal Commission established in 1966 to examine the role of tribunals of inquiry. Other amending Acts were promulgated to deal with specific problems that arose with tribunals during the later 1990s and will be discussed in conjunction with those tribunals.

Tribunals of Inquiry (Evidence) (Amendment) Act, 1979

This Act bolstered the original statute in Ireland by permitting a tribunal to make such orders 'as it considers necessary for the purposes of its functions', as well as to pursue prosecutions for non-compliance. This was later to become significant when the legitimacy of tribunals (given that the legislation was passed prior to the state's foundation) was challenged in the courts. It also provided that a tribunal did not have to consist of a judge. The 'sole member' could be a layperson who could use 'assessors' to aid an investigation. While a tribunal is powerless to impose sanctions based on its findings, it may impose penalties based on witnesses' conduct during the course of its hearings.[13] The Act also allowed for the non-admissibility of evidence given in subsequent criminal proceedings.[14]

Royal Commission on Tribunals of Inquiry

In what was later to become a reference point for tribunals of inquiry in Ireland, the Royal Commission of Tribunals of Inquiry (Salmon Commission) undertook a review of tribunals and the criteria for their establishment in Britain in 1966. Without specifying or setting

---

[12]   Brady, R. (1997) 'Reflections on Tribunals of Inquiry', *Bar Review* Vol. 3(3), 122.

[13]   O'Neill, B. (2000) 'Political and Legal Issues Arising out of Recent Tribunals of Inquiry', *Irish Political Studies* Vol. 15, 204.

[14]   Public Accounts Committee (2001) *Sub-Committee on Certain Revenue Matters: Parliamentary Inquiry into D.I.R.T. – Final Report Vol. 1.* Dublin, p. 100.

boundaries, the commission found that inquiries 'should always be confined to matters of vital public importance concerning which there is something in the nature of a nation-wide crisis of confidence'. This interpretation was has been followed by not only the British legal establishment but also the Irish Supreme Court when called on to assess legal challenges to the work of tribunals.[15] Interestingly, among the findings of the commission was that while the 1921 Act provides immunity to witnesses, it omits to confer it on members of the tribunal or lawyers for anything said by them in the course of the tribunal.[16]

Tribunals and other forms of inquiry

Tribunals must be established by legislation, which will set out the powers of the tribunal and the procedures that will be applied. Tribunals of inquiry are to be distinguished from rights tribunals. A rights tribunal is normally established by government to interpret and apply the law in order to make binding decisions on disputes between parties. Examples of such tribunals include the Labour Court, the Refugee Appeals Tribunal and the Valuation Tribunal. A tribunal of inquiry investigates a specific matter of public importance and submits a report to the Oireachtas setting out findings of fact.

The principal difference between tribunals of inquiry and other forms of inquiry such as non-statutory and committee inquiries is that tribunals are essentially inquisitorial in nature and there are no litigants.[17] Tribunals are not involved in the administration of justice and cannot determine civil or criminal liability.[18] Also, unlike a statutory inquiry, a tribunal of inquiry is a public affair. Nonetheless, the danger of witnesses becoming the accused has led to several legal challenges in Ireland during the course of tribunals of inquiry and has also caused problems for inquiries by parliamentary committees, as seen in the Abbeylara case (see above). Taken as a whole, these inquiries have significantly altered the public perception of accountability and its provision in Irish political life. Table 6.1 sets out the

---

[15] Corcoran, M. P. and White, A. (2000) 'Irish Democracy and the Tribunals of Inquiry' in E. Slater and M. Peillon (eds) *Memories of the Present: a Sociological Chronicle of Ireland, 1997–1998*. Dublin: IPA, p. 186.

[16] O'Flaherty, H. (1975) 'Tribunals and tribulations', *Irish Press*, 18 July, 9.

[17] Public Accounts Committee (2001) *Sub-Committee on Certain Revenue Matters: Parliamentary Inquiry into D.I.R.T. – Final Report Vol. 1*. Dublin, p. 105.

[18] Law Reform Commission (2005) *Report on Public Inquiries including Tribunals of Inquiry*. Dublin, p. 15.

Table 6.1: Principal features of various methods of inquiry

	Features	Powers	Personnel	Examples
Tribunal of inquiry	Established by Houses of the Oireachtas (on the government's request) but independent of both legislature and executive	Can compel witnesses, presents findings to parliament, refers matters to courts for legal action	Although not required to be, normally chaired by a judicial figure	Beef, McCracken, Moriarty, Flood/Mahon, Finlay, Lindsay, Barr, Morris
Statutory inquiry/commission	Established by government, specific legislation required, publishes report to general public and not parliament	Similar to court, discovery of documents, compellability and privilege of witnesses, sits in private	Chaired by judicial figure	Laffoy Commission* (child abuse)
Non-statutory inquiry	Established by government	No power to compel witnesses, discover documents, etc.	Chaired by judicial figure	Kilkenny Incest Inquiry, Dunne/Madden Inquiry (illegal organ retention**), Murphy Inquiry (handling of child sex abuse), Clarke Inquiry (events at Lourdes Hospital)

Type	Establishment	Powers	Chaired by	Examples
Commission of investigation	Established by government following recommendation of minister, requires consent of Oireachtas		Chaired by judicial figure***	Garda investigation into 1974 Dublin & Monaghan bombings
High Court inspector (under Companies Acts 1963, 1990 and Merchant Shipping Acts)	Established by High Court on minister's request	Inspects documents, subpoenas and questions witnesses	Inspector	National Irish Bank (overcharging of customers), Ansbacher (tax evasion)
Parliamentary committee inquiry	Established by parliament (on government's request)	Can compel persons, papers, records; recommends only	Members of parliament	DIRT Inquiry, Abbeylara Inquiry
Court of law	Independent of legislature and executive	Can impose custodial sentence	Judge	Ordinary judicial processes

* The Laffoy Commission was originally non-statutory but legislation was passed in 2000 to put it on a statutory footing.

** The Dunne Inquiry was established in February 2000 to consider the issue of body organ retention in various hospitals. It was initially intended to last for six months; this was subsequently extended to eighteen months. However, after several deadlines for presenting a report had been missed and with costs reaching almost €11 million, the government requested a report from the chairperson in early 2005. For legal reasons it could not be published and a new chairperson was appointed in 2005 to bring the inquiry to completion.

*** Unlike tribunals of inquiry, commissions of investigation will be chaired by senior barristers rather than judges.

principal features of the various forms of inquiry currently used in Ireland.

Tribunals prior to 1991

Until the establishment of the Hamilton Tribunal on the beef industry in 1991, tribunals had been established intermittently to investigate matters of economic importance or specific public disasters that had little political background.[19] As Table 6.2 shows, in each decade prior to 1990 there were rarely more than two or three tribunals established. Tribunals of inquiry to investigate allegations of malpractice in politics were not unusual; three were established in the mid to late 1940s.

In 1944, Fianna Fáil minister Seán Lemass TD was accused of selling shares in a railway company on the eve of a Transport Bill that would decrease the value of the shares. Two years later, in 1946, a parliamentary secretary was found guilty of tax fraud and later that year Lemass again came under fire concerning alleged improper authorisation during the sale of Locke's whiskey distillery to non-national businessmen. A tribunal of inquiry was the vehicle used to investigate each of these matters, which did not result in prosecutions or findings of corruption. Also, unlike later tribunals investigating allegations of corruption, those of the mid-1940s sat for a very short period and came to their conclusions relatively quickly. However, three tribunals of inquiry in a row tainted the Fianna Fáil government, and Manning argues that the 'whiff of corruption' played a part in the ending of the party's sixteen-year period in power in 1948.[20]

As Corcoran and White note, what sets post-1991 tribunals apart from their predecessors is the focus on the internal workings of state agencies and government.[21] However, tribunals have also challenged the role and activities of politicians and political parties, including the manner in which their activities are financed. While they were

---

[19] O'Flaherty, H. (1975) 'Tribunals and tribulations', *Irish Press*, 18 July, 9; O'Halpin, E. (2000) '"Ah, they've given us a good bit of stuff ...": Tribunals and Irish Political Life at the Turn of the Century', *Irish Political Studies* Vol. 15, 184.

[20] Manning, M. (1972) *Irish Political Parties: an Introduction*. Dublin: Gill & Macmillan, p. 49.

[21] Corcoran, M. P. and White, A. (2000) 'Irish Democracy and the Tribunals of Inquiry' in E. Slater and M. Peillon (eds) *Memories of the Present: a Sociological Chronicle of Ireland, 1997–1998*. Dublin: IPA, p. 189.

Table 6.2: Tribunals of inquiry prior to 1991

Year	Title	Matter investigated
1928	Prices	Cost of goods in Irish Free State
1930	Marketing of Butter	Cost of butter in Irish Free State
1930	Free State, Ports and Harbours	Ports and harbours
1936	Pearse Street Fire	Fire in Dublin's Pearse Street
1938	Local Government	Town planning
1943	Fire at St Joseph's Orphanage	Fire in orphanage
1944	Great Southern Railways Stocks	Alleged improper leaking of government information
1946	Ward	Alleged tax irregularity by parliamentary secretary to Minister for Health
1947	Locke's Distillery	Alleged political collaboration in sale of distillery
1959	Cross-Channel Freight Rates	Cost of shipping transport
1968	Teachers' Salaries	Teachers' salaries
1968	Liam O'Mahony	Death of man in Garda custody
1970	Illegal Moneylending	Illegal moneylending in Dublin
1975	Minister for Local Government*	Alleged improper payments by Minister for Local Government
1979	Whiddy Island Oil	Fire at oil depot
1981	Stardust	Deaths resulting from nightclub fire
1985	Kerry Babies	Suspicious death of infants

* This tribunal was unusual in that the allegations, made by two members of the opposition, were withdrawn before the tribunal was established yet it went ahead. No action was taken against the minister involved.

not originally intended to do so, tribunals have necessitated detailed scrutiny of the institutions of state through which decisions are formulated, and have resulted in the creation of a range of new oversight mechanisms. Indeed, the Beef Tribunal's proceedings (see below) saw one of the core institutions of government – collective cabinet confidentiality and its *raison d'être* – coming under scrutiny in the Supreme Court.[22] Tribunals have become a habitual feature of contemporary Irish political life and have important responsibilities. In a Supreme Court challenge to the work of the Flood Tribunal

---

[22] Hogan, G. (1993) 'The Cabinet Confidentiality Case of 1992', *Irish Political Studies* Vol. 8, 131–7.

(see below), the Court suggested that tribunals also have a function in relation to 'matters of urgent public importance *when inquiries are necessary to preserve the purity and integrity of public life*'.[23] However, as the government (via parliament) appoints them, tribunals exist in a nebulous position between two of the three pillars of state – the judiciary and the legislature.

We examine here six tribunals of inquiry that have been conducted since 1991. Three are concerned with administrative oversight and three with the activities of politicians and political actors.[24] Table 6.3 sets out chronologically these six tribunals and their subject matter. What is striking is that in most cases the media were responsible for bringing the relevant issue to light; this shows the importance of external or non-parliamentary mechanisms of accountability in Irish political life. As will be detailed below, despite the very political nature of many of the issues, Dáil Éireann was not equipped to deal with them.

The tribunals concerned with administrative oversight and accountability are the Beef, Finlay and Lindsay Inquiries. At the core of these investigations, the failure of parliament to provide adequate oversight of aspects of the executive apparatus and the consequences of this are revealed. The tribunals concerned with actors in the political sphere are the McCracken, Flood and Moriarty Inquiries. Again, the inability of parliament to perform one of its key functions, that of regulating political life in the state, is exposed. In short, all the tribunals to be examined here have a common underlying theme – they are concerned with issues that, theoretically at least, could and should be dealt with by the legislature. Why Dáil Éireann was incapable of precluding the issues that created the necessity for tribunals, or dealing with them as the problems came to light, is inextricably linked to the parliamentary mechanisms of oversight detailed in the previous chapters.

Background to the re-emergence of tribunals of inquiry

Many of the incidents under investigation by contemporary tribunals of inquiry occurred during the 1980s, a period of significant social

---

[23] McGrath, D. (1999) 'Review of Moriarty and Flood Tribunals, to date', *Bar Review* Vol. 4(5), 234 (emphasis in original).

[24] The Law Reform Commission's *Report on Public Inquiries* argued that tribunals can be divided into three categories – general inquiries that consider system failures, specific inquiries that consider allegations against individuals or organisations, and mixed inquiries that consider both elements.

Table 6.3: Selected tribunals of inquiry 1991–2005

Name	Period	Subject under investigation	Outcome	How issue came to light
Beef Tribunal	1991–94	Export procedures (and indirectly the relationship between government members and business interests)	Fall of 1989–92 FF/PD government, EU sanctions, minor charges against some workers in industry but none against political/public figures	TV documentary, parliamentary questions (PQs)
McCracken Tribunal	1997	Payments from a leading business-man to politicians	No prosecutions, Moriarty Tribunal	Private litigation, subsequent investigation by government/ Dunne family
Finlay Tribunal	1996–97	Malpractice in executive agency	Redress and compensation for victims	Media reports, lobbying by in-terest groups
Moriarty Tribunal	1997–?	Payments to politicians, illegal offshore accounts	Ongoing, no prosecutions to date	Media investi-gation, McCracken Tribunal
Flood Tribunal	1997–?	Rezoning deci-sions, political interference in planning process, payments to politicians	Ongoing, second interim report found politician guilty of corruption, no prosecutions to date	Media investi-gation, legal action by individuals, PQs
Lindsay Tribunal	1999–2002	Malpractice in executive agency	Redress and compensation for victims	Finlay Tribunal, lobbying by interest groups

and economic malaise in Ireland. In the early part of that decade, several scandals unfolded around Fianna Fáil governments led by Charles Haughey. Haughey had entered political life along with a cadre of young Fianna Fáil TDs in the late 1950s and early 1960s, and had quickly risen to the upper echelons of the party. These 'young Turks' gradually replaced the older generation of politicians who had been pivotal to the state's foundation and who showed a clear commitment to integrity in public life. Among the new Fianna Fáil TDs were some 'who had fewer scruples, particularly about how funds were to be raised for the party'.[25]

As Sinnott points out, Haughey's accumulation of personal wealth during this period led many to believe that public office had been used for personal gain.[26] Furthermore, Fianna Fáil became associated with a 'golden circle' of wealthy businessmen whose values began to infuse those of the state's political elite. The party's funding by private business interests continued while it was in opposition from 1982 to 1987. In fact, in the weeks before the 1987 general election campaign, Fianna Fáil received over IR£100,000 from three leading Irish meat processing companies, including IR£50,000 from one, Goodman International. Goodman's donation amounted to approximately 10 per cent of Fianna Fáil's party headquarters spending during that campaign.[27] The relationship between Goodman and certain political actors, particularly in Fianna Fáil, came under greater scrutiny when it was revealed that his private jet was kept at Baldonnell military airport – a state-owned facility.

'Golden circles' and state-sponsored bodies

In the early 1990s, suspicions of favouritism and public unease with the integrity of elected officials were aroused following a series of media revelations concerning state-sponsored bodies and commercial businesses in Ireland. These revelations deepened the public perception that 'golden circles' existed in Irish politics between certain politicians and private interests. It is worth mentioning a few of these scandals in order to show the context in which the first tribunal of inquiry was established.

In 1991 it transpired that a group of managers in the recently privatised Irish Sugar Company had been involved in selling shares (at a large profit) to the company itself. These shares had originally been acquired using the Irish Sugar Company's money. Also that year, the state-owned telephone company, Telecom Éireann,

---

[25] FitzGerald, G. (2003) *Reflections on the Irish State*. Dublin: Irish Academic Press, p. 72.

[26] Sinnott, R. (1995) *Irish Voters Decide*. Manchester: Manchester University Press, p. 39.

[27] Collins, N. and O'Raghallaigh C. (1994) 'Political Sleaze in the Republic of Ireland', *Parliamentary Affairs* Vol. 48(4), 707.

purchased a building from a property company that had close links with Telecom's chairman. There was further public disquiet over the purchase of land by a state-funded university at an inflated price: the beneficiary was rumoured to be a close friend of Taoiseach Charles Haughey, and had purchased the land only months previously. Finally, it was revealed that sensitive information concerning a state-owned helicopter company was acquired by a rival, privately owned helicopter company owned by Haughey's son.[28]

Investigations into some of these matters were established using High Court inspectors, as provided for under the 1963 Companies Act. No political resignations ensued. This series of events contributed to public cynicism towards politics, fuelled demands for investigation of a decision-making process that appeared to favour well-placed and wealthy interests, and caused great unease among the Fianna Fáil/Progressive Democrat coalition government, particularly the junior partner. As discussed above, the party had been established on a platform that included increasing transparency and accountability in political life.

Tribunals and administrative oversight

As noted above, three tribunals that published final reports during the 1990s had at their core the issue of administrative structures and the processes of accountability within them. The first tribunal to be considered in detail here is one that still resonates in Irish politics and was a catalyst for subsequent inquiries. The Hamilton Inquiry into the Beef Processing Industry was concerned not only with administrative accountability but also with improper links between politicians and businessmen, as well as the wider issue of political party funding. It provided the first clear link between weak parliamentary oversight mechanisms and the need for tribunals of inquiry.

Hamilton Inquiry into the Beef Processing Industry

In May 1991, an ITV *World in Action* investigative documentary televised evidence of widespread malpractice in the issuing of export credit guarantees[29] and the illegal classification of meat in the Irish beef

---

[28]   Collins, N. and O'Shea, M. (2000) *Understanding Corruption in Irish Politics.* Cork: Cork University Press, pp. 33–5.

[29]   The state granted export credit insurance to Irish companies that feared default by foreign states on payment of goods. Its purpose was to stimulate the export trade.

processing industry. It also alleged that Albert Reynolds, as Minister for Industry and Commerce, had ignored official advice[30] and awarded a substantial share of export credit insurance to a company owned by a prominent financial supporter of his party, Larry Goodman; and that Goodman International was involved in massive tax fraud schemes, which were possible because it had 'the right connections in the right places'.[31] The company's subsidiary processing plants were accused of being engaged in falsification of documents. Even more surprising was the claim that in 1990, as Goodman International faced liquidation due to its inability to repay loans, the then Taoiseach, Charles Haughey, recalled the cabinet from its summer recess to discuss legislation that would aid the company.[32]

These were particularly serious allegations given that the meat processing industry was one of the most important sectors in the state's ailing economy[33] (in fact, the final report of the Beef Tribunal estimated the beef processing industry to be worth approximately 10.5 per cent of Ireland's GDP).[34] The outcome of this documentary was the establishment of a tribunal of inquiry by the coalition government.

The question of why a Fianna Fáil-led government would agree to the establishment of a tribunal that would investigate its own party members must be addressed. In an interview with this author, former Progressive Democrat TD and party leader Desmond O'Malley pointed out that:

> The tribunal was only set up in '91, not as a result of parliamentary pressure or accountability to parliament or anything like that. That tribunal was set up, simply and solely the proximate reason for it was a television programme made by Granada Television in Britain, *World in Action*.[35]

Indeed, the revelations by the documentary caused a public outcry that forced the junior partner in government, the Progressive Democrats, to insist that Fianna Fáil agree to the establishment of the tribunal of inquiry to investigate the matter. The party had split from

---

[30] The Insurance Corporation of Ireland had warned that providing cover for exports to Iraq was too risky.

[31] Hamilton, L. (1994) *Report of the Tribunal of Inquiry into the Beef Processing Industry*. Dublin: Stationery Office, p. 23.

[32] Ibid., p. 361.

[33] O'Toole, F. (1995) *Meanwhile, Back at the Ranch*. London: Vintage, pp. 20–1.

[34] Hamilton, L. (1994) *Report of the Tribunal of Inquiry into the Beef Processing Industry*. Dublin: Stationery Office, p. 31.

[35] Interview with Desmond O'Malley, 20 June 2003.

Fianna Fail only six years earlier, and with its commitment to transparency in politics had styled itself the 'honest broker' in the coalition government. It is arguable whether or not the tribunal would have been established had Fianna Fáil been in single-party government. Indeed, during the Dáil motion to establish the tribunal, the opposition leader, Fine Gael's John Bruton, argued that the Taoiseach, Charles Haughey TD, 'had to be dragged screaming to the decision to appoint a judicial inquiry'.[36] However, after the series of scandals concerning semi-state bodies during early 1991 (see above), the government was faced with little choice but to take action. In fact, the decision to establish the tribunal was only confirmed by the Fianna Fáil Minister for Agriculture and Food, Michael O'Kennedy, at the end of a speech during which he down-played the significance of the *World in Action* revelations.[37]

This tribunal, chaired by Chief Justice Liam Hamilton, sat for over two years and, as legal bills kept coming in, cost over IR£19.5 million by 2000.[38] It uncovered widespread abuse of the EU agriculture sub-sidy scheme and resulted in Irish government paying substantial fines to the European Commission. Indeed, the issue of costs has plagued subsequent tribunals, and the large fees commanded by legal repre-sentatives, for which the taxpayer is liable, have been a constant source of public unease. As recently as June 2003, independent socialist Joe Higgins TD noted in the Dáil that the work of the tribunals had moved 'from millionaires being investigated … to the creation of new millionaires'.[39] In July 2004 the government finally responded by proposing a new schedule of fees for sitting and future tribunals, which in some cases envisaged a 40 per cent decrease in barristers' fees.

The terms of reference of the Beef Tribunal were very broad and resulted in the tribunal taking a considerable period of time to con-duct its preliminary investigations. Part of the motion passed by both Houses establishing the tribunal requested it to inquire into:

> allegations regarding illegal activities, fraud and malpractice in and in connection with the beef processing industry made or referred to … in Dáil Éireann.[40]

This engendered a considerable trawl by the tribunal through the official parliamentary report to identify all allegations made concerning

---

[36] *Dáil Debates*, 24 May 1991, Vol. 408, Col. 2435.
[37] Ibid., 15 May 1991, Vol. 408, Cols 1213–25.
[38] Cullen, P. (2002) *With a Little Help from my Friends*. Dublin: Gill & Macmillan, p. 139.
[39] *Dáil Debates*, 24 June 2003, Vol. 569, Col. 323.
[40] Ibid., 24 May 1991, Vol. 408, Col. 2423.

Goodman International. Subsequent tribunals learned from this costly experience, and prepared preliminary reports as well as more specific terms of reference for their inquiries.

The failure of parliamentary questions

In relation to Dáil Éireann, ministers' disregard for parliamentary procedure and PQs was one of the most significant revelations of the tribunal. In a now famous statement that has been used to emphasise the failure of formal parliamentary mechanisms of accountability, Chief Justice Hamilton claimed at the Beef Tribunal that:

> I think that if the questions that were asked in the Dáil were answered in the way they are answered here, there would be no necessity for this inquiry and an awful lot of money and time would have been saved.[41]

Desmond O'Malley recalled that:

> One of the more significant things to come out of the Beef Tribunal was that a senior official in the Department of Industry and Commerce wrote on a file words of congratulations to a more junior official for 'having successfully confused the deputy'. I thought that was pretty appalling.[42]

As far back as April 1989, opposition deputies had attempted to question the Minister for Agriculture and Food, Michael O'Kennedy TD, about the granting of export credit insurance to Irish beef companies. The minister answered evasively, as this example shows:

> **Mr Spring [Labour Party]:** Will the Minister confirm that in respect of one company, arising from an investigation carried out by the relevant authorities, bank guarantees to the order of approximately £18 million are being withheld by his Department for whom he is responsible since the end of the 1986 season, and that in the case of another company, again because of suspected irregularities, close on £40 million in bank guarantees have been withheld since the end of last season? What are the requirements that must be fulfilled before the guarantees withheld for more than two years are discharged?
>
> **Mr O'Kennedy [Fianna Fáil]:** I am sure the Deputy is well aware from his period in Government that it has been long established practice under successive Governments not to discuss the individual affairs of any company in this House. I propose to adhere to that long established practice which I assume the Deputy in his time in Government was aware of and may even have practised.[43]

---

[41] O'Toole, F. (1995) *Meanwhile, Back at the Ranch.* London: Vintage, p. 241.

[42] Interview with Desmond O'Malley, 20 June 2003.

[43] *Dáil Debates*, 26 April 1989, Vol. 389, Col. 339.

Later in the same Question Time period, the frustrations of the opposition in their attempts to elicit information were compounded by the Ceann Comhairle's refusal to allow further questions on the matter.

> **An Ceann Comhairle:** Question No. 12. If you want to debate this matter you had better find another time. Question Time is not the appropriate time for it.
>
> **Mr Spring:** It is difficult to find another venue to debate it.[44]

The following month, again during Question Time, the issue of export credit insurance policies was raised with the Minister for Industry and Commerce, Ray Burke TD,[45] whose evasive answers drew the opposition's ire.

> **Mr D. O'Malley:** Would it not be better for the Minister to answer the questions he was asked?
>
> **Mr R. Burke:** Somebody said it was only for one day but I do not think Deputy O'Malley would be small enough to cast a man aside and have it all under his umbrella for the one day.
>
> **Mr D. O'Malley:** The Minister is only drawing attention to the fact that he is refusing to answer the questions.
>
> **An Ceann Comhairle:** Time for priority questions is exhausted and I am proceeding to deal with other questions. No. 10, please.
>
> **Mr R. Burke:** The Deputy put down 24 questions and every one of them has been answered straight. He is not getting the answers he wants – that is what is wrong with him.
>
> **Mr D. O'Malley:** I am getting plenty of information.[46]

The Progressive Democrat TD Desmond O'Malley was one of the principal figures in addressing the issue of the abuse of the export credit scheme. During the week following the above exchange, he complained during an adjournment debate on beef exports to Iraq that:

> I cannot elicit all the necessary information in this matter tonight, nor, I think, can Dáil Éireann, given its procedures, ever elicit all the necessary information. The Government have shown over the last month or so how reticent they are in giving information and how it has to be dragged out of them, even in very limited quantities. It is evident that some form of independent inquiry is required in the public interest.[47]

---

44 Ibid., Col. 343.
45 Raphael (Ray) Burke was later to become the first politician in the state's history to be accused of corruption by a tribunal (see below).
46 *Dáil Debates*, 3 May 1989, Vol. 389, Cols 1054–5.
47 Ibid., 10 May 1989, Vol. 389, Col. 2841.

In a written response to a PQ on the issue, the Minister for Industry and Commerce again did not reveal any substantive information when asked about an investigation by his department into export insurance on beef to Iraq. He stated in a response to a written PQ that:

> As I indicated in reply to Questions Nos. 59 of 20 April 1989 and 53 of 27 April 1989, the investigation referred to by the Deputy is being carried out by my Department in consultation with the Central Statistics Office, the Insurance Corporation of Ireland, plc, the Department of Agriculture and the exporters. The investigation is necessarily of a complex nature involving considerable documentation. While the matter is receiving priority attention and a considerable amount of work has been done, it is also essential that the investigation be thorough and comprehensive in every respect. Accordingly, I am not in a position to indicate when the investigation will be completed.[48]

The above passages reveal the inadequacy of the principal tool at the disposal of the opposition for scrutinising government – the parliamentary question in both oral and written formats. However, following the general election of 1989, the Progressive Democrats unexpectedly formed a coalition government with Fianna Fáil, which kept the latter party in power. Significantly, one of the principal figures in questioning the government over the issue of export credit insurance, Desmond O'Malley TD, became Minister for Industry and Commerce, whose remit included the administration of the export credit insurance. In an interview with this author, O'Malley noted that once he assumed his portfolio he was able to confirm his suspicions that non-Irish beef was being sold as Irish, a fact that the tribunal also uncovered. However, even he was later accused of being evasive with answers to PQs.

In November 1989, Mr O'Malley as newly installed Minister for Industry and Commerce was questioned by the opposition on whether or not favouritism had occurred in the awarding of export credit insurance to certain firms. His replies drew criticism from the opposition benches.

> **Mr Rabbitte [Workers Party]:** On 10 May the Minister said that the scale of the abuse was, in its potential to the State, unprecedented. I should like to know if the Minister stands over the statement he made then, that this state of affairs was due to governmental and ministerial intervention.
>
> **Mr O'Malley [Progressive Democrats]:** On 10 May 'the Minister' did not say; 'Deputy O'Malley' said, and that is a different matter. I have already dealt with the other matters. I cannot go into historical facts.

---

48 Ibid., Vol. 390, Col. 2041.

I have expressed my view on the quantity of cover that was given and the circumstances in which it was given.

Mr Taylor [Labour Party]: The Deputy's view changes depending on whether he is a Minister or not.[49]

Over a year later, the issue of which firms received export credit insurance and how much each was given still had not been resolved. The Gulf War had caused Iraq to default on payments, leaving the Irish exchequer at a substantial loss as companies claimed the insurance provided for such situations. During the course of the inquiry, the tribunal discovered that ministers had misled the Dáil when they claimed no knowledge of incidents that subsequent evidence proved they were in fact aware of. It also uncovered evidence of several cases of abuse of public and EU funds. Arguably the most indefensible decision by the government was to provide insurance cover for exports by a private company to a war zone (Iraq at the time had been engaged in a war with Iran). Also, as noted above, much of the beef exported was not in fact Irish, but drawn from EU intervention stocks. As the beef was presented for export as Irish, it allowed the processors to benefit from generous EU subsidies.

O'Malley later recalled one of the occasions when he raised the issue during an adjournment debate in the Dáil with the Minister for Industry and Commerce, Fianna Fáil's Ray Burke TD:

> The export figures as disclosed by the CSO didn't at all tally with the export credit insurance figures which were about three times higher than the amount of beef that we had exported to Iraq. I queried why this was and I speculated on some possible explanations for it … and I got a torrent of abuse from Ray Burke who was then Minister for Industry and Commerce. To my mind, it kind of epitomises the abuse of parliament in a sense because there were blatant lies told that night. Burke knew exactly what was going on because an inquiry had started in the department to try and reconcile these figures. And the preliminary indications were that they weren't reconcilable and that there was something very serious afoot and that the most likely explanation was that it was the use of non-Irish beef which, in fact turned out to be the case.[50]

During the debate in question, Burke told the House:

> The records of the House will show that since March last 24 questions have been asked concerning the operation of the export credit insurance and finance schemes. In all cases I have answered the questions as thoroughly and as accurately as possible and again the records of the House will clearly demonstrate this … almost every

---

49   Ibid., 1 November 1989, Vol. 392, Cols 1014–15.
50   Interview with Desmond O'Malley, 20 June 2003.

conceivable question has been asked and answered fully. What has come out tonight is nothing new from Deputy O'Malley. It is merely a rehash of the position and personal abuse in relation to the Government and in relation to one company. I must say I am surprised at the continuation of these reckless charges from Deputy O'Malley. One thing that came out loud and clear is that the country should really want to know and be aware of the fact that Deputy O'Malley is out to get the Goodman Group.[51]

The tribunal's proceedings drew public attention to the inefficiency of parliamentary questions and debates, but no action was taken to improve the situation. Indeed, during the tribunal's evidence-taking, Burke, on being accused of being evasive in his answering of parliamentary questions prior to the inquiry, replied:

If the other side don't ask the right questions, they don't get the right answers. And it's not for me to lead them as to where they figure they want to go.[52]

Legal challenges to the jurisdiction of tribunals

The terms of reference of the Beef Tribunal were shaped by the recommendations of the Salmon Commission (see above), including the extension of privilege to all legal teams present. Nonetheless, lawyers for Larry Goodman applied for judicial review of the tribunal's powers on no fewer than seven occasions during the sittings. While the content of these cases is not relevant here, they resulted in a significant expansion to the case law relating to tribunals of inquiry. A later report by the Office of the Attorney-General on the outcome of these legal challenges revealed, for example, that:

- tribunals could sit in private as required
- tribunals did not encroach on the judicial domain as specified in the Constitution
- tribunals did not interfere with the administration of justice in civil matters.[53]

Cabinet confidentiality

During the course of the inquiry, Justice Hamilton requested that the cabinet minutes of 21 October 1988 be revealed to the tribunal. This was the date on which the decision to provide Goodman International with export credit insurance was taken. The Attorney-General

---

[51] *Dáil Debates*, 10 May 1989, Vol. 389, Col. 2043.
[52] O'Toole, F. (1995) *Meanwhile, Back at the Ranch*. London: Vintage, p. 256.
[53] Office of the Attorney General (2000) *Comparative Study of Tribunals of Inquiry and Parliamentary Inquiries*. Dublin: Stationery Office, p. 11.

immediately challenged this request in the High Court. For the first time in the state's history, the issue of cabinet confidentiality and its importance for the functioning of the administration came under scrutiny. During the High Court appeal, the Attorney-General's request was dismissed on the grounds that the public interest was served better by disclosure of the minutes.[54]

On appeal to the Supreme Court, however, it was decided that while the government was accountable to parliament for decisions taken at cabinet, it was not required to disclose cabinet discussions.[55] The majority verdict also ruled that the tribunals were not discharging judicial powers and were simply an instrument of the Oireachtas.[56] The Supreme Court decision was somewhat excessive, as it gave the doctrine of cabinet confidentiality an 'unexpected force and vibrancy'.[57] It was put to the people in a referendum in 1997.[58]

The seventeenth amendment to the Constitution rolled back the Supreme Court decision by permitting disclosure of such minutes in certain extenuating circumstances. However, it did not grant such powers to either House of the Oireachtas, but to tribunals of inquiry. Dáil Éireann has no mechanism for obtaining such minutes. In effect, the amendment perpetuated the practice whereby cabinet deliberations remained closed to public access for a period of thirty years.

The Beef Tribunal report

Justice Hamilton's final report, published in 1994, met with mixed and predictably partisan reactions. By this stage, a coalition government consisting of Fianna Fáil and the Labour Party was in power. The Labour Party had been very active in pushing for the establishment of the tribunal and was committed to increasing transparency in the decision-making process. The Fianna Fáil members of government, and particularly their leader and Taoiseach, Albert Reynolds TD, feared that the report would severely damage the party. The Labour Party had threatened to leave government if Reynolds was censured in it.[59]

---

[54] *Attorney General* v. *Hamilton Ir* [1993] H.C. (1993) *Irish Reports*. High Court, Dublin. Vol. 2, p. 259.

[55] Ibid., pp. 259–304.

[56] Hogan, G. (1993) 'The Cabinet Confidentiality Case of 1992', *Irish Political Studies* Vol. 8, 136.

[57] Ibid., 131.

[58] The amendment was approved by 53 per cent.

[59] Duignan, S. (1996) *One Spin on the Merry-Go-Round.* Dublin: Blackwater Press, p. 112.

Controversy surrounded the release of the report from the Department of Agriculture to Fianna Fáil's legal advisers before their coalition partners could see it, and the Taoiseach's swift claim to have been 'vindicated' by its contents. In a subsequent memoir by an adviser to the Labour Party, the way in which Fianna Fáil handled the tribunal report's contents was identified as a contributory factor to the breakdown in trust and the subsequent downfall of the coalition government.[60] Such partisan interpretation of tribunal reports was also a feature of later tribunals. Much of the report's impact was lost, however, when the day set for its debate in the Dáil in September coincided with the announcement of an IRA ceasefire.

In the Dáil debate on the tribunal report, Desmond O'Malley TD returned to the failure of PQs and drew attention to the lack of parliamentary accountability in the Irish parliament in comparison to Westminster:

> Over the past 30 to 40 years, there have been numerous British ministerial resignations arising out of different and sometimes bizarre affairs, but frequently the proximate cause of the resignation was not the personal misconduct of individual Ministers but the fact that they misled the House of Commons. In this country misleading the House is the least culpable of aberrations. Certain Members and former Members of this House feel they can sleep easily in their beds tonight. They do not live in a country where in practice any real accountability to Parliament is widely demanded.
>
> Why is there no such real accountability? There is none because the development of our constitutional institutions over the past 70 years, and in particular over the past 30 years, has led to a growth in the undoubted primacy of the Government, some increase in the powers of the courts and a marked diminution in the standing of the only directly elected and popularly accountable institution, the Legislature.[61]

The report found evidence of tax evasion and fraudulent practices, but failed to draw conclusions about the wider issues of corruption, unregulated party funding and the failure of parliamentary mechanisms of accountability. Despite its accounts of meetings between Goodman and ministers, including the Taoiseach, which revealed Goodman's privileged access to the highest levels of power, it found that this did not influence the decisions of the cabinet members involved.[62] It also found no basis to allegations made by the

---

[60] Finlay, F. (1998) *Snakes and Ladders*. Dublin: New Island Books, pp. 232–6.

[61] *Dáil Debates*, 1 September 1994, Vol. 445, Cols 339–40.

[62] Hamilton, L. (1994) *Report of the Tribunal of Inquiry into the Beef Processing Industry*. Dublin: Stationery Office, pp. 358, 360.

then Workers Party TD Pat Rabbitte that Goodman benefited from advance knowledge of certain business issues as he was on the 'inside political track'.[63]

However, the accounts of those meetings by Goodman and the ministers at the tribunal seem to contradict other conclusions drawn by the tribunal's chair. On examining the evidence concerning a meeting of Goodman with the Minister for Industry and Commerce, Hamilton noted that:

> It is difficult to understand how nobody recollects the circumstances under which notice was given to the Minister for Industry and Commerce that the Goodman Group would be making an application for Export Credit Insurance in respect of the largest contract for the export of beef ever negotiated by an exporter within the State.[64]

Furthermore, none of the of the report's recommendations were concerned with parliamentary reform or regulating finances in public life; they focused instead on agricultural and beef production issues.[65] There were also some unstructured recommendations that the export credit insurance scheme should be more closely monitored.[66] The only state institution to be criticised was the Department of Agriculture for not having enough staff to oversee the work of the meat processing industry.[67]

The report was criticised from several quarters. In his autobiography, former Labour Party minister Barry Desmond, who had been prominent in asking PQs on the matter prior to the tribunal's establishment, referred to it as 'a sloppy piece of work'.[68] In interviews conducted by the present author it was referred to variously as 'a judicial disgrace' and 'a lousy report'.

Aftermath of the Beef Tribunal report

In the aftermath of the publication of the Beef Tribunal's report, former Fine Gael leader and Taoiseach, Garret FitzGerald, argued that the remit of the tribunal's investigation was so wide that its

---

[63] *Dáil Debates*, 28 August 1990, Vol. 401, Cols 2097–8.
[64] Hamilton, L. (1994) *Report of the Tribunal of Inquiry into the Beef Processing Industry*. Dublin: Stationery Office, p. 71.
[65] Ibid., pp. 703–17.
[66] Ibid., pp. 235–6.
[67] Ibid., pp. 477–8.
[68] Desmond, B. (2000) *Finally and in Conclusion*. Dublin: New Island, p. 336.

findings were too broad to trigger decisive action.[69] However, it was surprising that no prosecutions resulted from its work considering the range of fraudulent activities uncovered. There were mixed public reactions to the Beef Tribunal; in the aftermath of the report 41 per cent of people said that it was a bad thing that the tribunal had been held and 46 per cent were in favour.[70] In the same survey, 70 per cent of respondents claimed that they did not feel that people had a reasonable knowledge of what the findings of the tribunal were, while only 22 per cent said they did. Later, further revelations concerning donations from Larry Goodman to political figures emerged at another tribunal of inquiry (Moriarty – see below). The fact that this information was not discovered by the Beef Tribunal raises the question of how a fact-finding inquiry can ensure that it has received full information and can therefore be in a position to present an objective account of events.

For all the criticisms levelled at it, the Beef Tribunal was a watershed in Irish politics for many reasons. It was a catalyst for the introduction of legislation and codes of practice designed to regulate the finances of political parties and to provide state funding for parties. It was instrumental in the creation of the Ethics in Public Office Act in 1995 and the Freedom of Information Act in 1997. However, its financial cost led to criticism of tribunals as a method of inquiry. As a result, subsequent tribunals have had much more clearly defined terms of reference. In terms of the accountability of the executive, the Beef Tribunal represented a significant departure in the creation of alternative mechanisms of oversight. For the first time, the inner workings of government, from cabinet discussions to the meetings of the Taoiseach with business interests, had been revealed, in a manner that parliamentary procedures might never have achieved.

Tribunal of Inquiry into the Blood Transfusion Supply Board

As with the Beef Tribunal, poor administrative oversight and the inability of parliament to monitor the activity of an executive agency were core issues in two subsequent tribunals. The first of these, the Tribunal of Inquiry into the Blood Transfusion Supply Board

---

[69] FitzGerald, G. (1994) 'Paying too high a price for techniques of obfuscation', *Irish Times*, 13 August, 14.

[70] Marsh, M. and Wilford, R. (1995) 'Data Section for Republic of Ireland', *Irish Political Studies* Vol. 10, 286.

(the Finlay Tribunal), was established in October 1996 to inquire into a matter described as 'the greatest health scandal in the history of the state'[71] – the infection of Irish women with hepatitis C through the administration of a blood product known as anti-D in the late 1970s. The product was administered by the Blood Transfusion Supply Board (BTSB), a separate legal entity established in 1961 by the government and ultimately under the aegis of the Minister for Health. The series of events leading up to the tribunal are not relevant here; instead the principal details are focused on.

One of the issues at the heart of this tribunal, and which is common to Westminster-style parliaments elsewhere, is the accountability of state agencies such as the BTSB to parliament. State-sponsored bodies became increasingly common in Ireland during the 1960s as a political and legal device for providing a degree of operational autonomy and independence in the performance of certain executive functions. The accountability of such bodies to parliament became problematic when ministers refused to answer questions on their performance, particularly when reasons of 'commercial confidentiality' or 'professional autonomy' were cited as justification.[72] As noted in Chapter 4, a joint committee had been established in the Oireachtas in 1976 to oversee the work of commercial state-sponsored bodies, but no equivalent committee to investigate non-commercial bodies was ever established. In fact it was not until 1999 that the Dáil debated one of the joint committee's reports. The BTSB therefore provides a classic example of a non-commercial semi-state body operating free of parliamentary scrutiny, as well as the distance between the Dáil and the operation of elements of the public administration.

In the years before the establishment of the tribunal, and as details of the scandal emerged, successive governments were able to use the narrow doctrine of ministerial responsibility to insulate both themselves and the BTSB from parliamentary scrutiny. As the Beef Tribunal demonstrated, it was only when investigation of the matter became politically imperative that the government (this time led by

---

[71] Department of Health (1997) *Report on behalf of the Government by Brian Cowen T.D., Minister of Health and Children on the Legal Strategy adopted by the Defence in the Case of the Late Mrs Bridget McCole.* Dublin: Department of Health, p. 7.

[72] Farrell, A. M. (1997) *The State and the Policy Process. A Case Study of Viral Contamination in Ireland: the Hepatitis C/Anti-D Episode: 1976–1997* (unpublished MA thesis). Department of Politics, University College Dublin, p. 40.

Fine Gael[73]) decided to act and establish a public inquiry into the matter. However, in light of the experience of the Beef Tribunal, the coalition government was reluctant to give the tribunal too much scope, and its terms of reference were strictly defined.

In the parliamentary debates prior to the tribunal's establishment, opposition TDs accused the Minister for Health, Fine Gael's Michael Noonan TD, of not being accountable for the actions of services under his control. The minister rejected this, arguing that the opposition did not question the matter until it became politically expedient:

> If we are discussing accountability, I have a responsibility to provide answers to the House. However, the Deputies calling on me to be accountable have a responsibility to table questions.[74]

While formal methods of accountability such as PQs kept the government under pressure and the issue in the public eye, other mechanisms of scrutiny such as committee investigations were less successful. The Select Committee on Social Affairs requested the Chief State Solicitor to attend the committee to explain the legal strategy of the state in the McCole case (below). He refused to do so, but no penalty was incurred.

An initial report into the matter by the Attorney-General had been presented to the Minister for Health in January 1995, in which the BTSB was criticised and found to have been negligent. This left the state open to subsequent legal action. In response, the government established in April an ad hoc compensation tribunal that it hoped would deal with the issue, and continued to emphasise the BTSB's independence in an attempt to disavow its responsibility for the body. However, the death in October 1996 of Bridget McCole – a victim of hepatitis C and at the time of her demise involved in a legal case against the state over her infection – caused a public outcry and mobilised the media in pressurising the government to investigate the matter further. During a Dáil motion following the death of Mrs McCole, opposition deputies criticised what they said was the attempt by the government to insulate itself from questioning. For example, Progressive Democrat TD Liz O'Donnell argued that:

---

[73] Following the collapse of its coalition with Fianna Fáil in 1994, the Labour Party had crossed the floor of the House and formed a new coalition with Fine Gael and the small socialist Democratic Left party.

[74] *Dáil Debates*, 8 October 1996, Vol. 469, Col. 1655.

This débâcle has highlighted the impotence of Dáil Éireann as an inquiring body and as one which holds the Executive and its State agencies to account. This House has failed from the beginning to extract the truth. It is entitled to the truth in response to questions legitimately put in the public interest. Because the State was a defendant – and it seems it is still one – this House will not extract the truth. The truth in so far as we know it, the fact that the board has admitted liability, has only come out because of a court action. It highlights yet again how this House has no role and has been denied one in extracting the truth in public affairs.

This Government which came into office on the wreckage of an Administration which fell because of a lack of openness and accountability has used the same tactics in all the debates in the House in seeking to avoid the truth.[75]

The issue was extremely sensitive and politically charged, and became even more so following the death of Mrs McCole. The Rainbow Coalition government was left with little choice but to concede to the opposition's demand for an independent tribunal of inquiry. A motion to establish the tribunal was passed by both Houses of the Oireachtas on 17 October 1996.

The tribunal that was established, chaired by Justice Thomas Finlay, was given more limited terms of reference than the Beef Tribunal, and was not required to investigate allegations made in Dáil Éireann concerning the culpability of government in the matter. During its proceedings, it uncovered serious operational malpractice in the BTSB as well as a lack of accountability and supervision of its work by the Department of Health.[76] It published a succinct and technical report in March 1997, which included recommendations for several restructuring changes to that body and also to the Irish Medicines Board.[77] However, somewhat confusingly, while the report criticised the Department of Health, it found that ministers had taken 'adequate and appropriate' action in many areas when the extent of the problem became clear.[78]

Unlike the findings of the Beef Tribunal report, which the Fianna Fáil-led government used as justification that its senior members were innocent of any wrongdoing, the Finlay Tribunal report and its recommendations were completely accepted by the Rainbow

---

[75] Ibid., 3 October 1996, Vol. 469, Col. 1400.

[76] Finlay, T. (1997) *Report of the Tribunal of Inquiry into the Blood Transfusion Supply Board.* Dublin: Stationery Office, p. 104.

[77] Ibid., pp. 143–6.

[78] Ibid., p. 151.

Coalition. As part of this, the ad hoc compensation tribunal was put on a statutory footing. Furthermore, having vigorously resisted financial liability, the government accepted full liability for damages caused.[79] The speed with which the tribunal completed its inquiry (six months) demonstrated the benefit of clear terms of reference and the availability of a preliminary report before the taking of evidence, the lack of which had been identified as a reason for the slow pace of the Beef Tribunal.

However, in the parliamentary debate subsequent to the Finlay Tribunal's report, the Fianna Fáil opposition spokesperson on Health, Brian Cowen TD, severely criticised what he viewed as the tribunal's limited terms of reference, which, he argued, had prevented it from identifying that the minister had avoided his accountability to the Dáil:

> The terms of reference of the tribunal circumscribed the ability of Mr Justice Finlay to make any comment on issues relating to political accountability in this House or the primary responsibility of Ministers for Health to answer this House for the way they carried out their responsibilities during their tenure of office throughout this crisis.[80]

Adopting a similar view of open government, Progressive Democrat TD Liz O'Donnell queried the need for a tribunal of inquiry to investigate the matter. She again challenged the Minister for Health as to why Dáil Éireann had not been capable of dealing with the matter:

> Why was this information revealed in a tribunal as distinct from Dáil Éireann? The answer is that the Dáil failed because it was misled by Ministers who, in turn, were misled by State authorities. The Dáil failed in one of its primary functions, to hold the Government of the day accountable for its stewardship of State authorities, and that is very dangerous.[81]

As with later tribunal reports, it was clear that the executive could insulate itself from a potentially damaging tribunal by using its parliamentary majority to limit the terms of reference. It can also be argued that tribunals provide a buffer between ministers and the matter under investigation and deflect the accountability of the executive to parliament. Notwithstanding the devolution of issues of administrative scrutiny to tribunals of inquiry, only the Dáil can ultimately enforce ministerial responsibility.

---

[79] *Dáil Debates,* 20 March 1997, Vol. 476, Col. 1222.
[80] Ibid., Col. 1230.
[81] Ibid., Col. 1261.

Lindsay Tribunal

The final tribunal of inquiry concerned with the issue of administrative oversight to be considered here produced its final report in 2002, having been established in 1999. As with the Finlay Tribunal, the Lindsay Tribunal was concerned with the infection of persons through the use of blood products. The victims in this case were haemophiliacs, and were infected not just with hepatitis C but also with HIV.

The Irish Haemophiliac Society had walked out during the Finlay Tribunal's proceedings of 1996/7, protesting that its terms of reference did not include haemophiliacs infected with hepatitis C. This new tribunal of inquiry established by the newly elected Fianna Fáil/ Progressive Democrat government addressed its concerns. The Fianna Fáil 1997 general election manifesto had committed the party to initiating an investigation into the matter of HIV contamination of blood and blood products. Also, its programme for government included a commitment to implement the Finlay Tribunal's recommendations.

As with the Finlay Tribunal, the subject matter of the Lindsay Tribunal was politically very sensitive, not least because of the lives lost as a result of the maladministration. The decision by the coalition to resort to an extra-parliamentary mechanism of accountability again demonstrates the importance of multiple veto players within government for opening up the mechanics of the executive to better scrutiny (the Rainbow Coalition was responsible for the establishment of the McCracken Tribunal – see below). It appears less likely that a single-party government would have established an independent investigation. More specifically, it would have been reluctant to allow such a body to make a potentially critical judgement on an agency under its control or on the work of one of its ministers.

Among its terms of reference, the Lindsay Tribunal was requested to investigate:

> The adequacy and timeliness of the response of the Minister, the Department of Health and Children and other relevant persons in the State, when they became aware of the fact that there were infected persons.[82]

After more than two years of public sitting, the tribunal's final report was presented on 4 September 2002. It did not find fault with

---

[82] Lindsay, A. (2002) *Report of the Tribunal of Inquiry into the Infection with HIV and Hepatitis C of Persons with Haemophilia and Related Matters*. Dublin: Stationery Office, p. 17.

the Ministers for Health who had been in office during the period of the infections; instead, it found that when answering parliamentary questions on blood products they were 'simply putting on the record of the House information supplied ... by ... civil servants'.[83] However, the report did find that the Department of Health's supervision of the BTSB was 'lacking in a number of respects'.[84]

Following its publication, opposition deputies queried aspects of how the tribunal had conducted its business. For example, despite criticising it throughout the report, the tribunal never took evidence from the BTSB.[85] Opposition deputies also voiced their dissatisfaction with the lack of clear conclusions in the document, contrasting this with the second interim report of the Flood Tribunal (see below) which appeared later in September and unambiguously found that a former minister had acted corruptly. Fine Gael's Olivia Mitchell TD commented on the Lindsay Tribunal report:

> When I first saw the report, I, in common with everyone else, was appalled at the absence of clear and concise conclusions. On reading it, I realise it is not that there are no conclusions ... the conclusions, such as they were, were buried in the body of the report. The report is not well produced or laid out. The conclusions were difficult to find and very easy to miss.[86]

The Labour Party's Dr Mary Upton TD complained that:

> Conclusions are dispersed throughout the document and it is an exercise in perseverance to try to extract the concise findings. Furthermore, and more importantly, many questions still remain unanswered.

She also argued that:

> The softness of the report's language defies credibility. The report does not remotely attribute a reasonable level of responsibility or accountability. The terms used are frequently woolly and meaningless and warrant a degree of scepticism. I refer to terms such as 'steps should have been taken', 'should have been pursued with greater urgency', 'it might also be thought', 'regrettable', 'unsatisfactory' and 'a missed opportunity'. That is hardly the language of a robust tribunal attempting to establish straightforward facts when it was clear that 79 people died and many more continue to suffer. It is in stark contrast to the language used in the interim report of the Flood tribunal.[87]

---

[83] Ibid., p. 233.
[84] Ibid., p. 224.
[85] *Dáil Debates*, 23 October 2002, Vol. 556, Cols 129, 136.
[86] Ibid., Col. 123.
[87] Ibid., 6 November 2002, Vol. 556, Col. 975.

Even a member of the government coalition partners, the Progressive Democrats' Fiona O'Malley TD, spoke out against the lack of clarity in the report:

> I am glad of the opportunity to speak in this debate, but my appreciation does not extend to the report of the Lindsay tribunal itself ... The failure of Ms Justice Lindsay to apportion blame or responsibility is disappointing.[88]

The Minister for Health and Children undertook to implement the report's recommendations, including the creation of a body to be called the National Haemophilia Council. This council was eventually established in 2004. Among the principal functions envisaged for it was the provision for increased communications between service providers, and a sub-group of the council will monitor the procurement of blood products. The government submitted the tribunal's report to the Director of Public Prosecutions but, as with the Beef and Finlay Tribunals, no prosecutions have resulted.

The impact of tribunals on administrative oversight

None of the reports of the three tribunals considered above succeeded in gaining cross-party support. Instead, each raised questions concerning the use of tribunals as a method of ensuring the accountability of the state's administrative structures, and demonstrated the importance of establishing adequate terms of reference for such inquiries. However, the tribunals did have some success, particularly in increasing pressure on government to provide for more accountability within certain government departments and in the administration of public affairs. Indeed, the Beef and Finlay reports coincided with the processing of the Freedom of Information Bill in the Dáil (between 1994 and 1997), which increased the accountability and transparency of the decision-making process.

The reports also contributed to the pressure on government to create wider powers of investigation into public administration for the Oireachtas. For example, coupled with the recommendations in another tribunal (McCracken – see below), the government instituted the Houses of the Oireachtas (Compellability, Privileges and Immunities) Act, 1997. As Chapter 5 has detailed, this Act provided new powers to allow parliamentary committees to perform inquiries, including the ability to compel the attendance of witnesses.

At the taking of evidence in the DIRT Inquiry, the Secretary-General at the Department of Finance noted that the Finlay Tribunal's

---

[88] Ibid., Col. 970.

findings had led to a major upgrade of procedures, standards and equipment in the BTSB.[89] An interim report in 2004 by another tribunal of inquiry (the Morris Tribunal), established in 2002 to investigate complaints against Gardaí in County Donegal, has resulted in significant appraisal of the methods for overseeing police work in Ireland.[90] In this respect, it may be argued that the tribunals have had an impact on improving standards of accountability within various arms of the state administration that the Dáil on its own could not have brought about so quickly. However, tribunals do not increase the ability of the Lower House to hold the executive to account and, if anything, prevent the legislature from developing this capacity in its own right. This is particularly true in the matter of regulating the activities of actors within the state institutions, which are now considered.

Tribunals and political actors

The second cluster of tribunals to be examined is those concerned with the activities of politicians and political parties. A by-product of the local and clientelist nature of Irish politics has been a perception that public representatives and even the political parties have been open to influence by wealthy interests. This has frequently been blamed on a combination of the proportional electoral system (PR-STV) and intra-party competition in constituencies with between three and five seats. Carey and Shugart found that in electoral systems that produce intra-party competition, as the number of seats in a constituency grows, so does the value of personal reputation.[91]

Prior to the 1997 Electoral Act, the financial affairs of political actors were largely unregulated and certain public representatives were suspected of engaging in improper practices to fund increasingly expensive election campaigns. The disclosure at several tribunals of donations of large sums of money to political representatives as bribes, as well as revelations of favouritism in the decision-making process, fuelled these perceptions of corruption in the body politic.[92]

---

[89] Public Accounts Committee (2001) *Sub-Committee on Certain Revenue Matters: Parliamentary Inquiry into D.I.R.T. – Final Report, Vol. 3*. Dublin, p. 160.

[90] This 2005 Garda Síochána Act contains provision for a Garda Ombudsman Commission and a Garda Inspectorate to oversee the work of the police.

[91] Carey, J. M. and Shugart, M. S. (1995) 'Incentives to Cultivate a Personal Vote: a Rank Ordering of Electoral Formulas', *Electoral Studies* Vol. 14(4), 417–39.

[92] Collins, N. and O'Shea, M. (2000) *Understanding Corruption in Irish Politics*. Cork: Cork University Press, p. 26.

In his work on the US Congress, Thompson distinguishes between institutional and personal corruption.[93] He argues that the latter is a corrosive force whereby office holders use their positions for public gain, while the former is often an unavoidable consequence of political life, where representatives act in ways that do not involve personal enrichment. Institutional corruption for Thompson is evident in campaign funding, when parties or candidates promote the values or goals of their financial supporters – something the democratic process requires them to do as public representatives and legislators. This is a dilemma faced by politicians everywhere, and has resulted in many Western states passing ethics legislation to try to halt the merging of business interests with political ones. Ireland has recently had to face this challenge, and the tension between the two types of corruption described by Thompson is evident in many of the tribunals of inquiry.

The McCracken Tribunal (Dunnes Payments)

As a result of a family dispute within one of Ireland's leading retail business chains, Dunnes Stores, donations of large sums of cash to politicians by one member of the family, Ben Dunne, came to public attention. The family feud had come before the courts and an investigation into the financial affairs of Dunne revealed donations by him to figures from each of the three main political parties. The Dunne family and the government agreed in December 1996 to the appointment of an independent judicial figure to make a preliminary investigation into allegations of improper influencing of the decision-making process. The parties wished to see a report on these donations before deciding whether or not to take the matter further.

Judge John Buchanan completed this report and presented it to a sub-committee of the Dáil Committee on Procedure and Privileges early the following year.[94] The Rainbow Coalition government subsequently established the Dunnes Payments Tribunal with Justice Brian McCracken as the sole member.[95] The coalition government partners had made a commitment to improving integrity in public life and in his inaugural parliamentary speech the new Taoiseach, Fine Gael's John Bruton TD, committed the government to

---

[93] Thompson, D. F. (1995) *Ethics in Congress.* Washington, DC: The Brookings Institute.
[94] *Dáil Debates,* 4 February 1997, Vol. 474, Col. 435.
[95] Ibid., Cols 890–909.

're-establishing the damaged trust between people and Government'.[96] The Buchanan Report's findings left it with little option but to establish a tribunal of inquiry into the matter.

Furthermore, by this stage the coalition government had introduced the 1995 Ethics in Public Office Act with a view to applying a more open and co-operative form of parliamentary governance. It was therefore politically imperative that it, and particularly Fine Gael, be prepared to deal with the allegations even if this involved investigating its own party members. Recalling that the Beef Tribunal's unclear terms of reference had resulted in lengthy initial investigations, the government asked McCracken to investigate specifically any payments from Dunnes Stores or Ben Dunne to:

1   persons who were between 1 January 1986 and 31 December 1996 Members of the Houses of the Oireachtas
2   their relatives or connected persons as defined in the Ethics in Public Office Act, 1995
3   political parties.[97]

As part of this role, McCracken had to investigate many allegations of corruption such as that Dunne had made payments totalling over a million pounds to Charles Haughey during 1988 and 1991, at a time when the latter was Taoiseach.[98] By this stage a member of the government, Fine Gael's Michael Lowry TD, had already been forced to leave office as media reports revealed that Dunne had paid for renovations to his family home. At the time of the revelations, Lowry was Minister for Transport, Energy and Communications and chairman of the Fine Gael parliamentary party. As ministers are obliged to make a declaration of their tax affairs to the Taoiseach on appointment, Lowry's abdication of this responsibility forced his resignation and he made a statement to the Dáil admitting receipt of the money. He also recorded that he had availed of a tax amnesty, in effect admitting that he had engaged in tax evasion.[99] The resignation of Lowry, who had been credited with reducing Fine Gael's large

[96]   Ibid., 15 December 1994, Vol. 447, Col. 1180.
[97]   Ibid., 6 February 1997, Vol. 474, Col. 891.
[98]   McCracken, B. (1997) *Report of the Tribunal of Inquiry (Dunnes Payments)*. Dublin: Stationery Office, p. 6.
[99]   *Dáil Debates*, 19 December 1996, Vol. 473, Cols 689–701. In the aftermath of the McCracken Tribunal report Deputy Lowry made another statement to the House admitting that he had omitted other financial transactions between himself and Dunnes from this original statement (*Dáil Debates*, 10 September 1997, Vol. 480, Cols 615–16).

financial debt only a few years previously, severely damaged the party's self-image of 'clean government' and high standards in public office. Lowry's fundraising activities were to come under further scrutiny in a later tribunal.

In the parliamentary motion establishing the McCracken Tribunal, the Taoiseach pointed out that a tribunal of inquiry rather than a parliamentary committee was the preferred vehicle for investigating the matter. He argued that:

> The advantage of a tribunal under the 1921 Act is that its powers are well established, and have withstood a number of tests in the courts, not least arising from litigation in connection with the beef tribunal. The process does not involve novelty: it is both tried and tested.
>
> Furthermore, it is preferable that where one of the categories or persons being inquired into is a politician, the investigator should come from outside the political sphere.[100]

The opposition Fianna Fáil leader, Bertie Ahern TD, supported the establishment of a tribunal of inquiry to investigate the matter fully. He commented that:

> It was obvious from the beginning that a committee of the House would be inadequate for the purpose and would be given neither the necessary powers nor protections.[101]

The McCracken Tribunal presented its report to parliament six months later. Leaders of the opposition parties greeted it as restoring public confidence in tribunals, which had been eroded due to the expense, length and unclear conclusions of the Beef Tribunal.[102] In his report, McCracken found that legitimate 'ordinary political donations' had been made to politicians and constituency organisations of Fianna Fáil, Fine Gael and the Labour Party.[103] The report was satisfied that there was no 'further motive behind those payments' and instead focused on payments to Lowry and Haughey.

The tribunal found that payments (in cash and in kind) from Dunnes Stores to Michael Lowry were 'extraordinary' and left a government minister 'vulnerable to all kinds of pressures from Dunnes Stores'.[104] However, the discovery of payments to Haughey

---

[100] *Dáil Debates*, 6 February 1997, Vol. 474, Col. 896.

[101] Ibid., Cols 901–2.

[102] Ibid., 10 September 1997, Vol. 480, Cols 684–710.

[103] McCracken, B. (1997) *Report of the Tribunal of Inquiry (Dunnes Payments)*. Dublin: Stationery Office, p. 17.

[104] Ibid., p. 32.

and the method through which the money was laundered was the most significant outcome of the tribunal. Along with other (unnamed) depositors, Haughey had lodged significant sums of money into offshore accounts in the Ansbacher (Cayman) Limited Bank, avoiding domestic taxes at a time when the economy was in great difficulty.[105] Desmond Traynor, who died shortly before the tribunal could take evidence from him, managed these accounts from Ireland.

The tribunal discovered that between 1987 and 1991 Ben Dunne had given Charles Haughey hundreds of thousands of pounds, but found no evidence that favours were asked of Haughey by Dunne. Nonetheless, the tribunal found it:

> quite unacceptable that Mr Charles Haughey, or indeed any member of the Oireachtas, should receive personal gifts of this nature, particularly from prominent businessmen within the State.
>
> If such gifts were to be permissible, the potential for bribery and corruption would be enormous.[106]

The McCracken Tribunal did not make recommendations in terms of parliamentary reform or the use of parliamentary tools of oversight to prevent future breaches of public office. Instead, the report welcomed the Ethics in Public Office Act, 1995 and the recent Electoral Act, 1997 as steps in the right direction towards preventing future financial impropriety among public figures. It recommended that sanctions for breaches of the former Act be increased and that consideration be given to increasing the powers of the Ombudsman to allow him or her to investigate breaches of the Ethics in Public Office Act. It also suggested that candidates for election to either House of the Oireachtas prove their tax affairs to be in order.

Furthermore, McCracken recommended that false declarations of interest by members of parliament should be considered a criminal offence, and members in contravention of the Ethics in Public Office Act should be ineligible to be a member of either House.[107] However, in a final note, Justice McCracken argued that if the sanctions were strong enough, there would be no need to ban political contributions completely and rely on state funding of political parties. This was, in effect, the situation after the 1997 Electoral Act passed into law.

[105] Keena, C. (2003) *The Ansbacher Conspiracy.* Dublin: Gill & Macmillan.

[106] McCracken, B. (1997) *Report of the Tribunal of Inquiry (Dunnes Payments).* Dublin: Stationery Office, p. 50.

[107] Ibid., pp. 75–6.

The Dáil debate on the tribunal report was principally concerned with issues of ethics in public life. Only one TD, Fianna Fáil's Conor Lenihan, identified weak parliamentary procedures as a core issue necessitating tribunals of inquiry. He argued that:

> It is clear from the McCracken and beef tribunals that if there were proper procedures and standards in the House, these expensive tribunals would be unnecessary.

Praising the role of the media in uncovering many of the issues investigated by tribunals, he noted that:

> it is no accident the media, not this House or a Member, have led many of the revelations which have occurred in the scandals we are discussing.[108]

Moriarty Tribunal

In 1997, the newly elected Fianna Fáil/Progressive Democrat government committed itself to implementing McCracken's recommendations, including the establishment of a new tribunal to follow the 'money trail' revealed during the Dunnes Payments Tribunal. In particular, this new tribunal was to investigate the sources of money paid into the Ansbacher accounts and to inquire further into financial transactions uncovered at the McCracken Tribunal but outside its remit. This tribunal was to be popularly known as the Moriarty Tribunal after its chairman, Mr Justice Michael Moriarty. In conjunction with its establishment, further amendments were added to the 1921 Tribunals of Inquiry (Evidence) Act. The key feature of the Tribunals of Inquiry (Evidence) (Amendment) Act, 1997 was to allow a tribunal to make an order for costs where it found that an individual failed to co-operate or provide assistance, or knowingly gave false or misleading information to the tribunal.[109] This Act was in response to the difficulties McCracken encountered in receiving information from Haughey and Lowry during its sittings.

The Moriarty Tribunal was established in September 1997, less than three months after the Fianna Fáil/Progressive Democrat coalition assumed power. As of 2005, it has not yet released an interim report or drawn conclusions from its work. Its terms of reference, as approved by both Houses of the Oireachtas, were to investigate:

---

108 *Dáil Debates*, 11 September 1997, Vol. 480, Col. 808.
109 Public Accounts Committee (2001) *Sub-Committee on Certain Revenue Matters: Parliamentary Inquiry into D.I.R.T. – Final Report, Vol. 1.* Dublin, p. 100.

- the sources of any 'substantial payments' made to Charles Haughey between 1979 and 1996 with which there may be 'a reasonable inference that the motive for making the payment was connected with any public office held by him or had the potential to influence the discharge of such office'
- the sources of any 'substantial payments' to Michael Lowry during the periods when he held public office and with which there might be 'a reasonable inference that the motive for making the payment was connected with any public office held by him or had the potential to influence the discharge of such office'
- the source of any money held in the Ansbacher accounts (or any other accounts discovered during the tribunal) for the benefit or in the name of Mr Charles Haughey or any other person who holds or has held ministerial office.[110]

At its first public hearing the chair proposed to complete his report by the following July, but extensive investigations and the wide terms of reference have led to considerable slippage.[111] This tribunal's work was also hampered by several legal challenges by the witnesses under investigation. For example, Haughey challenged the constitutionality of the 1921 Act in both the High and Supreme Courts, including the tribunal's right to make orders of discovery and production. The Supreme Court ruled in July 1998 that the Oireachtas had inherent power to appoint tribunals such as Moriarty, but the tribunal was ordered to give notice of intentions to make such orders of discovery.[112]

The Moriarty Tribunal was required to investigate the source of £38 million discovered in the Ansbacher accounts, but its terms of reference did not require it to disclose the names of the holders of the accounts. Instead the tribunal was asked to 'make broad recommendations for enhancing the role of the Central Bank and for protecting the State's tax base from fraud or evasion'. When it became clear that the tribunal could not name account holders, the Progressive Democrat leader, Mary Harney TD, appointed an inspector to investigate the matter independently using power under the 1963 Companies Act. This was in keeping with the Progressive Democrats' self-image as the party that would 'clean up' political life. The names

---

[110] http://www.moriarty-tribunal.ie

[111] McGrath, D. (1999) 'Review of Moriarty and Flood Tribunals, to date', *Bar Review* Vol. 4(5), 230.

[112] *Haughey v. Moriarty Ir* [1999] S.C. (1999) *Irish Reports*. Supreme Court, Dublin. Vol. 3, 27–78; Office of the Attorney General (2000) *Comparative Study of Tribunals of Inquiry and Parliamentary Inquiries*. Dublin: Stationery Office, p. 15.

of 190 Irish individuals and companies who had evaded tax by using the Ansbacher accounts were eventually made public in 2002.[113] Among those named were former TDs Charles Haughey and Denis Foley of Fianna Fáil. Hugh Coveney of Fine Gael was identified as an account holder but his involvement later transpired to be legitimate.

The range of issues, public figures and institutions of state investigated during the course of the Moriarty Tribunal significantly increased the amount of time needed by the chairman to prepare his report. For example, the tribunal felt it necessary to examine the awarding of the country's third mobile phone licence, as it occurred when Lowry was Minister for Communications. Also, the Moriarty (and McCracken) Tribunals' findings of tax evasion led to criticism of one executive branch, the Revenue Commissioners, for failing to pursue tax evaders and in particular Haughey and Lowry. The tribunal also spent considerable time attempting to untangle various 'money trails', and has even heard allegations from former Taoiseach John Bruton that he believed a newspaper group had threatened his coalition government with negative coverage if it did not respond to certain commercial demands.[114] However, the tribunal's pursuit of these matters has had certain negative consequences for Dáil Éireann – not least, the impression that the accountability of public representatives is best pursued through tribunals of inquiry rather than parliament.

While the final outcome of the Moriarty Tribunal remains uncertain, it has been a catalyst for legislation dealing with issues of corruption, standards in public office and party financing. Its work has been conducted in tandem with another tribunal of inquiry that has investigated the actions of local government politicians and property developers. Coupled with the Moriarty Tribunal, the Tribunal of Inquiry into Certain Planning Matters and Payments (the Flood Tribunal) has been responsible for amendments to the 1995 Ethics in Public Office Act as well as new codes of conduct for public representatives. It has also been the first tribunal to use the term 'corrupt' in relation to the activities of former government ministers.

The Moriarty and Flood Tribunals have resulted in significant contributions to the jurisprudence of tribunals of inquiry.[115] The

---

[113] Not all of those named had been involved in defrauding the state, however.

[114] Keena, C. (2004) 'Bruton felt threatened by Independent Group', *Irish Times* 24 March, 8. The newspaper group was Independent Newspapers.

[115] McGrath, D. (1999) 'Review of Moriarty and Flood Tribunals, to date', *Bar Review* Vol. 4(5), 230–6.

strengthening of judicial forms of executive accountability is in sharp contrast to the slow progress of parliamentary reform for the purpose of strengthening oversight of the executive in Ireland. The fact that both tribunals (as well as several others established since 1997) are some time from presenting final reports forestalls progress in this area, and means that a culture of parliamentary accountability in the Oireachtas remains undeveloped.

Tribunal of Inquiry into Certain Planning Matters and Payments

More commonly referred to as the Flood Tribunal, this inquiry arose out of an anonymous reward offered to anyone who could produce evidence that decisions concerning residential housing planning in County Dublin were influenced by corrupt payments. James Gogarty, a retired builder, became the whistle-blower on improper financial transactions between his former employer and certain politicians, including the incumbent Fianna Fáil Minister for Foreign Affairs, Raphael Burke TD.[116] In a twist of irony, on the same date that the Dáil began to debate the McCracken report (see above), Burke made a statement to the House rejecting allegations made in the print media that he had received large sums of cash from property developers. He vigorously denied the allegations but evaded subsequent questions from the opposition:

> **Mr Shatter [Fine Gael]:** I deliberately asked two very simple straightforward questions.
> **Mr R. Burke:** Yes, and I am responding.
> **Mr Shatter:** I am anxious to be fair to the answerer. For reasons I do not understand, the Minister seems to be evading answering both questions by delivering a form of soliloquy on a Kerry newspaper article.
> **Mr Spring [Labour Party]:** It is a great newspaper.
> **Mr Shatter:** Perhaps the Minister could respond to the questions which I am trying to raise in a fair and simple way.
> **Mr R. Burke:** And I am trying to answer in a fair and simple way. There is a view in relation to contributions in this House and I am making the point that it is not just my view. As I have already outlined, it is the view of the Fine Gael Party, with which I know the Deputy will not disagree. I am trying to be fair and reasonable. I want to make the point also in relation to the Labour Party and, similarly, I am sure I will get the opportunity to quote Deputy Rabbitte in relation to The Workers Party and a contribution of £28,000.

---

[116] Accusations of corruption were famously made against Burke by journalist Joe McAnthony in 1974 but despite a subsequent Garda investigation, no prosecutions resulted.

Mr Shatter: On a point of order and in case the Minister forgets, I repeat my
questions. Did the Minister ask Mr Gogarty why he was a recipient of
such largesse, and second, did he address the issue of why he was
receiving this money in cash? Was that something of a surprise to the
Minister? Will the Minister indicate in what notes the money was
received, as I previously requested? Perhaps the Minister would just
reply to the questions asked.[117]

Burke resigned from his ministerial post less than a month later. An
interim report (see below) by the Flood Tribunal in 2002 found that
Burke lied to the Dáil on this occasion and that the payments he
had received were corrupt. He was eventually jailed for six months in
January 2005 for tax evasion (not corruption), the first former
minister to receive a custodial sentence. However, as in the case of the
Beef and other tribunals, the very need to establish the Moriarty Tribunal demonstrates again how parliamentary questions were
virtually impotent in terms of eliciting information from members of
the government.

The tribunal eventually established by the Fianna Fáil/Progressive
Democrat government in October 1997 was asked not only to
investigate a particular decision to rezone lands for housing in north
County Dublin, but also to ascertain whether any acts associated with
the planning process (after June 1985) amounted to corruption.[118] As
a consequence of the wide terms of reference, several senior political
figures and business elites have been asked to present evidence before
the tribunal. This has resulted in a drip-feed of scandal and innuendo
through the media as the curtain has been lifted on many behind-the-
scenes incidents and meetings involving these figures.

As with previous tribunals, the opposition criticised the terms of
reference. Fine Gael's Alan Dukes TD argued that they were too
broad in this case and accused the government of trying to 'cast the
net wide in the hope of finding other unspecified matters which
would divert attention from the main issue'.[119] Later evidence by
former lobbyist Frank Dunlop showed that these fears of incompleteness
were warranted. He informed Justice Flood that councillors who had
been bribed believed that the tribunal had been established because
of political pressures and that it would deal with one issue only. Then
'it would be all wrapped up and forgotten about'.[120] However, the

---

[117]   *Dáil Debates*, 10 September 1997, Vol. 480, Cols 622–3.
[118]   Ibid., 7 October 1997, Vol. 481, Cols 49–52.
[119]   Ibid., Col. 63.
[120]   Cullen, P. (2003) 'Dunlop lied in belief case would be forgotten about', *Irish
        Times*, 6 February, 9.

first interim report of the tribunal in February 1998 requested that its terms of reference be expanded following the disclosure of further payments to Burke. The government acceded to the request and two Acts of the Oireachtas were passed to allow this. These were the Tribunals of Inquiry (Evidence) (Amendment) Act, 1998 and the Tribunals of Inquiry (Evidence) (Amendment) (No. 2) Act, 1998.

Strengthening tribunals: the 1998 Acts and tribunals of inquiry jurisprudence

The first of these Acts permitted the Flood Tribunal to extend the scope of its inquiries when more evidence of corrupt payments came to light soon after the tribunal began to take evidence.[121] The Act also facilitated an amendment to the instrument by which a tribunal is appointed by a resolution of the two Houses. The second Act built on this by granting any government minister the power to amend such an instrument.[122] These Acts were deemed necessary as evidence came to light that fell outside the time period specified in its terms of reference. After some legal wrangling, the Oireachtas passed the Tribunals of Inquiry (Evidence) (Amendment) (No. 2) Act, 1998, which enabled the Flood Tribunal to investigate Raphael Burke's financial transactions in a similar way to the Moriarty Tribunal's inquiries into Lowry and Haughey. In effect, the amending Act allowed the tribunal to discover whether the actions of Burke and other public officials amounted to corruption.

The tribunal's work, which as of 2005 is ongoing, has been seriously hampered by legal proceedings mounted by several former and sitting public office holders who sought to curb its investigations. In 1999 George Redmond, a former senior official in Dublin City and County Council, challenged the tribunal's right to conduct its preliminary investigations in private. The Supreme Court ultimately found against him.[123] Sitting Fianna Fáil TD, Liam Lawlor, who was the subject of allegations of improper payments in return for favourable planning decisions,[124] challenged the tribunal's right to order discovery and production, and succeeded in achieving a judicial review. The

---

[121]   www.flood-tribunal.ie

[122]   Public Accounts Committee (2001) *Sub-Committee on Certain Revenue Matters: Parliamentary Inquiry into D.I.R.T. – Final Report, Vol. 1.* Dublin, p. 100.

[123]   *Redmond* v. *Flood Ir* [1999] S.C. (1999) *Irish Reports.* Supreme Court, Dublin. Vol. 3, 79–96.

[124]   Lawlor had in fact voted in favour of establishing the Flood Tribunal.

Supreme Court considered his case taking account of the Haughey case of 1971 (see Chapter 5), and ultimately decided in favour of the tribunal.[125] This decision was in contrast with the judgment in the Abbeylara case.

In 2001 Frank Dunlop, a former Fianna Fáil press secretary, admitted that he had participated in an elaborate scheme whereby property developers 'bought' the votes of county councillors for the purposes of rezoning land pockets in Dublin. Members of both Fianna Fáil and Fine Gael were implicated in the matter and both parties established internal party investigations. The tribunal continues to find evidence of corrupt activity by local politicians and this has contributed to public cynicism *vis-à-vis* the devolution of responsibilities to local government in Ireland.

The Second Interim Report of the Flood Tribunal

Unlike the Moriarty Tribunal (which has released none), the Flood Tribunal has released four interim reports since it began its work in 1997. As detailed above, the first report was concerned with expanding the terms of reference of the tribunal. This increased the tribunal's workload and in June 2001, Justice Flood requested two extra judges and a substitute to assist him in the ongoing work of the tribunal.[126] The second interim report was a watershed for Irish politics and the tribunals of inquiry and became a bestseller, selling over 100,000 copies. The unambiguous content and findings of the 'devastatingly clear report'[127] earned the praise of the media and opposition political parties that had been critical of previous tribunal reports. Justice Flood found that Burke and certain property developers called before the tribunal had not co-operated with it and that the reason for this was that their actions 'would not withstand public scrutiny'.[128] The report also found that former Fianna Fáil government press secretary and confidant of Charles Haughey, P. J. Mara, had 'failed to co-operate with the Tribunal' by not disclosing the existence of an offshore account he held in the Isle of Man.[129]

---

[125] *Lawlor* v. *Flood Ir* [1999] S.C. (1999) *Irish Reports.* Supreme Court, Dublin, pp. 107–44.

[126] Cullen, P. (2002) *With a Little Help from my Friends.* Dublin: Gill & Macmillan, p. 277.

[127] Hennessy, M. (2002) 'Burke corruption findings put pressure on Taoiseach', *Irish Times*, 27 September, 4.

[128] Flood, F. (2002) *The Second Interim Report of the Tribunal of Inquiry into Certain Planning Matters and Payments.* Dublin: Stationery Office, p. 15.

[129] Ibid., p. 144.

Flood asserted throughout the report that several donations of money to Burke were corrupt.[130] For example, on one donation by developer Tom Brennan to Burke:

> The Tribunal concludes, on the balance of probabilities, that Mr Brennan did not make the payment of stg£50,000 in 1982 in the belief that he was making a legitimate political donation as claimed by him to 'Ray Burke/Fianna Fáil', but made it in the knowledge that it was a payment to Mr Burke which would not withstand public scrutiny because, in the opinion of the Tribunal, it was a corrupt payment.[131]

The tribunal also found that Burke had taken decisions in his capacity as Minister for Communications that benefited private actors rather than the public interest.[132]

From the time of the allegations in Dáil Éireann that resulted in the Beef Tribunal's establishment until this report's publication, the perception that certain figures had acted corruptly was widespread in public discourse. Indeed, if the definition of 'corruption' is the abuse of public office for private gain, it is surprising that both the Beef and McCracken Tribunal reports failed to use the term and recommend prosecutions. This, as well as their spiralling cost, had fuelled public cynicism towards tribunals of inquiry. The Flood Tribunal's second interim report had legal implications for those accused, and, under the tribunals of inquiry Acts, made them liable for prosecution in the courts proper.

The tribunal's findings were especially damning for Fianna Fáil. In particular, the judgement of the party's leader and Taoiseach, Bertie Ahern TD, in appointing Burke as Minister for Foreign Affairs was called into question. Despite the significance of the report, the Dáil did not meet until two weeks after its publication and the government easily stifled debate and opposition attacks on it.

Using its prerogative, the government refused to allow a full questions and answers session on the Flood Tribunal's interim report, allowing only statements from the opposition. This provoked the opposition parties into claims that the government was attempting to ignore the matter.

---

[130] Ibid., pp. 23, 34, 51, 65.
[131] Ibid., p. 23.
[132] Flood, F. (2002) *The Second Interim Report of the Tribunal of Inquiry into Certain Planning Matters and Payments*. Dublin: Stationery Office, p. 46.

Mr G. Mitchell [Fine Gael]: On the question of the late sitting, we are seeing the greatest scandal since the Arms Trial, when this House sat throughout the night and on Saturdays. To suggest that we should put a time limit on this debate and have no questions and answers at the end is unacceptable and does not meet the requirements of the public. Around 100,000 people bought this report. The reason we are having tribunals at all is that questions were not answered in this House. It is imperative that the points made by Deputy Kenny be accommodated by the Taoiseach and the Government, and we will not accept anything less.

The Taoiseach: I will answer the questions.

Mr Gormley: He will answer a question now.

The Taoiseach: I will answer the two questions together as it will save me repeating myself later. The reports of all previous tribunals presented to the Dáil were dealt with in a similar way. As no individual Minister is responsible for the establishment of the tribunals, no question and answer session has ever been taken. That is the precedent in the House.

[Interruptions]

Mr Howlin: On a point of order, a Cheann Comhairle, you are allowing the Taoiseach to answer a question you would not allow.

An Ceann Comhairle: Deputy Howlin, I ask you to resume your seat and hear the Taoiseach and then I will take your point of order.

Mr Howlin: He is answering a question that you would not allow to be put. I tabled an amendment about this.

Mr Coveney: This is about the late sitting.

An Ceann Comhairle: Taoiseach, perhaps we will wait until the next item.

The Taoiseach: There is a question on a time motion and it is as easy for me to answer the two together, but I could just –

Ms O. Mitchell: It is not as easy for us to ask.

[Interruptions]

The Taoiseach: Would Deputies like me to be helpful on the time motion, or do they just want to make noise generally?

Mr Timmins: Questions and answers.

Mr Connaughton: The Taoiseach should come on and answer the question.

The Taoiseach: At least Deputy Timmins is honest. The Deputies do not really care about the tribunal and they do not really care about the time and they want answers to questions I answered before, so they can forget about it.[133]

The sitting was tempestuous but, given the bias in the standing orders towards government business in the House, the opposition failed in its attempts to get the government to answer questions concerning the appointment of Burke to ministerial office. The refusal to allow parliamentary questions to be put to the Taoiseach concerning the appointment represented Westminster-type adversarial government taken to its extreme. The government's offer to allow only two days of statements, with no time for opposition questions,

---

[133] *Dáil Debates*, 9 October 2002, Vol. 554, Cols 503–4.

led to a temporary breakdown in 'pairing' arrangements,[134] demonstrating the weak powers of sanction available to the opposition.

As with previous tribunal reports, the government accepted the findings of the chairperson but attempted to distance itself from the subject under investigation, in this case former minister Raphael Burke. The Progressive Democrat leader and Tánaiste, Mary Harney TD, claimed that she had raised the matter of alleged donations to Burke prior to his appointment as minister in 1997 but had not objected to it following assurances from the Fianna Fáil leadership. During the debate on the report, the Fianna Fáil Minister for Arts, Sport and Tourism, John O'Donoghue TD, attempted to insulate his party leader from accusations of corruption and bribery, arguing that:

> Every person who has read this report is aware of one unassailable and uncontradictable fact. There is not a single syllable of criticism of the Taoiseach contained in the report.[135]

Despite the opposition parties' outrage, the Taoiseach claimed that a questions and answers session was not possible on the Flood Tribunal Report as it might prejudice any future legal action.[136] Lawyers for Charles Haughey had successfully argued in the High Court that comments by the Tánaiste concerning their client meant that he could not receive a fair hearing at the Moriarty Tribunal in relation to some allegations. This decision also led to the creation of the Tribunals of Inquiry (Evidence) (Amendment) Act in 2002.

This Act had two main purposes. The first was to allow tribunals to exclude members of the public from their hearings, so that no evidence could be claimed to prejudice any pending criminal trial. This followed the abovementioned court ruling that Charles Haughey could not be subject to legal prosecution. Secondly, it provided a clear legal basis for the appointment of additional and reserve members of tribunals, as recommended and required by the Flood Tribunal in the previous year. Interestingly, such a development was also recommended by the Public Accounts Committee's sub-committee inquiry (see below), also on the basis that a tribunal's work should not be delayed.[137]

---

[134] Hennessy, M. (2002) 'Government still blocking Dail questions for Taoiseach', *Irish Times*, 4 October, 1.

[135] *Dáil Debates*, 9 October 2002, Vol. 554, Col. 606.

[136] Ibid., Col. 508.

[137] Public Accounts Committee (2001) *Sub-Committee on Certain Revenue Matters: Parliamentary Inquiry into D.I.R.T. – Final Report, Vol. 1*. Dublin, p. 104.

The use of reserve members has proved necessary in the Flood Tribunal as its chairman stood down in June 2003 and was replaced by one of the reserve judges, Alan Mahon. The 2002 Act also provided that a tribunal could appoint investigators to assist it in carrying out its functions.[138] The Flood Tribunal's work had been hampered by legal challenges, and this Act was intended to allow another member to continue with hearing evidence if a similar legal challenge arose in the future. Another amending Act in 2004 allowed the new chair to award costs to those who gave evidence before he or she assumed the role of chairperson. The Tribunals of Inquiry (Evidence) (Amendment) Act 2004 also allowed the Mahon Tribunal to divide its time between concurrent modules in order to speed up the investigative process.

In September 2002, Flood presented his third interim report, which found that former Dublin City and County Assistant Manager George Redmond had received corrupt payments from developers. Redmond subsequently became the first person in the tribunal era to be convicted of corruption and jailed,[139] but he was released on appeal in July 2004. During 2003 and 2004, the Flood/Mahon Tribunal continued to uncover sordid details concerning a large property development and demands for cash made on the developer by senior government ministers in 1989. Indeed, at one stage the current Taoiseach gave evidence at the tribunal. An *Irish Times* editorial the following day noted that 'Mr Ahern was subjected to the kind of rigorous cross-examination that Dáil procedures do not admit.'[140]

Judge Mahon released a fourth interim report in June 2004, in which he asked for a reduction in its workload and an increase in legal staff. He estimated that without increased resources and amended terms of reference, its work could continue for another ten or eleven years.[141] A target of March 2007 has now been established for presentation of a final report, and the tribunal will attempt to divide its staff in order to conduct several lines of inquiry concurrently. In June 2005, Judge Mahon ruled that witnesses who had co-operated

---

[138] *Dáil Debates*, 22 March 2002, Vol. 551, Col. 4.

[139] The Dublin Circuit Criminal Court found him guilty in December 2003 on two counts of corruption, including accepting a cheque for IR£10,000 from an individual in return for a favourable planning decision. Redmond was also found guilty of tax evasion later that year, but avoided a jail sentence.

[140] *Irish Times* (2004) 'Ahern shifts his ground at tribunal' (editorial), 8 April, p. 12.

[141] Mahon, A. (2004) *The Fourth Interim Report of the Tribunal of Inquiry into Certain Planning Matters and Payments*. Dublin: Stationery Office, p. 9.

with the tribunal and given truthful evidence to it, and against whom no adverse findings had been made, should be awarded their costs. This has substantially increased the overall cost of completing the tribunal's work.

The impact of tribunals of inquiry on political actors

As two of the tribunals of inquiry discussed in this section are ongoing at time of writing, it is difficult to draw any final conclusions as to their impact on politicians and political parties. The McCracken Tribunal embarrassed Fianna Fáil and Fine Gael, and exposed further the secretive financial relationship between business and political interests that the Beef Tribunal had uncovered. Legal challenges and the ever-increasing length of time they are taking to draw final conclusions have marred the Flood and Moriarty Tribunals, but the Flood Tribunal's second interim report represented a milestone in Irish politics.

As a result of these three tribunals (as well as the Beef Tribunal), a range of regulatory bodies and oversight legislation has been introduced both within and outside the Oireachtas. Also, many of the political parties have established internal checks, including booklets on ethics and standards for members, to ensure that they not be left open to accusations of impropriety. Therefore, the principal impact of tribunals on political actors has been to make potential transgressors 'think twice' about engaging in corrupt activity. It is significant that tribunals of inquiry rather than a strong ethos of parliamentary accountability have had this result. The contrast with Westminster, where ministers and MPs increasingly fear being called before a parliamentary committee or being accused of misleading the House of Commons, is stark. In fact, misleading the Dáil technically does not breach any of its standing orders.

It can be argued that tribunals have been a less effective mechanism of holding political actors to account than was expected. As with the Beef, Finlay and Lindsay Tribunal reports, the ministers involved in the McCracken, Moriarty and Flood Tribunals were quick to point out that the matters under consideration occurred at a time in their departments when they were not in office. Also, opposition parties tend to use such reports to berate government and to advocate accountability via ministerial responsibility as the proper method of scrutinising the executive administration. This was particularly evident in the McCracken and Flood Tribunals, where issues of political party financing and the scruples of individual parliamentarians were called into question.

Tribunals of inquiry – a balance sheet

The wide variety in the quality of tribunal reports reveals the potential weakness of such investigations. Of the six tribunals considered above, five have produced at least one report, but only the McCracken and Flood second interim reports were credited with being unambiguous in their findings. Indeed, the McCracken Tribunal was also commended for its brevity, due in part to its precise terms of reference. Unlike routine legal hearings, which are conducted in an adversarial manner, tribunals are inquisitorial and are supposed to produce findings of fact on which future action may be taken. However, the partisan manner in which the political parties treat their reports calls tribunals' efficacy into question, particularly if their recommendations do not lead to clear and unequivocal actions.

Although the consent of both Houses of the Oireachtas is required in order to establish a tribunal, the government has the initiative in presenting an account of the details of the inquiry, and will do so in a way that favours it. Indeed, Flinders argues that in Britain, judicial inquiries such as tribunals are not instruments of parliament but of the government, as ministers and their officials decide whether or not to establish an inquiry.[142] Similarly, Winetrobe notes that the government in Westminster is more likely to allow a statutory inquiry such as a tribunal when ministerial culpability is not an issue.[143]

Furthermore, experience in Ireland reveals how members of the government tend to welcome tribunal reports as independent assessments of events. This allows them to distance themselves from any potentially damaging findings, particularly when tribunals are investigating issues of administrative oversight and accountability. In recent years governments have also used the tribunals as an excuse for not commenting on allegations of corruption and malpractice in public life. In other words, there is a strong argument that tribunals of inquiry allow government to deflect attempts at parliamentary

---

[142] Flinders, M. (2001) 'Mechanisms of Judicial Accountability in British Central Government', *Parliamentary Affairs* Vol. 54(1), 68.

[143] Winetrobe, B. (1997) 'Inquiries after Scott: the Return of the Tribunal of Inquiry', *Public Law*, spring, 18–31.

accountability, and thus undermine one of the core functions of Dáil Éireann.

At the start of 2003 no fewer than nine separate judicial inquiries were sitting, most of which were tribunals of inquiry rather than statutory or non-statutory inquiries (see Table 6.1). As Fine Gael's Alan Shatter TD pointed out prior to the 2002 election:

> There have been more motions before the Houses of the Oireachtas relating to the establishment of tribunals of inquiry, the amendment of their terms of reference and provision for new statutory mechanisms concerning tribunals of inquiry, during the lifetime of the Government than ever before in the history of the State.[144]

In contrast, the impetus for parliamentary reform that began in the mid-1990s has decreased significantly since 2002. Another reason why the experience with tribunals of inquiry in Ireland has been far from satisfactory has been the number of legal challenges they have encountered. This has created lengthy delays in their proceedings, as well as ever-increasing jurisprudence. The principal reason for this is that the 1921 Act came into law at a time when the concept of fair procedures was undeveloped. As Brady notes, the jurisprudence created by successive tribunals of inquiry since the early 1990s has placed the public right to know above the right of citizens to privacy.[145] Also, as Fianna Fáil's Mary Hanafin TD pointed out, the creation of a constitutional superstructure and its imposition on a pre-independence statute have resulted in frictions between the legal and parliamentary spheres.[146] While lessons have been learned as to the costs and benefits of tribunals of inquiry, the financial cost of the ongoing Flood and Moriarty Tribunals has led to public disenchantment with both the legal profession[147] and the inquiries themselves.

Just as the parliamentary committee of 1912 was found to have been an unsatisfactory and partisan mechanism for investigating matters of public concern, almost a century later, tribunals of inquiry are also falling out of favour. At the time of writing, it is reported that

---

[144] *Dáil Debates*, 22 March 2002, Vol. 551, Col. 12.
[145] Brady, R. (2000) 'Tribunals and Politics: a Fundamental Review', *Contemporary Issues in Irish Law and Politics* Vol. 3, 157.
[146] *Dáil Debates*, 2 June 1999, Vol. 505, Col. 1445.
[147] In 2004 the director-general of the Law Society, the regulatory and representative body for solicitors, described the tribunals of inquiry and their associated legal fees as 'the greatest disaster to befall the legal profession in Ireland' (Reid, L. (2004) 'Law Society says high tribunal fees have hurt legal profession', *Irish Times*, 3 April, 6).

legislation is being drafted that will empower the government to dissolve a tribunal with a resolution of both Houses of the Oireachtas. The length and cost[148] of sitting tribunals have been the two most influential factors in the government's decision to produce legislation providing for a new format of inquiry. Rather than sitting in public as tribunals do, a principal feature of these new pared-down 'commissions of investigation' is that they may take evidence in private. As a form of statutory inquiry, they are designed to investigate matters of 'significant public concern' and offer a cheaper and more efficient method of inquiry than tribunals of inquiry. However, deciding the need to create such a commission and its terms of reference will be in the domain of government alone; parliamentary approval will be the last stage in its establishment. As with tribunals, any reports produced by commissions of inquiry will be presented to ministers before being presented to the Houses of the Oireachtas.[149] In effect, this further reduces the input of the legislature into the decision-making process and hinders the evolution of parliamentary bodies to carry out similar investigation. It also ensures that the judicial sphere maintains a strong involvement in both political and parliamentary affairs.

---

[148] Private correspondence from the government to the Public Accounts Committee in 2004 showed that the state had spent almost €190m on tribunals since 1991, with lawyers' fees accounting for approximately 70 per cent of the costs. The Law Reform Commission's publication on public inquiries estimated the cost to be €200 million as of 2005.

[149] Section 32 (4) of the Commissions of Investigation Act, 2004.

CHAPTER 7

Public accountability

B y definition, the pursuit of public accountability does not directly involve parliament. Rather it exists alongside – and is in some respects in competition with – parliamentary (and judicial) forms of executive oversight. Indeed, Oliver refers to such accountability as administrative'[1] and Flinders categorises it as 'managerial'.[2] The term 'public' is used here because unlike other extra-parliamentary modes of oversight, such as tribunals of inquiry, public accountability devices can bypass government and make information available, usually through a report presented to the Houses of the Oireachtas (see Table 1.2). In other words, institutions of public accountability are accountable directly to citizens.

However, while such institutions increase the flow of information between government and governed, they also reduce the effectiveness and inhibit the development of parliamentary methods of oversight. The two most significant developments in relation to public accountability in contemporary Ireland are the increased profile of the Office of the Ombudsman and the development of freedom of information (FOI) legislation, which provide the background to the creation of other extra-parliamentary and parliamentary devices of accountability.

The Office of the Ombudsman

The concept of an independent Ombudsman for oversight of the public administration was discussed as early as the mid-1960s. In a speech to the Solicitors' Apprentices Debating Society of Ireland, originally meant to be delivered by Charles Haughey, prominent civil servant T. K. Whitaker argued that:

> The basic reason ... why we do not need an official Ombudsman is because we have so many unofficial but nevertheless effective ones.[3]

---

[1] Oliver, D. (1991) *Government in the United Kingdom: the Search for Accountability, Effectiveness and Citizenship.* Milton Keynes: Open University Press.
[2] Flinders, M. (2001) *The Politics of Accountability in the Modern State.* Aldershot: Ashgate.
[3] *Irish Times* (1966) 'An Irish Ombudsman' (editorial), 12 November, 13.

This was a clear reference to the clientelist role of Dáil deputies in solving constituents' grievances with the bureaucracy. The personalised and competitive intra-party context of the Irish electoral system is partly responsible for this, but the impartiality of the public service appeared to be undermined as a consequence. Removing from political actors the role of broker between voter and state administration, and vesting it in an independent body, was a logical step to remedy this situation.

Following developments in other Westminster-style democracies and Scandinavia, the concept of an Ombudsman increased in popularity in Ireland during the 1970s. In response to a Private Member's motion from a government backbencher, the Fine Gael/ Labour Party government established an all-party informal committee on administrative justice in 1976. Its report of May 1977 recommended the establishment of such an office; the drafting process for a Bill to provide for it had begun when the general election of 1977 occurred. Having won this election, Fianna Fáil did not display enthusiasm for the project and it was a further two-and-a-half years before the Ombudsman Bill began its life in the Dáil.[4] The Bill was eventually passed in 1983.

Under the Ombudsman Act, the office has the status of a High Court judge, and can demand information, documents or files from government departments, local authorities and many other arms of the administration. It can also require any official to give information about a complaint. The Ombudsman can look into all administrative actions including decisions, refusal or failure to take action, and administrative procedures. However, the office is precluded from investigating issues such as court decisions; functions exercised by the elected members of local authorities; complaints relating to recruitment, pay and conditions of employment; non-commercial state agencies; and medical institutions including hospitals.

Fianna Fáil's lack of enthusiasm for the creation of an Ombudsman meant that the appointment of one was delayed until 1984, by which time Fine Gael and the Labour Party had again formed a coalition. The first incumbent of the new office, journalist Michael Mills, held it until 1994, when former civil servant Kevin Murphy took over. During Mills's tenure, the Haughey administration that returned to power in 1987 attempted to 'starve the watchdog into submission by

---

[4] *Dáil Debates*, 20 November 1979, Vol. 316, Cols 2056–7.

malnutrition' and reduced staffing and resources available to the office.[5] The reduction of the Ombudsman's budget by a quarter of a million pounds in 1987 was justified as necessary given the crisis in public expenditure. However, as Gwynn Morgan points out, 'cuts in other sections of the public service did not amputate nearly a half of the establishment.'[6]

This incident reflects how the 'Fianna Fáil versus the rest' dynamic in Irish politics extended to supposedly independent institutions of state. The reluctance of single-party Fianna Fáil governments until 1989 to concede powers of oversight to independent bodies reflected a majoritarian tendency within the party when in government. Since then the party has only been in coalition governments and its suspicion of the Office of the Ombudsman has dissipated, allowing the institution to develop.

In Britain, the equivalent of the Ombudsman is the Office of the Parliamentary Commissioner for Administration, who is an officer of parliament. It may therefore be argued that the office forms part of the machinery of parliamentary oversight.[7] In Ireland, the statutory independence of the Ombudsman is formalised through his or her appointment by the President following nomination by the government and a resolution of both Houses of the Oireachtas. However, the Office of the Ombudsman has been very much dependent on the Department of Finance for its resources, and this situation persists as of 2005.

In recent years, the Office of the Ombudsman has become a better resourced and institutionalised part of the Irish administration, particularly with the incorporation of the Office of Information Commissioner (see below). Just as the Comptroller and Auditor-General is responsible for financial accountability, the Ombudsman

---

[5] Interview with former Ombudsman Kevin Murphy, 27 November 2002. The office's budget was reduced by IR£100,000 in 1987 and four investigative staff had to be removed, as well as some support personnel. The Ombudsman presented a special report on the matter to the Oireachtas, which received significant media coverage. The cutbacks were reversed by 1989 (Mills, M. (2004) 'The Office of the Ombudsman in Ireland' in T. Garvin, M. Manning and R. Sinnott (eds) *Dissecting Irish Politics: Essays in Honour of Brian Farrell*. Dublin: UCD Press, pp. 103–15).

[6] Gwynn Morgan, D. (2001) 'Ireland's Ombudsman' in J. Sarkin and W. Binchy (eds) *Human Rights, the Citizen and the State: South African and Irish Perspectives*. Dublin: Round Hall Sweet & Maxwell, p. 96.

[7] Pyper, R. (1996) 'Parliamentary Accountability' in R. Pyper (ed.) *Aspects of Accountability in the British System of Government*. Liverpool: Tudor Business Publishing, pp. 64–8.

regards his/her role as 'a mechanism to help parliament hold the executive accountable in the area of what I call administrative accountability'.[8] Indeed, the Constitution Review Group recommended an amendment to the Constitution to insert a constitutional guarantee for the office;[9] while all the political parties endorsed this at the time, no action has been taken.

While the Irish Ombudsman has considerable operational independence, in the absence of constitutional recognition the office is accountable to the Houses of the Oireachtas. This makes it similar to the British Parliamentary Commissioner for Administration, who is accountable to parliament at Westminster and not a creature of government. However, there is a substantial difference between the two as in Britain, only MPs can approach the Commissioner with a case for investigation. MPs may therefore be regarded as 'filters' for the work received by the Parliamentary Commissioner.

Reflecting the growth in confidence and competence of the Office of the Ombudsman, during the 1990s its annual reports departed from specific concerns with public administration and local authorities to concentrate on the sphere of national and central government. For example, annual and other reports now tend to criticise the government for not extending the remit of the Ombudsman to include public voluntary hospitals and agencies.[10] Also, the office has been prepared to criticise the governing process in the Dáil, and did so most explicitly in an ad hoc report on nursing home subventions.

Nursing home subventions

In 2001 the Ombudsman's Office published a report on its investigation into the payment of nursing home subventions by the local health authorities[11] following complaints that the Department of Health was not fully subsidising geriatric patients in private nursing homes, although legislation to do so had been enacted. As with

---

[8] Interview with former Ombudsman Kevin Murphy, 27 November 2002.
[9] Constitution Review Group (1996) *Report of the Constitution Review Group*. Dublin: Stationery Office, pp. 425–7.
[10] Office of the Ombudsman (2002) *Annual Report*. Dublin: Office of the Ombudsman, p. 30; Office of the Ombudsman (2004) *20th Anniversary of the Office of the Ombudsman in Ireland*. Dublin: Office of the Ombudsman, p. 8.
[11] The report was titled *Nursing Home Subventions: an Investigation by the Ombudsman of Complaints regarding Payment of Nursing Home Subventions by Health Boards*.

the tribunals of inquiry and parliamentary committee inquiries, accountability and oversight within the Irish system of parliamentary democracy were called into question.

In his report, the then Ombudsman Kevin Murphy criticised the nature of the governing process in Ireland, which was so at odds with the theoretical constitutional separation of powers between the executive and the legislature. He found this to be one of the main factors in the failure of adequate procedures of accountability in the governing process. Within the executive, the report criticised the extensive power granted to ministers, which 'precludes the possibility of independent action by senior civil servants'.[12] This was despite the fact that the Public Service Management Act, 1997 had sought to delegate more responsibility to departmental staff. Furthermore, the report argued that the increased tendency of ministers not to put their views explicitly in writing undermined accountability within departments, and led to uncertainty concerning responsibility.

The nursing home subvention report stated that there are no guarantees that a similar failure in accountability will not occur in the future, because of three features of the parliamentary system:

1   the difficulties faced by the Oireachtas in monitoring all secondary legislation and regulations
2   the weakness of the link between the legislation for new entitlements and the allocation of resources to fund these entitlements
3   the difficulties faced by Oireachtas members in feeding their concerns into the administration.[13]

Though it did not receive much publicity on its release, the PAC DIRT inquiry report recognised this publication as a 'damning indictment of our public administration system'.[14] Indeed, the nursing home subvention report demonstrated the confidence of the Office of the Ombudsman, which was prepared to attack the system of parliamentary accountability in a manner not often seen in the Oireachtas itself. The Office of the Ombudsman has become an integral part of Irish administrative and political life, and while there is much room for development, it would be politically unwise for any

---

[12]   Office of the Ombudsman (2001) *Nursing Home Subventions: an Investigation by the Ombudsman of Complaints regarding Payment of Nursing Home Subventions by Health Boards.* Dublin: Office of the Ombudsman, p. 67.

[13]   Ibid., p. 71.

[14]   Public Accounts Committee (2001) *Sub-Committee on Certain Revenue Matters: Parliamentary Inquiry into D.I.R.T. – Final Report*, Vol. 1. Dublin, p. 12.

administration to be seen to reduce its powers of inquiry, as in the period of cutbacks of the late 1980s.

Freedom of information

The second institution to be considered when examining the development of public accountability is the Freedom of Information Act. Even more than the Office of the Ombudsman, the Act has presented challenges for Dáil Éireann. The Official Secrets Act, 1963 set out prohibitive rules on the disclosure of information into the public domain by members of the civil service. However, beginning in the 1980s, with the backdrop of severe economic difficulties imposed by management of the national debt, there was 'a breakdown of trust in the traditionally secretive and autonomous functioning of Governmental institutions'.[15] The need for more open information flows between the executive and the public was also identified as a key area for development under the programme of public sector reform known as the Strategic Management Initiative. As the tribunals of inquiry unfolded in the early 1990s, the issue of striking a balance between the need for official secrecy and the right of citizens to have access to information concerning themselves and the decision-making process became even more pressing.

The National Archives Act of 1986 had provided for all government and departmental records, including cabinet minutes, to be open to the public after thirty years.[16] There were some exceptions, principally in relation to sensitive material on Northern Ireland and the administration of justice, and matters of state security. This Act facilitated for the first time a closer look at the decision-making process and the influences that led to courses of action taken by governments since the state's foundation. The 1997 Freedom of Information Act enhanced this increase in the transparency of the administration.

---

[15] Cooke, P. (1985) 'Why We Need Open Government in Ireland', *Seirbhis Phoibli* Vol. 6(3), 28.

[16] The Act also obliged departments to keep records and to lodge them with the National Archives. Prior to this Act, it was not unusual for government departments to destroy records in order to clear space. For more on this see the recent volume by Gerard O'Brien (2004, *Irish Governments and the Guardianship of Historical Records 1922–72*. Dublin: Four Courts Press), which also examines difficulties in the early decades of the state's independence in accessing parliamentary debates from the 1919–22 period.

This new Act drew on best practice from Canada, Australia and New Zealand,[17] and established three new statutory rights:

- a legal right for each person to access information held by public bodies
- a legal right for each person to have official information relating to himself/herself amended where it is incomplete, incorrect or misleading
- a legal right to obtain reasons for decisions affecting oneself.

The legislation also provided for the establishment of an Information Commissioner whose role is to provide an independent review of decisions taken by public bodies in relation to requests for access to records. This office was subsequently combined with that of the Ombudsman: the two offices share premises but employ separate staffs and computer systems. There is some confusion between them, as the remit of the Information Commissioner is broader than that of the Ombudsman, and the Ombudsman's annual reports have called for amending legislation to clear up the anomaly. Unlike the Ombudsman's office, which can only make recommendations, the Information Commissioner can also make binding decisions.

The Information Commissioner is appointed by the President on the advice of the government following a resolution of both Houses of the Oireachtas. The decision to make the Ombudsman also hold the office of Information Commissioner was due to the fact that the Ombudsman's office had considerable expertise in the area of disclosure of public records. The Information Commissioner's office was presented with significant powers under the Act, such as the ability to authorise the release of information that might previously have been withheld in response to a citizen's request. In this respect, it breaches the 'corporation sole' doctrine (see below), which renders each minister solely responsible for his or her department.[18]

While the Act provides protection for public servants who disclose any wrongdoing in the public administration, there has been some debate as to whether or not it will result in less recording and documentation of information by the civil service. In an interview with this author, the Clerk of Dáil Éireann said he believed a possible outcome might be that less information would be committed to paper.[19] However, the Information Commissioner found such fears

---

[17] The British Freedom of Information Act of 2000 came into operation only in 2005.

[18] Zimmerman, J. F. (2001) 'The Irish Ombudsman–Information Commissioner', *Administration* Vol. 49(1), 79.

[19] Interview with Kieran Coughlan, 16 May 2002.

to be unwarranted following an investigation by his office into the progress of the new regulations.[20] Nonetheless, the report on this investigation expressed concern that the standard of record-keeping was inadequate in some departments, and queried the consequent 'ability of public bodies to conduct their business efficiently', noting that this 'also has implications for accountability'.

In an interview with this author, the Ombudsman/Information Commissioner noted that:

> we always expected Freedom of Information to have a spin-off in that officials would be more careful in what they say or write, and that is generally seen as a good thing in that officials don't recklessly commit things to paper without having thought it out. And in terms of policy advice I think Freedom of Information in other countries has been seen to have tightened up and improved the quality of the advice.[21]

A consultancy report into the progress of the Strategic Management Initiative corroborated this, and found that the Freedom of Information Act:

> has generated additional workloads across Departments/Offices, but it has undoubtedly improved the accountability of the civil service to the wider public.[22]

Less transparency? The Freedom of Information (Amendment) Act, 2003

The 1997 Act was a landmark for public accountability. It also had important implications for parliamentary accountability and oversight of the executive. In early 2003, the re-elected Fianna Fáil/ Progressive Democrat government decided to amend the Act, but the amending legislation was a significant curtailment on one of the most important mechanisms of public accountability in the state. Among the principal amendments were:

- an extension of the period after which the public could access government records from five to ten years

---

[20] Office of the Information Commissioner (2001) *Presentation to the Joint Oireachtas Committee on the Strategic Management Committee.* Dublin: Oireachtas Éireann – Joint Oireachtas Committee on the Strategic Management Committee.

[21] Interview with Kevin Murphy, 27 November 2002.

[22] PA Consulting (2002) *Evaluation of the Progress of the Strategic Management Initiative/Delivering Better Government Modernisation Programme.* Dublin: PA Consulting Group, p. 88.

- an extension of the type and number of official documents to which the original Act could not apply – this included parliamentary briefing records, including briefings in relation to the answering of parliamentary questions
- the introduction of fees for all FOI requests, reviews and appeals.

While the government insisted that it was amending the Act in light of experience gained since its introduction, more political reasons were suspected, especially when it emerged that the Information Commissioner and users of the legislation such as academics and journalists were not consulted over the amendments. The amending legislation was rushed through both Houses of the Oireachtas, causing consternation in the media and on opposition benches. The parliamentary debate that surrounded the amending legislation provides a clear example of the ongoing tension between the adversarial and co-operative views of parliamentary accountability in Dáil Éireann.

For example, defending the amendment that extended the period before which cabinet minutes could be released, former government adviser turned Fianna Fáil Senator Martin Mansergh argued that:

> It is a reasonable change, the purpose of which is to balance the need for good Government and freedom of deliberation within the Government with the right to freedom of information.[23]

Similarly, the Minister for Finance, whose department sponsored the Bill, argued in the Seanad that 'the Government is … committed to effective government.'[24] During the second stage in the Dáil, Fianna Fáil TD Peter Kelly noted that:

> The major responsibility of a Government is to govern. That should overshadow all other aspects of responsibility. *Where possible* it is essential that we be governed in a manner that has due regard for the concepts of accountability and transparency.[25]

This reflected the traditional majoritarian view of government most closely associated with Fianna Fáil, a party that has spent more time in government than any other. This view emphasises the necessity of government insulation from parliamentary and extra-parliamentary mechanisms of oversight, as well as the right of the government to govern. Simultaneously, the opposition parties advocated a more consensual view of accountability and berated the government, and

---

[23] *Seanad Debates*, 12 March 2003, Vol. 171, Col. 1688.
[24] Ibid., 4 March 2003, Vol. 171, Col. 1134.
[25] *Dáil Debates*, 26 March 2003, Vol. 563, Col. 1211 (emphasis added).

particularly the Progressive Democrats, for reneging on promises of a more open and transparent administration.

Despite the fundamental importance of FOI, like other issues it became embroiled in the adversarial politics of the parliament. Restrictive parliamentary procedures, as detailed in Chapter 4, meant that opposition deputies could do little to halt the proposed amendments, and instead attempted to score points off their counterparts on the government benches.

The speedy progress of the Bill though the Oireachtas demonstrated the government's unfettered ability to control parliament as well as the impotence of the opposition in attempting to oppose the legislation. Indeed, so sure was the Minister for Finance of the Bill's passage that it was left to various ministers of state to push it through most of the parliamentary stages. Although the opposition parties used every opportunity to oppose the amending legislation, the Bill passed through both Houses in less than seven weeks, with some stringent use of the guillotine. During the second stage of its passage through the Seanad, Fine Gael Senator Jim Higgins referred to its swift progress as 'a smash and grab raid on a key pillar of accountability and transparency of Government'.[26]

Following the enactment of the amending legislation, the government introduced a €150 fee for all appeals to the Information Commissioner. The office's new incumbent and Ombudsman, Emily O'Reilly, stated that 'the progressive nature of the charges could act as a financial disincentive to requesters exercising their rights of appeal'.[27] It was also noted that in other jurisdictions such charges did not apply. A study by the Information Commissioner found that as a result of the charges, between the first quarter of 2003 and the first quarter of 2004 the number of requests fell by 83 per cent. This included a 75 per cent drop in FOI requests for non-personal information. It also found that the media were now less likely to use the Act.[28]

In spite of the amendments, the FOI legislation remains an important mechanism of public accountability, and supplements the work of the Office of the Ombudsman. Both institutions have provided for unprecedented public access to administrative records

---

[26] *Seanad Debates*, 4 March 2003, Vol. 171, Col. 1144.

[27] www.oic.gov.ie/press.htm

[28] In fact, media requests prior to the 2003 amending legislation had given rise to a considerable part of the workload of staff at the Information Commissioner's office, due to their wide-ranging nature. Requests by journalists and public commentators are now more focused and time-specific.

and therefore greater opportunity for executive oversight. They have also had an influence on parliamentary accountability that has not received much public attention.

Freedom of information and the Ombudsman: complementing or supplanting parliament?

The two institutions of public accountability detailed above have significantly increased the amount of information available to the public concerning the decision-making process. They also represent a significant step away from the secretive bureaucratic style that characterised the preceding decades of Irish government. However, these developments have not been paralleled by the development of more transparent practices in the Dáil.

In the first instance, it is plausible that the power of the Ombudsman's office to probe into the administrative structures of state reduces the Dáil's ability to present itself as the watchdog of the public interest. As Zimmerman notes, parliamentarians' power to enquire into the public service through parliamentary questions does not guarantee the resolution of a complaint in the manner that the Ombudsman's extensive powers do.[29] Also, the Clerk of Dáil Éireann noted that FOI requests received more comprehensive answers than parliamentary questions. He pointed out that:

> there's much better information flows and so on, much more information around in all walks of life and that's reflected in the parliament itself and the backbencher himself is probably a bit more … empowered is not the word, but he is certainly more in the know about a much broader range of issues than he was, say, before. But I have my doubts, this is my own personal view … but I think there's not a whole lot of change in the real sense of accountability. It might be a contradiction in terms but there's more information around but in some cases less accountability.[30]

Similarly, when asked whether these institutions reduce the influence of parliamentary mechanisms of accountability, former Progressive Democrat leader Desmond O'Malley stated that:

> They do and it devalues parliament and the parliamentary system. And that's why it's essential I think to continually update it. I don't think those external institutions would have prospered to the extent that they have if the parliamentary system were working properly.[31]

---

[29] Zimmerman, J. F. (2001) 'The Irish Ombudsman–Information Commissioner', *Administration* Vol. 49(1), 78.

[30] Interview with Kieran Coughlan, 30 April 2002.

[31] Interview with Desmond O'Malley, 20 June 2003.

In contrast, some interviewees see these institutions as supplementing rather than threatening parliament. For example, according to a former Ombudsman:

> I think they [TDs] should use offices like mine more and more to try to claw back some degree of control over the executive because they've lost so much now.[32]

Agreeing with this view, Fine Gael's Alan Shatter argued that:

> Freedom of Information provides an additional mechanism for members of the Oireachtas to gain access to information that they may never otherwise have got. So I see that not as damaging parliament but as adding something additional to the parliamentary weapon.
>
> I also think the Ombudsman was a huge advance; I think if the Ombudsman can provide real answers to some of the questions that were previously dealt with on a sort of clientelist basis – I much prefer to see an official Ombudsman's office dealing with issues and producing an independent report on areas of life that aren't being dealt with properly.[33]

The Office of the Ombudsman and the Freedom of Information Act are properly regarded as progressive and necessary steps towards a more transparent and accountable democracy. However, the dichotomy of views expressed above raises questions as to how they influence the development of parliamentary accountability. From a parliamentary standpoint, these institutions remove from Dáil Éireann certain powers of oversight, even though the House had difficulty asserting them in its own right. This narrows the range of goals towards which the Dáil can aspire in attempting to assert itself as a check on the executive.

While both the Ombudsman and the Freedom of Information Act are key institutions in creating a more open decision-making culture in Ireland, the tribunals of inquiry examined in Chapter 6 have inspired the creation of other mechanisms of public accountability. These mechanisms are concerned with party funding and standards in public office, and form part of a new regulatory regime within which Irish political and administrative life now operates.

Party funding

The desire to regulate and account for the financing of political parties is not unique to Ireland; it has been a feature of many Western

---

32 Interview with Kevin Murphy, 27 November 2002.
33 Interview with Alan Shatter, 24 June 2003.

democracies, particularly in the light of corruption scandals in Italy, France and Germany. Britain has also witnessed an ongoing public debate over the issue of state funding of parties. Following several political scandals in the early 1990s, the Conservative government established the Committee on Standards in Public Life under the chairmanship of Lord Nolan in 1994.[34] The committee published several wide-ranging reports concerning issues such as ethics in the public service, party financing and the accountability of non-departmental public bodies.[35] Many of the issues and recommendations of the committee resonate with recent developments in Ireland.

As noted above, political parties are the medium through which politics operates in Ireland. The absence of any recognition of political parties in the Constitution is in contrast to the standing orders of both Houses of the Oireachtas, which grant speaking and questioning rights to parliamentary party groupings (of seven or more TDs) rather than individual members. The lack of rules concerning the financing of political parties gave an unfair advantage to parties that could form governments and were more attractive to business interests seeking to influence government decisions. It also caused huge lacunae in the public accountability of the principal political actors in the state.

A core issue at the Beef, McCracken, Flood and Moriarty Tribunals has been the sources of funding for party finances, particularly for Fine Gael and Fianna Fáil during the 1980s and early 1990s. Until 1997, there were no limits or controls on the receipt of funds by political parties in the state. Concern over this issue is not new, and the fundraising methods used by the parties (particularly Fianna Fáil) have caused public disquiet in the past.

As far back as 1947 Fianna Fáil placed advertisements in national broadsheets calling for donations to the party and providing addresses of prominent Irish businesses as locations for posting such donations.[36] Indeed, as FitzGerald points out, Fianna Fáil's introduction of industrial protection as early as the 1930s had left it better placed than others to secure financial support from Irish business.[37] In 1957, Seán Lemass made public appeals for finances that were to be

---

34 Lord Neill succeeded him in November 1997 and subsequently Sir Nigel Wicks has chaired the committee since 2001.

35 www.public-standards.gov.uk

36 Desmond, B. (2002) *Funding Political Parties in Ireland*, UCD Department of Politics Seminar, 22 March.

37 FitzGerald, G. (2003) *Reflections on the Irish State*. Dublin: Irish Academic Press, p. 75.

channelled through the party secretary's office, then in the hands of a young accountant, Charles Haughey, who would later become the party's most infamous figure.

By the 1960s, elections, campaigning and advertising were becoming considerably more expensive in Ireland, and the numbers of party volunteers (while still significant) was decreasing. In response, Fianna Fáil moved from using what it called its business election committee to creating in 1966 a permanent fund-raising network known as Taca ('Support'), which quickly became embroiled in controversy. It was established to raise finances for the party from the business community but, as Murphy indicates, it gained a reputation for seeking to influence ministerial decisions inappropriately and was quickly wound up.[38] Nonetheless, it was a reminder of the close personal relationship between politicians and business interests that had existed since the state's foundation. Indeed, Fianna Fáil's press officer during this period noted in his autobiography that while Taca disappeared, the 'goal of raising money from the business community didn't; the party just found more discreet ways of doing it'.[39] Indeed, as recently as March 2005 media reports claimed that the party was offering membership of its 'Forum for Opportunity' to private individuals for €4,500, payable over three years.[40]

While Taca was associated with Fianna Fáil, Fine Gael was also close to prominent members of Ireland's business community, who privately donated sums of money. The party has traditionally garnered support from the more privileged sections in Irish society, as well as those in professional occupations, and this provided a ready source of funding at election time. The involvement of both parties with Ireland's business community was to continue for some time, and increasingly involved large sums of money. It once again showed the powerlessness of the Dáil to regulate political activity and to cope with political parties, especially those in government.

While the activities of certain members of Fianna Fáil have been subject to intense scrutiny by various tribunals of inquiry, how Fine Gael rapidly alleviated debts of over IR£1 million during the early 1990s remains unclear. The McCracken Tribunal heard that in 1989

---

[38] Murphy, G. (1999) 'The Role of Interest Groups in the Policy Making Progress' in J. Coakley and M. Gallagher (eds) *Politics in the Republic of Ireland*. London: PSAI Press, p. 284.

[39] Dunlop, F. (2004) *Yes, Taoiseach*. Dublin: Penguin, p. 19.

[40] Sheahan, F. (2005) '€4,500 fee to join FF's golden club', *Irish Independent*, 29 March, 1.

the Fine Gael leader, Alan Dukes TD, wrote to several prominent businessmen seeking financial support for the party and received substantial amounts of money from Ben Dunne. The subsequent leader of the party, John Bruton TD, appointed Michael Lowry as one of the party's chief fundraisers; Dunne was successfully approached for finances again in 1991.[41] At the time of writing, this issue is yet to be considered by the Moriarty Tribunal.

The accountability of elected actors

The Electoral Act, 1997

The 1997 Electoral Act was the first attempt in the history of the state to hold political parties to account by placing a limit on the amount of money they could spend on Seanad, Dáil, European and presidential elections. The limits were linked to the Consumer Price Index to allow for increases in costs. The Act came soon after the Supreme Court judgment in the McKenna case, which found it unconstitutional that the government spend exchequer funds in the promotion of one viewpoint in referendums. For general elections, the stipulations of the Act came into effect nationally for the 2002 election,[42] but not before the Fianna Fáil/Progressive Democrat government raised the limits substantially (Table 7.1).

Of course, it is not unusual for incumbent administrations to attempt to manipulate the 'rules of the game' in their favour. Fianna Fáil had attempted to introduce a plurality electoral system in 1959 and again in 1968, which would have theoretically ensured its dominance of government and parliament. In 1974, during the Fine Gael/Labour Party 'National' Coalition, the Labour Minister for Local Government, James Tully, successfully passed an act allowing him to redraw constituency boundaries in favour of the coalition. The 'Tullymander' backfired in Fianna Fáil's favour, but it was not until 1997 that the power to redraw constituency boundaries was given to a permanent, independent Constituency Commission.[43]

---

[41] McCracken, B. (1997) *Report of the Tribunal of Inquiry (Dunnes Payments)*. Dublin: Stationery Office, pp. 19–20.

[42] There were six by-elections prior to the 2002 general election, which were subject to the regulations introduced under the Act.

[43] Ad hoc constituency commissions had been used in 1983, 1988, 1990 and 1995.

Table 7.1: Expenditure limits of party candidates for general elections[44]

Seats in constituency	Electoral Act, 1997 (IR£/€)	Electoral (Amendment) Act, 2001 (IR£/€)	Increase (%)
Three	14,000/ 17,776	20,000/25,395	43
Four	17,000/ 21,586	25,000/31,743	47
Five	20,000/ 25,395	30,000/38,092	50

While constituency sizes were removed from political interference, the new spending limits under the 1997 Act were not. An amending Act in 2001 allowed increases in spending limits that certainly favoured the larger government party, Fianna Fáil. As Table 7.1 shows, the largest spending limit increases were in the five-seat constituencies, where Fianna Fáil would be most likely to win extra seats, as it duly did in the 2002 election.

The 1997 Electoral Act also required candidates to declare any donations over €635 (IR£500) to their campaign; donations to political parties over the value of €5,079 (IR£4,000) were to be registered with the (Standards in) Public Offices Commission (Table 7.2). Similarly, in Britain, the Neill Committee's Fifth Report recommended that individual candidates should register donations over STG£200 (€323). Furthermore, donations to political parties in Britain over the value of STG£5,000 (€8,076), or to local constituency organisations of STG£1,000 (€1,615) or over must also be declared. The smaller amount permitted for individual donations in Britain compared with Ireland is offset by the frequency of donations to local constituency organisations, which is a result of the focus on party rather than candidate in the electoral system.

While the 1997 Electoral Act required disclosure of donations, no limits were placed on the value of those donations. However, in 2001, an Electoral (Amendment) Act was introduced which placed a limit of IR£5,000 (€6,349) on the amount of money a political party could receive as a donation. These donations would subsequently be made public by the Standards in Public Office Commission (see below).

---

[44] As of 2004, the limit for candidates in European elections is €230,000, an increase on the €190,461 allowed in 1999.

Table 7.2: Maximum undeclarable individual donations to politicians and political parties in Ireland and Britain (€)

	Ireland: Electoral Act, 1997	Britain: Political Parties, Elections and Referendums Act, 2000
Maximum undeclarable donation to individual politician	634.87	323
Maximum undeclarable donation to political party	5,078.95	8,076 (HQ) 1,615 (local)

Mirroring developments in Ireland, in Britain the Political Parties, Elections and Referendums Act, 2000 established:

- an Electoral Commission to oversee the implementation of the law relevant to party finance, oversight of electoral boundaries and the use of advertising
- the regulation of political donations
- limits to campaign spending at national level in general elections.

The Neill Committee rejected calls for comprehensive state funding, arguing that the election spending caps would be sufficient to reduce the need for income.[45] However, despite the new regulations, political party financing remains a contentious issue in Britain and demonstrates the difficulties in attempting to set a 'level playing field' for political competition.

The 1997 Electoral Act also provided for state funding of Irish political parties in proportion to their electoral results. To be eligible for such funding, a party must have achieved a minimum of 2 per cent of first preference votes nationally at the last general election. Table 7.3 shows that the three largest parties received almost 79 per cent of the total funding available in 2004 (down from the 86 per cent received in 2000).[46] This gives them a clear advantage over the

---

[45] Fisher, J. (2002) 'Next Step: State Funding for the Parties?' *Political Quarterly* Vol. 73(4), 393.

[46] Standards in Public Office Commission (2005) *Annual Report 2004*. Dublin, p. 44; MacCarthaigh, M. (2001) 'Political Data for Republic of Ireland, 2000', *Irish Political Studies* Vol. 16, 343.

Table 7.3: Allocation of state funding to political parties in 2004 (€)

Party	Share of eligible funding (%)	Amount (€)
Fianna Fáil	41.92	2,049,876
Fine Gael	23.9	1,168,924.23
Labour	12.81	626,481
PDs	6.36	310,678
Green Party	6.25	305,311
Sinn Féin	8.77	428,743
Total		4,890,013.23

Source: Standards in Public Office Commission (2005), p. 48

smaller parties, which have to research and develop policies over as many issues as the larger parties, on a much smaller budget. The allocation of almost 5 million is quadruple the amount received in 2000,[47] due to changes brought about by the 2001 Standards in Public Office Act (see below). All parties over the 2 per cent first preference threshold now receive a basic sum of €126,974; the balance consists of an annual sum divided proportionally to the total first preference vote of each party.[48]

The parties must present audited accounts to the Standards in Public Office Commission every year showing under several sub-headings how they spent the money allocated to them. Table 7.4 details the breakdown of €4,924,478 spent by the parliamentary parties for the year 2004. Interestingly, it demonstrates that all the parties spend most of their allocation on internal administration and co-ordination activities and comparatively little on research and policy formulation. Independent Dáil members, though also eligible for state funding under the 2001 legislation, are not required to present such accounts.

---

[47] MacCarthaigh, M. (2001) 'Political Data for Republic of Ireland, 2000', *Irish Political Studies* Vol. 16, 343.

[48] Standards in Public Office Commission (2004) *Annual Report 2003*. Dublin, p. 33.

Table 7.4: Spending of exchequer funding for 2004 by political parties (€)

Qualified political party	General admin.	Research, education and training	Policy formulation	Co-ordination of activities of branches and members	Promotion of participation of women	Promotion of participation of young people	Total funding spent
Fianna Fáil	1,893,820	Nil	Nil	11,250	18,930	Nil	1,924,000
Fine Gael	586,741	1,069	24,901	583,008	50,961	87,057	1,333,737
Labour	415,425	50,575	31,365	51,770	34,235	38,639	622,009
PDs	235,040	8,360	43,103	24,175	Nil	Nil	310,678
Green Party	238,923	Nil	484	47,680	3,729	14,495	305,311
Sinn Féin	184,541	25,340	30,783	143,677	11,189	33,213	428,743
Total	3,554,490	85,344	130,636	861,560	119,044	173,404	4,924,478*

*The difference between this figure and the total in Table 7.3 is the amount of money carried forward to the following year by Fianna Fáil, Fine Gael and the Labour Party.
Source: Standards in Public Office Commission (2005), p. 45

Obliging political parties to publish details of how they spend their exchequer allocations is regarded as another method of introducing transparency and accountability into the electoral process in Ireland. In presenting records of income and expenditure, parties are now subject to more public scrutiny than ever before. However, a debate over corporate funding of political parties continues, with mixed views among the principal parties.

Fianna Fáil and the Progressive Democrats prefer regulation to a blanket ban on such donations, from which they have traditionally benefited. The Labour Party (which has traditionally received financial support from trade unions) has consistently opposed corporate donations and introduced in 2000 the Electoral (Amendment) (Donations to Parties and Candidates) Bill. This Private Member's Bill attempted to reduce further the amount of money that could be donated to political parties and politicians, but was defeated by the government. Fine Gael, having initially sided with the Labour Party, has recently performed an about-face on the issue. In 2002, the party's newly elected leader, Enda Kenny TD, overturned a ban on such donations introduced by his predecessor following tribunal revelations linking business and political interests.

Local Elections (Disclosure of Donations and Expenditure) Act, 1999

The introduction of regulations in the 1997 Electoral Act for the funding of parties and candidates at elections was followed by similar legislation concerning local elections in Ireland. The revelations at the Flood Tribunal concerning the bribing of local politicians were the principal motivating factor in the creation of the Local Elections (Disclosure of Donations and Expenditure) Bill, 1999. When passed, the Act drew on the principles of the Electoral Act (see above) and obliged all candidates and parties to record and declare donations during campaigns for local government office. Non-compliance by a successful candidate could result in suspension from the local authority. However, there are no limits for local election campaign spending.

Oireachtas (Ministerial and Parliamentary Offices) (Amendment) Act, 2001

The Oireachtas (Ministerial and Parliamentary Offices) Act, 2001, involved further regulation of the use of funds by political parties.

State funding for the leaders of parliamentary parties had been introduced in 1938. Although still referred to as the party leader's allowance, in fact the money is for the use of the political party in question. Prior to the 2001 Act, the only stipulations tied to these allowances were that such funding be for parliamentary purposes only and, following the McKenna judgment (see above) in 1995, that such funding not be used for electoral purposes.

The new Act was concerned with how such funding should in future be computed and audited, and how it would be adjusted following a merger of parliamentary parties. The sum received by each party depends on the number of party members elected to the Dáil at the preceding general election. The legislation was partly in response to the discovery at the McCracken Tribunal that former Fianna Fáil leader and Taoiseach, Charles Haughey, had been using his party's allowance for personal expenditure, often with the knowledge and compliance of senior party members. Haughey had drawn from this account using cheques pre-signed by Bertie Ahern TD, then a front-bench member of the party. During a Dáil debate on the McCracken Tribunal report, by which time Ahern was Taoiseach, he was markedly reluctant to confirm this co-signatory role. He was the 'senior party member' to whom he referred in the following Dáil speech:

> Deputy Spring [leader of the Labour Party] has raised the issue of the party leader's allowance during Fianna Fáil's period in Opposition. In so far as I could with little available records I am satisfied, having spoken to the person who administered the account, that it was used for bona fide party purposes, that the cheques were prepared by that person and countersigned by another senior party member. Their purpose was to finance personnel, press and other normal supports for an Opposition leader.[49]

The new Act required party leaders to have their accounts audited and presented to the (Standards in) Public Offices Commission. The political parties must provide accounts of how money they receive under the party leader's allowance is spent; a series of headings is provided ranging from policy formulation to entertainment. Table 7.5 sets out how much each of the parties received between 2002 and 2004.

Despite the plethora of new regulations, links between large business interests and the political parties in Ireland persist and are not easily subjected to parliamentary scrutiny. One of the most public examples of this (often criticised by Fine Gael and the Labour

---

[49] *Dáil Debates*, 10 September 1997, Vol. 480, Col. 677.

Table 7.5: Party leaders' allowances for 2002–4 (€)

	2002	2003	2004
Fianna Fáil	1,562,205	2,257,361	2,348,308
Fine Gael	1,718, 843	1,754,506	1,825,203
Labour Party	956,454	1,175,537	1,222,907
Progressive Democrats	182,055	423,401	440,463
Green Party	102,344	319,596	332,475
Sinn Féin	51,172	266,325	277,062
Socialist Party	51,172	53,265	55,413
Total	4,624,245	6,249,991	6,501,831

Source: Standards in Public Office Commission (2003), p. 40; (2004), p. 48; (2005), p. 48.

Party) is the large sums paid by prominent business figures to sit beside government ministers during lunches at the Fianna Fáil tent at the Galway Races. Indeed, figures released by the Standards in Public Office Commission for the election year of 2002 reveal that the party received almost three-quarters of all donations to political parties.[50]

Fianna Fáil is not alone in having question marks over its money-raising activities. As the McCracken and Moriarty Tribunals have shown, Fine Gael's reputation for honesty and integrity has been tarnished by revelations concerning a former minister from the party, Michael Lowry. Apart from his tax evasion, it was revealed in 2001 that a member of a communications business consortium had donated IR£50,000 to Fine Gael.[51] As Minister for Communications during the Fine Gael-led 'Rainbow' Coalition, Lowry had awarded a mobile communications licence to this company.

Following the 2001 limit on donations to political parties, the Standards in Public Office Commission recorded that the totals received by the political parties fell from €947,768 in 2001 to €265,799.52 in 2002. However, as they are not required to disclose

---

[50] Standards in Public Office Commission (2004) *Annual Report 2003*. Dublin, p. 25.

[51] The consortium was ESAT and the Norwegian firm Telenor had written the cheque.

donations under €5,078.95 (Table 7.2), these figures may understate the actual amounts of money received by the parties. As shown above, there is no agreement among the parties as to how the issue of corporate donations should be dealt with.

Individual politicians as well as political parties have encountered difficulties in achieving a level playing field for elections. Following the 2002 general election, the Standards in Public Office Commission admitted that it had had difficulty in completing its role, as some TDs refused to disclose fully the sources of their election donations. The commission also complained that, because a complete list of candidates is not finalised until two weeks before the election, it is left with little time to inform all candidates adequately of the rules involved concerning disclosure.[52]

In June 2003, the Standards in Public Office Commission released details of spending by candidates during the 2002 general election. It found that fifty-six of the incoming 166 TDs had over-spent their quota as established under the Electoral (Amendment) Act, 2001 (Table 7.1), among them the Taoiseach and most of the cabinet ministers. Some of this overspending was the result of a court decision on the eve of the election, which held that Oireachtas members must include in their spending estimation services such as mail and secretarial services. Indeed, a major factor in Fianna Fáil's electoral success since 1987 has been its ability to use such facilities.[53] Nonetheless, no sanctions were imposed. The use of state facilities by incumbent TDs in Ireland contrasts with Westminster, where parliamentarians do not have access to parliamentary facilities during an election campaign.

A further difficulty in regulating election spending is that candidates need only submit details of expenditure from the time the official announcement of the polling date or 'writ' is passed in the Dáil. During two concurrent by-elections in March 2005, candidates were openly campaigning in advance of the writ being passed, yet no declaration had to be made of expenses incurred during this period. This gives an obvious advantage to the party with the right to pass the writ.

In short, the attempt to regulate the financial affairs of the political classes has been problematic and has suffered many teething

---

[52] Hennessy, M. (2002) 'Unsuccessful SF candidates received largest donations', *Irish Times*, 1 November, 6.

[53] Collins, S. (2003) 'Government broke the law and got away with it', *Sunday Tribune*, 22 June, 17.

difficulties. The historical legacy of financial support for the main parties from private interests will prove a difficult challenge for the new regulatory mechanisms. However, the system does provide for significantly more transparency in the political process than existed previously, and certainly more than the Dáil could elicit. In this respect, therefore, it may be argued that legislation resulting from the tribunals of inquiry has strengthened political actors' public accountability.

The accountability of non-elected actors: political lobbying

When analysing elected actors' accountability to the public, we must also consider the influence of non-elected actors, i.e. private lobbyists, on the political process. In recent years, many former political advisers in Ireland have embarked on careers in this industry, which seeks to sway political decisions in favour of certain organised groups. In part, lobbyists have occupied a vacuum left by the absence of media interest in the work of the Dáil, and they have featured at tribunals of inquiry that have particular political import.[54] As with issues of party funding until recently, the work of lobbyists is unaccountable to the public or parliament, and has been an underlying feature of recent tribunals of inquiry.

During the course of the Flood Tribunal, revelations concerning the activities of political lobbyists led to calls for a register of lobbyists, as exists in other European jurisdictions, including Britain. In particular, the distinction between bribery and the legitimate lobbying of public representatives came under scrutiny. While no relevant legislation has been promulgated, several Private Members' Bills have been proposed in recent years concerning the registration of lobbyists. These Bills would have required all paid lobbyists to register their interests with the Public Offices Commission (later the Standards in Public Office Commission). The Labour Party introduced the first such Bill in the Seanad in 1999, noting that 'lobbying has become established as a permanent feature of our system of parliamentary democracy'.[55] The government defeated the Bill at the second stage, arguing that the forthcoming Standards in Public Office Bill and

---

[54] Collins, S. (2004) 'The Parliamentary Lobby System' in T. Garvin, M. Manning and R. Sinnott (eds) *Dissecting Irish Politics: Essays in Honour of Brian Farrell.* Dublin: UCD Press, pp. 198–211.

[55] *Seanad Debates*, 30 June 1999, Vol. 160, Col. 88.

codes of conduct being drafted as part of the civil service Strategic Management Initiative (see below) would deal adequately with the matter.[56]

Following revelations at the Flood Tribunal by a former Fianna Fáil press secretary turned political lobbyist, Frank Dunlop, that he took bribes from property developers, the Labour Party proposed a second Bill in the Seanad in 2000. Proposing the Bill, Senator Joe Costello argued that had such a register existed fifteen years previously 'it would probably have made the Flood tribunal unnecessary'.[57] The government requested that the reading of the Bill be postponed on the basis that it proposed to establish an all-party committee to consider the issue of lobbyists as well as other relevant legislation. Similarly, another Private Member's Bill introduced by the Labour Party in 2003 dealing with lobbyists made little progress. Despite government assurances that the matter would be dealt with, the Standards in Public Office Act, 2001 did not require lobbyists to register their interests.

Lobbying remains an area of political life that has not been penetrated by either parliamentary or public forms of accountability, although certain aspects of it have been made public by tribunals of inquiry, particularly the Flood Tribunal. A government-commissioned report into regulating lobbyists was submitted to an all-party committee of TDs and Senators to consider in 2004. At time of writing, no recommendation had appeared.[58] This is an issue that the Dáil must pursue, particularly as it seeks to scrutinise the process by which government decisions are made.

Standards in public office

The regulations outlined above have been created in parallel with others concerning a fundamental matter in political life – standards in public office. The concept of ethics and standards is more difficult to measure and therefore to regulate than a tangible matter such as finance. Along with accountability, standards in public office have become part of the public and political discourse surrounding the tribunals of inquiry, as revelations concerning questionable political

---

[56] Ibid., Cols 93–6.
[57] Ibid., 24 May 2000, Vol. 163, Col. 639.
[58] In anticipation of future legislation, the Public Relations Institute of Ireland – the representative organisation for lobbyists – released a *Code of Professional Practice for Public Affairs* for its members in October 2004.

decision-making at both national and local level continue. Several pieces of legislation introduced since 1995 have resulted in some new extra-parliamentary institutions to monitor behaviour in public office.

O'Toole considers ethics in government to be 'the application of moral standards in the course of official work'.[59] He argues that unethical behaviour occurs when, for example, ministers do not disclose full information in answering parliamentary questions, thus causing a breakdown in parliamentary accountability, or when members do not disclose personal interests concerning a matter before parliament. Most legislatures attempt to avoid such conflicts of interests by creating what in other sectors is often referred to as 'professional' accountability or self-regulation. An example of such accountability in a legislature is a requirement on parliamentarians to register their assets.

In Ireland, the concept of a register of members' interests can be traced back at least as far as Barry Desmond's *The Houses of the Oireachtas – a Plea for Reform* in 1975. Among a wide range of proposals, he called for members to declare fully their business and professional interests and beneficiary holdings.[60] However, he later noted that at the time:

> I regret to record that my proposal and argument in favour were greeted with almost unanimous hostility. I do not recall receiving any support.[61]

While in Opposition in 1991, Labour TD Brendan Howlin proposed a Private Member's Bill titled the Ethics in Government and Public Office Bill. Its main goals were:

1   the regulation of gifts to office holders
2   a register of interests in both Houses of the Oireachtas
3   a declaration of income by political parties.

The Bill was supported in principle by Fine Gael but was defeated by the Fianna Fáil/Progressive Democrat government, which argued that standing orders and the Dáil Committee on Procedure and Privileges, rather than legislation, would be appropriate to regulate the financial interests of Dáil members.

---

[59]   O'Toole, B. (1997) 'Ethics in Government', *Parliamentary Affairs* Vol. 50(1), 130.

[60]   Desmond, B. (1975) *The Houses of the Oireachtas – a Plea for Reform*. Leinster House, Dublin: Parliamentary Labour Party, p. 31.

[61]   Downey, J. (1975) 'T.D. puts Dáil reform plea to government', *Irish Times*, 6 March, 5.

Three years later, in 1994, Labour TD Eithne FitzGerald, as minister of state at the reconstituted Department of the Tánaiste, began to steer the Ethics in Public Office Bill through the Oireachtas. The creation of such legislation had been part of the Fianna Fáil/ Labour Programme for Government. Girvin notes that Fianna Fáil was reluctant to introduce both the Ethics Bill and the register of interests.[62] The progress of the Bill was undoubtedly eased by the public demand for greater accountability in political life during this period, in response to the revelations of improper relationships between business and government at the Beef Tribunal.

The Fianna Fáil/Labour Party coalition also initiated the Electoral Bill later that year, before the collapse of this government and its replacement by the Rainbow Coalition. This Bill was promulgated during the subsequent Rainbow Coalition's term of office, revealing the Labour Party's commitment to a more open form of government. It was also during this government that the Freedom of Information Act was introduced.

Introducing standards: the Ethics in Public Office Act, 1995

Ethics legislation and codes of conduct for members have become a common feature of public bodies, including legislatures, in Western democracies. It is interesting to note the simultaneous development of ethical guidelines for parliamentarians in Westminster-style democracies globally during the 1990s. As part of these guidelines, the creation of a monitoring body independent of parliament has been a common development. In Canada, for example, an Ethics Councillor was appointed in 1994 and renamed the Ethics Commissioner in 2003. Similarly in Britain, following the recommendation of the Nolan Committee (see above), the new office of Parliamentary Commissioner for Standards was created, whose remit included keeping a register of members' interests.[63]

As well as updating the law on the prevention of corruption, the 1995 Ethics in Public Office Act provided for the annual registration

---

[62] Girvin, B. (1999) 'Political Competition, 1992–1997' in M. Marsh and P. Mitchell (eds) *How Ireland Voted 1997*. Oxford: Westview/PSAI Press, p. 4.

[63] Silk, P. and Walters, R. (1998) *How Parliament Works*. London: Longman, p. 28. Controversially, the second holder of the post, Elizabeth Filkin, claimed in late 2001 that the Speaker of the House of Commons had failed to ensure that the office had the necessary independence and resources. Her accusations came in the light of revelations that she was not being automatically reappointed to the post, as her predecessor had been.

of interests by people in key public positions. These include Oireachtas members and ministers, the Attorney General, senior civil and public servants, board members and senior executives of state enterprises as well as special advisers to ministers. It also obliged members speaking or voting on an issue to make a formal declaration if the issue involved a potential conflict of interest. For ministers, the Act went further, obliging members of the government to declare if a close relative or business partner had an interest in a matter under debate. A simple statement that the member has an interest is sufficient to meet the requirements of the Act. The Act also provided for the establishment of a Public Offices Commission to oversee compliance by those affected.

Public Offices Commission

The Public Offices Commission was a new body established under the 1995 Act; its membership comprised the:

- Ceann Comhairle (Speaker) of Dáil Éireann
- Comptroller and Auditor General
- Ombudsman
- Clerks of the Dáil and Seanad Éireann.

Its role was to monitor compliance with the provisions of the Act by the public office holders mentioned above. The Electoral Act, 1997 and the subsequent Electoral (Amendment) Act, 1998 extended the commission's remit, giving it the power to monitor the disclosure of political donations, the limiting of election expenditure, public funding of qualified political parties, and the reimbursement of expenses incurred by certain election candidates.

Members of the Oireachtas who did not hold any of these offices were responsible to the Committee on Members' Interests of the Dáil or Seanad. The Ethics in Public Office Act and the later Standards in Public Office Act established these committees to monitor the implementation of its requirements, as well as to sanction members who broke the guidelines. This was a significant development as it introduced a new mechanism of oversight for parliament and empowered its members to make decisions concerning their peers.

Standards in Public Office Act, 2001

Following the publication of the McCracken Tribunal report in August 1997, the government made a commitment to amend the

Ethics in Public Offices Act to incorporate the report's recommendations. Taoiseach Bertie Ahern TD said that among these new addi-
tions to the Act would be:

> the creation of a criminal offence for breaches of the legislation and the conse-
> quent barring of a convicted person from standing for subsequent election.[64]

The new Act promulgated in 2001 created financial penalties for
breaches of the Act by those falling within its remit. Following suggestions from the Public Offices Commission, the new legislation
also put on a statutory footing the ability of the commission to
appoint an inspector to make an initial investigation into a matter of
concern to the commission.

Standards in Public Office Commission

The Standards in Public Office Commission was established under
the Standards in Public Office Act, 2001, and built on the work of the
existing Public Offices Commission. Its terms of reference were
amended by the Electoral Acts from 1997 to 2002 and the Oireachtas
(Ministerial and Parliamentary Offices) (Amendment) Act, 2001.
Members are appointed for a six-year term. Unlike the Public Offices
Commission, the Standards in Public Office Commission did not
include in its membership the Ceann Comhairle: he or she was to be
replaced by a member of the judiciary appointed by the President on
the advice of the government, who would fulfil the role of chairperson.

The reason for excluding the Ceann Comhairle was that an
anomalous situation arose when the Public Offices Commission
produced reports that had to be submitted to the Ceann Comhairle,
as he was already a member of the commission. Also, in an interview
conducted with this author, a former Ombudsman noted that both
he and the Comptroller and Auditor-General were concerned
that a future situation might arise involving legal action.[65] As the
commission would need legal advice in such a situation, they
recommended that a senior judicial figure replace the Ceann
Comhairle. The government also appointed a former minister (the
Labour Party's Liam Kavanagh) to the commission. The former
Ombudsman said that this was because they 'still have this feeling that
people like myself don't understand political life'.[66] He went on to

---

[64] *Dáil Debates*, 10 September 1997, Vol. 480, Col. 680.
[65] Interview with Kevin Murphy, 27 November 2002.
[66] Ibid.

note that Kavanagh was 'a great addition to the commission because he does bring a perspective to the commission of what's going on at the ground'.

International anti-corruption standards

While evidence has mounted in recent years of corrupt activity in Irish politics, successive governments have been afraid to tackle this issue. Indeed, at the time of writing, no elected officials have been convicted of the offence and a proper study of corruption in Irish politics has yet to be undertaken. As detailed above, a plethora of legislation indirectly related to corruption in the political and administrative processes was enacted in the 1990s, but it was not until the Prevention of Corruption (Amendment) Act, 2001 that the issue was directly addressed. The Act was signed into law following the government's rejection of two Private Members' Bills of the same name from Fine Gael in 1999 and the Labour Party in 2000.

The Act was the first new anti-corruption legislation in the state in 85 years.[67] It strengthened the law on corruption, but the driving force behind it was not domestic but international; its principal purpose was to allow the state to ratify three international agreements on combating international corruption: the 1997 EU Convention against Corruption, the 1997 OECD Convention on Combating Bribery and the 1999 Council of Europe Criminal Law Convention on Corruption.

The legislation allows, for the first time, a presumption of corruption in the case of undeclared donations to a candidate above the amount set out in the Electoral Act, 1997 or the Local Elections (Disclosure of Donations and Expenditure) Act, 1999 (see above). The Act amended and broadened pre-Independence anti-corruption legislation, including the new offence of corruption in office, whereby decisions are made to benefit the office holder or persons close to him or her. It also brought within its scope MEPs, members and officials of the EU, judges of national, foreign and international courts, and certain other foreign public officials. At time of writing, none of these measures has been called on. A Proceeds of Crime (Amendment) Act was signed into law in 2005, a section of which allows the Criminal Assets Bureau to confiscate goods it believes were obtained through corruption, subject to a High Court order.

---

[67] Previous anti-corruption legislation included the Public Bodies Corrupt Practices Act, 1889 and the Prevention of Corruption Acts, 1906 and 1916.

Difficulties in enforcing standards

As with the regulations concerning party funding, the new legislation and oversight bodies described above and created for the purposes of improving standards in public life have not been successful to date. It can be argued that some of the new regulations were knee-jerk reactions to the tribunals of inquiry and have had difficulty in taking root in a traditionally secretive political culture. Experience to date would seem to demonstrate that institutions of public accountability are as difficult to legislate for and operate as institutions of judicial accountability.

It is not just parliamentarians that find difficulty with the creation of new public institutional checks on their activities. Members of the Public Offices Commission encountered difficulties in trying to interpret the Ethics in Public Office Act. There was also recorded general discontent among parliamentarians about the new regulations that arose in response to the tribunals of inquiry, and few amendments to the legislation were proposed during its passage through the Oireachtas as members feared being accused of corruption. As with its predecessor, the Standards in Public Office Commission has encountered difficulties in fulfilling its remit.

In 2003 the commission was alerted to the fact that a TD had not given full details of his assets in a tax compliance certificate. However, as no complaint was made against the TD in question, the commission found itself unable to investigate the issue.[68] In late 2004 the commission considered an issue that had arisen in the context of a minister awarding a public relations contract for his department to a constituent. At first glance it appeared to be exactly the type of issue the commission was established to investigate, but it found itself unable to so.[69] Concerns were also expressed by TDs that with because of the commission's very existence, 'tit for tat' allegations might develop between deputies before full investigations were conducted.[70]

As with the issue of enforcing standards in public office, the new regulations for increasing the financial accountability of political actors have been problematic, as described above. This again

---

[68] Standards in Public Office Commission (2005) Annual Report 2004. Dublin, p. 15.

[69] Ibid., p. 16.

[70] Gay, O. (2002) *The Regulation of Parliamentary Standards – a Comparative Perspective* (commissioned on behalf of the Committee on Standards in Public Life). London: The Constitution Unit, University College London, p. 76.

demonstrates the difficulty faced by mechanisms of public account-ability in attempting to regulate political life. In particular, it raises questions as to the commission's ability to ensure that public office holders act in accordance with loosely defined codes of conduct.

Interviewees pointed out the difficulty of enforcing the new regulations under the Ethics and Standards in Public Office Acts. Cullen argues that in the Oireachtas, the register does not receive full co-operation from members. He found that 'most TDs record "nil" interests and even where information is provided it is so vague as to be useless.'[71] This is in contrast to the voluntary register of members' interests in Westminster, where MPs traditionally disclose accurate details of their interests for fear of being 'discovered' by the media.

Setting the bar too high?

Public accountability has emerged in Ireland as a form of executive oversight that does not involve Dáil Éireann. However, it can be argued that the unprecedented number of regulatory and institutional mechanisms facing parliamentarians today raise as many difficulties as they attempt to solve. There is an element of 'locking the gate after the horse has bolted', and many former parliamentarians and public figures will never be reprimanded for their corrupt actions. Furthermore, it is impossible to regulate for every eventuality in political life, and it may be argued that the new regulatory regime has raised the bar too high.

Indeed, a strong case can be made for improving existing tools of parliamentary accountability instead of creating new extra-parliamentary ones. However, having failed in their duty, traditional parliamentary devices of executive oversight have not been considered as suitable mechanisms on which to build a stronger culture of parliamentary accountability. Instead, the lack of respect for such devices has produced a situation whereby, unlike Westminster, no parliamentarian in Ireland is likely to resign for the offence of 'misleading parliament'.[72]

While the Ombudsman/Information Commissioner and Freedom of Information Act have provided for unprecedented levels of

---

[71] Cullen, P. (2002) *With a Little Help from my Friends.* Dublin: Gill & Macmillan, p. 285.

[72] As recently as 2002, two ministers in Westminster (Stephen Byers and Estelle Morris) resigned in recognition of the fact that they had failed in the oversight or supervision of their departments.

administrative scrutiny, they have also presented challenges for parliamentary accountability. Likewise, the innovations in the areas of party funding and standards in public office inhibit Dáil Éireann to some degree, and present difficulties for the bodies responsible for managing them. The restructured Standards in Public Office Commission has existed only for a short period at the time of writing, but has made its presence felt in the Irish political arena. Its growth and success, however, depend on parliamentary support and the functioning of new institutions within parliament designed to support its work (see below). This commission, the Office of the Ombudsman and the Freedom of Information Act offer new opportunities for public accountability. Given clear boundaries, they can complement rather than undermine parliamentary accountability.

CHAPTER 8

Towards a new parliamentary environment? Recent reforms in Dáil Éireann

Reforms within parliament

By their very nature, parliaments are the most difficult institution of all to reform. Politicians do not like departing from the status quo or altering the environment in which they have been politically socialised. In rational choice institutionalist terms, there may be many 'sunken costs' in an institution, which make any benefits of reform too costly. Again one must ask why governments in Westminster-style parliaments such as the Oireachtas engage in parliamentary reform that might weaken their dominance of the decision-making process.

In discussing electoral system change, Shugart and Wattenberg identify two reasons why governments change the 'rules of the game' that got them into power.[1] Firstly, inherent factors, whereby it is perceived that the existing system causes failures, act as a catalyst for change. Secondly, contingent factors – events and interests – cause actors to introduce reforms, usually because not introducing them would be electorally damaging in the future.

The same logic elucidates the increased tempo in Dáil reform since the mid-1990s. The tribunals of inquiry implicitly and explicitly drew unprecedented public attention to the failure of Dáil mechanisms of executive oversight. The government was forced to reform aspects of the Dáil and its procedures, even if this was to its disadvantage. Also, it became politically dangerous for the government not to be seen to take action on eliminating corruption and malpractice from political and administrative life – a 'contingent' reason for reform.

With these factors in mind, it becomes less surprising that Fianna Fáil-led administrations have been responsible for recent developments. As noted above, the party has traditionally been the most reactionary in relation to altering legislative–executive relations,

---

[1] Shugart, M. S. and Wattenberg, M. P. (2001) 'Conclusion' in M. S. Shugart and M. P. Wattenberg (eds) *Mixed-Member Electoral Systems: the Best of Both Worlds?* Oxford: Oxford University Press, p. 571.

favouring an adversarial rather than a consensual form of parliamentary politics. However, since 1989, when it entered the first of a series of coalition governments, it has proved amenable to several institutional reforms.

Paralleling recent extra-parliamentary reforms such as the Standards in Public Office Commission has been the establishment of new institutions *within* the Oireachtas. Some of these institutions act as supports for the external bodies; others aim to alter the functioning of parliament itself. It is worth reconsidering here the constitutional prerogative that provides for the prevention of corruption in the Oireachtas. Article 15.10 of Bunreacht na hÉireann states that:

> Each House shall make its own rules and standing orders, with power to attach penalties for their infringement, and shall have power to … *protect itself and its members against any person or persons interfering with, molesting or attempting to corrupt its members in the exercise of their duties.*[2]

Many of the recent reforms in Dáil Éireann have attempted to adhere to this constitutional aspiration. These institutions have been created as responses to the allegations (and exposure) of corruption in political life, as well as to support the new mechanisms of oversight for party funding and ethics in public life described above.

While there have been significant developments in the public sector under the Strategic Management Initiative for the purposes of increasing administrative accountability, the same cannot be said of the parliamentary arena. A recent OECD report notes that 'compared to the pace of change in the executive branch, the Parliament has been slow to assume its new regulatory accountability responsibilities.'[3] However, while reforms designed to increase the accountability of the executive and parliamentarians have proceeded slowly, their creation is significant and demonstrates concern about the condition of parliamentary accountability in Dáil Éireann.

Parliamentary committees

The increased use of parliamentary committees since their re-establishment in 1992, and their role as oversight bodies, provides the most prominent example of recent internal institutional design in the Oireachtas. However, their success in moving beyond strictly defined

---

[2] Emphasis added.
[3] Organisation for Economic Cooperation and Development (2001) *Regulatory Reform in Ireland.* Paris: OECD, p. 57.

roles has been limited, and they have not yet fundamentally altered the legislative–executive balance of power. The zero-sum politics still operating in the Lower House, as well as the institutional logic of the Westminster system, makes it unlikely that committees will, for example, have the power to force a ministerial resignation. While this finding concurs with the analysis presented earlier, we must examine here the establishment of two committees that have played an important role in the development of standards in public office and parliamentary reform in Dáil Éireann.

Dáil Committee on Members' Interests

The Ethics in Public Office Act, 1995 and its successor, the Standards in Public Office Act, 2001 legislated for the creation of a Committee on Members' Interests in both Houses of the Oireachtas to ensure members' compliance with that legislation. In fact, the Dáil Committee on Members' Interests is the only select committee of that chamber with a non-government majority,[4] as well as being one of only two created by virtue of statute law rather than standing order.[5] It does not have the power to alter, revise or otherwise change the findings of the Standards in Public Office Commission. It has encountered difficulties in institutionalising itself into the machinery of the Oireachtas, and its five members have been difficult to recruit. We must consider here two cases with which the committee has had to deal as evidence of how effective it has been and can expect to be. The first was referred to the committee by the Standards in Public Office Commission; the committee itself initiated the second.

Suspension of Ned O'Keeffe TD

In 2001, members of the opposition complained to the Public Offices Commission[6] that the Minister of State for Food at the Department of Agriculture, Fianna Fáil's Ned O'Keeffe TD, had not declared a relevant family business interest during a Private Member's motion on agricultural matters. Neither had he noted in the Register of Interests shareholdings held by his family in this business. O'Keeffe resigned as minister of state after the complaints were made, and the

---

4   The chair was, however, held by a member of the government.
5   As noted above, the other committee established by statute is the Sub-Committee on European Scrutiny.
6   The Standards in Public Office Act had not yet passed into law.

commission conducted an investigation into the matter under the 1995 Ethics in Public Office Act. The commission concluded that O'Keeffe had not intentionally breached the requirements of the Act, and forwarded its report to the Dáil's Committee on Members' Interests. It recommended that he be suspended with pay for ten days.

During the ensuing Dáil debate on his suspension, O'Keeffe protested that he was victimised by the media, and indeed members of his own party, who he said had conducted a 'concerted campaign' to force his resignation.[7] Somewhat bizarrely, he claimed that he was a scapegoat and that the:

> story was massaged, embellished and primed by senior members of Fianna Fáil and their masterful minders into an issue of national importance. The political pressure was skilfully, wilfully and, with masterful precision, communicated to the nation via a prominent journalist.[8]

He also criticised the decision of the Committee on Members' Interests to sit in private and questioned its impartiality, saying:

> How could I expect a committee made up of members with party interests, political interests and self-promotion interests to come forward with anything other than today's proposed suspension?[9]

What is significant about this episode is that the members of the committee that censured O'Keeffe claimed that they found their task 'distasteful'. One member, the Labour Party's Brendan Howlin TD, revealed that:

> None of us took satisfaction in any of this and none of us will queue up to sit on this committee again.[10]

Indeed, the previous week, during a debate introducing a new code of conduct for parliamentarians, Howlin had also recorded his lack of enthusiasm for membership of the committee, saying:

> It has enabled me to have an overview of the workings and minutiae of the House in a way one would probably not get unless one were a party Whip. It is a committee of which I will not be queuing up to be a member in the next Dáil, assuming I am returned as a Member.[11]

---

[7] *Dáil Debates*, 7 March 2002, Vol. 550, Col. 404.
[8] Ibid., Col. 405.
[9] Ibid., Col. 408.
[10] Ibid., Col. 411.
[11] Ibid., 28 February 2002, Vol. 550, Col. 77.

Similarly, the chair of the five-member committee, Fianna Fáil's Tony Killeen TD, revealed that he had not relished his task of enforcing the standards established by the Ethics in Public Office Act:

> I thank the committee members for having undertaken a most unpleasant task and for having observed confidentiality in this and all other matters. I assure the House, on my own behalf and on behalf of the members of the committee, that they will not serve on this committee if they are returned to this House.[12]

Following the general election later that year, the Dáil Committee on Members' Interests was the last committee to be filled due to reluctance among TDs to sit on it. Former Ombudsman Kevin Murphy commented on the significance of this debate:

> If they can't hold a member, a peer accountable, how can we ever expect them to hold a minister accountable? I mean there was a washing of hands in public. I said to myself, under the constitution this is the body [the Dáil] that's supposed to be the cutting edge of accountability as far as ministers are concerned. It [made me wonder] is there the will in parliament to hold the executive accountable.[13]

Thompson argues that because of the political nature of a legislature, it is not desirable that politicians act in a judicial manner, as when judging colleagues they must 'assess not only their institutional norms and practices but also public confidence in those norms and practices'.[14] In other words, self-regulation is not the optimal way to reach an impartial decision, and leaves bodies such as Ethics Committees open to accusations of partisan decisions.

Suspension of Denis Foley TD

The Dáil Committee on Members' Interests has initiated investigations into members of the Lower House. It heard its first complaints by one TD against another in 2000. The Labour Party leader, Ruairi Quinn TD, wrote to the committee complaining that Fianna Fáil TD Denis Foley had voted against a motion in which he had a material interest that he had not declared. The motion, in 1997, concerned the extension of the terms of reference of the Moriarty Tribunal, which would allow it to further its investigations into the identity of Ansbacher account holders. As noted in Chapter 5,

---

[12] Ibid., 7 March 2002, Vol. 550, Col. 404.

[13] Interview with Kevin Murphy, 27 November 2002.

[14] Thompson, D. F. (1995) *Ethics in Congress*. Washington, DC: The Brookings Institute, p. 135.

it subsequently transpired that Deputy Foley held one of the accounts, putting him in breach of the requirements of the 1995 Ethics in Public Office Act. Foley resigned his position as vice-chair of the Public Accounts Committee[15] and, while he accepted that he had been in breach of the Act, in a statement to the committee he claimed that he was following the party whip on the matter.[16]

During the debate on the motion to suspend Deputy Foley, the committee's chair drew attention to the difficulties that it faced in its role:

> The principle at stake is that of self-regulation by this House of the Oireachtas and whether it has the capacity to undertake such an inquiry. Many of us would have harboured doubts about whether that was possible.[17]

Following the committee's recommendation, the Dáil voted to suspend Foley for fourteen days.[18]

Resignation of Liam Lawlor TD

In an unusual turn of events, during the committee's investigation into Foley one of its members was forced to resign his position. Fianna Fáil's Liam Lawlor TD became the focus of public attention as, despite legal threats, he refused to co-operate satisfactorily with the Flood/Mahon Tribunal that was sitting at the time.[19] As the evidence mounted of Lawlor's involvement with improper planning decisions in County Dublin, he was refused the Fianna Fáil parliamentary whip and was eventually forced to resign from the party, saving it from further embarrassment. A subsequent investigation by Fianna Fáil's internal Standards in Public Life committee accused him of being uncooperative and contradictory in his evidence.[20]

---

[15] He had been a member of the PAC when it conducted the DIRT inquiry into tax evasion.

[16] Dáil Committee on Members' Interests (2000) *Report of the Results of an Investigation into a Complaint Concerning Deputy Denis Foley*. Dublin: Stationery Office. Foley resigned from the Fianna Fáil parliamentary party but contined to vote with the government.

[17] *Dáil Debates*, 23 May 2000, Vol. 519, Col. 995.

[18] Ibid., Cols 994–9.

[19] In 1991, Lawlor had been forced to resign from the Joint Committee on State-Sponsored Bodies after his involvement with a company owned by Larry Goodman, who at the time wanted to buy the state-sponsored Irish Sugar, became public.

[20] Cullen, P. (2002) *With a Little Help from my Friends*. Dublin: Gill & Macmillan, p. 160.

In January 2001 Lawlor also resigned his position as vice-chairman of the Oireachtas Finance and Public Service Committee (which considered legislation relating to standards in public office), but remained an ordinary member of that committee, and of two others. Fianna Fáil deselected him by choosing two newcomers to contest his electoral constituency of Dublin Mid-West in the 2002 election. Lawlor also served two seven-day prison sentences for contempt of the Flood/Mahon Tribunal and became the first sitting politician in the state's history to be jailed. Nonetheless, the inability of either his parliamentary party or Dáil Éireann to remove him from parliament revealed the impunity with which the legislature could be treated and the absence of powers to sanction members.

The Dáil Committee on Members' Interests has had a difficult birth, and the lack of enthusiasm among its members, as detailed above, does not bode well for its future. As noted above, following the 2002 general election there was difficulty in finding the five members required to serve on it; it has met infrequently since. Nonetheless, the committee is now a permanent feature of the Irish parliamentary infrastructure, and its potential power to sanction members remains significant.

Standing Sub-Committee on Dáil Reform

Another important development within Dáil Éireann has been the establishment of the Committee on Procedure and Privileges Sub-Committee on Dáil Reform. Its origins lie in the Beef Tribunal's exposure of ineffective parliamentary mechanisms of oversight during its 1991–94 sitting and the subsequent collapse of the Fianna Fáil/Labour government. The Rainbow Coalition's programme for government – 'A Government of Renewal' – committed the government to Oireachtas reform in conjunction with the introduction of extra-parliamentary institutions of oversight as detailed in the previous chapter. This commitment reflected Fine Gael and Labour's belief that a more co-operative form of parliamentary practice was required. In July 1995, the Dáil Committee on Procedure and Privileges appointed a sub-committee 'to undertake a comprehensive review of the Standing Orders of Dáil Éireann relative to public business'.[21]

The sub-committee's existence was recognition in itself that substantial reform of the internal working of the Dáil was necessary in

---

[21] Standing Sub-Committee on Dáil Reform (1996) *First Report on Reform of Dáil Procedure.* Dublin: Stationery Office, p. 1.

order to tackle the root causes of corruption in public life. It also reflected a more consensual mode of policy-making as the government decided not to simply push its parliamentary reforms through parliament, instead referring matters to a committee for non-partisan consideration. The sub-committee's creation is not dissimilar to the development in 1976 of a Procedure Committee in Westminster – a recognition of MPs' deep concern regarding the poor public reputation of parliament and the power of the executive.[22] Permanent officials within the Oireachtas, including the Clerk of the Dáil, were heavily involved in the work of the sub-committee and were anxious that its work not be abandoned with a change of government. The sub-committee managed to convince the Rainbow Coalition government to make it a permanent (standing) sub-committee of the Committee on Procedure and Privileges. Furthermore, the sub-committee was empowered to report directly to the Dáil without seeking its parent committee's prior approval.[23]

First report

The sub-committee has produced three substantial reports, whose recommendations have been accepted into Dáil standing orders (DSOs). Some of these amendments have been referred to in Chapter 4, but it is worth considering here the amendments that have attempted to provide for a more consensual parliamentary environment. The sub-committee's first report, in particular, was debated extensively in the Dáil in October 1996, with a range of speakers from all parties expressing their views on the need for even more substantial parliamentary reform. Even the Fianna Fáil party, which has traditionally been slow to introduce such reforms while in power, noted that it had set up a party sub-committee on Dáil reform; front-bench TD Dermot Ahern claimed that:

> The majority of [the Dáil sub-committee's] proposals emanated from suggestions made at meetings of the Fianna Fáil subcommittee which examined all documents and Government proposals on the question of Dáil reform.[24]

---

[22] Flinders, M. (2001) *The Politics of Accountability in the Modern State.* Aldershot: Ashgate, p. 64.

[23] Standing Sub-Committee on Dáil Reform (1997) *Consensus Positions on Areas for Reform of Dáil Procedure.* Dublin: Stationery Office, p. 5.

[24] *Dáil Debates*, 9 October 1996, Vol. 469, Col. 1710.

However, the chief whip, Jim Higgins TD (Fine Gael), argued that Fianna Fáil had 'graciously acknowledged that many of its proposals had previously been proposed by the parties now in Government when in Opposition'.[25]

Among the changes introduced to the procedures of Dáil Éireann were:

- extension of the remit of the Joint Committee on State-sponsored Bodies
- allowing existing committees to investigate matters of serious public concern
- formalisation of the role of Dáil and Seanad Committees on Procedure and Privileges in overseeing the procedures of committees
- creation of a format for debating committee reports
- provision for second contributions on report stages of Bills and Financial Resolutions
- financial aid for preparing up to five Private Members' Bills each year
- rationalisation of the system for PQs
- relaxation of the rule concerning the disallowing of PQs that are anticipatory of debate
- provision of twenty extra minutes for Taoiseach's questions on Wednesdays
- provision for interventions during, and on, Dáil debates
- provision for a question-and-answer facility in debates
- creation of affirmations in respect of the offices of the Ceann Comhairle and Leas-Cheann Comhairle
- revision of the format for the Order of Business.[26]

The adoption of these amendments on 15 October 1996 was a significant and genuine move towards more co-operative parliamentary practices in the chamber as well as better parliamentary accountability. Higgins noted that 'many of the changes being introduced have been debated for years but consensus has only recently been achieved'[27] – a clear reference to the fact that Fianna Fáil-led administrations since 1987 had not been prepared to engage in substantial parliamentary reform that might forestall Fianna Fáil's first preference, majoritarian government.

The sub-committee's work was informed by the Beef Tribunal's revelations concerning the inability of the Dáil to hold members of the executive accountable. Therefore, many of the amendments focused on creating more opportunities for opposition deputies to

---

[25] Ibid., Col. 1702.
[26] Ibid., Cols 1703–4.
[27] Ibid., Col. 1707.

access information. For example, amendment to DSOs 26, 35, 38 and 39 provided for more time and opportunity for questioning members of the government. Amendments to DSOs 21, 56 and 58 provided more opportunities for the opposition to raise matters in the chamber and to intervene in speeches to 'query or comment on points made' (DSO 47 (1)).

Second report

In March 1997 the sub-committee produced its second report, recommending further areas for Dáil reform. Many of the recommendations in this report were technical, with a particular focus on the area of parliamentary privilege. There was further elaboration on the scheme for providing financial support for Private Members' Bills, with a lottery system being proposed. However, this provision was instituted by a sessional order only, which meant that it would expire with that Dáil.

Unlike the first report, this report was not debated in the House and was passed by a simple motion on 25 March 1997.[28] However, following the general election later that year and the return to power of a Fianna Fáil-led coalition, the proposal for financing Private Members' Bills was dropped. Again, this emphasised Fianna Fáil governments' majoritarian tendency to limit the opportunities available to the opposition parties to control the legislative agenda.

In April 1997, fearful that its work (if not its very existence) would not feature following a change of government in the upcoming general election, the sub-committee had produced a short report titled *Consensus Positions on Areas for Reform of Dáil Procedure*, proposing five specific areas where work should progress under the incoming government:

- a review of the Order of Business
- a review of the committee system
- a review of the effectiveness of PQs
- the establishment of an Oireachtas Commission
- the creation of sessional work programmes.[29]

Only the second and fourth of these proposals were taken up by the new Fianna Fáil/Progressive Democrat administration. The committee system was the subject of the sub-committee's third report.

---

[28]   Ibid., Vol. 476, Col. 1448.
[29]   Standing Sub-Committee on Dáil Reform (1997) *Consensus Positions on Areas for Reform of Dáil Procedure*. Dublin: Stationery Office, pp. 3–5.

Third report

In November 1997, in line with the sub-committee's proposals at the time of the Dáil's dissolution, it produced a report on parliamentary committees proposing that they become a more permanent feature of the Oireachtas. These recommendations were largely a 'tidying up exercise'[30] to rationalise the committees' work. This would be achieved through embedding their procedures in standing orders and the redesignation of many of them as permanent committees, i.e. that they would be re-established automatically after a general election.[31] The changes brought about by this report made the DIRT and Abbeylara Inquiries (discussed above) possible.

While the sub-committee is now a standing one, it has not produced a report since 1997 and the frequency of meetings has declined considerably. As of 2005, it has not made further progress in terms of restructuring standing orders in the Dáil, and the impetus for parliamentary reform has slipped substantially. The only area where there has been movement in Dáil reform is in the establishment of the Oireachtas Commission. This would appear to indicate that Dáil reform remains a low priority for Fianna Fáil-led governments.

Oireachtas Commission

The concept of an independent body charged with ensuring the proper functioning of parliament has become normal in many European democracies, including Westminster. In Ireland, the level of funding and personnel available to the Office of the Houses of the Oireachtas has traditionally been subject to the whims of the Department of Finance. However, following the Public Accounts Committee's much-publicised report on the DIRT Inquiry, which recommended the creation of a 'Parliamentary House Commission', pressure increased on government to initiate such a body as outlined in previous reports by the Sub-Committee on Dáil Reform. It duly initiated the Houses of the Oireachtas Bill in 2001; this passed into law in July 2003 and came into effect on 1 January 2004.

---

[30] Interview with Kieran Coughlan, 16 July 2003.
[31] Standing Sub-Committee on Dáil Reform (1997) *First Report of the Standing Sub-Committee on Dáil Reform on Establishment of Committees in the 28th Dáil.* Dublin: Stationery Office, pp. 1–4.

The purpose of the Oireachtas Commission is to provide the Irish parliament with financial independence and the power to decide how to spend its budget. The commission can decide how much funding will be made available for matters ranging from the level of secretarial expenses available to members to research undertaken by a committee. It has also funded new-technology-based developments in the Houses, such as an electronic voting mechanism in the Dáil chamber.[32] The traditional reluctance of the Department of Finance to release funds was a cause of complaint for parliamentarians, especially those in opposition who felt that it gave the government a further veto point on any initiatives they might have. The commission offers the potential for parliament to develop its oversight function, by allocating funds for matters such as better research facilities or specific studies on government spending.

During the debate on the Bill to establish the commission, many members drew attention to the historically inadequate resources available to members, which had hampered their ability to hold the executive to account. Interestingly, a member of the Sub-Committee on Dáil Reform, Fianna Fáil's Tony Killeen (who also chaired the Dáil Committee on Members' Interests) argued that:

> It is not stretching the point too far to say that many of the tribunal difficulties which Parliament and the country has had to face and is facing are a direct result of the fact that this Parliament did not have the resources to hold the Executive to account. Many Members would say that those who have been before tribunals played a role in depressing pay and support systems for Members of the Oireachtas … I do not doubt that a lack of resources is the reason why the Executive has not been held to account as effectively here as has been the case in other countries.[33]

The Office of the Houses of the Oireachtas had commissioned an international benchmarking report in 2002, which found that the Oireachtas was 'significantly underresourced' compared with nine other selected legislatures.[34] As a consequence, funding has improved and is now presented to the commission at three-year intervals.[35]

---

[32] This was introduced to allow members to vote in their seats, rather than waste time queuing to go through the voting lobbies.

[33] *Dáil Debates*, 16 October 2002, Vol. 555, Cols 789–90.

[34] Houses of the Oireachtas Commission (2005) *Annual Report*. Dublin: Stationery Office, p. 7.

[35] The first allocation for 2004–6 is for €295 million.

However, there are still limits to what the commission can finance: as the DIRT inquiry, which cost over IR£1 million, has shown, committee investigations can be expensive. The commission is obliged to present an annual report to the House, as well as to present a strategic plan and customer service action plan as per all public bodies.[36] This provides the Oireachtas with a regular opportunity for a general debate on its finances. The commission will also be able to fund the provision of legal advice to members.

Furthermore, while the commission provides new opportunities and facilities for members, particularly from the opposition parties, there remain certain veto points that prevent the opposition parties from using it to usurp the government agenda. Firstly, membership of the commission is heavily weighted in favour of the government party or parties. The eleven-member body consists of:

- the Chairperson of Dáil Éireann
- the Chairperson of Seanad Éireann
- the Clerk of Dáil Éireann (to be designated Secretary General of the Commission)
- a member appointed by the Minister for Finance
- seven members of whom four will be from the Dáil and three from the Seanad.

The seven members appointed by the Dáil and Seanad are to be selected by a committee appointed by those Houses, which will normally contain a government majority. This allocation of membership ensures that the government will hold a majority on the commission, thus providing a veto over any work it might fund that would be potentially damaging to an incumbent administration.

The appointment of the chairpersons from Dáil Éireann and Seanad Éireann to the commission increases the profiles of those positions. Furthermore, the fact that the Minister for Finance is allowed to appoint a member ensures that the Department of Finance continues to have an input into the running of the Oireachtas. The Clerk of the Dáil has noted that the role of the commission under the legislation was to replace the Department of Finance as the 'service agency'.[37] However, while the commission might initially have been seen as a significant departure for the Oireachtas, there is good reason to suspect that its existence and role will not substantially

---

[36] The creation of such plans in all government departments and state agencies is part of the public service modernisation agenda.

[37] Interview with Kieran Coughlan, 16 July 2003.

improve the policy formulation and evaluation capacity of parliamentarians, partly because members have tended to use the significant additional administrative and research personnel now
available to them for constituency rather than policy matters. As of
2005 plans are in place to initiate a non-partisan research service for
the committee system, which should provide significant assistance
in increasing the influence of the committees on domestic and EU
legislation.

Legal advisers and parliamentary inspectors

As the judicial pillar of state has increasingly encroached on the
legislative arena, the Oireachtas has attempted to increase its ability
to provide legal support to members. Following recommendations
in the DIRT Inquiry's report, a parliamentary legal adviser was
appointed in 1999 with competence for offering legal advice to
members of the Oireachtas.[38] This was because legal advice would
be a prerequisite in order for parliamentary committees (or individual members) to pursue an investigation. The office also provides
legal advice to the chairpersons of both Houses on issues such as
parliamentary privilege and constitutional law in a parliamentary
context.

In addition, parliamentary inspectors with powers similar to those
of High Court inspectors were appointed. Their role was to prepare
a preliminary investigation for any future inquiries by the Oireachtas
or its committees, similar to a preliminary investigation by a tribunal
of inquiry. However, following the Abbeylara Supreme Court judgment, the government decided to discontinue the use of such inspectors, as the constitutional position of such investigations remains
unclear. The new commissions of investigation may also involve
the introduction of further permanent legal facilities into future
inquiries.

Codes of conduct

As mentioned above, the 2001 Standards in Public Office Act
required the government to develop codes of conduct that would
provide guidelines for ethical behaviour as well as 'professional

---

[38] A *Protocol for the Use of the Services of the Parliamentary Legal Adviser* was created
in 2000. There is now also an assistant legal adviser. Both advisers offer particular help to the joint committees.

accountability' for those in public life.[39] As well as complementing the legislation, these codes were to ensure that ministers and other office holders, members of the Oireachtas and employees of public bodies acted in the public interest at all times. A code of conduct for non-office-holding members of the Oireachtas was duly introduced in 2001 (Appendix B). However, it was not until 2003 that a code of conduct for members of the Oireachtas who are office holders, i.e. members of the government and committee chairpersons, was published (Appendix C). It is admissible in any proceedings before a court, tribunal of inquiry, either Committee on Members' Interests or the Standards in Public Office Commission. Significantly, while it is up to the Standards in Public Office Commission to investigate breaches of the 2001 Act, the power to sanction is in the hands of the Oireachtas. In this respect, the codes may be seen as another method of improving parliamentary accountability.

Code of conduct for members of Dáil Éireann

Section 10 (1) of the Standards in Public Office Act, 2001 required both of the Committees on Members' Interests to 'from time to time draw up codes of conduct for the guidance of members (other than office holders) of the House concerned'. However, the Labour Party had already taken the initiative on this in April of that year, when it laid a draft code of conduct before the Dáil and had it debated during Private Members' Business.[40] Following some amendments the motion to draft the code was approved without government opposition.[41]

The proposal for the creation of the code was a direct result of the failure of the Dáil to remove Liam Lawlor (see above) from the chamber, which made it seem a weak institution that could not even reprimand its own members. Indeed, as the Progressive Democrat minister of State Liz O'Donnell pointed out:

> Members, and the public generally, were extremely frustrated that, notwithstanding a raft of ethical provisions on the Statute Book, there was no effective mechanism through which the House as Parliament could indicate its disapproval or sanction misconduct which fell short of criminality or insolvency.[42]

---

[39] Codes of conduct were introduced for local authority staff and elected members in 2004 and a *Civil Service Code of Standards and Behaviour* was released in 2005.

[40] *Dáil Debates*, 6 February 2001, Vol. 529, Cols 1310–11.

[41] Ibid., 7 February 2001, Vol. 530, Col. 160.

[42] Ibid., Col. 137.

The draft was subsequently referred to the Dáil's Committee on Members' Interests, which took submissions from deputies and from the major parliamentary parties on the issue. During its deliberations, the committee noted that:

> The broad political context in which the preparation of a Code of Conduct is taking place is, firstly, marked by a cathartic process in which, through tribunals, courts and the House itself, aspects of the political system and alleged abuses by a number of people within that system over two decades are, quite properly, being held up to public scrutiny in an unprecedented way.[43]

As the then Labour Party leader, Ruairi Quinn TD, pointed out, the Ethics in Public Office Act (and subsequent Standards in Public Office Act) defined the limits of public representatives' actions. Conversely, he argued, the point of a code of conduct 'is to establish an agreed set of standards to which we should all aspire'.[44]

The Committee on Members' Interests forwarded the code to the newly established Standards in Public Office Commission for its comments, as it was required to do. The commission recommended certain changes to the draft but the committee decided not to accept any of these, leading to public criticism by the Ombudsman of the absence of any real consultation in the process.[45] Subsequently, there was a much greater degree of consultation with the commission on the code for ministers and the code for civil servants.

The resulting eleven-point *Code of conduct for members of Dáil Éireann* (Appendix B) was a first attempt at establishing a standard for political behaviour in the Oireachtas. The committee presented the code to the Dáil a week before it censured Fianna Fáil TD Ned O'Keeffe (see above). On proposing the code, the chairman of the committee, Fianna Fáil's Tony Killeen TD, pointed out that during submissions to the committee:

> Some were of the view that a code should be extremely prescriptive and detailed, but one of the difficulties of going down that road is that it is hard to prepare an exhaustive code. It was decided that the legislation clearly provided for a code which would act as a guide.[46]

---

[43] Dáil Committee on Members' Interests (2002) *Report on a Draft Code of Conduct for Members of Dáil Éireann.* Dublin: Stationery Office, transcript of 12 April.

[44] *Dáil Debates,* 6 February 2001, Vol. 529, Col. 1312.

[45] Interview with Kevin Murphy, 27 November 2002.

[46] *Dáil Debates,* 28 February 2002, Vol. 550, Col. 72.

Commenting on the code, Fine Gael TD Jim O'Keeffe, a member of the committee that drafted it, noted that even with this new set of standards the onus to resolve conflicts of interest remained with the members individually. He argued that 'the code of conduct will be the yardstick or benchmark against which performance will be measured.'[47]

Deputy Jim Mitchell, also of Fine Gael, queried the inactivity of the Committee on Procedure and Privileges in matters concerning standards and ethics in the House. He noted that previously, that committee had had the power to compel a member to make a statement to the House if it judged that the member had acted in an unparliamentary fashion.[48] Progressive Democrat TD Desmond O'Malley raised a similar point during the deliberations over the code of conduct by the Committee on Members' Interests. He noted that while the Committee on Procedure and Privileges used to sit 'thirty or forty times a year', it now met only occasionally. He went on to argue that:

> Power is shifting and we must ensure that it shifts fairly. An advantage of that committee is that it accurately reflects party numbers in the House because of its size. This small Sub-Committee cannot do so. There are political and individual interests in the House not represented.[49]

While the code of conduct for members of Dáil Éireann represents a milestone in Irish parliamentary development, it has some inherent flaws. In particular, it fails to address the reality of party discipline and the adversarial nature of politics, which lay behind the failure of traditional oversight mechanisms. Section 3 of the code states that:

(i) Members have a particular obligation to behave in a manner which is consistent with their roles as *public representatives and legislators*, save where there is a *legitimate and sustainable conscientious objection*.

(ii) Members must interact with authorities involved with public administration and the enforcement of the law in a manner which is consistent with their roles as *public representatives and legislators*.[50]

Both of these demands are based on a presumption that the Dáil is composed of independently minded parliamentarians free from party

---

[47] Ibid., Col. 75.

[48] Ibid., Cols 79–81.

[49] Dáil Committee on Members' Interests (2002) *Report on a Draft Code of Conduct for Members of Dáil Éireann.* Dublin: Stationery Office, transcript of 12 April.

[50] Emphasis added.

and constituency constraints. The reality, as Chapter 4 has shown, is that the Dáil functions as the government allows it to, and that 'legitimate and conscientious objections' will be voiced by backbench TDs at parliamentary party meetings rather than in public.

Furthermore, during his submissions on behalf of his party to the Dáil Committee on Members' Interests, Deputy O'Malley pointed out that it might be wrong to interact with public bodies if one believes they are working against the public interest. He used the example of the beef authorities in Ireland in the years before the Beef Tribunal, and wondered whether a deputy should have been expected to co-operate with the malpractice that occurred.[51]

Code of Conduct for Office Holders

In July 2003, following consultation with the Standards in Public Office Commission, the government introduced a new code of conduct, this time for office holders (Appendix C). As with the members' code, the new code was required under the Standards in Public Office Act, 2001. Its purpose was to 'ensure [the] highest ethical standards' among the Taoiseach, Tánaiste, ministers, ministers of state and committee chairs.

Again, reflecting the finding that evasion of parliamentary accountability by former ministers was responsible for several tribunals of inquiry, the code stated that:

> Office holders, who are members of the Houses of the Oireachtas, are accountable to the Houses of the Oireachtas in accordance with the arrangements set out in the Constitution or in the Standing Orders of the respective Houses. It is of paramount importance that office holders give accurate and truthful information to the Houses of the Oireachtas, correcting any inadvertent error at the earliest opportunity.

The code disallows office holders from holding positions in private companies that could cause a conflict of interest. Also, office holders who leave to take up employment elsewhere are required not to reveal information from their former position that would provide their new employers with an unfair advantage. As noted above, it is in the domain of the Houses to impose sanctions on members who breach the codes. However, as the codes have yet to be tested, it is not clear what these sanctions would be.

---

[51] Dáil Committee on Members' Interests (2002) *Report on a Draft Code of Conduct for Members of Dáil Éireann*. Dublin: Stationery Office, transcript of 12 April.

The production of the codes of conduct for members mirrored developments within the political parties themselves. As noted above, following revelations at the tribunals of inquiry concerning certain of its members, Fianna Fáil had initiated an internal inquiry with its Standards in Public Life committee. One outcome of this inquiry was that the party introduced a *Code of Principles in Public Life* for its members. As well as providing a means to sanction transgressing members that had not been available during the Lawlor fiasco, this allowed the party to demonstrate publicly its commitment to probity in public life.

A new legislative–executive relationship?

Dáil Éireann has experienced an unprecedented period of internal change since 1995, but it is difficult and perhaps too early to assess how effective these reforms have been in altering the legislative–executive balance of power. Much of the focus has been on the new system of joint committees and their potential ability to expand the limits of parliamentary work. However, the Abbeylara judgment, combined with an institutional bias in favour of the governing parties, means that short of a constitutional amendment, the jurisdiction of committees at the time of writing is substantially constrained.

The principal dynamic underlying recent Dáil reforms has been to ensure that the government's agenda-setting position is not considerably weakened, while at the same time allowing for more information about the executive to be subject to scrutiny. In December 2000 the Fianna Fáil/Progressive Democrat minority government published a set of proposals for parliamentary reform titled *A Dáil for the New Millennium*, which included:

- provision for a new 'current affairs time' every Tuesday, Wednesday and Thursday
- provision for a 'citizens' petition' that would allow a one-hour debate on a subject if 10,000 signatures were collected supporting it
- a new 'backbenchers' hour' to allow ordinary members to raise issues
- the Taoiseach to take questions on one day per week instead of two
- the House to sit only three weeks in every month, the fourth week being reserved for committee work.

None of these reforms were subsequently implemented, except for the reduction in the amount of time the Taoiseach has to spend taking questions, which occurred in October 2002. The disappearance of the reform proposals has never been adequately explained and has not been commented on in the media. Indeed, since the return of the Fianna Fáil/Progressive Democrat government in 2002 with a majority of seats, the government has in many respects reverted to operating in a traditionally adversarial manner in respect of parliamentary politics.

The Ned O'Keeffe case embodies core questions concerning the problem of accountability within the Oireachtas. Can parliamentarians regulate their own activities without the help of an external body such as the Standards in Public Office Commission? Does parliamentary accountability require external institutions to ensure that public representatives adhere to standards they set for themselves? As with the tribunals discussed in the previous chapter, the inability of parliament to hold members of government to account has resulted in many such regulatory bodies being created, but often without any consideration of their potential outcomes. The creation of new institutional rules and structures therefore creates a new context within which corrupt practices can occur.

Self-regulation poses difficulties for all professions; for parliamentarians, members' democratic mandate to represent their constituencies compounds the difficulty. As was made clear during the creation of the code of conduct for members, sanctioning of transgressors should not interfere with their constitutional right to represent their electorate. Progressive Democrat TD Desmond O'Malley pointed out during the drafting of the code of conduct that:

> One of the fundamental things that you have to remember is that everyone in this House is here because he or she was elected. The Constitution makes it clear, at least by implication, that while this House can make its own rules for the governance and regulation of Deputies and their affairs and activities, it does not envisage their being removed from office. To do that would be a direct interference in the political process and in the democratic process. So, the sanctions have to be short of that.[52]

Similarly, the Labour Party's Emmet Stagg TD identified the problem of enforcing 'professional accountability' in the Oireachtas, noting that while his party had drafted the document:

> we have never called for and do not now call for a situation whereby a majority of the Members of Dáil Éireann could effectively decide upon the composition of the House by expelling those with whom they have a disagreement.[53]

---

[52]   Ibid.
[53]   Ibid.

This issue became particularly pertinent during the Liam Lawlor débâcle. The public outrage at Lawlor's activities was augmented by his refusal to resign his Dáil seat and his insistence on portraying himself as a victim rather than a perpetrator. The Dáil's inability to sanction him or force his resignation made both the chamber and the legislation designed to improve standards in public office seem toothless. It remains to be seen whether the new codes of conduct for members and office holders will be sufficient to prevent future such incidents.

> There is nothing more difficult to plan, more doubtful of success, nor more dangerous to manage than the creation of a new system. For the initiator has the enmity of all who would profit by the preservation of the old system and merely lukewarm defenders in those who would gain by the new one.
>
> Niccolò Machiavelli, *The Prince*, 1513

The conventional wisdom that the Irish political system presents a chronic case of 'strong government, weak parliament' remains undeniably true. A combination of institutional design and choices taken at critical junctures by political actors has meant that government control of the decision-making process in Ireland is virtually unrivalled anywhere in Europe. A corollary is that mechanisms of executive oversight are weak in order that the government can pursue its agenda as efficiently as possible. The long-term effect of this has been to erode confidence in the system of parliamentary accountability.

Reports by tribunals of inquiry, committee investigations, and constant revelations of corrupt activity in public life provide a damning pathology of many aspects of Irish public governance over the past two decades. However, the failure to link these phenomena to ineffective mechanisms of parliamentary oversight has meant that prescribed remedies have not dealt with root causes. Instead, Ireland has witnessed the introduction of a new layer of regulatory and oversight legislation that has further complicated accountability relationships. It is argued here that a more fruitful approach to the recent accountability deficits would have been to consider strengthening existing mechanisms of parliamentary accountability.

Recasting Dáil Éireann in order to weaken the executive is not a panacea. Indeed, it may be argued that Dáil Éireann is a successful chamber as it has traditionally elected strong governments that have, on average, lasted for over three years. Similarly, as King identified in his seminal paper, 'How to Strengthen Legislatures – Assuming That We Want To', the legislature-dominated politics of the German Weimar Republic or the French Fourth Republic were far from a political or parliamentary nirvana.[1] A more comprehensive

---

[1] King, A. (1981) 'How to Strengthen Legislatures – Assuming That We Want To' in N. J. Ornstein (ed.) *The Role of the Legislature in Western Democracies.* London: American Enterprise Institute, pp. 77–89.

understanding of corruption and administrative failings in Ireland demands consideration of wider issues of political culture and public trust, and of the role of parliament in contemporary society.

As the 2003 annual report of the Standards in Public Office Commission argued:

> Principal among the factors that give rise to corrupt practices are poor levels of remuneration of senior public officials, including elected representatives, ineffective supervision and audit of public finances, control over resources being exercised by governments and officials who are not accountable for their actions and, very importantly, a culture which does not embrace a public service ethos.[2]

One of the principal revelations of the tribunal and committee inquiries has been the massive scale of tax evasion in Ireland in all strata of society.[3] This is significant for many reasons, not least the contempt it demonstrates for public institutions and the well-being of fellow citizens. As Rothstein demonstrates, if citizens feel that their fellow citizens are corrupting government institutions, not only will their trust in those institutions fall, but also their trust in *each other*.[4] Those elected to public office are obliged to set an example and subject themselves and their work to constitutional structures of accountability, and to ensure that parliament is capable of carrying out its oversight and inquiry functions. After all, 'trust in our leaders and in the institutions of the State is the bedrock on which our parliamentary democracy is founded.'[5]

Notwithstanding the continuing deficiencies in parliamentary accountability, there are now several alternative avenues of political and administrative executive oversight in Ireland. As a consequence, the volume of information in the public domain concerning executive activity has increased substantially and acts as a deterrent to future malpractice in public life. Public awareness has been augmented by legislation such as the Freedom of Information, Electoral, and Standards in Public Office Acts. Investigative journalism, which

---

[2] Standards in Public Office Commission (2004) *Annual Report 2003*. Dublin, p. 5.

[3] In September 2004, the Comptroller and Auditor-General revealed that investigations by the Revenue Commissioners following the DIRT Inquiry and other tax avoidance issues uncovered by the tribunals had generated 1.56 billion.

[4] Rothstein, B. (2003) 'Social Capital in a Working Democracy: the Causal Mechanisms' in O. Osterud (ed.) *Power and Democracy: Critical Interventions*. London: Ashgate, pp. 115–41.

[5] Standards in Public Office Commission (2004) *Annual Report 2003*. Dublin, p. 5.

played a significant role in the establishment of tribunals of inquiry, also continues to be a major source of public knowledge concerning government activity. Nevertheless, Dáil Éireann faces great challenges if it is to assert its role as principal government watchdog. The question arises of how to provide inducements for TDs to develop a deeper interest in parliamentary accountability.

As this study has demonstrated, institutions unequivocally shape the activities and choices of actors. The design of governing institutions is therefore crucial, and as Lijphart's typology informs us, there are significant differences in how we can expect legislatures (and parliamentary accountability) to operate depending on whether they are closer to the Westminster or the consensual model. It is possible to have a strong culture of parliamentary accountability in Westminster-style parliamentary democracies, but there are internal and external requirements for this. Since no single measure can guarantee effective oversight, it is worth considering a range of factors that have a bearing on the Irish culture of parliamentary accountability.

Electoral system

The electoral system is often identified as inhibiting the ordinary backbencher from developing his or her role of holding government to account. One interviewee noted that 'the thinking [among TDs] is – if you want to get elected to the Dáil, don't go near the bloody Dáil.' The emphasis on constituency service means that much of political life in Ireland appears to be based on personality rather than policy, on constituency issues rather than national issues, and on delivery of services and favours rather than reform of institutions that would make these personal interventions unnecessary. Others argue that changing the rules by which parliamentarians are elected will not alter how they conduct their work within parliament. Nonetheless, it is interesting to note the success of electoral reform, and particularly the adoption of mixed-member systems as a response to localism, in other jurisdictions.[6] FitzGerald[7] and Laver[8] have presented alternatives to the current system along these lines.

---

[6] Shugart, M. S. and Wattenberg, M. P. (eds) (2001) *Mixed-Member Electoral Systems: the Best of Both Worlds?* Oxford: Oxford University Press.

[7] FitzGerald, G. (2003) *Reflections on the Irish State.* Dublin: Irish Academic Press, pp. 89–102.

[8] Laver, M. (1998) *A New Electoral System for Ireland?* The Policy Institute, Trinity College Dublin.

One recent development that may contribute to the development of parliamentarians' interest in national rather than local political issues is the 2003 Local Government (No. 2) Act. This contained a provision to end the 'dual mandate' whereby sitting TDs could also be a member of their local authority. Removing the necessity for TDs to attend local government meetings should free up time for further engagement in national issues. However, it is equally possible that the effect will be to encourage TDs to devote more time to constituency service in order to prevent local politicians from developing rival support bases.

Recesses

Dáil Éireann cannot oversee the government and its work if the parliament itself is not in session. The long summer and Christmas recesses decided on by governments are inimical to regular parliamentary accountability, particularly since the cabinet meets during part of these periods. In Westminster, the cabinet does not sit when the Houses are in recess. There is therefore a clear case for increasing the annual number of Dáil sitting weeks. The comparatively recent development whereby committees meet when the parliament has risen is welcome, but needs to be followed with more frequent sittings of the plenary. In 2002 the outgoing Fianna Fáil/Progressive Democrat government proposed that the Houses of the Oireachtas sit in two-week cycles for the whole year, with a two-week recess after each cycle. This proposal was modelled on the successful experience of the Norwegian Storting. However, it was not discussed in the debate of Dáil reform that took place in February 2004. As the Dáil broke for a summer recess in 2005, an *Irish Times* editorial criticised the three-month absence, arguing that:

> In spite of many shortcomings, primary Dáil sessions provide citizens with the clearest picture of the quality of administration and of decision-making being provided by government in their names.[9]

Procedures

A core argument of this study has been that the influence of Dáil standing orders is under-appreciated, and that the 'rules of the game' in the Oireachtas ultimately serve to protect the prerogative of the

---

[9] *Irish Times* (2005) 'Dáil break not in the public interest' (editorial), 2 August, 13.

executive and have a deleterious effect on political and administrative oversight. A substantial study of these standing orders and a genuine attempt to provide more opportunities for ordinary non-government members to become involved in parliamentary work are crucial to improving the Lower House's profile.

It is worth recalling that the most significant recent change to the parliamentary timetable – the introduction of leaders' questions – was not the result of the combined efforts of the opposition parties. Since the 2002 general election, the impetus for Dáil reform has subsided considerably. In part this is due to the fact that some senior Fine Gael members who had a genuine interest in Dáil reform failed to be re-elected. At time of writing, the issue of parliamentary reform is not a priority for any political party and the operation of the Dáil does not receive the attention it deserves. Indeed, in June 2003 Dáil Éireann had to be adjourned when the government could not raise a quorum for a debate on its own legislation. This situation contrasts sharply with Westminster, where the Select Committee on Public Administration and its predecessor, the Public Service Committee, have produced several reports on the impact of parliamentary procedures and the changing nature of ministerial accountability.

Committees

As in other European parliaments, committees offer considerable opportunity for parliamentarians to assert their role as national representatives and scrutinisers of government. Committees in the Oireachtas have allowed members to engage more productively with legislation and political actors such as interest groups, and offer much potential for better policy-making. How successful parliamentary committees can expect to be in opening up government and holding it to account, however, is still unclear, and there is great variation in attendance and output.

What is certain is that the adversarial party system and the institutional logic of the government-dominated Oireachtas are strong disincentives to a flourishing and influential committee system. And yet the committees have developed quite significantly from the issue-based and relatively weak committees of the 1982–87 administration. In an interview, the Director of Committees noted that:

> The principle of a committee shadowing a government department is one which has found a safe haven. People are comfortable with it now. The system

we have at the moment is very neat from a legislative point of view, an estimate point of view and from an accountability point of view.[10]

However, the fact remains that parliamentarians do not tend to exercise the full range of powers available to them in the committees.

In this light, calls for a reduction in the number of TDs may be misplaced. For the committee system and parliamentary oversight to function effectively, a critical mass of parliamentarians is necessary. Furthermore, committees still offer the best opportunity for TDs to restore influence to the Oireachtas by engaging with issues of administrative and financial oversight.

Seanad Éireann

The issue of the abolition of the Upper House is frequently addressed in Irish politics. As a small, unitary and largely ethnically homogeneous state, most of the conventional reasons for having a second parliamentary chamber do not apply to Ireland, and the chamber's role is confined to legislation. In 2002, building on the work of the all-party Oireachtas Committee on the Constitution,[11] the Seanad Committee on Procedure and Privileges established a Sub-Committee on Seanad Reform. Its report in 2004 proposed an increase in Seanad membership (to sixty-five) new methods of electing Senators, and that the Seanad be allowed to review the activities of government departments, state agencies and the social partnership agreements, as well as to scrutinise senior public appointments. It remains to be seen whether these recommendations will be implemented, but there is a strong case for allowing the Upper House to play a more active role in overseeing key aspects of the public administration, as well as examining secondary legislation.

Public awareness and the media

The subject of Dáil and parliamentary reform does not capture the imagination of the electorate. This is partly because of the frequent portrayal of Dáil Éireann as a 'rubber stamp' for government decisions. This lack of appreciation of the centrality of the legislature to the process of governing and political life in Ireland facilitates governments' unwillingness to engage in substantial reform. As

---

10   Interview with Art O'Leary, 17 July 2003.
11   All-Party Oireachtas Committee on the Constitution (1997) *Seanad Éireann.* Dublin: Stationery Office.

this study has shown, the short-term interest of successive govern-ments in controlling parliaments has had a detrimental effect on the standing of parliamentary politics in the state. Governments must be made aware that there are substantial long-term benefits to an effective Dáil. However, favourable public opinion is a prerequisite for a government to embark on reform of the Lower House.

The media could play a role in improving public awareness of what actually happens in the Oireachtas. If parliamentary and com-mittee work were more accurately and comprehensively reported, this would undoubtedly curtail the partisan sniping that currently characterises much television and print media reporting. One of the reasons often cited by long-serving parliamentarians for the decline in quality of parliamentary debate is members' use of prepared scripts. This developed in the late 1960s, when parliamentary report-ers ceased to use shorthand and members could get reported only if they spoke before 6.30 p.m. and provided a script.[12] Up to the mid-1980s there were up to twenty media correspondents covering the work of the Dáil, but now only a handful do so while the main body of political correspondents compete for political news elsewhere. As a consequence, with one notable exception, reporting on the work of the Houses of the Oireachtas and its committees has declined to a minimum in the national newspapers.[13] This vicious cycle whereby TDs do not take their parliamentary duties seriously due to a lack of media coverage, and media correspondents in turn ignore the Dáil, must be addressed if the national assembly is to develop its relevance in a political environment with multiple actors and alternative deci-sion-making venues.

This is particularly true in respect of EU matters. Media coverage of the work of the Joint Committee on EU Affairs and its Sub-Committee on European Scrutiny is negligible; this has significant consequences for public understanding of Ireland's obligations and entitlements as a member of the Union. Indeed, it can be argued that the public Forum on Europe, established following the rejection of the Nice Treaty referendum in 2001, would not have been necessary had there been better media coverage of the work of the committee system in respect of EU affairs.

---

[12] Interview with Garret FitzGerald, 8 August 2003.
[13] Collins, S. (2004) 'The Parliamentary Lobby System' in T. Garvin, M. Manning and R. Sinnott (eds) *Dissecting Irish Politics: Essays in Honour of Brian Farrell.* Dublin: UCD Press, pp. 208–9.

The role of parliamentarians

Providing multiple incentives for elected representatives does not guarantee that the Dáil will become a more effective institution. The will of TDs themselves is the most important factor in this regard. In Britain the Commission to Strengthen Parliament, established in 1999, has identified such willingness as a key issue. During a debate on the Houses of the Oireachtas Commission Bill, Fine Gael's Richard Bruton picked up on this theme of parliamentary will:

> We need, as a group of 166 people, to get our act together and decide what will benchmark Dáil Éireann against best practice in any parliament in the world. We are unacceptably far off the pace.[14]

In a similar vein, the Director of Committees indicated that 'the effectiveness of a committee to a large extent depends on the dynamism of the chairman and the members'.[15]

While this study has drawn comparisons between the structural features of the British and Irish parliaments, the most difficult feature for Dáil Éireann to emulate is a culture of respect. This applies not only for parliamentarians but for media commentators, academics and the public as well. Labelling Dáil Éireann a 'rubber stamp' does nothing to enhance our understanding of why this national institution has failed to perform some of its core tasks, and how this failure has had an enormous influence on decisions that affect every citizen in Ireland.

The 2002 general election saw a third of the House (fifty-five TDs) being replaced by new members. Further turnover at the next election will mean that that Dáil will contain a new generation of parliamentarians who have seen the catastrophic effect of weak parliamentary accountability on public confidence in the state and its institutions. It will be their task to restore such confidence and to ensure that Dáil Éireann is given due recognition in Irish political and administrative life.

As stated at the outset of this study, a healthy democracy requires an active and effective legislature and an executive that is not only efficient but accountable as well. In order to earn the public confidence on which its authority rests, it is vital that Dáil Éireann be adequately equipped to hold government to account. Events since the early 1990s have demonstrated how an unchecked executive and

---

[14] *Dáil Debates*, 26 June 2002, Vol. 553, Col. 1354.
[15] Interview with Art O'Leary, 17 July 2003.

political elite can be acutely detrimental to good and accountable governance. There is some distance to go before adequate parliamentary oversight is achieved. As one interviewee argued, 'one key institution is just not functioning really as it should – and I don't think that can be a good thing for democracy'.[16] If a genuine will exists to close the era of tribunals and corruption in Irish politics, and to connect citizens with the institutions of government, both the modus operandi of Dáil Éireann and its structures and methods of executive oversight require immediate attention.

[16] Interview with Kevin Murphy, 27 November 2002.

Proposals for parliamentary reform by the Labour Party and Fine Gael

Main recommendations	Labour Party 1968	Labour Party 1975	Fine Gael 1980	Fine Gael 1990	Fine Gael 2000	Labour Party 2003
Introduction of committee system	Yes	Yes	Yes	Including specialist business committees; increase powers of PAC	Reduce number but increase powers	–
Individual estimates to be dealt with by committee	Yes	Yes	–	Yes	Yes	–
Increase in sitting hours	Yes	Yes		Yes	Yes	Yes
Decrease in recess periods	Yes	–	Yes	Yes	Yes	Yes
Official recognition of opposition leaders	–	–	–	–	Yes	–
Better facilitation of Private Members' Business and Bills	Yes	–	Yes	Yes	Yes	Yes
Review of Question Time format	–	Yes	–	Yes	Yes	Yes
Longer hours for PQs, and ministers to answer questions on state agencies	–	–	Yes	Yes	–	Yes

Main recommendations	Labour Party 1968	Labour Party 1975	Fine Gael 1980	Fine Gael 1990	Fine Gael 2000	Labour Party 2003
Cutting the length of debates and contributions	–	Yes	–	Yes	–	–
New provision for raising topical matters of public importance	–	–	–	Yes	Yes	Yes
Allow TV and radio broadcasts of the Dáil and Seanad	–	Yes (subsequently introduced)	–	–	–	Improved coverage, including committees
State assistance to parties for work outside parliament	–	Yes	–	Yes	Yes	–
Declaration of members' interests	–	Yes	–	–	Yes	–
Financial independence for Oireachtas	–	–	–	–	Yes	–
Better resources for deputies and parties	–	Yes	Yes	Yes	Yes	Oireachtas to open for longer hours and Saturdays
Remuneration for committee members	–	–	–	Yes	Yes	–
Introduce new officer to Oireachtas	–	–	–	Oireachtas information officer	Oireachtas legal officer	Parliamentary investigator
Regularise role of whips	–	–	–	–	Yes	–
Better scrutiny of government estimates and the Capital Budget	–	–	Yes	Yes	Yes	–
Establishment of a committee on delegated/secondary legislation	–	–	Yes	–	–	Committee system to scrutinise such legislation

Main recommendations	Labour Party 1968	Labour Party 1975	Fine Gael 1980	Fine Gael 1990	Fine Gael 2000	Labour Party 2003
Code of practice to allow public access to government files	–	–	Yes	–	–	–
Committee witnesses to have privilege	–	–	–	Yes	1997 Act provided for this	–
Monthly 'committee week'	–	–	–	–	–	Yes
Regular debating time for committee reports	–	–	–	–	–	Yes
Fewer restrictions on legislative amendments	–	–	–	–	–	Yes
Constitutional protection of right of the Dáil to hold inquiries into the executive	–	–	–	–	–	Yes
Introduce a Committee of Investigations, Oversight and Petitions	–	–	–	–	–	Yes

Code of conduct for members of Dáil Éireann

Preamble

Members of Dáil Éireann recognise that it is in their individual and collective interest to foster and sustain public confidence and trust in their integrity as individuals and in Dáil Éireann as an institution. To this end, Members should at all times be guided by the public good and ensure that their actions and decisions are taken in the best interests of the public. Members are in the unique position of being responsible to the electorate which is the final arbiter of their conduct and has the right to dismiss them from office at regular elections. Accordingly, and as a matter of principle, individual Members are not answerable to their colleagues for their behaviour, except where it is alleged to breach the obligations to answer to them which have been placed on Members by law, by Standing Orders or by Codes of Conduct established by the House. To this end and in exercise of the powers conferred by Article 15.10 of the Constitution, the Members of Dáil Éireann have adopted this Code of Conduct, the purpose of which is to assist Members in the discharge of their obligations to the House, their constituents and the public at large, without, however, trespassing into areas where Members more properly submit themselves to the judgement of their electors rather than the jurisdiction of this House.

Code

1 Members must, in good faith, strive to maintain the public trust placed in them, and exercise the influence gained from their public office to advance the public interest.
2 Members must conduct themselves in accordance with the provisions and spirit of the Code of Conduct and ensure that their conduct does not bring the integrity of their office or the Dáil into serious disrepute.
3 (i) Members have a particular obligation to behave in a manner which is consistent with their roles as public representatives and legislators, save where there is a legitimate and sustainable conscientious objection.

(ii) Members must interact with authorities involved with public administration and the enforcement of the law in a manner which is consistent with their roles as public representatives and legislators.

4 (i) Members must base their conduct on a consideration of the public interest and are individually responsible for preventing conflicts of interest.

(ii) Members must endeavour to arrange their private financial affairs to prevent such conflicts of interest arising and must take all reasonable steps to resolve any such conflict quickly and in a manner which is in the best interests of the public.

5 (i) A conflict of interest exists where a Member participates in or makes a decision in the execution of his or her office knowing that it will improperly and dishonestly further his or her private financial interest or another person's private financial interest directly or indirectly.

(ii) A conflict of interest does not exist where the Member or other person benefits only as a member of the general public or a broad class of persons.

6 Members may not solicit, accept or receive any financial benefit or profit in exchange for promoting, or voting on, a Bill, a motion for a resolution or order or any question put to the Dáil or to any of its committees.

7 Members must fulfil conscientiously the requirements of the Dáil and of the law in respect of the registration and declaration of interests and, to assist them in so doing, should familiarise themselves with the relevant legislation and guidelines published from time to time by the Committee on Members' Interests and the Public Offices Commission as appropriate.

8 (i) Members must not accept a gift that may pose a conflict of interest or which might interfere with the honest and impartial exercise of their official duties.

(ii) Members may accept incidental gifts and customary hospitality.

9 In performing their official duties, Members must apply public resources prudently and only for the purposes for which they are intended.

10 Members must not use official information which is not in the public domain, or information obtained in confidence in the course of their official duties, for personal gain or the personal gain of others.

11 Members must co-operate with all tribunals of inquiry and other bodies inquiring into matters of public importance established by the Houses of the Oireachtas.

Code of conduct for office holders

Part 1

1.1. Purpose of the Code of Conduct

This Code of Conduct for the guidance of office holders has been drawn up by the Government in accordance with Section 10 (2) of the Standards in Public Office Act 2001 (2001 Act). In accordance with Section 10(6) of the 2001 Act, it is designed to 'indicate the standards of conduct and integrity for the persons to whom it relates in the performance of their functions and in relation to any matter connected with or affecting or likely or appearing to affect such performance and in relation to such other matters (if any) as may be specified in the code.' This Code does not make provision in relation to matters for which adequate provision is made in existing guidelines and will apply prospectively, i.e. from the date of publication.

1.2. Persons to whom the Code of Conduct applies

In accordance with the terms of the Ethics in Public Office Acts, 1995 & 2001 (Ethics Acts) this Code applies to office holders, namely:

- the Taoiseach
- the Tánaiste
- a minister
- a minister of State
- an Attorney General who is a member of Dáil Éireann or Seanad Éireann
- a person who is Chairman or Deputy Chairman of Dáil Éireann or Chairman or Deputy Chairman of Seanad Éireann
- a person who holds the office of Chairman of a Committee of either House of the Oireachtas, being an office that stands designated, for the purpose of the Ethics in Public Office Act, 1995 (1995 Act), for the time being by resolution of that House or

- a person who holds the office of Chairman of a Joint Committee of both Houses of the Oireachtas, being an office that stands designated, for the purposes of the 1995 Act, for the time being by resolution of each House.

1.3. Requirement to observe the Code of Conduct

In accordance with the provisions of the Ethics Acts, office holders shall, in so far as it is relevant, have regard to and be guided by the Code in the performance of their functions and in relation to any other matters specified in the Code. This Code seeks to ensure that office holders must at all times observe, and be seen to observe, the highest standards of ethical behaviour in the carrying out of the functions of their office. Office holders are obliged to act in accordance with advice given and guidelines published by the Standards in Public Office Commission (Standards Commission) unless to do so would constitute a contravention of another provision of the Ethics Acts. Pursuant to Section 10(8) of the 2001 Act, codes of conduct will be admissible in proceedings before a Court or other tribunal or a Committee or the Standards Commission and any relevant provision may be taken into account in determining a matter.

1.4. Principles of ethical conduct

Holders of public office have a duty to keep faith with the public trust placed in them by the manner in which they carry out their official responsibilities. This is a personal responsibility and requires them at all times to promote the common good, fairly and impartially, to conscientiously and prudently apply the resources of their office in furtherance of the public interest and to observe the highest ethical standards in the performance of their duties. The Standards Commission has described ethical behaviour in the following terms: 'A successful ethics regime is one which provides mechanisms whereby the sensitivities of political/public life can be handled, where competing interests can be reconciled and where individual legislators/executives can be guided in their difficult decisions by reference to the general principle that the public interest should always take precedence over the interests of the individual and, perhaps more importantly, over the interests of a political party whether in power or in opposition.' These are the principles which should guide office holders.

1.5. Highest ethical standards to be applied at all times

In addition to complying with those formal requirements, office holders should at all times observe the highest standards of behaviour and act in good faith with transparency, fairness and impartiality to promote the common good in the performance of their official functions. Ministerial office holders, in the performance of their functions, need to respect the particular requirements of the many different and distinct roles that they hold, e.g. as a member of cabinet, as a Minister of a Department of State, as an elected public representative. Ministers also have a responsibility to ensure that special advisers are accountable to them for the performance of their functions in accordance with the provisions of the Public Service Management Act, 1997. Special advisers cease to hold their position when the relevant Minister ceases to hold office as outlined in the Public Service Management Act, 1997.

Office holders in particular should

- act only by reference to and dedicate the resources of their offices in furtherance of the public interest
- make decisions and encourage and support the making of decisions on merit and without discrimination
- not be influenced in their official duties by personal considerations
- be accountable for their decisions
- protect the integrity of the offices they hold
- respect confidences entrusted to them in the course of their official duties
- respect at all times the role of the Accounting Officers of their Departments and the obligations of staff under the Civil Service Code of Conduct.

1.6. Chairs of Committees

The increasing role and importance of Committees in the Houses of the Oireachtas has placed the chairs of such Committees in a more prominent role. There is a need for the chairs of Committees to be mindful of this increased responsibility in the conduct of their business.

Part 2

Section 1 – Statutory Framework

2.1. Statutory obligations relating to conduct in public life

There is already in place a comprehensive statutory framework for the regulation of conduct in public life. It is a requirement of this

Code of Conduct that office holders comply fully with all of the requirements in that framework as well as any requirements which may be introduced in the future. The following are key elements of the statutory framework in relation to the conduct of office holders:

The Ethics in Public Office Act, 1995 and the Guidelines for Office Holders concerning the steps to be taken by them to assist compliance with the provisions of the Ethics in Public Office Act, 1995

- The 1995 Act includes provisions in relation to office holders for the disclosure of interests, for the treatment of gifts, and for the fulfilment of their responsibilities in relation to special advisers appointed by them or on their behalf.
- Information on the steps office holders need to take in order to comply with the provisions of the 1995 Act is set out in the Guidelines, a copy of which is contained in the attached Appendix.

The Standards in Public Office Act, 2001

- The 2001 Act established the Standards Commission, which subsumed the Public Offices Commission established by the 1995 Act. The Standards Commission has enhanced powers under the 2001 Act and an offence of obstruction of the Standards Commission or its agents has been created.
- The 2001 Act also requires the Government, from time to time, to draw up codes of conduct for the guidance of office holders. The 2001 Act provides that the Guidelines drawn up pursuant to the 1995 Act (referred to above) continue in force.
- Additional requirements are imposed by the 2001 Act on members of the Houses of the Oireachtas in respect of tax compliance. These also apply to an Attorney General who is not a member of either House.

Prevention of Corruption Acts

- The 1995 Act amended the Prevention of Corruption Acts in a number of respects, such as increasing the penalties for corruption to a maximum of 7 years' imprisonment and a fine of up to €63,486.90.
- The 1995 Act increased corruption penalties to 10 years and unlimited fine(s). It also introduced a presumption of corruption, in certain circumstances, from a failure to disclose political donations, and secondly where a person exercising certain functions receives money or other benefit from a person who has an interest in the exercise of those functions.

- The 1995 Act also makes liable to an offence of corruption, third parties who seek to corrupt others, in addition to persons who are directly involved in an activity.

Other provisions

Office holders must also have regard as appropriate to

- The Code of Conduct for Members of Dáil Éireann and Seanad Éireann
- The Electoral Act, 1997, as amended
- The Local Government Act, 2001, which sets out an ethical framework for the local government service

Section 2 – Additional requirements

2.2. Additional guidance for office holders

In addition to requirements which are legislatively prescribed, office holders should observe the following requirements:

2.2.1. Tribunals of inquiry

Tribunals of inquiry established by the Houses of the Oireachtas have a crucial role in maintaining and in some cases restoring public confidence in the political and administrative organs of Government. Office holders (as is the case, of course, for the general public) are required by law to co-operate fully with tribunals of inquiry and all other lawfully constituted investigations or inquiries.

2.2.2. Accountability to the Houses of the Oireachtas

Office holders, who are members of the Houses of the Oireachtas, are accountable to the Houses of the Oireachtas in accordance with the arrangements set out in the Constitution or in the Standing Orders of the respective Houses. It is of paramount importance that office holders give accurate and truthful information to the Houses of the Oireachtas, correcting any inadvertent error at the earliest opportunity.

2.2.3. Public resources

Office holders are provided with facilities at public expense in order that public business may be conducted effectively. The use of these facilities should be in accordance with this principle. Holders of public office enjoy an enhanced public profile and should be mindful of the need to avoid use of resources in a way that could reasonably be construed as an inappropriate raising of profile in the context of a General Election. Official facilities should be used only for official purposes. Office holders should ensure that their use of officially provided facilities are designed to give the public value for money and to avoid any abuse of the privileges which, undoubtedly, are attached to office.

2.2.4. *Business and other interests*

Office holders should not engage in any activities that could reasonably be regarded as interfering or being incompatible with the full and proper discharge by them of the duties of their office. Office holders should not hold company directorships carrying remuneration. Even if remuneration is not paid, it is regarded as undesirable for them to hold directorships. A resigning director may enter into an arrangement whereby a company would agree to his/her re-appointment as a director upon ceasing to be an office holder.

An office holder should not carry on a professional practice while an office holder but may make arrangements for the maintenance of a practice until such time as s/he ceases to be an officer holder and returns to the practice. Office holders should not take any part in the decision-making or management of the affairs of a company or practice and should dispose of, or otherwise set aside for the time-being, any financial interests which might conflict, or be seen to conflict, with their position as an office holder.

Office holders, in taking up appointments on leaving office, should be careful to avoid any real or apparent conflict of interest with the office they formerly occupied. Particular care should be taken in the first few months following departure from office. Office holders should give careful consideration to the type of occupation chosen having left office. Although it is in the public interest that former office holders are able to move into business or other areas of public life, it is equally important that there should be no cause for any suspicion of impropriety when taking up a particular appointment. In this context, office holders should act in a way which ensures it could not be reasonably concluded that an office holder was influenced by the hope or expectation of future employment with the firm or organisation concerned or that an unfair advantage would be conferred in a new appointment by virtue of, for example, access to official information the office holder previously enjoyed.

2.2.5. Lobbyists

It is an integral part of a functioning democracy that particular sections of society will endeavour to highlight issues of sectoral importance with office holders. In this respect contact between office holders and lobbyists is to be expected. However, as guidance, such dealings should be conducted so that they do not give rise to a conflict between public duty and private interest.

2.2.6. Records of official meetings

In all cases where meetings are arranged for the purpose of transacting official business, office holders should be accompanied by an official who would act as a note-taker in the office holder's own interest. In any event, it is advised that an official or adviser should attend before the conclusion of a meeting to record details of any decisions reached.

2.2.7. Appointments

Subject to provisions in legislation or other formal requirements for the establishment of Government bodies or the filling of positions, appointments by members of the government should be made on the basis of merit, taking into account the skills, qualifications and experience of the person to be appointed, as well as any other relevant criteria including, for example, requirements in relation to gender balance.

2.2.8. Gifts

The Government Guidelines for Office Holders published pursuant to Section 15(4) of the 1995 Act and the Guidelines for Office Holders, in relation to the acceptance of gifts by office holders, produced by the Standards Commission provide a framework in relation to the acceptance of gifts. A copy is contained at Appendix 3 to the Guidelines for Office Holders (as attached in the Appendix to this Code).

Additionally, office holders should not accept offers to meet the costs of travel facilities and/or commercial accommodation in connection with official activities (including of a spouse/partner if so accompanied), where such offers are made by private citizens or private enterprises. Discretion may be used where an office holder is the official guest of another Government or official body, or of a not for profit representative organisation or the like. Office holders should be particularly sensitive of acceptance of gifts or hospitality from friends, or connected persons, as defined in the 1995 Act, where such persons have, or are likely to obtain, a benefit or suffer a loss arising from a decision made, or to be made, by an office holder or by the Government, of which the office holder is aware.

2.2.9. Constituency matters

In their capacity as elected representatives, Ministers (including Ministers of State) are free to make representations on behalf of constituents, including to other Ministers, provided that the responses sought or expected to their representations or given to the representation of other office holders are in keeping with responses which would be given to members of the Houses of the Oireachtas generally. Ministers are free to receive representations from other office holders on a similar basis.

Books, journal articles and theses

Alivizatos, N. C. (1995) 'Judges as Veto Players' in H. Döring (ed.) *Parliaments and Majority Rule in Western Europe*. New York: St Martin's Press, pp. 566–89.

Andeweg, R. B. and Nijzink, L. (1995) 'Beyond the Two-Body Image: Relations between Ministers and MPs' in H. Döring (ed.) *Parliaments and Majority Rule in Western Europe*. New York: St Martin's Press, pp. 152–78.

Arkins, A. (1988) 'The Committees of the 24th Oireachtas', *Irish Political Studies* Vol. 3, 91–7.

Arrow, K. J. (1963 [1951]) *Social Choice and Individual Values*. New York: Wiley.

Ayearst, M. (1971) *The Republic of Ireland: Its Government and Politics*. London: University of London Press.

Bachrach, P. (1967) *The Theory of Democratic Elitism*. London: Little, Brown & Co.

Bachrach, P. and Baratz, M. S. (1971) *Power and Poverty*. Oxford: Oxford University Press.

Bagehot, W. (2001 [1867]) *The English Constitution*. Cambridge: Cambridge University Press.

Barrington, T. J. (1970) *Discussion Paper – Parliamentary Study Group*. Dublin: Tuairim.

Bartholomew, P. C. (1971) *The Irish Judiciary*. Dublin: Institute of Public Administration.

Bax, M. (1976) *Harpstrings and Confessions: Machine Style Politics in the Irish Republic*. Assen, The Netherlands: Van Gorcum.

Beattie, A. (1995) 'Ministerial Responsibility and the Theory of the British State' in R. Rhodes and P. Dunleavy (eds) *Prime Minister, Cabinet and Core Executive*. London: Macmillan, pp. 158–81.

Becker, R. and Saalfeld, T. (2004) 'The Life and Times of Bills' in H. Döring and M. Hallerberg (eds) *Patterns of Parliamentary Behaviour*. Aldershot: Ashgate, pp. 57–90.

Beer, S. H. (1990 [1966]) 'The British Legislature and the Problem of Mobilizing Consent' in P. Norton (ed.) *Legislatures*. Oxford: Oxford University Press, pp. 62–81.

Berger, P. and Luckman, T. (1966) *The Social Construction of Reality*. London: Penguin Books.

Bew, P., Hazelkorn, E. and Patterson, H. (1989) *The Dynamics of Irish Politics*. London: Lawrence and Wishart.

Birch, A. H. (1989) 'Responsibility in British Politics' in G. Marshall (ed.) *Ministerial Responsibility*. Oxford: Oxford University Press, pp. 25–9.

Blondel, J. (1969/70) 'Legislative Behaviour: Some Steps towards a Cross-National Measurement', *Government and Opposition* Vol. 5(1), 67–85.

Blondel, J. (1973) *Comparative Legislatures*. London: Prentice Hall.

Borthwick, R. L. (1993) 'On the Floor of the House' in M. Franklin and P. Norton (eds) *Parliamentary Questions*. Oxford: Clarendon Press, pp. 73–103.

Bourke, T. (1996) 'Irish Public Service Reform: a Review of Current Developments', *Parliamentary Affairs* Vol. 49(3), 485–94.

Bowler, S., Farrell, D. M. and Katz, R. S. (1999) 'Party Cohesion, Party Discipline, and Parliaments' in S. Bowler, D. M. Farrell and R. S. Katz (eds) *Party Discipline and Parliamentary Government*. Columbus: Ohio State University Press, pp. 3–22.

Bracken, P. M. (1995) *The Role of the Whip in the Oireachtas* (unpublished MA thesis). Department of Politics, University College Dublin.

Brady, R. (1997) 'Reflections on Tribunals of Inquiry', *The Bar Review* Vol. 3(3), 121–3.

Brady, R. (2000) 'Tribunals and Politics: a Fundamental Review', *Contemporary Issues in Irish Law and Politics* Vol. 3, 157–66.

Bryce, Lord (1990 [1921]) 'The Decline of Legislatures' in P. Norton (ed.) *Legislatures*. Oxford: Oxford University Press, pp. 47–56.

Cameron, C. M. (2000) *Veto Bargaining: Presidents and the Politics of Negative Power*. Cambridge: Cambridge University Press.

Carey, J. M. and Shugart, M. S. (1995) 'Incentives to Cultivate a Personal Vote: a Rank Ordering of Electoral Formulas', *Electoral Studies* Vol. 14(4), 417–39.

Carty, R. K. (1981) *Party and Parish Pump: Electoral Politics in Ireland*. Waterloo, Ontario: Wilfred Laurier Press.

Chubb, B. (1963) '"Going About Persecuting Civil Servants": the Role of the Irish Parliamentary Representative', *Political Studies* Vol. 11(3), 272–86.

Chubb, B. (1982) *Cabinet Government in Ireland*. Dublin: Institute of Public Administration.

Chubb, B. (1983) *Source Book of Irish Government*. Dublin: Institute of Public Administration.

Chubb, B. (1992) *The Government and Politics of Ireland*. London: Longman.

Coakley, J. (2005) 'Appendices' in J. Coakley and M. Gallagher (eds) *Politics in the Republic of Ireland*. London: Routledge/PSAI, pp. 462–90.

Coakley, J. (2005) 'Society and Political Culture' in J. Coakley and M. Gallagher (eds) *Politics in the Republic of Ireland*. London: Routledge/PSAI, pp. 36–71.

Coakley, J. and Gallagher, M. (eds) (2005) *Politics in the Republic of Ireland*. London: Routledge/PSAI.

Cohan, A. S. (1972) *The Irish Political Elite*. Dublin: Gill & Macmillan.

Collier, R. B. and Collier, D. (1991) *Shaping the Political Arena: Critical Junctures, the Labor Movement, and Regime Dynamics in Latin America*. Princeton, NJ: Princeton University Press.

Collins, N. and O'Raghallaigh, C. (1994) 'Political Sleaze in the Republic of Ireland', *Parliamentary Affairs* Vol. 48(4), 697–710.

Collins, N. and O'Shea, M. (2000) *Understanding Corruption in Irish Politics*. Cork: Cork University Press.

Collins, S. (2000) *The Power Game: Fianna Fáil since Lemass*. Dublin: O'Brien Press.

Collins, S. (2004) 'The Parliamentary Lobby System' in T. Garvin, M. Manning and R. Sinnott (eds) *Dissecting Irish Politics: Essays in Honour of Brian Farrell*. Dublin: UCD Press, pp. 198–211.

Cooke, P. (1985) 'Why We Need Open Government in Ireland', *Seirbhís Phoiblí* Vol. 6(3), 23–30.

Copeland, G. W. and Patterson, S. C. (eds) (1994) *Parliaments in the Modern World: Changing Institutions*. Ann Arbor: University of Michigan Press.

Corcoran, M. P. and White, A. (2000) 'Irish Democracy and the Tribunals of Inquiry' in E. Slater and M. Peillon (eds) *Memories of the Present: a Sociological Chronicle of Ireland, 1997–1998*. Dublin: Institute of Public Administration, pp. 185–96.

Cox, G. W. (1987) *The Efficient Secret*. Cambridge: Cambridge University Press.

Cox, G. W. (2002) 'On the Effects of Legislative Rules' in G. Loewenberg, P. Squire and D. R. Kiewiet (eds) *Legislatures: Comparative Perspectives on Representative Assemblies*. Ann Arbor: University of Michigan Press, pp. 247–68.

Cox, G. W. and McCubbins, M. D. (1993) *Legislative Leviathan*. Berkeley: University of California Press.

Crenson, M. A. (1971) *The Un-Politics of Air Pollution*. Baltimore, MD: Johns Hopkins University Press.

Crossman, R. H. S. (1964) 'Introduction' in W. Bagehot, *The English Constitution*. London: C.A. Watts, pp. 1–57.

Cullen, P. (2002) *With a Little Help from My Friends*. Dublin: Gill & Macmillan.

Daly, M. (1981) *Social and Economic History of Ireland since 1800*. Dublin: The Educational Company.

Daly, M. (1987) *Accountability amongst Senior Civil Servants*. Dublin: Institute of Public Administration.

Damgaard, E. (ed.) (1992) *Parliamentary Change in the Nordic Countries*. Oslo: Scandinavian University Press.

Damgaard, E. (1994) 'Parliamentary Questions and Control in Denmark' in M. Wiberg (ed.) *Parliamentary Control in the Nordic Countries*. Jyväskylä, Finland: Gummerus Printing, pp. 44–76.

Damgaard, E. (1995) 'How Parties Control Committee Members' in H. Döring (ed.), *Parliaments and Majority Rule in Western Europe.* New York: St Martin's Press, pp. 308–325.

Day, P. and Klein, R. (1987) *Accountabilities: Five Public Services.* London: Tavistock.

Delaney, E. (2001) *An Accidental Diplomat.* Dublin: New Island.

Deleon, L. (1998) 'Accountability in a "Reinvented" Government', *Public Administration* Vol. 76(3), 539–58.

Deleon, L. (2003) 'On Acting Responsibly in a Disorderly World: Individual Ethics and Administrative Responsibility' in B. G. Peters and J. Pierre (eds) *Handbook of Public Administration.* London: Sage, pp. 569–80.

Della Porta, D. (2001) 'A Judges' Revolution? Political Corruption and the Judiciary in Italy', *European Journal of Political Research* Vol. 39(1), 1–21.

Desmond, B. (1975) *The Houses of the Oireachtas – a Plea for Reform.* Leinster House, Dublin: Parliamentary Labour Party.

Desmond, B. (2000) *Finally and In Conclusion.* Dublin: New Island.

De Winter, L. (1995) 'The Role of Parliament in Government Formation and Resignation' in H. Döring (ed.) *Parliaments and Majority Rule in Western Europe.* New York: St Martin's Press, pp. 115–51.

Dooney, S. and O'Toole, J. (1998) *Irish Government Today.* Dublin: Gill & Macmillan.

Döring, H., (ed.) (1995) *Parliaments and Majority Rule in Western Europe.* New York: St Martin's Press.

Döring, H. (1995) 'Institutions and Policies: Why We Need Cross-National Analysis' in H. Döring (ed.) *Parliaments and Majority Rule in Western Europe.* New York: St Martin's Press, pp. 27–50.

Döring, H. (1995) 'Time as a Scarce Resource: Government Control of the Agenda' in H. Döring (ed.) *Parliaments and Majority Rule in Western Europe.* New York: St Martin's Press, pp. 223–48.

Döring, H. & Hallerberg, M. (eds) (2004) *Patterns of Parliamentary Behaviour.* Aldershot: Ashgate.

Döring, H. (2001) 'Parliamentary Agenda Control and Legislative Outcomes in Western Europe', *Legislative Studies Quarterly* Vol. 26(1), 145–65.

Downs, A. (1957) *An Economic Theory of Democracy.* New York: Harper & Row.

Duignan, S. (1996) *One Spin on the Merry-Go-Round.* Dublin: Blackwater Press.

Dunleavy, P. and Rhodes, R. A. W. (1990) 'Prime Minister, Cabinet and Core Executive – Introduction', *Public Administration* Vol. 68(1), 3–28.

Dunlop, F. (2004) *Yes, Taoiseach.* Dublin: Penguin.

Dunne, J. (1989) 'The Politics of Institutional Reform in Ireland: Lessons of the 1982–87 Government', *Irish Political Studies* Vol. 4, 1–20.

Dunphy, R. (1995) *The Making of Fianna Fáil Power in Ireland: 1923–48.* Oxford: Clarendon Press.

Duverger, M. (1964) *Political Parties.* Cambridge: Cambridge University Press.

Elgie, R. and Stapleton, J. (2004) 'The Parliamentary Activity of the Head of Government in Ireland (1923–2002) in Comparative Perspective', *Journal of Legislative Studies* Vol. 10(2, 3), 154–73.

Evans, P. B., Rueschemeyer, D. and Skocpol, T. (1985) 'On the Road toward a More Adequate Understanding of the State' in P. B. Evans, D. Rueschemeyer and T. Skocpol (eds) *Bringing the State Back In.* Cambridge: Cambridge University Press, pp. 347–66.

Fahey, T., Hayes, B. C. and Sinnott, R. (2005) *Conflict and Consensus: a Study of Values and Attitudes in the Republic of Ireland and Northern Ireland.* Dublin: Institute of Public Administration.

Farrell, A. M. (1997) *The State and the Policy Process. A Case Study of Viral Contamination in Ireland: the Hepatitis C/Anti-D episode: 1976–1997* (unpublished MA thesis). Department of Politics, University College Dublin.

Farrell, B. (1969) 'A note on the Dáil Constitution, 1919', *The Irish Jurist* Vol. 4, 127–38.

Farrell, B. (1970) 'The Drafting of the Irish Free State Constitution: I', *The Irish Jurist* Vol. 5, 115–40.

Farrell, B. (1973) 'The First Dáil and After' in B. Farrell (ed.) *The Irish Parliamentary Tradition.* Dublin: Gill & Macmillan, pp. 208–20.

Farrell, B. (1988) 'From First Dáil through Irish Free State' in B. Farrell (ed.) *De Valera's Constitution and Ours.* Dublin: Gill & Macmillan, pp. 18–32.

Farrell, B. (1993) 'The Formation of the Partnership Government' in M. Gallagher and M. Laver (eds) *How Ireland Voted 1992.* Dublin: Folens/PSAI Press, pp. 146–61.

Farrell, B. (1994) 'The First Dáil and its Constitutional Documents' in B. Farrell (ed.) *The Creation of the Dáil.* Dublin: Blackwater Press, pp. 61–74.

Farrell, D. M. (1999) 'Ireland: a Party System Transformed' in D. Broughton and M. Donovan (eds) *Changing Party Systems in Western Europe.* London: Pinter, pp. 30–47.

Fenno, R. F. (1973) *Congressmen in Committees.* Boston: Little, Brown.

Finer, H. (1941) 'Administrative Responsibility in Democratic Government', *Public Administration Review* Vol. 1, 335–50.

Finlay, F. (1998) *Snakes and Ladders.* Dublin: New Island.

Fisher, J. (2002) 'Next Step: State Funding for the Parties?', *Political Quarterly* Vol. 73(4), 392–9.

FitzGerald, G.(1992) *All in a Life.* Dublin: Gill & Macmillan.

FitzGerald, G. (2003) *Reflections on the Irish State.* Dublin: Irish Academic Press.

Flinders, M. (2001) 'Mechanisms of Judicial Accountability in British Central Government', *Parliamentary Affairs*, Vol. 54(1), 54–71.

Flinders, M. (2001) *The Politics of Accountability in the Modern State.* Aldershot: Ashgate.

Flinders, M. (2002) 'Shifting the Balance? Parliament, the Executive and the British Constitution', *Political Studies* Vol. 50(2), 23–42.

Flintermann, L., Heringa, A. W. and Waddington, L. (eds) (1994) *The Evolving Role of Parliaments in Europe.* Antwerp: Maklu.

Franklin, M. and Norton, P. (eds) (1993) *Parliamentary Questions.* Oxford: Clarendon Press.

Friedrich, C. J. (1940) 'Public Policy and the Nature of Administrative Responsibility' in C. J. Friedrich and E. S. Mason (eds) *Public Policy.* Cambridge, MA: Harvard University Press, pp. 3–24.

Gallagher, M. (1982) *The Irish Labour Party in Transition 1957–82.* Manchester: Manchester University Press.

Gallagher, M. (1985) *Political Parties in the Republic of Ireland.* Manchester: Manchester University Press.

Gallagher, M. (2005) 'Parliament' in J. Coakley and M. Gallagher (eds) *Politics in the Republic of Ireland.* London: Routledge/PSAI, pp. 211–41.

Gallagher, M. and Laver, M. (eds) (1993) *How Ireland Voted 1992.* Dublin: Folens/PSAI Press.

Gallagher, M., Laver, M. and Mair, P. (1995) *Representative Government in Modern Europe.* Maidenhead: McGraw-Hill.

Gallagher, M., Laver, M. and Marsh, M. (1997) *The Oireachtas Committee System.* Dublin: The Policy Institute, Trinity College Dublin.

Gallagher, M. and Marsh, M. (2002) *Days of Blue Loyalty: the Politics of Membership of the Fine Gael Party.* Dublin: PSAI Press.

Gallagher, M., Marsh, M. and Mitchell, P. (eds) (2003) *How Ireland Voted 2002.* Basingstoke: Palgrave.

Gamm, G. and Huber, J. (2002) 'Legislatures as Political Institutions: Beyond the Contemporary Congress' in I. Katznelson and H. V. Milner (eds) *Political Science: State of the Discipline.* New York: W.W. Norton, pp. 313–41.

Garvin, T. (1974) *Political Parties in a Dublin Constituency* (unpublished PhD thesis). Department of Political Science, University of Georgia, Athens, GA.

Garvin, T. (1981) *The Evolution of Irish Nationalist Politics.* Dublin: Gill & Macmillan.

Garvin, T. (1981) 'The Growth of Faction in the Fianna Fáil Party, 1966–80', *Parliamentary Affairs* Vol. 34(1), 110–23.

Garvin, T. (1999) 'Democratic Politics in Independent Ireland', in J. Coakley and M. Gallagher (eds) *Politics in the Republic of Ireland.* London: Routledge, pp. 350–63.

Garvin, T., Manning, M. and Sinnott, R. (eds) (2004) *Dissecting Irish Politics: Essays in Honour of Brian Farrell.* Dublin: UCD Press.

Gay, O. (2002) *The Regulation of Parliamentary Standards – a Comparative Perspective* (commissioned on behalf of The Committee on Standards in Public Life). London: The Constitution Unit, University College London.

Gellner, E. (1977) 'Patrons and Clients' in E. Gellner and J. Waterbury (eds) *Patrons and Clients*. London: Duckworth, pp. 1–6.

Gellner, E. and Waterbury, J. (eds) (1977) *Patrons and Clients*. London: Duckworth.

Girvin, B. (1993) 'The Road to the General Election' in M. Gallagher and M. Laver (eds) *How Ireland Voted 1992*. Dublin: Folens/PSAI Press, pp. 1–20.

Girvin, B. (1999) 'Political Competition, 1992–1997' in M. Marsh and P. Mitchell (eds) *How Ireland Voted 1997*. Oxford: Westview/PSAI Press, 3–28.

Green, D. and Shapiro, I. (1994) *Pathologies of Rational Choice Theory*. New Haven, CT: Yale University Press.

Griffith, J. A. G. (1974) *Parliamentary Scrutiny of Government Bills*. Oxford: Alden Press.

Griffith, J. A. G. and Ryle, M. (1989) *Parliament: Functions, Practice and Procedures*. London: Sweet & Maxwell.

Gwynn Morgan, D. (1990) *The Constitutional Law of Ireland*. Dublin: Round Hall Press.

Gwynn Morgan, D. (1997) *The Separation of Powers in the Irish Constitution*. Dublin: Round Hall Sweet & Maxwell.

Gwynn Morgan, D. (2001) 'Ireland's Ombudsman' in J. Sarkin and W. Binchy (eds) *Human Rights, the Citizen and the State: South African and Irish Perspectives*. Dublin: Round Hall Sweet & Maxwell, pp. 94–107.

Hall, P. A. (1997) 'The Role of Interests, Institutions and Ideas in the Comparative Political Economy of Industrialised Nations' in M. I. Lichbach and A. S. Zuckermann (eds) *Comparative Politics: Rationality, Culture and Structure*. Cambridge: Cambridge University Press, pp. 174–207.

Hall, P. A. and Taylor, R. (1996) 'Political Science and the Three New Institutionalisms', *Political Studies* Vol. 44(5), 936–57.

Hall, P. A. and Taylor, R. (1998) 'The Potential of Historical Institutionalism', *Political Studies* Vol. 46(5), 958–62.

Hansard Society Commission (2001) *The Challenge for Parliament: Making Government Accountable*. London: Vacher Dod.

Hardiman, A. (2004) 'The Role of the Supreme Court in our Democracy' in J. Mulholland (ed.) *Political Choice and Democratic Freedom in Ireland*. Dublin: Transcripts of 2004 MacGill Summer School, Glenties, Co. Donegal, pp. 32–44.

Hardiman, N. and Whelan, C. (1994) 'Politics and Democratic Values' in C. Whelan (ed.) *Values and Social Change in Ireland*. Dublin: Gill & Macmillan, pp. 100–35.

Hardiman, N. and Whelan, C. (1998) 'Changing Values' in W. Crotty and D. E. Schmitt (eds) *Ireland and the Politics of Change*. London: Longman, pp. 66–85.

Hay, C. and Wincott, D. (1998) 'Structure, Agency and Historical Institutionalism', *Political Studies* Vol. 46(5), 951–7.

Headlam-Morley, A. (1928) *The New Democratic Constitutions of Europe*. London: Oxford University Press.

Heringa, A. W. (1994) 'Democracy in Europe: the Evolving Role of Parliaments. Is there a European Parliamentary Model?' in L. Flintermann, A. W. Heringa and L. Waddington (eds) *The Evolving Role of Parliaments in Europe*. Antwerp: Maklu, pp. 99–109.

Higgins, M. D. (1982) 'The Limits of Clientelism: Towards an Assessment of Irish Politics' in C. Clapham (ed.) *Private Patronage and Public Power*. London: Frances Pinter, 114–41.

Hogan, G. (1993) 'The Cabinet Confidentiality Case of 1992', *Irish Political Studies* Vol. 8, 131–7.

Huber, J. D. (1992) 'Restrictive Legislative Procedures in France and the United States', *American Political Science Review* Vol. 86(3), 675–87.

Humphreys, R. F. (1991) 'Legislative Obstruction: How to Do It', *Administration* Vol. 39(1), 55–69.

Immergut, E. M. (1992) 'The Rules of the Game: the Logic of Health Policy-making in France, Switzerland and Sweden' in. S. Steinmo, K. Thelen and F. Longstreth (eds) *Structuring Politics: Historical Institutionalism in Comparative Analysis*. Cambridge: Cambridge University Press, pp. 57–89.

Immergut, E. M. (1998) 'The Theoretical Core of the New Institutionalism', *Politics and Society* Vol. 26(1), 5–34.

Inter-Parliamentary Union (1962) *Parliaments*. London: Cassell.

Irwin, H., Kennon, A., Natzler, D. and Rogers, R. (1993) 'Evolving Rules' in M. Franklin and P. Norton (eds) *Parliamentary Questions*. Oxford: Clarendon Press, pp. 23–72.

Jennings, I. (1957) *Parliament*. Cambridge: Cambridge University Press.

Jordan, G. (1994) *The British Administrative System: Principles versus Practice*. London: Routledge.

Joyce, J. and Murtagh, P. (1983) *The Boss: Charles J. Haughey in Power*. Dublin: Poolbeg Press.

Judge, D. (ed.) (1983) *The Politics of Parliamentary Reform*. London: Heinemann Educational.

Keatinge, P. and Laffan, B. (1999) 'Ireland: a small open polity' in J. Coakley and M. Gallagher (eds) *Politics in the Republic of Ireland*. London: Routledge/PSAI, pp. 320–49.

Keena, C. (2001) *Haughey's Millions: the Full Story of Charlie's Money Trail*. Dublin: Gill & Macmillan.

Keena, C. (2003) *The Ansbacher Conspiracy*. Dublin: Gill & Macmillan.

Keeton, G. W. (1960) *Trial by Tribunal*. London: Museum Press.

Kiewiet, D. R., Loewenberg, G. and Squire, P. (2002) 'The Implications of the Study of the US Congress for Comparative Legislative Research' in G. Loewenberg, P. Squire and D. R. Kiewiet (eds) *Legislatures: Comparative Perspectives on Representative Assemblies.* Ann Arbor: University of Michigan Press, pp. 3–22.

Kiewiet, D. R. and McCubbins, M. D. (1988) 'Presidential Influence on Congressional Appropriation Decisions', *American Journal of Political Science* Vol. 32(August), 713–36.

Kiewiet, D. R. and McCubbins, M. D. (1991) *The Logic of Delegation. Congressional Parties and the Appropriations Process.* Chicago: University of Chicago Press.

King, A. (1976) 'Modes of Executive–Legislative Relations: Great Britain, France and West Germany', *Legislative Studies Quarterly* Vol. 1(1), 11–34.

King. A. (1981) 'How to Strengthen Legislatures – Assuming That We Want To' in N. J. Ornstein (ed.) *The Role of the Legislature in Western Democracies.* London: American Enterprise Institute, pp. 77–89.

King, G., Keohane, R. O. and Verba, S. (1994) *Designing Social Inquiry: Scientific Inference in Qualitative Research.* Princeton, NJ, Princeton University Press.

Kissane, B. (2002) *Explaining Irish Democracy.* Dublin: UCD Press.

Komito, L. (1984) 'Irish Clientelism: a Reappraisal', *Economic and Social Review* Vol. 15(3), 173–94.

Krehbiel, K. (1991) *Information and Legislative Organization.* Ann Arbor: University of Michigan Press.

Laffan, B. (2001) 'The Parliament of Ireland: a Passive Adapter Coming in from the Cold' in A. Maurer and W. Wessels (eds) *National Parliaments on their Ways to Europe: Losers or Latecomers?* Baden-Baden, Germany: Nomos, pp. 251–68.

Laffan, B. and O'Mahony, J. (2003) *Managing Europe from Home: the Europeanisation of the Irish Core Executive.* Dublin: Dublin European Institute.

Lane, J. E. (1993) *The Public Sector: Concepts, Models and Approaches.* London: Sage.

Lane, J. E. and Ersson, S. (1998) *Politics and Society in Western Europe.* London: Sage.

Lane, J. E. and Ersson, S. (2000) *The New Institutional Politics. Performance and Outcomes.* London: Routledge.

Laundy, P. (1989) *Parliaments in the Modern World.* Aldershot: Dartmouth.

Laver, M. (1986) 'Ireland: Politics with Some Social Bases: an Interpretation Based on Survey Data', *The Economic and Social Review* Vol. 17(3), 193–213.

Laver, M. (1997) *Private Desires, Political Action.* London: Sage.

Laver, M. (1998) *A New Electoral System for Ireland?* Dublin: The Policy Institute, Trinity College Dublin.

Laver, M. (2002) 'Divided Parties, Divided Government' in G. Loewenberg, P. Squire and D. R. Kiewiet (eds) *Legislatures: Comparative Perspectives on Representative Assemblies*. Ann Arbor: University of Michigan Press, pp. 201–23.

Laver, M. and Shepsle, K. A. (eds) (1994) *Cabinet Ministers and Parliamentary Government*. Cambridge: Cambridge University Press.

Laver, M. and Shepsle, K. A.(1996) *Making and Breaking Governments*. Cambridge: Cambridge University Press.

Lawton, A. and Rose, A. (1994) *Organisation and Management in the Public Sector*. London: Pitman.

Lee, J. J. (1989) *Ireland 1912–85: Politics and Society*. Cambridge: Cambridge University Press.

Lees, J. D. and Shaw, M. (eds) (1979) *Committees in Legislatures: a Comparative Analysis*. Durham, NC: Duke University Press.

Lijphart, A. (1984) *Democracies*. New Haven, CT: Yale University Press.

Lijphart, A. (1994) 'Democratization and Constitutional Choices in Czechoslovakia, Hungary and Poland, 1989–1991' in I. Budge and D. McKay (eds) *Developing Democracy*. London: Sage, pp. 202–17.

Lijphart, A. (1999) *Patterns of Democracy: Government Forms and Performance in Thirty-Six Countries*. New Haven, CT: Yale University Press.

Linz, J. J. and Valenzuela, A. (eds) (1994) *The Failure of Presidential Democracy*. Baltimore, MD: Johns Hopkins University Press.

Lipset, S. M. and Rokkan S. (1967) 'Cleavage Structures, Party Systems, and Voter Alignments: an Introduction' in S. M. Lipset and S. Rokkan (eds) *Party Systems and Voter Alignments: Cross-National Perspectives*. London: Collier Macmillan, pp. 1–64.

Litton, F., McNamara, T. and O'Connor, T. (1996) 'A New Constitutional Balance?' *Administration* Vol. 44(1), 3–11.

Loewenberg, G., Squire, P. and Kiewiet, D. R. (eds) (2002) *Legislatures: Comparative Perspectives on Representative Assemblies*. Ann Arbor: University of Michigan Press.

Longley, L. D. and Ágh, A. (1997) 'On the Changing Nature of Parliamentary Committees' in L. D. Longley and A. Ágh (eds) *The Changing Roles of Parliamentary Committees*. Lawrence University, Appleton, WI, Research Committee of Legislative Specialists. Working Papers II, pp. 3–13.

Longley, L. D. and Davidson, R. H. (eds) (1998) *The New Roles of Parliamentary Committees*. London: Frank Cass.

Longley, L. D. and Davidson R. H. (1998) 'Parliamentary Committees: Changing Perspectives on Changing Institutions' in L. D. Longley and R. H. Davidson (eds) *The New Roles of Parliamentary Committees*. London: Frank Cass, 1–20.

Lukes, S. (1983) *Power: a Radical View*. London: Macmillan.

Lustik, I. (1993) *Unsettled States, Disputed Lands: Britain and Ireland, France and Algeria, Israel and the West Bank–Gaza*. Ithaca, NY: Cornell University Press.

MacCarthaigh, M. (1999) *Paying for Independence: George McGrath and the Development of the Office of the Comptroller and Auditor-General, 1923–44* (unpublished MA thesis). Department of Politics, University College Dublin.

MacCarthaigh, M. (2001) 'Political Data for Republic of Ireland, 2000', *Irish Political Studies* Vol. 16, 287–351.

MacCarthaigh, M. (2002) 'The Establishment of the Office of the Comptroller and Auditor-General in the Irish Free State', *The History Review* Vol. XIII, 123–8.

McCracken, J. L. (1958) *Representative Government in Ireland.* London: Oxford University Press.

McCullagh, D. (1998) *A Makeshift Majority.* Dublin: Institute of Public Administration.

McGowan Smyth, J. (1973) *The Houses of the Oireachtas.* Dublin: Institute of Public Administration.

McGrath, D. (1999) 'Review of Moriarty and Flood Tribunals, to date', *The Bar Review* Vol. 4(5): 230–6.

Magaloni, B. (2002) 'Horizontal Accountability, the Rule of Law and the Judiciary: Mexico in Comparative Perspective' in S. Mainwaring and C. Welna (eds) *Democratic Accountability in Latin America.* Oxford: Oxford University Press, pp. 1–32.

Mair, P. (1987) *The Changing Irish Party System.* London: Pinter.

Mair, P. (1993) 'Fianna Fáil, Labour and the Irish Party System' in M. Gallagher and M. Laver (eds) *How Ireland Voted 1992.* Dublin: Folens/PSAI Press, pp. 162–73.

Mair, P. (1999) 'Party competition and the changing party system' in J. Coakley and M. Gallagher (eds) *Politics in the Republic of Ireland.* London: PSAI Press, pp. 127–51.

Maitland, F. W. (1908) *The Constitutional History of England.* Cambridge: Cambridge University Press.

Majone, G. (1994) 'Independence vs. Accountability? Non-Majoritarian Institutions and Democratic Government in Europe', *EUI Working Papers in Political and Social Sciences.* Florence: European University Institute.

Majone, G. (1998) *The Regulatory State and Its Legitimacy Problems.* Vienna: Institute for Advanced Studies.

Malone, S. (1947) *Oireachtas Procedure.* Dublin: The Stationery Office.

Manning, M. (1972) *Irish Political Parties: an Introduction.* Dublin: Gill & Macmillan.

Manning, M. (2000) *James Dillon: a Biography.* Dublin: Wolfhound Press.

Mansergh, N. (1934) *The Irish Free State: Its Government and Politics.* London: G. Allen & Unwin.

March, J. G. and Olsen, J. (1989) *Rediscovering Institutions: the Organizational Basis of Politics.* London: Free Press.

Marsh, M. and Mitchell, P. (eds) (1999) *How Ireland Voted 1997.* Oxford: Westview Press/PSAI Press.

Marsh, M. and Wilford, R. (1995) 'Data Section for Republic of Ireland', *Irish Political Studies* Vol. 10, 262–301.

Marshall, G. (ed.) (1989) *Ministerial Responsibility*. Oxford: Oxford University Press.

Marshall, G. (1991) 'The Evolving Practice of Parliamentary Accountability: Writing Down the Rules', *Parliamentary Affairs* Vol. 44(4), 460–9.

Martin, S. (1998) *Discipline in Irish Parliamentary Parties* (unpublished PhD thesis). School of Law and Government, Dublin City University.

Mattson, I. (1994) 'Parliamentary Questions in the Swedish Riksdag' in M. Wiberg (ed.) *Parliamentary Control in the Nordic Countries*. Jyväskylä, Finland: Gummerus Printing, pp. 276–352.

Mattson, I. (1995) 'Private Members' Initiative and Amendments' in H. Döring (ed.) *Parliaments and Majority Rule in Western Europe*. New York: St Martin's Press, pp. 448–87.

Mattson, I. and Strøm, K. (1995) 'Parliamentary Committees' in H. Döring (ed.) *Parliaments and Majority Rule in Western Europe*. New York: St Martin's Press, pp. 249–307.

Maurer, A. and Wessels, W. (eds) (2001) *National Parliaments on Their Ways to Europe: Losers or Latecomers?* Baden-Baden, Germany: Nomos.

Mezey, M. (1979) *Comparative Legislatures*. Durham, NC: Duke University Press.

Mezey, M. L. (1991) 'Parliaments and Public Policy: an Assessment' in D. M. Olson and M. L. Mezey (eds) *Legislatures in the Policy Process*. Cambridge: Cambridge University Press, pp. 201–14.

Migdal, J. S. (1997) 'Studying the State' in M. I. Lichbach and A. S. Zuckermann (eds) *Comparative Politics: Rationality, Culture and Structure*. Cambridge: Cambridge University Press, pp. 208–35.

Mills, M. (2004) 'The Office of the Ombudsman in Ireland' in T. Garvin, M. Manning and R. Sinnott (eds) *Dissecting Irish Politics: Essays in Honour of Brian Farrell*. Dublin: UCD Press, pp. 103–15.

Mitchell, P. (2000) 'Ireland: from Single-party to Coalition Rule' in W. Müller and K. Strøm (eds) *Coalition Governments in Western Europe*. Oxford: Oxford University Press, pp. 126–57.

Moe, T. M. and Caldwell, M. (1994) 'The Institutional Foundations of Democratic Government: a Comparison of Presidential and Parliamentary Systems', *Journal of Institutional and Theoretical Economics* Vol. 150(1), 171–95.

Mulgan, R. (2000) 'Accountability: an Ever-Expanding Concept?', *Public Administration* Vol. 78(3), 555–73.

Mulgan, R. (2002) 'Accountability Issues in the New Model of Governance', *Graduate Programme in Public Policy Discussion Papers*, Australian National University, Canberra.

Mulgan, R. (2003) *Holding Power to Account: Accountability in Modern Democracies*. London: Macmillan.

Mulgan, R. and Uhr, J. (2000) Accountability and Governance. *Graduate Programme in Public Policy Discussion Papers*, Australian National University, Canberra.

Mulholland, J. (ed.) (2004) *Political Choice and Democratic Freedom in Ireland*. Dublin: Transcripts of 2004 MacGill Summer School, Glenties, Co. Donegal.

Müller, W. (2000) 'Political Parties in Parliamentary Democracies: Making Delegation and Accountability Work', *European Journal of Political Research* Vol. 37(3), 309–33.

Murphy, G. (1999) 'The Role of Interest Groups in the Policy Making Progress' in J. Coakley and M. Gallagher (eds) *Politics in the Republic of Ireland*. London: PSAI Press, pp. 271–93.

Murphy, G. (2000) 'A Culture of Sleaze: Political Corruption and the Irish Body Politic 1997–2000', *Irish Political Studies* Vol. 15, 193–200.

Murray, F. (1997) 'The Irish Political and Policy-making System and the Current Programme of Change', *Administration* Vol. 45(4), 39–48.

North, D. C. (1990) *Institutions, Institutional Change and Economic Performance*. Cambridge: Cambridge University Press.

Norton, P. (1983) 'The Norton View', in D. Judge (ed.) *The Politics of Parliamentary Reform*. London: Heinemann Educational Books, pp. 54–69.

Norton, P. (ed.) (1990) *Legislatures*. Oxford: Oxford University Press.

Norton, P. (ed.) (1990) *Parliaments in Western Europe*. London: Frank Cass.

Norton, P. (1993) 'Introduction: Parliament since 1960' in M. Franklin and P. Norton (eds) *Parliamentary Questions*. Oxford: Clarendon Press, pp. 1–22.

Norton, P. (1993) *Does Parliament Matter?* London: Harvester Wheatsheaf.

Norton, P. (1994) 'The Legislative Powers of Parliament' in L. Flintermann, A. W. Heringa and L. Waddington (eds) *The Evolving Role of Parliaments in Europe*. Antwerp: Maklu, pp. 15–35.

Norton, P. (ed.) (1996) *National Parliaments and the European Union*. London: Frank Cass.

Norton, P. (1997) *The Provision of Government Time for Private Members' Bills in the House of Commons*. Centre for Legislative Studies, University of Hull.

Norton, P. (1998) 'Nascent Institutionalisation: Committees in the British Parliament' in L. D. Longley and R. H. Davidson (eds) *The New Roles of Parliamentary Committees*. London: Frank Cass, pp. 143–62.

Norton, P. (ed.) (1998) *Legislatures and Legislators*. Aldershot: Ashgate.

Norton, P. (ed.) (1998) *Parliaments and Governments in Western Europe*. London: Frank Cass.

Norton, P. (1998) 'Introduction: The Institution of Parliaments' in P. Norton (ed.) *Parliaments and Governments in Western Europe*. London: Frank Cass, pp. 1–15.

Norton, P. (1998) 'Conclusion: Do Parliaments Make a Difference?' in P. Norton (ed.) *Parliaments and Governments in Western Europe.* London: Frank Cass, pp. 190–208.

Norton, P. (ed.) (1999) *Parliaments and Pressure Groups in Western Europe.* London: Frank Cass.

Norton, P. (ed.) (2002) *Parliaments and Citizens in Western Europe.* London: Frank Cass.

O'Brien, G. (2004) *Irish Governments and the Guardianship of Historical Records 1922–72.* Dublin: Four Courts Press.

O'Brien, P. and Webb, M. (eds) (1991) *The Executive State: WA Inc. & The Constitution.* Perth, Australia: Constitutional Press.

Ó Cinnéide, S. (1999) 'Democracy and the Constitution', *Administration* Vol. 46(4), 41–58.

O'Halloran, A. (2005) 'Transformation in Contemporary Ireland's Society, Economy and Polity: an Era of Post-Parliamentary Governance?' *Administration* Vol. 53(1), 54–79.

O'Halpin, E. (1987) 'Oireachtas Committees: Experience and Prospects', *Seirbhis Phoibli* Vol. 7(2), 3–9.

O'Halpin, E. (1997) 'Parliamentary Party Discipline and Tactics: the Fianna Fáil Archives, 1926–32', *Irish Historical Studies* Vol. XXX(120), 581–90.

O'Halpin, E. (1997) 'Partnership Programme Managers in the Reynolds/ Spring Coalition, 1993–4: an Assessment', *Irish Political Studies* Vol. 12, 78–91.

O'Halpin, E. (1998) 'A Changing Relationship? Parliament and Government in Ireland' in P. Norton (ed.) *Parliaments and Governments in Western Europe.* London: Frank Cass, pp. 123–41.

O'Halpin, E. (2000) '"Ah, They've Given Us a Good Bit of Stuff …": Tribunals and Irish Political Life at the Turn of the Century', *Irish Political Studies* Vol. 15, 183–192.

Oliver, D. (1991) *Government in the United Kingdom: the Search for Accountability, Effectiveness and Citizenship.* Milton Keynes: Open University Press.

Olson, D. M. (1980) *The Legislative Process: a Comparative Approach.* New York: Harper & Row.

Olson, D. M. and Mezey, M. L. (eds) (1991) *Parliaments and Public Policy.* Cambridge: Cambridge University Press.

Olson, D. M. and Mezey, M. L. (1991) 'Parliaments and Public Policy' in D. M. Olson and M. L. Mezey (eds) *Parliaments and Public Policy.* Cambridge: Cambridge University Press, pp. 1–24.

Olson, D. M. and Norton, P. (eds) (1996) *The New Parliaments of Central and Eastern Europe.* London: Frank Cass.

Olson, M. (1965) *The Logic of Collective Action: Public Goods and the Theory of Groups.* Cambridge, MA: Harvard University Press.

O'Neill, B. (2000) 'Political and Legal Issues Arising out of Recent Tribunals of Inquiry', *Irish Political Studies* Vol. 15, 210–12.

Ornstein, N. J. (ed.) (1981) *The Role of the Legislature in Western Democracies*. London: American Enterprise Institute.

Ostrow, J. M. (2000) *Comparing Post-Soviet Legislatures*. Columbus: Ohio State University Press.

O'Toole, B. (1997) 'Ethics in Government', *Parliamentary Affairs* Vol. 50(1), 130–42.

O'Toole, F. (1995) *Meanwhile, Back at the Ranch*. London: Vintage.

O'Toole, F. (1996) *The Ex-Isle of Erin*. Dublin: New Island.

Ozbudun, E. (1970) *Party Cohesion in Western Democracies: a Causal Analysis*. Beverly Hills, CA: Sage.

Patzelt, W. (2002) 'Recruitment and Retention in Western European Parliaments' in G. Loewenberg, P. Squire and D. R. Kiewiet (eds) *Legislatures: Comparative Perspectives on Representative Assemblies*. Ann Arbor: University of Michigan Press, pp. 80–118.

Peters, B. G. (1996) 'Political Institutions, Old and New' in R. E. Goodin and H. D. Klingemann (eds) *A New Handbook of Political Science*. Oxford: Oxford University Press.

Peters, B. G. (2000) *Institutional Theory: Problems and Prospects*. Vienna: Institute for Advanced Studies.

Pierson, P. (2000) 'Increasing Returns, Path Dependance, and the Study of Politics', *American Political Science Review* Vol. 94(2), 251–67.

Pierson, P. (2000) 'The Limits of Design: Explaining Institutional Origins and Change', *Governance* Vol. 13(4), 475–99.

Pierson, P. and Skocpol, T. (2002) 'Historical Institutionalism in Contemporary Political Science' in I. Katznelson and H. V. Milner (eds) *Political Science: State of the Discipline*. New York: W. W. Norton, pp. 693–721.

Polsby, N. W. (1968) 'The Institutionalization of the US House of Representatives', *American Political Science Review* Vol. 62, 144–68.

Powell, W. and DiMaggio, P. J. (eds) (1991) *The New Institutionalism in Organisational Analysis*. Chicago: University of Chicago Press.

Public Affairs (1969) 'Is the Dáil inefficient?' *Public Affairs* Vol. 1(4), 1–5.

Pyper, R. (1996) 'Parliamentary Accountability' in R. Pyper (ed.) *Aspects of Accountability in the British System of Government*. Liverpool: Tudor Business Publishing, pp. 45–81.

Rasch, B. E. (1994) 'Question Time in the Norwegian Storting' in M. Wiberg (ed.) *Parliamentary Control in the Nordic Countries*. Jyväskylä, Finland: Gummerus Printing, pp. 247–75.

Rasch, B. E. (1995) 'Parliamentary Voting Procedures' in H. Döring (ed.) *Parliaments and Majority Rule in Western Europe*. New York: St Martin's Press, pp. 488–527.

Rhodes, R. A. W. (1997) *Understanding Governance: Policy Networks, Governance, Reflexivity and Accountability*. Buckingham: Open University Press.

Robinson, M. T. W. (1971) *The Importance of Standing Committees for the Development of the Activity of Parliaments.* Inter-Parliamentary Union 59th Conference, Paris.

Robinson, M. T. W. (1974) 'The Role of the Irish Parliament', *Administration* Vol. 22(1), 3–25.

Rockman, B. A. (1984) 'Legislative–Executive Relations and Legislative Oversight', *Legislative Studies Quarterly* Vol. IX(3), 387–440.

Romzek, B. S. and Dubnik, M. J. (1987) 'Accountability in the Public Sector: Lessons from the Challenger Tragedy', *Public Administration Review* Vol. 47, 227–38.

Rose, R. (1974) 'Comparability in Electoral Studies' in R. Rose (ed.) *Electoral Behaviour: a Comparative Handbook.* London: Collier Macmillan, pp. 3–25.

Rothstein, B. (1996) 'Political Institutions: an Overview' in R. E. Goodin and H. D. Klingemann (eds) *A New Handbook of Political Science.* Oxford: Oxford University Press, pp. 133–66.

Rothstein, B. (2003) 'Social Capital in a Working Democracy: the Causal Mechanisms' in O. Osterud (ed.) *Power and Democracy: Critical Interventions.* London: Ashgate, pp. 115–41.

Rush, M. and Ettinghausen, C. (2002) *Opening Up the Usual Channels.* London: Hansard Society.

Saalfeld, T. (1995) 'On Dogs and Whips: Recorded Votes' in H. Döring (ed.) *Parliaments and Majority Rule in Western Europe.* New York: St Martin's Press, pp. 528–65.

Saalfeld, T. (2000) 'Members of Parliament and Governments in Western Europe: Agency Relations and Problems of Oversight', *European Journal of Political Research* Vol. 37(3), 354–76.

Sacks, P. M. (1976) *The Donegal Mafia.* New Haven, CT: Yale University Press.

Salmon, C. (1967) 'Tribunals of Inquiry', *The Hebrew University of Jerusalem Lionel Cohen Lectures,* Jerusalem.

Sartori, G. (1976) *Parties and Party Systems.* Cambridge: Cambridge University Press.

Schattschneider, E. E. (1960) *The Semi-Sovereign People: a Realist's View of Democracy in America.* New York: Holt, Rinehart and Winston.

Scott, C. (2000) 'Accountability in the Regulatory State', *Journal of Law and Society* Vol. 27(1), 38–60.

Scott, J. C. (1972) *Comparative Political Corruption.* Englewood Cliffs, NJ: Prentice Hall.

Scott, W. R. (1995) *Institutions and Organizations.* Thousand Oaks, CA: Sage.

Shaw, M. (1979) 'Conclusion' in J. D. Lees and M. Shaw (eds) *Committees in Legislatures: a Comparative Analysis.* Durham, NC: Duke University Press, pp. 361–434.

Shaw, M. (1997) 'Committee Patterns in Parliaments: a Global Perspective' in L. D. Longley and A. Ágh (eds) *The Changing Roles of Parliamentary Committees.* Appleton, WI, Research Committee of Legislative Specialists. Working Papers II, pp. 505–13.

Shaw, M. (1998) 'Parliamentary Committees: a Global Perspective' in L. D. Longley and R. H. Davidson (eds) *The New Roles of Parliamentary Committees.* London: Frank Cass, pp. 225–51.

Shepsle, K. A. and Weingast, B. R. (1982) 'Institutionalising Majority Rule: a Social Choice Theory with Policy Implications', *American Economic Review* Vol. 72, 367–73.

Shugart, M. S. and Carey, J. M. (1992) *Presidents and Assemblies: Constitutional Design and Electoral Dynamics.* Cambridge: Cambridge University Press.

Shugart, M. S. and Wattenberg, M. P. (2001) 'Conclusion' in M. S. Shugart and M. P. Wattenberg (eds) *Mixed-Member Electoral Systems: the Best of Both Worlds?* Oxford: Oxford University Press, pp. 571–95.

Shugart, M. S. and Wattenberg, M. P. (eds) (2001) *Mixed-Member Electoral Systems: the Best of Both Worlds?* Oxford: Oxford University Press.

Silk, P. and Walters, R. (1998) *How Parliament Works.* London: Longman.

Silkin, A. (1989) 'The "Agreement to Differ" of 1975', in G. Marshall (ed.) *Ministerial Responsibility.* Oxford: Oxford University Press, pp. 55–67.

Sinclair, B. (1997) *Unorthodox Lawmaking.* Washington, DC: Congressional Quarterly Press.

Sinnott, R. (1995) *Irish Voters Decide.* Manchester: Manchester University Press.

Skocpol, T. (1985) 'Bringing the State Back In: Strategies of Analysis in Current Research' in P. B. Evans, D. Rueschemeyer and T. Skocpol (eds) *Bringing the State Back In.* Cambridge: Cambridge University Press, pp. 3–37.

Smyth, S. (1997) *Thanks a Million Big Fella.* Dublin: Blackwater Press.

Stone, B. (1993) 'Accountability reform in Australia', *Australian Quarterly* Vol. 65(2), 17–30.

Strøm, K. (1990) *Minority Government and Majority Rule.* Cambridge: Cambridge University Press.

Strøm, K. (1995) 'Parliamentary Government and Legislative Organisation' in H. Döring (ed.) *Parliaments and Majority Rule in Western Europe.* New York: St Martin's Press, pp. 51–82.

Strøm, K. (1997) 'Democracy, Accountability and Coalition Bargaining', *European Journal of Political Research* Vol. 31(1–2), 47–62.

Strøm, K. (1998) 'Parliamentary Committees in European Democracies' in L. D. Longley and R. H. Davidson (eds) *The New Roles of Parliamentary Committees.* London: Frank Cass, pp. 21–59.

Strøm, K. (2000) 'Delegation and Accountability in Parliamentary Democracies', *European Journal of Political Research* Vol. 37(3), 261–86.

Suleiman, E. N. (ed.) (1986) *Parliaments and Parliamentarians in Democratic Politics.* London: Holmes & Meier.

Teahon, P. (1997) 'The Irish Political and Policy-making System and the Current Programme of Change', *Administration* Vol. 45(4), 49–58.

Thatcher, M. and Stone Sweet, A. (2002) 'Theory and Practice of Delegation to Non-Majoritarian Institutions', *West European Politics* Vol. 25(1), 1–22.

Thelen, K. (1999) 'Historical Institutionalism in Comparative Politics', *Annual Review of Political Science* Vol. 2, 369–404.

Thelen, K. and Steinmo, S. (1992) 'Historical Institutionalism in Comparative Analysis' in K. Thelen, S. Steinmo and F. Longstreth (eds) *Structuring Politics: Historical Institutionalism in Comparative Perspective.* Cambridge: Cambridge University Press, pp. 1–32.

Thomas, P. G. (2003) 'Accountability' in B. G. Peters and J. Pierre (eds) *Handbook of Public Administration.* London: Sage, pp. 549–56.

Thompson, D. F. (1995) *Ethics in Congress.* Washington, DC: The Brookings Institute.

Tomkins, A. (1998) *The Constitution after Scott: Government Unwrapped.* Oxford: Clarendon Press.

Troy, T. (1959) 'Some Aspects of Parliamentary Questions', *Administration* Vol. 7(3), 251–9.

Tsebelis, G. (1995) 'Veto Players and Law Production in Parliamentary Democracies' in H. Döring (ed.) *Parliaments and Majority Rule in Western Europe.* New York: St Martin's Press, pp. 83–114.

Tsebilis, G. and Money, J. (1997) *Bicameralism.* Cambridge: Cambridge University Press.

Tsebilis, G. and Rasch, B. (1995) 'Patterns of Bicameralism' in H. Döring (ed.) *Parliaments and Majority Rule in Western Europe.* New York: St Martin's Press, pp. 365–90.

Tutty, M. G. (1998) 'Implications of New Organisational Structures' in R. Boyle and T. McNamara (eds) *Governance and Accountability.* Dublin: Institute of Public Administration, pp. 83–109.

Uhr, J. (1993) 'Redesigning Accountability', *Australian Quarterly* Vol. 65(2), 1–16.

Ward, A. J. (1974) 'Parliamentary Procedures and the Machinery of Government in Ireland', *Irish University Review* Vol. 4(2), 222–43.

Ward, A. J. (1994) *The Irish Constitutional Tradition: Responsible Government and Modern Ireland, 1782–1992.* Dublin: Irish Academic Press.

Ward, A. J. (1996) 'The Constitution Review Group and the "Executive State" in Ireland', *Administration* Vol. 44(4), 42–63.

Ware, A. (1996) *Political Parties and Party Systems.* Oxford: Oxford University Press.

Webb, M. and O'Brien, P. (1991) 'The Ghost in the System' in P. O'Brien and M. Webb (eds) *The Executive State: WA Inc. and the Constitution.* Perth, Australia: Constitutional Press, pp. 341–52.

Weingast, B. R. (1996) 'Political Institutions: Rational Choice Perspectives' in R. E. Goodin and H.-D. Klingemann (eds) *A New Handbook of Political Science*. Oxford: Oxford University Press, pp. 167–90.

Weingast, B. R. (2002) 'Rational-Choice Institutionalism' in I. Katznelson and H. V. Milner (eds) *Political Science: the State of the Discipline*. New York: W. W. Norton, pp. 660–92.

Wheare, K. C. (1955) *Government by Committee*. Oxford: Clarendon.

Wheare, K. C. (1963) *Legislatures*. London: Oxford University Press.

Wheare, K. C. (1968) *Legislatures* (2nd edn). London: Oxford University Press.

Whyte, J. (1974) 'Politics without Social Bases' in R. Rose (ed.) *Electoral Behaviour: a Comparative Handbook*. London: Collier Macmillan, pp. 619–51.

Wiberg, M. (1994) 'Introduction' in M. Wiberg (ed.) *Parliamentary Control in the Nordic Countries*. Jyväskylä, Finland: Gummerus Printing, pp. 9–18.

Wiberg, M. (1994) 'To Keep the Government on Its Toes: Behavioural Trends in Parliamentary Questioning in Finland 1945–1990' in M. Wiberg (ed.) *Parliamentary Control in the Nordic Countries*. Jyväskylä, Finland: Gummerus Printing, pp. 103–201.

Wiberg, M. (1994) 'Conclusions' in M. Wiberg (ed.) *Parliamentary Control in the Nordic Countries*. Jyväskylä, Finland: Gummerus Printing, pp. 357–64.

Wiberg, M., (ed.) (1994) *Parliamentary Control in the Nordic Countries*. Jyväskylä, Finland: Gummerus Printing.

Wiberg, M. (1995) 'Parliamentary Questioning: Control by Communication?' in H. Döring (ed.) *Parliaments and Majority Rule in Western Europe*. New York: St Martin's Press, pp. 179–222.

Wiberg, M. and Koura, A. (1994) 'The Logic of Parliamentary Questioning' in M. Wiberg (ed.) *Parliamentary Control in the Nordic Countries*. Jyväskylä, Finland: Gummerus Printing, pp. 19–43.

Winetrobe, B. (1997) 'Inquiries after Scott: the Return of the Tribunal of Inquiry', *Public Law* (spring), 18–31.

Woodhouse, D. (1994) *Ministers and Parliament*. Oxford: Clarendon Press.

Zimmerman, J. F. (1988) 'An Oireachtas Innovation: Backbench Committees', *Administration* Vol. 36(3), 265–89.

Zimmerman, J. F. (2001) 'The Irish Ombudsman–Information Commissioner', *Administration* Vol. 49(1), 78–102.

Conference and seminar proceedings

Desmond, B. (2002) *Funding Political Parties in Ireland*. UCD Politics Department Seminar, 22 March.

Farrell, A. M. (2001) *Contaminated Blood and Political Scandal in Ireland*. Political Scandals: Past and Present Conference, European Studies Research Institute, University of Salford, Manchester, 22 June.

Gallagher, M. (2000) *Parliamentary Control of the Executive in Ireland: Non-Party, Inter-Party, Cross-Party and Intra-Party.* Workshop on Parliamentary Control of the Executive, European Consortium of Political Research Joint Sessions, Copenhagen, 14–19 April.

MacCarthaigh, M. (2001) *Scandal and Accountability in Irish Parliamentary Politics.* Political Scandals: Past and Present Conference, European Studies Research Institute, University of Salford, Manchester, 22 June.

MacCarthaigh, M. and Martin, S. (2002) *Majoritarian Government and Parliamentary Committees.* Research Committee of Legislative Specialists, Bilgi University, Istanbul, 24 June.

Official publications

All-Party Oireachtas Committee on the Constitution (1997) *Seanad Éireann.* Dublin: Stationery Office.

All-Party Oireachtas Committee on the Constitution (2002) *Parliament.* Dublin: Stationery Office.

Committee on Foreign Affairs Sub-Committee on European Scrutiny (2002) *First Report.* Dublin: Stationery Office.

Constitution Review Group (1996) *Report of the Constitution Review Group.* Dublin: Stationery Office.

Co-ordinating Group of Secretaries (1996) *Delivering Better Government.* Dublin: Department of the Taoiseach.

Dáil Committee on Members' Interests (2000) *Report of the Results of an Investigation into a Complaint concerning Deputy Denis Foley.* Dublin: Stationery Office.

Dáil Committee on Members' Interests (2002) *Report on a Draft Code of Conduct for Members of Dáil Éireann.* Dublin: Stationery Office.

Department of Health (1997) *Report on behalf of the Government by Brian Cowen T.D., Minister of Health and Children on the Legal Strategy adopted by the Defence in the Case of the Late Mrs. Bridget McCole.* Dublin: Department of Health.

Eurobarometer Surveys 1980–2004.

Finlay, T. (1997) *Report of the Tribunal of Inquiry into the Blood Transfusion Supply Board.* Dublin: Stationery Office.

Flood, F. (2002) *The Second Interim Report of the Tribunal of Inquiry into Certain Planning Matters and Payments.* Dublin: Stationery Office.

Group of States Against Corruption (GRECO) (2003) *First Evaluation Round: Compliance Report on Ireland.* Strasbourg: Council of Europe.

Hamilton, L. (1994) *Report of the Tribunal of Inquiry into the Beef Processing Industry.* Dublin: Stationery Office.

Houses of the Oireachtas Commission (2005) *Annual Report.* Dublin: Stationery Office.

Informal Committee on Reform of Dáil Procedure (1972) *Final Report.* Dublin: Stationery Office.

Joint Committee on Health and Children (2000) *Annual Report.* Dublin: Stationery Office.

Joint Committee on Health and Children (2005) *Interim Report on the Report on Certain Issues of Management and Administration in the Department of Health & Children associated with the Practice of Charges for Persons in Long-Stay Care in Health Board Institutions and Related Matters.* Dublin: Stationery Office.

Joint Committee on Public Enterprise and Transport (2001) *Verbatim Transcript of the Sub-Committee on the Mini-CTC Signalling Project.* Dublin: Stationery Office.

Lindsay, A. (2002) *Report of the Tribunal of Inquiry into the Infection with HIV and Hepatitis C of Persons with Haemophilia and Related Matters.* Dublin: Stationery Office.

McCracken, B. (1997) *Report of the Tribunal of Inquiry (Dunnes Payments).* Dublin: Stationery Office.

Mahon, A. (2004) *The Fourth Interim Report of the Tribunal of Inquiry into Certain Planning Matters and Payments.* Dublin: Stationery Office.

Office of the Attorney General (2000) *Comparative Study of Tribunals of Inquiry and Parliamentary Inquiries.* Dublin: Stationery Office.

Office of the Information Commissioner (2001) *Presentation to the Joint Oireachtas Committee on the Strategic Management Committee.* Dublin: Oireachtas Éireann – Joint Oireachtas Committee on the Strategic Management Committee.

Office of the Ombudsman (1999) *Annual Report.* Dublin: Office of the Ombudsman.

Office of the Ombudsman (2001) *Nursing Home Subventions. An Investigation by the Ombudsman of Complaints regarding Payment of Nursing Home Subventions by Health Boards.* Dublin: Office of the Ombudsman.

Office of the Ombudsman (2002) *Annual Report.* Dublin: Office of the Ombudsman.

Office of the Ombudsman (2004) *20th Anniversary of the Office of the Ombudsman in Ireland.* Dublin: Office of the Ombudsman.

Oireachtas Committee on the Constitution (1967) *Report of the Committee on the Constitution* (Pr. 9817). Dublin: Oireachtas Éireann.

Organisation for Economic Cooperation and Development (2001) *Regulatory Reform in Ireland.* Paris: OECD.

PA Consulting (2002) *Evaluation of the Progress of the Strategic Management Initiative/Delivering Better Government Modernisation Programme.* Dublin: PA Consulting Group.

Parliamentary Bulletin (2002) Issue 1: January to December 2001. Dublin: Leinster House.

Public Accounts Committee (1970) *Interim Report – December 1970.* Dublin: Stationery Office.

Public Accounts Committee (1999) *Sub-Committee on Certain Revenue Matters: Parliamentary Inquiry into D.I.R.T. – First Report.* Dublin: PAC.

Public Accounts Committee (2001) *Sub-Committee on Certain Revenue Matters: Parliamentary Inquiry into D.I.R.T. – Final Report Vol. 1.* Dublin: PAC.

Public Accounts Committee (2001) *Sub-Committee on Certain Revenue Matters: Parliamentary Inquiry into D.I.R.T. – Final Report Vol. 3.* Dublin: PAC.

Returns relating to Sittings and Business of the Dáil. Dublin: Oireachtas Éireann.

Seanad Éireann Committee on Procedure and Privileges Sub-Committee on Seanad Reform (2004) *Report on Seanad Reform.* Dublin: Stationery Office.

Standards in Public Office Commission (2003) *Annual Report 2002.* Dublin.

Standards in Public Office Commission (2004) *Annual Report 2003.* Dublin.

Standards in Public Office Commission (2005) *Annual Report 2004.* Dublin.

Standing Sub-Committee on Dáil Reform (1996) *First Report on Reform of Dáil Procedure.* Dublin: Stationery Office.

Standing Sub-Committee on Dáil Reform (1997) *Second Report on Reform of Dáil Procedure.* Dublin: Stationery Office.

Standing Sub-Committee on Dáil Reform (1997) *First Report of the Standing Sub-Committee on Dáil Reform on Establishment of Committees in the 28th Dáil.* Dublin: Stationery Office.

Standing Sub-Committee on Dáil Reform (1997) *Consensus Positions on Areas for Reform of Dáil Procedure.* Dublin: Stationery Office.

Sub-Committee of the Select Committee on Legislation and Security (1995) *Report of the Sub-Committee.* Dublin: Stationery Office.

The Law Reform Commission (2003) *Consultation Paper on Public Inquiries including Tribunals of Inquiry.* Dublin: LRC.

The Law Reform Commission (2005) *Report on Public Inquiries including Tribunals of Inquiry.* Dublin: LRC.

Tribunal of Inquiry into Certain Planning Matters and Payments (2002) *The Second Interim Report – September 2002.* Dublin: Stationery Office.

Law reports

Attorney General v. *Hamilton Ir* [1993] H.C. (1993) *Irish Reports.* High Court, Dublin. Vol. 2, 250–59.

Attorney General v. *Hamilton Ir* [1993] S.C. (1993) *Irish Reports.* Supreme Court, Dublin. Vol. 2, 259–304.

Haughey v. *Moriarty Ir* [1999] S.C. (1999) *Irish Reports.* Supreme Court, Dublin. Vol. 3, 27–78.

In re Haughey [1971] 217 (1971) *Irish Reports.* Dublin.

Lawlor v. *Flood Ir* [1999] S.C. (1999) *Irish Reports*. Supreme Court, Dublin: 107–44.

Maguire v. *Ardagh* [2001] H.C. (2002) *Irish Reports*. High Court, Dublin. Vol. 1, Part II, 385–447.

Maguire v. *Ardagh* [2002] S.C. (2002) *Irish Reports*. Supreme Court, Dublin. Vol. 1, Part II, 447–742.

Redmond v. *Flood Ir* [1999] S.C. (1999) *Irish Reports*. Supreme Court, Dublin. Vol. 3, 79–96.

Newspaper and magazine articles

Brennock, M. (2003) 'Code of conduct to "ensure highest ethical standards" by office holders', *Irish Times*, 4 July, 9.

Browne, V. (2001) 'Politicians must take blame for inquiry fiasco', *Irish Times*, 28 November, 16.

Carolan, M. (2001) 'Court ruling called "attack on democracy"', *Irish Times*, 19 January, 6.

Collins, S. (2003) 'Government broke the law and got away with it', *Sunday Tribune*, 22 June, 17.

Collins, S. (2004) 'Politics', *Sunday Tribune*, 25 January, 12.

Coulter, C. (2001) 'Court's ruling not a major setback to committee system', *Irish Times*, 12 April, 8.

Cullen, P. (2003) 'Dunlop lied in belief case would be forgotten about', *Irish Times*, 6 February, 9.

Desmond, B. (1979) 'Dail reform before Dail expansion', *Hibernia*, 13 September, 13.

Downey, J. (1975) 'T.D. puts Dail reform plea to Government', *Irish Times*, 6 March, 5.

FitzGerald, G. (1994) 'Paying too high a price for techniques of obfuscation', *Irish Times*, 13 August, 14.

FitzGerald, G. (2002) 'Seanad has key role in scrutinising legislation', *Irish Times*, 22 June, 12.

Hennessy, M. (2002) 'Burke corruption findings put pressure on Taoiseach', *Irish Times*, 27 September, 4.

Hennessy, M. (2002) 'Government still blocking Dail questions for Taoiseach', *Irish Times*, 4 October, 1.

Hennessy, M. (2002) 'Unsuccessful SF candidates received largest donations', *Irish Times*, 1 November, 6.

Irish Times (1966) 'An Irish Ombudsman' (editorial), 12 November, 13.

Irish Times (1976) 'Disputed section deleted from Bill setting up Oireachtas inquiry committee' (editorial), 26 March, 8.

Irish Times (1990) 'Machine needs overhaul' (editorial), 19 July, 13.

Irish Times (2001) 'The Abbeylara Inquiry' (editorial), 24 November, 13.

Irish Times (2004) 'Ahern shifts his ground at Tribunal' (editorial), 8 April, 12.

Irish Times (2005) 'Dáil break not in the public interest' (editorial), 2 August, 13.

Keena, C. (2004) 'Bruton felt threatened by Independent Group', *Irish Times*, 24 March, 8.

Keery, N. (1971) 'The Dail traffic jam: is the committee the answer?', *Sunday Press*, 28 March, 8.

Maddock, J. (2001) 'Oireachtas "has no power to investigate Abbeylara"', *Irish Independent*, 18 July, 5.

Manning, M. (1975) 'Making Dail and Seanad more democratic and effective', *Irish Press*, 6 March, 9.

O'Doherty, C. (2001) 'Court rules Oireachtas rail inquiry can proceed', *Irish Times*, 16 October, 4.

O'Flaherty, H. (1975) 'Tribunals and tribulations', *Irish Press*, 18 July, 9.

Reid, L. (2004) 'Law Society says high tribunal fees have hurt legal profession', *Irish Times*, 3 April, 6.

Reid, L. (2005) 'Plan to cut time Ahern must spend facing Dáil questions', *Irish Times*, 27 June, 1.

Sheahan, F. (2005) '€4,500 fee to join FF's golden club', *Irish Independent*, 29 March, 1.

Political party publications

Desmond, B. (1975) *The Houses of the Oireachtas – a Plea for Reform.* Leinster House, Dublin: Parliamentary Labour Party.

Fine Gael (1980) *Reform of the Dail: Fine Gael Policy on Reform of the Dail.* Leinster House, Dublin: Fine Gael Parliamentary Party.

Fine Gael (1990) *Dáil Reform.* Leinster House, Dublin: Fine Gael Parliamentary Party.

Fine Gael (2000) *A Democratic Revolution.* Leinster House, Dublin: Fine Gael Parliamentary Party.

The Labour Party (1968) *Proposals for the Reform of Parliamentary Procedure in Dail Eireann.* Leinster House, Dublin: Parliamentary Labour Party.

The Labour Party (2003) *Putting Our House in Order: Dáil Reform, Parliamentary Oversight and Government Accountability.* Leinster House, Dublin: Parliamentary Labour Party.

Archival material

Desmond, B. (1971) Report to Parliamentary Party of Meeting on Reform of Dail Eireann Procedures on 29th January, 1971. Leinster House, Dublin: Parliamentary Labour Party.

Fianna Fáil Parliamentary Party, Minutes of Party Meetings 1927–81. University College Dublin Archives (P176/446–51).

Interviews

Bruton, J. (2002) Kildare House, Dublin, 12 February.
Coughlan, K. (2002) Office of the Clerk of Dáil Éireann, Leinster House, Dublin, 30 April.
Coughlan, K. (2002) Office of the Clerk of Dáil Éireann, Leinster House, Dublin, 16 May.
Coughlan, K. (2003) Office of the Clerk of Dáil Éireann, Leinster House, Dublin, 16 July.
Desmond, B. (2003) Goatstown, Dublin, 9 June.
FitzGerald, G. (2003) Ranelagh, Dublin, 8 August.
Murphy, K. (2002) Office of the Ombudsman, Dublin, 27 November.
O'Leary, A. (2003) Office of the Director of Committees, Kildare House, Dublin, 17 July.
O'Malley, D. (2003) Ballsbridge, Dublin, 20 June.
Shatter, A. (2003) Ely Place, Dublin, 24 June.

Internet resources

- http://debates.oireachtas.ie (Dáil and Seanad Debates)
- www.sipo.gov.ie (Standards in Public Office Commission)
- http://ombudsman.gov.ie (Office of the Ombudsman)
- www.oic.gov.ie (Office of the Information Commissioner)
- www.moriarty-tribunal.ie (Moriarty Tribunal)
- www.public-standards.gov.uk (Westminster Committee on Standards in Public Life)

Miscellaneous

Tuairim (1968) Minutes of meetings of Dublin Branch. Dublin.

INDEX